Handbook of Pragmatics
21st Annual Installment

# *Handbook of Pragmatics*

ISSN 1877-9611

Prepared under the scientific auspices of the **International Pragmatics Association (IPrA;** https://pragmatics.international).

# Handbook of Pragmatics

21st Annual Installment

*Edited by*

Jan-Ola Östman
IPrA & University of Helsinki

Jef Verschueren
IPrA & University of Antwerp

John Benjamins Publishing Company
Amsterdam / Philadelphia

The paper used in this publication meets the minimum requirements of the American National Standard for Information Sciences – Permanence of Paper for Printed Library Materials, ANSI z39.48-1984.

DOI 10.1075/hop.21

ISBN 978 90 272 6308 7 (HB)
ISBN 978 90 272 6307 0 (E-BOOK)



John Benjamins Publishing Co. · https://benjamins.com

# Table of contents


Editors' note VII

User's guide IX

**Traditions**

Language psychology 3
*Jacob Thøgersen, Søren Beck Nielsen, Lian Malai Madsen & Christina Fogtmann Fosgerau*

Linear Unit Grammar 25
*Anna Mauranen*

Truth-conditional pragmatics 49
*Jacques Moeschler*

**Handbook A–Z**

Benedict Anderson's imagined communities 81
*William O. Beeman*

Emotions: A philosophical and cognitive perspective 111
*Claudia Strey*

Language maintenance and shift 125
*Louisa Willoughby*

*Mianzi/lian*: Chinese notions of face 141
*Ling Zhou & Shaojie Zhang*

Roman Jakobson 159
*Manfred Bierwisch*

Stance 173
*Hiroko Takanashi*

Style and styling 201
*Janus Mortensen & Nikolas Coupland*

Superdiversity 221
*Zane Goebel*

Tactile sign languages 239
*Louisa Willoughby, Shimako Iwasaki, Meredith Bartlett & Howard Manns*

Cumulative index 259

# Editors' note

When we launched the idea of a ***Handbook of Pragmatics*** under the auspices of the **International Pragmatics Association** (IPrA; https://pragmatics.international) in the early 1990s, we wanted to create a format that would be indefinitely moldable for and by the readership. The very essence of scientific research is that scientific insights change constantly. In a field like pragmatics, with the functioning and use of constantly changing styles and registers of language as its focus of research, we did not want to produce a single book as the ultimate 'handbook of pragmatics.' Since we saw this venture as a task that would take decades, if we wanted to do it properly, we also did not want to start with categories and traditions beginning with "A" and after a couple of decades finally reaching "Z".

At that time, we settled for a loose-leaf publication format, relatively unorthodox in the humanities and social sciences. The idea was that this would enable us to gradually build up a changeable and expandable knowledge base for the users of the Handbook. Moreover, each individual reader would be able to group and re-group the entries according to his or her own preferences and particular interests, which no doubt would themselves be changing over time. So, with every three or four annual installment of the Handbook, the subscriber received a new ring binder in which to collect and order the new entries. The series of loose-leaf installments was preceded in 1995 with a hardback bound **Manual** which provided background information on a wide range of traditions and research methods underlying much of the pragmatic research described in the more topical entries of the annual installments. Needless to say that also this background information has evolved and has necessitated numerous new entries on traditions and methods in the loose-leaf installments. So far we have published 20 installments of some 300 pages each, in addition to the 658-page Manual. Subscribers to the loose-leaf version of the *Handbook of Pragmatics* should by now have a bookshelf filled with Manual plus 7 ring binders, reflecting the state of the art in the science of language use.

Meanwhile, the world has gradually become more and more digital. In the early 1990s hardly anyone could have foreseen the radical changes that have come to take place on the publishing scene. The *Handbook of Pragmatics* quickly followed suite, went online, and is available for readers as, precisely, the *Handbook of Pragmatics Online* (https://benjamins.com/online/hop/). The online version has been continuously updated with new material whenever and as soon as a new installment of the Handbook was published; and in cases where an entry has been totally rewritten, the older version has been retained in the Archive – all in the interest of giving readers a feeling of how the discipline itself has changed and evolved over the decades. It is also the case that the online version has become the most often used version of the Handbook, both by individual scholars (especially by members of the International

Pragmatics Association), and by many of their institutions and universities. The loose-leaf version on paper is nowadays seldom subscribed to by individuals, but we are happy to say that it does attract libraries and research groups. It is, however, challenging for libraries to make loose-leaf versions of books available for the general readership in a shape where all leaves/pages are physically "a-loose".

Faced with this situation, we have in close discussions with John Benjamins Publishing Company decided to produce further installments of the ***Handbook of Pragmatics*** in the form of bound publications, of which the one you are now holding in your hands is the first volume. One consequence of this change is that there was no installment in 2017. The annual regularity will be restored from this year onwards. We are convinced that this will make the Handbook easier to handle and more attractive not only for libraries, but also for scholars who still cherish the feel and satisfaction of reading a concrete book. Meanwhile, the online version continues to integrate all additions and changes.

The gist of the User's Guide for the *Handbook of Pragmatics* and its online version will largely remain the same as before – see below. As in the loose-leaf version, we will have a cumulative index (at the end of each volume), covering not only the present installment, but linking it to the entire *Handbook of Pragmatics*.

## Acknowledgments

A project of this type cannot be successfully started, let alone completed, without the help of dozens, or even hundreds, of scholars. First of all, there are the authors themselves, who sometimes have had to work under extreme conditions of time pressure, especially since all contributions also undergo peer reviewing. Further, most members of the IPrA Consultation Board have occasionally, and some repeatedly, been called upon to review contributions. Innumerable scholars could have been added, whose input was essential for authors of the individual contributions; for reasons of space, we decided to take out most of the acknowledgments appended to the articles.

Last but not least, the present editors want to make sure that the contribution made by the co-editors of the Manual and the first eight annual installments, is not forgotten: Jan Blommaert and Chris Bulcaen were central to the realization of the project. Similarly, Eline Versluys acted as editorial assistant for a five-year period ending in 2009. Our sincerest thanks to all of them.

We hope the 21st installment of the Handbook in its new format will meet with your approval.

Uppsala & Antwerp, June 2018.
Jan-Ola Östman & Jef Verschueren, editors

# User's guide

## Introduction

For the purpose of this publication, ***pragmatics*** can be briefly defined as *the cognitive, social, and cultural study of language and communication*. What this means exactly, and what it entails for the scientific status of linguistic pragmatics, was explained in detail in the introductory chapter, 'The pragmatic perspective' by Jef Verschueren, of the **Manual** (*Handbook of Pragmatics: Manual*, edited by Jef Verschueren, Jan-Ola Östman & Jan Blommaert, 1995).

The overall purpose of the **Handbook of Pragmatics** is that it should function as a tool in the search for coherence, in the sense of cross-disciplinary intelligibility, in this necessarily interdisciplinary field of scholarship. The background of the Handbook and its historical link with the International Pragmatics Association (IPrA), as well as its basic options, were described in the preface to the Manual. The Handbook format, although described in the same preface, will be presented anew in this **User's Guide** for the sake of clarity.

The **Handbook of Pragmatics** will continue to be available ***online*** (see https://benjamins.com/online/hop). The printed version will continue to be expanded with *new articles* and will also incorporate *revised versions* of older entries. *Updates* that require minimal changes will be published only in the annual online releases. In addition, ***Highlights*** from the Handbook have been published in ten thematically organized paperbacks (in 2009, 2010, and 2011; cf. https://benjamins.com/catalog/hoph), making the contents accessible in an affordable way for use as practical teaching tools and reading materials for a wide range of pragmatics-related linguistics courses focusing specifically on general pragmatic, philosophical, cognitive, grammatical, social, cultural, variational, interactive, applied, or discursive aspects, respectively.

## The handbook format

The printed edition of the **Handbook of Pragmatics** contains three clearly distinct parts: the *Manual*, the *Handbook* proper, and the *Cumulative index*.

In addition to a preface and a general introduction, the ***Manual*** gathers basic instrumental information that the authors and readers of all the articles and entries in the Handbook proper should be able to rely on, thus eliminating repetitions and extensive digressions. The following three areas are dealt with in the Manual:

i. The major *traditions* or approaches in, relevant to, or underlying pragmatics, either as a specific linguistic enterprise or as a scientific endeavor in general. The articles in this section give an overview of the traditions and approaches in question, with historical background information and a description of present and potential interactions with other traditions or approaches and the field of pragmatics as a whole.
ii. The major *methods of research* used or usable in pragmatics or pragmatics-related traditions.
iii. Different kinds of *notational systems*, including the most widespread transcription systems.

Obviously, these areas are closely interrelated and cannot be separated for any other than presentational purposes.

Even though methods change and traditions get reinterpreted constantly, the topics dealt with in the main body of the Handbook find a relatively stable frame of reference in the Manual; hence the bound format of the Manual. Yet, already at the time of its publication we were aware of a number of gaps which we are constantly – due to the changing field itself – trying to fill systematically. Therefore, the Installments of the Handbook over the years have also contained loose-leaf sections labeled in accordance with the three sections of the Manual: *Traditions*, *Methods*, and *Notational systems*. Articles in these sections were marked (in the upper right corner of the title page) '*TRADITIONS update*', etc. In the volumes that are to be published in bound format in the future, there will be separate TRADITIONS (etc.) sections whenever relevant, in addition to an alphabetically organized topical HANDBOOK A–Z section.

The main body of the ***Handbook*** consists of articles of various sizes, organized around entry-like key-words, alphabetically presented. They range in generality: some provide a general overview of a particular field (which cannot be captured under the label of a 'tradition'; see above), others discuss a specific topic in quite some detail. They present a state-of-the-art overview of what has been done on the topic. Where necessary, they also mention what has not been dealt with extensively (e.g. acquisitional and diachronic aspects), thus suggesting topics for further research. Important research in progress is mentioned where appropriate. In addition, some references to major works are given; these reference lists are kept reasonably restricted because of space limitations.

A different type of article in the body of the Handbook is devoted to the contributions made by an individual influential scholar and may contain interesting biographical information as well.

The Handbook attempts to document pragmatics dynamically. Consequently, a *loose-leaf* publication format was initially chosen for maximum flexibility and expandability (see the Editors' Note above) – properties that are even more characteristic of the **Handbook of Pragmatics** ***online***, which has therefore taken over that specific functionality to the point of rendering the loose-leaf printed format superfluous and replaceable by bound annual installments. By definition, there is no point in time when it is possible to say that the main body of the Handbook will be complete, though a reasonably comprehensive overview could be said to have been obtained after the eighth annual installment published in 2002, so that from then onwards, in addition to further *expansion*, there have been regular *revisions* and (in the online version) *updates* of older contributions. In the case of articles that are being replaced completely, the older versions are kept in the Archive section of the online version.

Even though we are now giving up paper publication in loose-leaf format, the very idea of continuous flexibility and expandability is retained. Being a vibrant field, pragmatics sees new openings and coherent subfields emerging constantly. Thus, every annual installment of the **Handbook of Pragmatics** will naturally also contain entries on such new directions of research.

## About the cumulative index

At the end of each printed annual installment of the *Handbook of Pragmatics*, you will find a complete index, with all necessary cross-references to ensure easy access to the available information (which continuously accumulates over the years). The index thus does not only contain references to concepts and matters to be found in the annual installment at hand, but cross-references to all Handbook entries that have appeared in the *Handbook of Pragmatics*. Needless to say, this cumulative index is also continuously updated in the online version of the Handbook, where it also contains direct links to relevant articles.

In addition to references to specific handbook entries, the index also contains lists of terms which are not used as entry headings but which do occur as alternative labels in the literature, with an indication of where exactly the topics in question are treated in the Handbook.

# Traditions

# Language psychology

Jacob Thøgersen, Søren Beck Nielsen, Lian Malai Madsen & Christina Fogtmann Fosgerau
University of Copenhagen

## 1. Overview

The purpose of this article is to describe the field of language psychology which – in a general sense – may be described as a cross-disciplinary concern with the question of how human beings achieve 'intersubjectivity' through communication. For the purposes of this article, we define intersubjectivity as individuals' shared understanding of each other and of the world surrounding them. The questions addressed by language psychology are in many cases also of central concern for other areas of language studies, but intersubjectivity through linguistic interaction has arguably been overlooked as a specialized field of study.

An initial clarification of terminology may be in order. Efforts to combine the field of linguistics with its focus on language structure and language use, with the field of psychology with its focus on human perception and cognition has led to different research foci and different compound names for the resulting disciplines. The combination of psychology and linguistics will for most readers probably be associated with *psycholinguistics*, a discipline which seeks "to achieve insight into the mental infrastructure that makes language use possible" (see Sandra 2010), focussing on the mind as a language processing entity. We propose *language psychology* as a compound name for the discipline that investigates language as a means for human beings to grasp the world around them, and as a means for achieving shared understanding between humans as social beings.[1] In cases where a shared term is needed, covering both disciplines, we will be referring to the *psychology of language*. As we will show, both disciplines have extensive histories in linguistic, psychological, sociological and philosophical theory; the suggestion that linguistics

1. Language psychology is, as we will show, rooted in 'continental' philosophy and linguistics, so a better term might in fact be the German *Sprachpsychologie* (to indicate the association with mainland Europe). In Copenhagen, which has a tradition spanning more than 40 years of teaching language psychology, the term used is *Sprogpsykologi*, i.e. the equivalent of the German compound.

https://doi.org/10.1075/hop.21.lan11

and psychology only met after 'the Chomskyan revolution' is but one version of the history of the language sciences.

The article is organised in three parts. In the first section, we briefly present the history and theoretical background of language psychology; in the second, we bring out some of the similarities and differences between language psychology and psycholinguistics, showing that although they are related, the disciplines have different points-of-departure and somewhat different epistemological interests. In the third and most extensive part of the article, we aim to illustrate how the classic questions of language psychology are still being addressed in various forms within linguistics and neighbouring disciplines. The disciplinary name of *language psychology*, or *Sprachpsychologie*, may not be widely used, but its research questions are undoubtedly still central to many areas of language studies.

## 2. History

Since time immemorial, linguists, philosophers, psychologists and like-minded thinkers have pondered the nature of language and the nature of the interface between language and mind, constituting central questions in what we might call *the psychology of language*. Blumenthal (1970) traces the modern, scientific study of *Sprachpsychologie*, or as he translates it 'psycholinguistics', to the days of the earliest proponent of modern psychology, Wilhelm Wundt (1832–1920) (see also Hermann & Gregersen 1978: 11–34 for a historical overview). Wundt was aware of and inspired by the linguists of his time, and he produced significant works on language production, language perception and the interplay between thought and language (e.g. Wundt 1900). An important element in Wundt's psychology (including his language psychology) was the concept of *apperception*, the discovery that the mind is active and selective, not passive in its perception of the world. In terms of language production and perception the concept highlights the listener's active search for meaning as well as the speaker's attempt to present material for meaningful interpretation. The human capacity for intersubjectivity thus took centre stage in language psychology from the outset.

A second foundation for language psychology comes from the language theory of Karl Bühler (1879–1963). His *Organon* model (Bühler 1965 [1934], 1990; Innis 1982) places language – or, more correctly, the linguistic sign – in a triangular field between a sender, a receiver and some state of affairs being communicated. This model has been the starting point for many similar models within the field of communication (e.g. Shannon & Weaver's mathematical model and Jakobson's functional communication model), but a central insight is easily overlooked, namely that language in Bühler's conception is essentially an *organon* – a tool for communication between human subjects, not a *structure* as in de Saussure's linguistic theory, or a mental faculty as in Chomsky's.

Finally, Hörmann's (1970, 1981, 1986) semantic theory should be mentioned as a significant theoretical inspiration in the development of language psychology. Hörmann combines contemporary linguistic and pragmatic theories with Bühlerian semiotics and considers intersubjective meaning-making the central concern of his work. As he phrases it (1986: 242), "the thesis which runs through this whole book [is]: the speaker makes an utterance in order to change the listener's consciousness". An overlooked but fundamental question to theoreticians and language users alike is what it means 'to understand an utterance': "Does the listener understand what the speaker says, or what the utterance means, or even what the speaker means?" (ibid.: 241f.). Hörmann (and language psychology) tends to focus on the last option listed here, 'what the speaker means'. Linguistics traditionally seems to have looked more at the first two options and thus has been more interested in looking at the linguistic sign abstracted away from the speaker's intentions. A basic premise in language psychology is that humans are capable of making sense of the world around them including the actions of their interactants. Indeed they are destined to do so. We cannot *not* ascribe intentions to an interactant's actions and utterances. Because we are always scanning input for the actor's intentions, the situational context is given as much weight as the linguistic signal in language psychological theory: the listener's understanding of an utterance is an understanding of the whole sign-speaker-context constellation, not of a sentence *in vacuo*.

In a sense, Bühler's *organon* model's focus on language as a communicative and expressive medium mirrors the language theory of Bakhtin and Voloshinov (and their criticism of de Saussure's structural linguistics with its focus on *langue* over *parole*). As Voloshinov (1973: 68) points out, "what is important for the speaker about a linguistic form is not that it is a stable and always self-equivalent signal, but that it is an always changeable and adaptable sign", and (ibid.: 70) "the linguistic form [...] exists for the speaker only in the context of specific utterances, [it] exists, consequently, only in a specific ideological context". The points raised so far are brought nicely together in a third quote from Voloshinov (1973: 102), "there is no reason for saying that meaning belongs to a word as such. In essence, meaning belongs to a word in its position between speakers; that is, meaning is realized only in the process of active, responsive understanding" (see Linell 1994).

We can see, then, that questions of the psychology of language including language psychology's questions of intersubjective meaning-making have been with us since the birth of modern psychology and modern linguistics (irrespective of whether we place this birth with e.g. de Saussure 1976 [1916] or Chomsky 2002 [1957]). The meeting of linguistics and psychology is not a new thing; the two were never truly separated.

## 3. Language psychology, psycholinguistics and related perspectives

In a programmatic article, Rommetveit[2] (1979a: 17) describes the 'current paradigm' of psycholinguistics, as exemplified by Chomsky's concept of Deep Structure (Chomsky 2015 [1965]), as "the child of structural linguistics and individual (as contrasted to *social*) psychology". In contrast to this paradigm, Rommetveit presents his alternative approach in which the situational context and joint orientation of the interactants are given primacy. A point of great importance to Rommetveit (1979a: 25) was that linguistic "encoding and decoding are complementary processes" (see also Rommetveit 1972). When composing an utterance, the speaker has in mind "the tacitly assumed shared social reality" between himself and the listener as well as the "free information" which has already been established or can be implied from previous interaction. Only on the basis of this information which the speaker assumes the listener has or can deduce, is the utterance, or as Rommetveit says "what is made known", presented. The listener's task is complementary. He or she will interpret the utterance based on knowledge they assume to be shared or deducible (and which they assume that the speaker will also assume to be shared and deducible). "Intersubjectivity has thus in some sense to be taken for granted in order to be achieved" (Rommetveit 1979b: 96, a point also made by Prætorius 2004, and one which may indeed be said to go back to Schütz' (1967) phenomenological sociology and Heidegger's phenomenology). We see that interaction is based on interactants' *keeping the other person's mind in mind* (to use a phrase we will return to below in our treatment of *social cognition research*). What matters to interactants is understanding what their interlocutors might be thinking and doing, and how they might change this through their own contributions.

A central element in understanding the listener's interpretation of an utterance is captured by the hermeneutic concept of *prejudice* or 'fore-meaning' (Gadamer 1989 [1975]: 271f.). As indicated by Wundt's notion of *apperception*, human beings are not passive in their approach to stimuli. We selectively orient towards certain things in our surroundings. In terms of language interaction, this means that we orient towards an utterance already expecting what it will be. Rommetveit (1979b) gives the example of an incoherent utterance, – "I too was invited. I went to the ball. And it rolled. And rolled away" – which may be a sign of schizophrenia, given one particular set of fore-meanings, or simply an instance of poetry given another set of expectations. Indeed, this focus on 'the understanding before the stimulus' is the basis of Stanley Fish's (1980) reader-response theory of literary criticism.

2. A fascinating introduction to Rommetveit's work and his influence is presented in a special issue of *Mind, Culture, and Activity* in 2003, edited by James Wertsch.

The intersubjective view on communication broadens the scope of what we may term 'language' and what the decoding of linguistic messages might involve. Voloshinov (1973: 103f.) cites a story from Dostoyevsky in which six men conduct a conversation using only one word, "a widely used obscenity". By using variable intonation and relying on the changing sequential context, they seem fully capable of interpreting communicative intentions and making communicative intentions known using only one and the same lexeme. This example may be used to highlight differences in epistemological points-of-departure between (interpretative and pragmatic) language psychology and the cognitivism of early psycholinguistics. From a psycholinguistic perspective, there is very little to learn about the cognitive and linguistic capacity for constructing sentences from the anecdote. From a language psychology perspective, on the other hand, there is nothing particularly remarkable about the exchange in itself: it is entirely common for everyday language interactions to be conducted (partly) by means of single syllable words, grunts, gestures and looks, and linguistics with focus on communication and intersubjectivity should be just as well suited to handle such interactions as the ones which rely on more elaborate linguistic structures. We are well aware that psycholinguistics since the post-Chomskyan era has come a long way towards including also pragmatic perspectives. The demarcation lines between the fields are considerably more blurred than in the rough sketch we are painting here.

Language psychology, then, is on the one hand a psychological discipline with focus on language and on the other a linguistic discipline with focus on meaning, and especially on how humans interpret each other's communicative intentions and make their own communicative intentions known. In terms of Morris' (1946) tripartite distinction between syntactics, semantics and pragmatics, language psychology sits somewhere between semantics, pragmatics and beyond, leaving syntactics to other linguistic disciplines. It should, however, also be clear that language psychology focuses more on 'the interpreting human being' than on the sign being interpreted – it is a psychology first and a linguistics second. It would be wrong to see language psychology as exclusively (or even primarily) theory of language. As a discipline, it borrows as much from social psychology, e.g. social cognition research, and from micro and macro sociology as it does from linguistics and pragmatics. We will discuss the interdisciplinary basis of language psychology further in the final sections of this article. In this section we will restrict ourselves to linking language psychology with current topics in linguistics (treated elsewhere in the *Handbook of Pragmatics*). It seems reasonable to point to *Construction Grammar* and *Frame Semantics* for obvious similarities (see the articles by Nikiforidou (2009) and Petruck (1996); and see also chapters in Hoffmann & Trousdale 2013). Like construction grammar, language psychology has little interest in distinguishing between meaning associated with lexicon vs. meanings associated with syntax. Its linguistic concerns are tied to the way 'form' and 'meaning' are associated in (more or less fixed) grammatical constructions and how these ready-made resources come to hold meaning for language users, rather than assuming that constructions and their interpretations are constructed anew in each instance. Again, the focus on the establishment of intersubjectivity takes precedence over interests in the human capacity for mental manipulation of symbols.

Language psychology shares with Frame Semantics the view that words must be understood as complex frames in which the understanding of a given word presupposes an understanding of related words and typical usage situations, including genres and registers (which we will develop further in the section on linguistic indexicality below). In a sense, this is congruent with the Russian formalists Bakhtin and Voloshinov mentioned earlier. Bakhtin wrote extensively on the meaning of genre and genre conventions and on heteroglossia, the 'foreignness' of the words we use. (See e.g. Bakhtin 1986.) To the complexity of word meanings analysed in frame semantics we should add the individual associations which William James (1950 [1890]), another early theorist in the psychology of language, presented. James would argue that meaning is always unique, located in our individual minds. The fact that we are able to make (apparently) meaningful communicative interactions in spite of that – and the way this is done – is perhaps the core interest to language psychology.

A final connection between language psychology and linguistic theory should be mentioned. Roy Harris's (1981, 1996, 1998, 2007) integrationist program has presented an iconoclastic attack on linguistics' attempt to isolate 'language' from the context in which language is used (see also Wolf & Love 1997; Duncker & Perregaard 2017). Different linguistic theories vary in the degree to which they assume that language(s) are stable structures. Integrationism would hold that there is no language, only language use (or in another parlance 'languaging') inseparable from contexts of use, and that the seemingly fixed structures described as 'languages' are more a product of linguistics and grammar books than of actual language use. The Voloshinov/Dostoyevsky anecdote presented above illustrates this point eloquently.

In the remainder of this article we will discuss research areas in which the questions posed by earlier generations of language psychologists are being investigated today. It is not our intention to suggest that these fields and schools of thoughts are 'really' language psychology. Our contention is rather that some of the questions that were raised in classic language psychology are still relevant to pursue today although they are now operationalized and treated differently. The traditions we point to do not comprise a unified theory or field; but we believe there is a benefit in exploring their connections, in an attempt to unify theoretical insights that are rarely discussed together. The discussion will refer to different disciplines, including micro and macro sociology, sociolinguistics and social psychology, to highlight different disciplinary perspectives that must, by necessity, be taken into consideration in addressing the fundamental questions of language psychology. Micro sociology provides central insights about human beings' ability to perform meaningful interactions; insights from macro sociology and sociolinguistics sketch the larger socio-historical backdrop against which meaning is projected; and from social psychology we learn about the mental states of human beings in interaction with other human beings, and human beings' capacity to make sense of each other's mental states. We have no intention of writing exhaustive research histories of any of the fields we draw on. Our aim is quite simply to explore how language psychology's central concern with intersubjectivity is shaped when discussed from a multi- or interdisciplinary perspective of this sort, and what we may learn about the establishment of intersubjectivity through interaction in doing so.

## 4. Micro sociology: Ethnomethodology and conversation analysis

Intersubjectivity lies at the heart of etnomethodological (EM) and conversation analytic (CA) research (see Firth 1994 on *Ethnomethodology*, especially Section 4, and Clift, Drew & Hutchby 2006 on *Conversation Analysis*). These research traditions – separately or in combination – are particularly valuable for language psychology because they, very concretely and always empirically anchored, illustrate how members use conversationally organized language and embodied resources to establish intersubjective understanding. We shall briefly illustrate this with some examples from the origins of EM and CA, respectively.

In an often-cited experiment by the founder of EM, sociologist Harold Garfinkel, an experimenter (E) asked a subject (S), who happened to be E's husband, to clarify even the most mundane and innocent remarks. When the experimenter did this in response to the subject's casual comments during television watching, it made subject react in this way (Garfinkel 1967: 42):

S: What's the matter with you? You know what I mean.
E: I wish you could be more specific.
S: You know what I mean! Drop Dead!

In this particular case, the husband displays an orientation towards his wife's inquiries as unnecessary or irrelevant; he implies that he thinks that she knows perfectly well what he means. Garfinkel's experiment illustrates that conversationalists may, and presumably tend to, treat their remarks as for-all-practical-purposes sufficiently self-explanatory. Crude violation of the tacit contract that remarks make good sense can lead to overt hostility and conversational breakdown. For language psychology, a simple experiment such as this one offers valuable insights. Seen in relation to the phenomenological philosophy of Alfred Schütz briefly mentioned above, it lends support to the assumption that actors by-and-large engage in interaction presupposing that shared understanding about thoughts, considerations, experiences, observations etc. is feasible for-all-practical-purposes, despite actors' different biographies and spatial positions.

CA is one of the dominant methods for the study of social organization *in situ*, that is, of orderly use of talk and embodied conduct in interaction. CA's main strength, not least for language psychology, lies in its empirical foundation, always using "observation as a basis for theorizing" as Harvey Sacks put it (1984: 25). As Emanuel Schegloff has argued, any orderly conversational resource which members use to make sense of one another deserves to be described in detail (Schegloff 1993). CA studies illustrate the highly attentive ways in which actors exploit detailed conversational organization to accomplish sufficient intersubjectivity to carry out joint businesses. For example, Sacks distinguished between actors' ways of claiming or demonstrating understanding when they respond to utterances such as answers to questions (Sacks 1992, Vol II: 141–142). In the third turn of the following example, A implies that he or she knows the whereabouts of the Pacific Palisades, in effect *claiming* understanding:

A: Where are you staying?
B: Pacific Palisades.
A: Oh Pacific Palisades.

But A could also have replied by saying the following, thereby *demonstrating* understanding:

A: Oh at the west side of town.

In this answer, A displays that she/he recognizes Pacific Palisades as a western district of Los Angeles. She/he *demonstrates* to B that they share an understanding of the location of Pacific Palisades – and makes it possible for A to confirm or challenge this shared knowledge.

Another way to describe the project of CA is to say that it investigates the concrete *architecture of intersubjectivity*, that is, the conversational organization by which "a context of publicly displayed and continuously up-dated understandings is systematically sustained" (Heritage 1984: 259). This architecture offers members resources to validate their understandings of one another and to react upon an anticipated or recognized misunderstanding by means of repair mechanisms. Sacks proposed that conversational organization offers *proof procedures* through which participants may check if they have been understood properly by monitoring how recipients respond to their own contributions (Sacks 1992, Vol II: 252; Sacks, Schegloff & Jefferson 1974: 728). This mechanism is vital for the accomplishment of intersubjectivity. When threats to intersubjectivity are detected (or anticipated), conversational organization offers participants possibilities to *repair* the talk in order to optimize the possibility of shared understanding. Repairs may be initiated by speakers themselves in anticipation of upcoming trouble (Schegloff, Jefferson & Sacks 1977), but it is also possible for recipients to pre-emptively address difficulties in understanding, and thereby have speakers express themselves more clearly in anticipation of upcoming problems to intersubjectivity. Schegloff (1992) suggests that a third position, that is, a repair after the next turn, which follows the trouble source, is the last structurally provided defence of intersubjectivity in conversation. It is possible to repair an understanding later than in a third position, but the sequential context no longer provides a structural possibility to do so. We will return to repair sequences and especially pre-emptive repair in the last section of this article because it turns out to be remarkably fruitful when we want to gain insights into interactants' understanding of each other's minds.

Using the conversation analytic method, a recent study within the framework of language psychology looks into dialogue between general practitioners and patients. The study concerns the duration of patients' symptoms (Beck Nielsen 2015). To paraphrase Schütz (1967), when patients explain the duration of symptoms they transcend from the natural state of 'living in time' to the radically different state of 'reflecting upon living in time'. Shared understanding of this issue is a matter of medical importance, for example in terms of relevant treatment options: do the symptoms require urgent treatment, or should patients go home and wait and see how the symptoms develop over time? Patients frequently explain the duration of their symptoms on their own initiative. When they do not, doctors may ask them. The following transcript offers an example of the latter scenario from a Danish context. It is transcribed following standard CA principles (Jefferson 2004) and accompanied by English paraphrases line by line. The patient has been examined for her stiff neck, and the doctor has consented to provide her with a referral to a physiotherapist. The parties, however, never got to talk about exactly how long the patient has suffered from a stiff neck, and here the doctor asks her how long she has had her symptoms:

01. DO: *er det ↑tre uger siden eller hvor længe har du cirka haft det?*
was it ↑three weeks ago or how long have you had it approximately?
02. PA: *.h det her har jeg haft en:::::: uges- (.3) °hva er det° nogle*
.h this here I've had fo:::::r a week- (.3) °what is it° some
03. *dage=↑fire dage.*
days=↑four days.

The doctor's initial yes/no question proposes three weeks as the most likely answer. However, the doctor asks in yet another way before the patient answers – now with a formally more open 'how long' question. The patient overtly answers the second question, that is, without a type-conforming initial 'yes' or 'no'. However, at the same time she arguably orients towards her answer as a dispreferred one: She displays hesitance towards answering the question, accomplished by means of an initial audible in-breath, prolonged vowel length, pause, and restarts. In other words: She treats 'four days' as a slightly inappropriate answer, perhaps because of the significant gap between three weeks, which the doctor's first question initially suggested as a likely answer, and a mere four days.

In general, doctors and patients tend to arrive at shared understandings of the duration of patients' symptoms (as well as the 'appropriate' or 'normal' length for symptoms to persist), at least sufficiently shared understandings for the practical purpose of reaching a diagnosis and settling upon a relevant treatment plan. But the road may be winding. It may be necessary for the participants to correct each other's assumptions, as in the example above, and doing so in ways which allow all parties involved to recognize that a potentially dispreferred correction takes place. Furthermore, it may be treated as appropriate to recognize that the duration is actually *shorter* than assumed. The latter is noteworthy in the light that the study in mention finds that patients overwhelmingly use categories that stress the persistence of their symptoms. It seems that emphasising the persistence of the symptoms means that the visit to the clinic is legitimate: more is more. Thus, 'reflecting upon living in time' implies using categories that are anything but neutral.

EM and CA are important for language psychology because research into the social organization of interaction provides insights about intersubjectivity as a practical accomplishment, mediated and conditioned by identifiable resources that unfold temporally and sequentially *in situ*. Two perspectives on intersubjectivity, with significance for language psychology, that are left unaddressed by EM and CA are how the identified processes relate to societal macro structures, and how intersubjective understanding is related to mental states and emotions. In the following section, we will look closer at these issues.

## 5. The macro in the micro: Discourse, conversational inference and linguistic indexicality

Language psychology, we have argued, is centrally concerned with how meaning is created between people through language in specific communicative contexts. In addressing the central questions of language psychology, it is relevant to look at how wider socio-historical relations play a part in the meaning-making between individuals, how language itself is embedded in wider societal structures, and how the relation between linguistic forms and societal structures can impact on and be exploited in the situated accomplishment of shared understanding. Pointing to the nature of language as inherently individual and contextual, Bakhtin (1986: 88; see also Björklund's 2000) states that "any word exists for the speaker in three aspects: as a neutral word of a language, belonging to nobody; as an *other's* word, which belongs to another person and is filled with echoes of the other's utterance; and, finally, as *my* word, for, since I am dealing with it in a particular situation, with a particular speech plan, it is already imbued with my expression" (italics in original). With the formulation "the echoes of the other's utterances" Bakhtin points to the relation of utterances to other people and to the lived cultural world in time and place and thereby to the embeddedness of utterances in a history of expressions, produced in chains of utterings at particular moments. Such a wider historical perspective on expressions has significance, of course, for both the meaning of the utterance and the language forms used.

To address the socio-historical dimensions of intersubjectivity, language psychology takes inspiration from various types of discourse analysis. Discourses, here referring to ways of using language to add meaning to phenomena and experiences from a particular perspective (e.g. Cameron 2001; Blommaert 2005; see also Wodak 2006), certainly involve shared understanding; and discourse analysis in this sense focuses on the circulation, repetition and transformation of shared meaning. Engaging with discourses from a language psychological point of view, however, requires attention to the actual articulations of discourses and their specific implementation in concrete communicative situations. Discursive psychology represents one such approach, very much in tune with the interests of language psychology. Rather than viewing discourses, like Foucault would do, as abstract statements, discursive psychology sees discourses as an important part of what makes up the common sense of a culture. It views discourse as a social practice, by focusing on how shared common understanding, or *interpretive repertoires*, are used in particular contexts of communication (Wetherell & Potter 1992; see also Potter 1994, especially Section 3.5). Below we discuss an example of how interpretive repertoires concerning parental educational aspirations, combined with ethno-linguistic stereotypes, are employed in a conversation among adolescents to comment on and regulate situated behaviour of a school friend in the schoolyard. In this case, the local implementation of a shared understanding of a particular social character – and the social values associated with this – crucially hinges on the imitation of a particular speech style.

The relation of language forms to human beings, social groups and the wider socio-cultural context is the key concern of sociolinguistics (see Romaine's 1995). While language psychology does not share variationist sociolinguists' concerns with the distribution and change of language forms, it clearly aligns with many questions addressed within interactional sociolinguistics (see Verschueren 2010) concerning the interactive accomplishment of meaning and the nature of inferencing in conversation, including how participants in interaction make assessments of each other's intentions based on the range of signs displayed, and how they coordinate their responses in line with such assessments (Gumperz 1982: Chapter 7). A significant point made by Gumperz is that people rely on socio-cultural knowledge in such inferencing, and the tradition of interactional sociolinguistics thereby attempts to incorporate attention to macro-social structures in the micro-analysis of specific interactional encounters. This is achieved by means of methods designed to investigate the links between semiotic practices in the here-and-now and the historical and socio-cultural embeddedness of the resources used, including language. CA has inspired interactional sociolinguistics in adopting an analytical focus on how turns-at-talk relate to one another in a stretch of conversation, combined with an interest in how utterances are meaningfully composed with respect to prosody, accent, grammar and word choice. Analyses of social interaction in this tradition also tend to take the types of activities relevant to the interaction into account. What are the participants engaged in during the conversation? Where does the interaction take place? Who are present? And what type of conversation is it? Interactional sociolinguists pay particular attention to how the linguistic resources used in a particular context relate to recognizable linguistic styles, codes or registers, which in turn are associated with particular social types and values (Rampton 2006; Coupland 2007; Agha 2007). Understanding these connections is important for the analysis of how particular utterances function in the here-and-now. The central point is that local interactions and language forms are always permeated by (common) socio-cultural assumptions involving macro-social relations. Micro-analysis is therefore typically combined with ethnographic research providing the empirical basis for considering contextual conditions in a wider sense, such as the social relationship between participants and their former interactional history, as well as institutional, moral or ideological codes, cultural conventions, values and social roles of currency in the communities in which the interaction takes place (Rampton 2006; Madsen 2015). Interactional sociolinguistics contributes to the understanding of intersubjectivity by demonstrating that many processes of interpretation in interaction cannot be explained without reference to implicit taken-for-granted socio-cultural assumptions, including the symbolic value of speaking styles (see Verschueren 2010). On a par with other communicative practices, (shifts in) speaking styles function as *contextualization cues* that constrain participants' interpretations of social activities relevant to a particular situation. When all participants understand and notice such cues they seem to go unnoticed (Gumperz 1982), but recent interactional sociolinguistic work has also taken an interest in situations where the seemingly situationally incongruous use of linguistic styles may point to and comment on taken-for-granted socio-cultural assumptions (Jaspers 2010; Madsen 2014).

Linguistic stylisations are examples of such marked self-conscious and non-routine linguistic practices (Coupland 2007; Rampton 2006). Stylisation is defined by Rampton (2009: 149) as instances of speech where speakers produce "specially marked and often exaggerated representations of languages, dialects, and styles that lie outside their own habitual repertoire (at least as this is perceived within the situation at hand)". Such practices implicitly or explicitly involve an evaluation of linguistic forms and their association with recognizable cultural models, identities and values. Stylisations acquire meaning by drawing on shared understanding of the (potential) indexical values of linguistic signs, as part of particular styles, rooted in the signs' historical and social relationships. So, on the one hand, stylisation as a speech practice complicates the relationship between language, speaker and social categories or stereotypes because a speaker uses language in an unexpected way. On the other hand, acts of stylisation perpetuate language ideological constructions by flagging sociolinguistic stereotypes and possibly forging new ones (Madsen 2014; Jaspers 2010). For language psychology, such practices are fruitful to study as an entry into how utterances comment on the situation in which they are produced. As such, they serve as illustrations of participants' perceptions of – and possibly their critical commentary on – ideological representations of language and social behaviour. Attending to stylised language use thus combines an interest in how widely circulated discourses about social types and language are used to generate meaning with an interest in the role of socio-historical associations related to linguistic forms and styles in practices of situated meaning-making. The following example of an adolescent's use of foreign-accented English in a conversation in a Danish schoolyard, otherwise carried out in Danish by pupils with minority ethnic background, may serve to illustrate these points (detailed analysis in Madsen & Svendsen 2015):

During break time in an urban public school in Copenhagen, Denmark, Kurima and Shahid have been discussing their results in a recent reading test where Shahid achieved a mid-level mark. He claims that next time he will achieve top marks. Bashaar, another boy also present in the schoolyard, then joins the conversation and begins a performance in English, stylised with an (Asian?) accent very different from Bashaar's typical (Danish) English accent:

> you (.) my friend you've got a very beautiful future in front of you you're gonna travel to Lon↑don (.) and stu↑dy you're gonna study in Bol↑ton I think it's gonna be a very good eh eh lesson for ↑you because you are are are a man with a heart of gold.

Bashaar's utterances are marked by a range of uncharacteristic pronunciation features. Apart from the codeswitch from Danish to English, the marked features include unrounded and fronted /ʌ/ in *London*, and *study*, approximately [ɜ], trilled alveolar [r] in *front* and *brain*, monophtong [e:] instead of diphtong in *brain*, aspirated final [$d^h$] in *friend* and a flapped alveolar [ɾ] instead of [t] in *beautiful*, as well as stress and pitch rise on the final syllables in certain words (*London* and *Bolton*). The pronunciation features function as contextualization cues, all pointing to a non-serious framing of the situation while stereotypically indexing an (adult) English learner (or a non-Anglo accent). In addition, the content, intonation and pauses function as contextualization cues indexing a performance of a public speech. That the speech genre and the accent are noticed and recognized by the other participants is indicated by Shahid reacting with a "thank you" (also in English), Bashaar further reacting to an interruption with the comment: "let me finish let me finish my speech with my boy with my son" and some girls adding "stop det der libanesisk" ('stop that Lebanese'). This episode can be seen as Bashaar reacting to a friend's academic boasting by performing the voice of a supportive fatherly persona, praising the heart and mind of his son, all the while assuming the shared understanding of such a character. In contrast to this evocation of high academic aspirations, the voice of the persona is performed with features associated with adult-learner English. This combination seems to invoke associations of a naivety on the part of the father figure, highlighting high ambitions in relation to the relatively poor academic value of the linguistic resources demonstrated here. Thereby Bashaar's performance seems to function locally as a playful sanctioning of a friend's behaviour and evokes a wider stereotype of (unrealistic) parental expectations for a successful future.

In this example we see how a shared interpretive repertoire, relating to a particular social character as well the mental/semiotic associations of the speech style, is activated in situated performance, being absolutely central to the generation of shared local meaning. However, it is also central that the local function of this language use contributes to the meaning it achieves in this particular situation. In this episode, the non-academic and incompetent associations stereotypically attached to adult and newcomer-accented speech are locally exploited in a playful manner to put a friend in his place after he has explicitly claimed a perhaps too-ambitious academic and linguistic status. Thereby the stereotypic ethnically-coloured language use is used to highlight a more general marginal social (and academic) positioning associated with linguistic incompetence, rather than a specific ethnic identity. (See similar examples in Jaspers 2011 among adolescents in Antwerp "talking illegal").

## 6. Perception of mental states in (inter)action

In the preceding sections, we have argued that language psychology investigates the achievement of intersubjectivity through language *in situ* as participants draw on (and renegotiate) shared socio-cultural knowledge. We have reflected on how human beings use linguistic resources in order to come to shared understandings of their (social) world. In the field of social cognition research[3] (SCR), psychologists and philosophers study a related problem, namely how people make sense of people by addressing the question: how are we able to know another person's mind? It is agreed within SCR that mental states (desires, emotions, beliefs etc.) matter when individuals attempt to make sense of others, and it is suggested that without any kind of perception of the mental states of co-interactants, establishment of intersubjectivity

3. Note that the concept of *social cognition* is used in a different sense in Potter (1994).

is challenged (Fonagy et al. 1998: 8; Krych-Appelbaum et al. 2007; Takahashi et al. 2013). Keeping the other person's mental states in mind has been shown to affect the relational experiences of intimacy and safety between interactants (Allen & Fonagy 2006: 16), and a general feeling of being met and understood. It has even been suggested that a therapist's ability to automatically perceive the mental states of a client is the most important component in psychotherapeutic treatment (Fonagy 2003: 271). Intersubjectivity is more than an intellectual understanding of interlocutors' thoughts. Shared understanding is also understanding interlocutors' emotional states and dispositions as well as feeling understood in one's own mental states. In the following section, we will discuss how insights from SCR on the ability to perceive another person's mental states may be linked with the perspectives on intersubjectivity developed within conversation analysis, as discussed above. The aim of combining insights from SCR and CA is twofold: First, it allows us to investigate how interactants' perceptions of co-interactants' mental states unfold *in real time* – what does it look like when an interactant displays the ability to keep another person's mind in mind in an ongoing interaction? Second, it broadens interaction-analytic studies to include a focus on the ways in which perceptions of other persons' mental states may affect the establishment of intersubjectivity and relational and emotional processes and outcomes.

### 6.1 Social cognition perspectives

SCR introduces a variety of concepts to account for the ability to know the other person's mental states, such as empathy, mentalizing and theory of mind. The concepts' theoretical underpinnings differ (Zahavi 2008; Davidsen & Fosgerau 2015a; Liljenfors & Lundh 2014). Basically, perception processes are attended to as either pre-reflective and automatic or as reflective and involving representational activity. Whereas phenomenologists consider immediate and pre-reflective processes as essential, theorized through concepts like *empathy* (Ratcliffe 2012) and *direct perception* (Gallagher 2008), researchers working within the general framework of *Theory of Mind* are concerned with reflective processes that are either inferential or imply simulation processes, to account for the understanding of other minds.

The concept of *mentalizing* captures both pre-reflective and reflective processes as it refers to "the mental processes by which an individual implicitly and explicitly interprets the actions of himself and others as meaningful on the basis of intentional mental states such as personal desires, needs, feelings, beliefs and reason" (Bateman & Fonagy 2004: 21). The explicit–implicit dimension introduced by the quote springs from the hypothesis that processes of keeping mind in mind are both automatic/unconscious and controlled/conscious in different contexts and possibly even at the same time. Understanding of minds mostly depends on implicit processes, but when intersubjectivity is challenged, explicit processes are needed (Allen et al. 2003). When studying people making sense of people, the mentalizing framework thus enables a focus on processes that are both reflective and pre-reflective in nature. Also, the mentalizing framework, in contrast to some of the above-mentioned theories under SCR, offers a perspective in which the ability to understand the other person's mind is considered highly dynamic. Mentalizing varies with co-interactants' ways of interacting, and it can, in line with ideas developed within dialogical approaches to communication, be considered as a co-constructed interactional phenomenon (Luyten et al. 2012). It seems obvious then, and it is a language psychological goal, to study the processes of keeping mind in mind from an interaction analytical perspective.

### 6.2 Studying mentalizing processes in situ

To study how mentalizing processes affect the establishment of intersubjectivity and relational processes, we need to consider what mentalizing processes look like and how they are enacted. Numerous methods exist within SCR in general and mentalizing research in specific that describe and assess the ability to perceive other minds (Luyten et al. 2012). However, none of them tap into mentalizing as it happens in interaction between people as exchanges unfold in real time, what we may call *online* mentalizing. Instead, established methods assess mentalizing experimentally, as a decontextualized phenomenon in which informants' answers and responses are studied without reference to their engagement in a social encounter (i.e. *offline* mentalizing) (Przyrembel et al. 2012; Antaki 2004).

Understanding online mentalizing processes is claimed to be challenged by methodological constraints (Schilbach 2014). However, one dominant view is that online social cognition is closely tied to interaction (Przyrembel et al. 2012; Gallagher 2001; Ratcliffe 2014), since the basis of both explicit and implicit processes of social cognition is suggested to lie in the process of interacting (De Jaegher 2009). To study online mentalizing we therefore need to conduct in-depth investigations of interacting. The (psychological) field of social cognition does not offer a method that allows us to consider such linguistic and interactional processes, so this is where linguistics plays a central role.

In line with interactional approaches to social cognition, a language psychological approach attends to both implicit and explicit online mentalizing, studied by means of CA-inspired interactional analyses. Traditionally, CA is not concerned with analysing interactants' mental states. However, aspects having to do with perspective taking and recipient sensitivity, and therefore also with social cognition, are already deeply embedded in the establishment of intersubjectivity as theorised within CA (Fosgerau et al. 2018). As we have touched upon, CA scholars view the establishment of intersubjectivity as an inherent element in the structure of conversation which can be observed by studying how interactants routinely display how they make sense of each other's utterances (i.e. proof procedures). We argue that such displays also project interactants' understanding of co-interactants' mental states. The displays can be *explicit*, as when interactants comment upon or ask co-interactants how they feel, think or what their intentions were. The latter is often enacted in sequences of repair. However, by including the knowledge accumulated in CA about rules and orders of interactions that interactants orient towards, *implicit* processes of mentalizing can also be identified. These processes display themselves in various ways through interactants' turn designs without being explicitly attended to by interactants. For example, when an interactant redesigns an utterance which is not immediately accepted by the co-interactant to whom it is directed, this might be seen as displaying a pre-reflective sensitivity towards the mental state of that co-interactant – an orientation to the understanding that the initial formulation might have offended, hurt or in other ways been unacceptable to the co-interlocutor. In specific sequential contexts, interactional activities such as pre-emptive completions, self-repairs in same turn, immediate modification of a response from preferred to dis-preferred design, and mirroring of a co-interlocutor's tone of voice might also be interpreted as displaying pre-reflective mentalizing, displaying the speaker's interpretation of the interlocutor's mental state (Davidsen & Fosgerau 2015b).

This approach in which perceptions of co-interactants' mental states are included as a focus of interest to inform interactional analysis of intersubjectivity and relational establishments brings new perspectives to interactional analysis by combining the tools of CA with contemporary social psychological theory. Among other things, it has been applied in studies of physicians' interactions with patients diagnosed with depression. Based on video recordings, Davidsen and Fosgerau (2014, 2015b) analyses and discusses how physicians display reflective and pre-reflective mentalizing of patients to different degrees, and with different relational and therapeutic effects. Also, based on recordings of dinner conversations at a residential care school, caregivers' online mentalizing of the adolescents was analyzed. Davidsen and Fosgerau found that when neither reflective nor pre-reflective mentalizing was displayed by the caregivers in sequential contexts in which disagreements were displayed, the interpersonal challenges were not resolved and the conflict often became entrenched. The absence of online mentalizing led to situations where the caregivers displayed annoyance and irritation, while the adolescents displayed rigidity, repeated their points of view without modification and became upset, often leaving the room or disrupting the interaction in others ways. On the other hand, when caregivers displayed online mentalizing, the young people started reflecting upon their own points of view and explained them and regulated their emotionality. Disagreements were not necessarily resolved, but the relations between caregivers and the adolescents were apparently not damaged (Fosgerau et al. 2018).

The language psychology approach outlined above not only broadens the scope of interaction analysis to aspects regarding relational and emotional outcomes by including a focus on perceptions of mental states, it also illuminates what has until now only been claimed but not accounted for in SCR, *viz.* the ways in which online social cognition is displayed in social interaction.

## References


Agha, A. 2007. *Language and Social Relations*. Cambridge: Cambridge University Press.

Allen, J. G., E. Bleiberg and T. Haslam-Hopwood. 2003. "Mentalizing as a compass for treatment." *Bullentin of the Menninger Clinic* 67: 1–11. https://doi.org/10.1521/bumc.67.1.1.23451

Allen, J. G. and P. Fonagy. 2006. *Handbook of Mentalization-Based Treatment*. Hoboken, NJ: John Wiley & Sons. https://doi.org/10.1002/9780470712986

Antaki, C. 2004. "Reading minds or dealing with interactional implications?" *Theory & Psychology* 14(5): 667–683. https://doi.org/10.1177/0959354304046178

Bakhtin, M. 1986. *Speech Genres and other Late Essays*. Austin: University of Texas Press.

Bateman, A. and P. Fonagy. 2004. *Psychotherapy for Borderline Personality Disorder: Mentalization-Based Treatment*. Oxford: Oxford University Press. https://doi.org/10.1093/med:psych/9780198527664.001.0001

Beck Nielsen, S. 2015. "'And how long have you been sick?': The discursive construction of symptom duration during acute general practice visits and its implications for 'doctorability'." *Time and Society*. Advance online publication. https://doi.org/10.1177/0961463X15609808

Björklund, M. 2000. "Mikhail Bakhtin." In *Handbook of Pragmatics*, vol. 6, ed. by J.-O. Östman and J. Verschueren. Amsterdam: John Benjamins. https://doi.org/10.1075/hop.6.bak1

Blommaert, J. 2005. *Discourse: A Critical Introduction*. Cambridge: Cambridge University Press. https://doi.org/10.1017/CBO9780511610295

Blumenthal, A. L. 1970. *Language and Psychology*. Hoboken, NJ: John Wiley and sons.

Bühler, K. 1965 [1934]. *Sprachtheorie*. Ullstein.

Bühler, K. 1990. *Theory of Language: The Representational Function of Language*. Amsterdam: John Benjamins. https://doi.org/10.1075/fos.25

Cameron, D. 2001. *Working with Spoken Discourse*. London: Sage Publications.

Chomsky, N. 2002 [1957]. *Syntactic Structures*. Berlin: Mouton de Gruyter.

Chomsky, N. 2015 [1965]. *Aspects of the Theory of Syntax*. Cambridge, Mass.: The MIT Press.

Clift, R., P. Drew and I. Hutchby. 2006. "Conversation analysis." In *Handbook of Pragmatics*, vol. 10, ed. by J.-O. Östman and J. Verschueren. Amsterdam: John Benjamins. https://doi.org/10.1075/hop.10.con4

Coupland, N. 2007. *Style: Language Variation and Identity*. Cambridge: Cambridge University Press. https://doi.org/10.1017/CBO9780511755064

Davidsen, A. S. and C. F. Fosgerau. 2014. "General practitioners' and psychiatrists' responses to emotional disclosures in patients with depression." *Patient Education and Counseling* 95: 61–68. https://doi.org/10.1016/j.pec.2013.12.018

Davidsen, A. S. and C. F. Fosgerau. 2015a. "Grasping the process of implicit mentalization." *Theory & Psychology* 25(4): 434–454. https://doi.org/10.1177/0959354315580605

Davidsen, A. S. and C. F. Fosgerau. 2015b. "Mirroring patients – or not: A study of general practitioners and psychiatrists and their interactions with patients with depression."*European Journal of Psychotherapy & Counselling* 17(2): 162–178. https://doi.org/10.1080/13642537.2015.1027785

De Jaegher, H. 2009. "Social understanding through direct perception? Yes, by interacting." *Consciousness and Cognition* 18: 535–542. https://doi.org/10.1016/j.concog.2008.10.007

Duncker, D. and B. Perregaard. 2017. "Communication: Creativity and continuity." In *Creativity and Continuity – Perspectives on the Dynamics of Language Conventionalization*, ed. by D. Duncker and B. Perregaard, 7–40. Copenhagen: UPress.
Firth, A. 1994. "Ethnomethodology." In *Handbook of Pragmatics: Manual*, ed. by J. Verschueren, J.-O. Östman and J.Blommaert, 269–278. Amsterdam: John Benjamins. https://doi.org/10.1075/hop.m.eth2
Fish, S. 1980. *Is there a Text in this Class?* Cambridge, Mass.: Harvard University Press.
Fonagy, P. 2003. "Epilogue." *Bulletin of the Menninger Clinic* 67: 271–280. https://doi.org/10.1521/bumc.67.3.271.23438
Fonagy, P., M. Target, H. Steele and M. Steele. 1998. *Reflective-Functioning Manual, Version 5.0, for Application to Adult Attachment Interviews*. London: University College London.
Fosgerau, C. F., A. Schöps, P. L. Bak and A. D. Davidsen. 2018. "Exploring implicit mentalizing as an online process." *Nordic Psychology* 70(2): 129–145. https://doi.org/10.1080/19012276.2017.1374204
Gadamer, H.-G. 1989 [1975]. *Truth and Method*. New York: Continuum.
Gallagher, S. 2001. "The practice of mind: Theory, simulation or primary interaction." *Journal of Consciousness Studies* 8: 83–108.
Gallagher, S. 2008. "Direct perception in the intersubjective context." *Consciousness and Cognition* 17: 535–543. https://doi.org/10.1016/j.concog.2008.03.003
Garfinkel, H. 1967. *Studies in Ethnomethodology*. Englewood Cliffs, NJ: Prentice-Hall.
Gumperz, J. 1982. *Discourse Strategies*. Cambridge: Cambridge University Press. https://doi.org/10.1017/CBO9780511611834
Harris, R. 1981. *The Language Myth*. London: Duckworth.
Harris, R. 1996. *Signs, Language and Communication*. London: Routledge.
Harris, R. 1998. *Introduction to Integrational Linguistics*. Oxford: Pergamon.
Harris, R. 2007. "Integrational linguistics." In *Handbook of pragmatics*, vol. 11, ed. by J.-O. Östman
Heritage, J. 1984. *Garfinkel and Ethnomethodology*. Cambridge: Polity Press.
Hermann, J. and F. Gregersen. 1978. *Gennem Sproget* [*Via language*]. Copenhagen: Gyldendal.
Hoffmann, T. and G. Trousdale (eds). 2013. *The Oxford Handbook of Construction Grammar*. Oxford: Oxford University Press.
Hörmann, H. 1970. *Psychologie der Sprache*. Berlin: Springer. https://doi.org/10.1007/978-3-662-28290-8
Hörmann, H. 1981. *To Mean – To Understand*. Berlin: Springer. https://doi.org/10.1007/978-3-642-67883-7
Hörmann, H. 1986. *Meaning and Context: An Introduction to the Psychology of Language*. New York: Plenum Press.
Innis, R. 1982. *Karl Bühler Semiotic Foundations of Language Theory*. Berlin: Springer Science and Business Media. https://doi.org/10.1007/978-1-4757-0923-0
James, W. 1950 [1890]. *The Principles of Psychology*, vol. 1–2. Mineola, NY: Dover Publications.
Jaspers, J. 2010. "Introduction – Society and language use." In *Society and Language Use*, ed. by J. Jaspers, J.-O. Östman and J. Verschueren, 1–20. Amsterdam: John Benjamins. https://doi.org/10.1075/hoph.7
Jaspers, J. 2011. "Talking like a zerolingual: Ambiguous linguistic caricatures at an urban secondary school. *Journal of Pragmatics* 43: 1264–1287. https://doi.org/10.1016/j.pragma.2010.05.012
Jefferson, G. 2004. "Glossary of transcript symbols with an introduction." In *Conversation Analysis: Studies from the First Generation*, ed. by G. H. Lerner, 13–31. Amsterdam: John Benjamins. https://doi.org/10.1075/pbns.125.02jef

Krych-Appelbaum, M., J. B. Law, D. Jones and J. P. Keenan. 2007. "'I think I know what you mean': The role of theory of mind in collaborative communication." *Interaction Studies* 8(2): 267–280. https://doi.org/10.1075/is.8.2.05kry

Liljenfors, R. and L.-G. Lundh. 2014. "Mentalization and intersubjectivity: Towards a theoretical integration." *Psychoanalytic Psychology* 32(1): 36–60.

Linell, P. 1994. "Dialogical analysis." In *Handbook of Pragmatics*, ed. by J.-O. Östman and J. Verschueren. Amsterdam: John Benjamins. https://doi.org/10.1075/hop.m.dia2

Luyten, P., P. Fonagy, B. Lowyck and R. Vermote. 2012. "Assessment of mentalization." In *Handbook of Mentalizing in Mental Health Practice*, ed. by A. Bateman and P. Fonagy, 43–65. American Psychiatric Publishing.

Madsen, L. M. 2014. "Heteroglossia, voicing and social categorisation." In *Heteroglossia as Practice and Pedagogy*, ed. by A. Blackledge and A. Creese, 41–58. Berlin: Springer. https://doi.org/10.1007/978-94-007-7856-6_3

Madsen, L. M. 2015. *Fighters, Girls and Other Identities: Sociolinguistics in a Martial arts Club*. Bristol: Multilingual Matters. https://doi.org/10.21832/9781783093991

Madsen, L. M. and B. A. Svendsen. 2015. "Stylized voices of ethnicity and social division." In *Language, Youth and Identity in the 21st Century*, ed. by J. Nortier and B. A. Svendsen, 207–230. Cambridge: Cambridge University Press. https://doi.org/10.1017/CBO9781139061896.015

Morris, C. W. 1946. *Signs, Language and Behavior*. Englewood Cliffs, NJ: Prentice-Hall. https://doi.org/10.1037/14607-000

Nikiforidou, K. 2009. "Constructional analysis." In *Handbook of Pragmatics*, ed. by J.-O. Östman and J. Verschueren. Amsterdam: John Benjamins. https://doi.org/10.1075/hop.13.con14

Petruck, M. R. L. 1996. "Frame semantics." In *Handbook of Pragmatics*, ed. by J.-O. Östman and J. Verschueren. Amsterdam: John Benjamins. https://doi.org/10.1075/hop.2.fra1

Potter, J. 1994. "Social psychology." In *Handbook of Pragmatics*, ed. by J.-O. Östman and J. Verschueren. Amsterdam: John Benjamins. https://doi.org/10.1075/hop.m.soc1

Prætorius, N. 2004. "Subjektets intersubjektivitet og intersubjektivitetens subjekt [The intersubjectivity of the subject and the subjectivity of intersubjectivity]." In *Subjektivitet og Videnskab* [*Subejctivity and Science*], ed. by D. Zahavi and G. Christensen. Roskilde: Roskilde Universitetsforlag.

Przyrembel, M., J. Smallwood, M. Pauen and T. Singer. 2012. "Illuminating the dark matter of social neuroscience: Considering the problem of social interaction from philosophical, psychological, and neuroscientific perspectives." *Frontiers in Human Neuroscience* 21(6). https://doi.org/10.3389/fnhum.2012.00190

Rampton, B. 2006. *Language in Late Modernity: Interaction in an Urban School*. Cambridge: Cambridge University Press. https://doi.org/10.1017/CBO9780511486722

Rampton, B. 2009. "Interaction ritual and not just artful performance in crossing and stylization." *Language in Society* 38(2): 149–175. https://doi.org/10.1017/S0047404509090319

Ratcliffe, M. 2012. "Phenomenology as a form of empathy." *Inquiry – An Interdisciplinary Journal of Philosophy* 55: 473–495.

Ratcliffe, M. 2014. "The phenomenology of depression and the nature of empathy." *Medicine Health Care and Philosophy* 17: 269–280. https://doi.org/10.1007/s11019-013-9499-8

Romaine, S. 1995. "Sociolinguistics." In *Handbook of Pragmatics*, ed. by J.-O. Östman and J. Verschueren. Amsterdam: John Benjamins. https://doi.org/10.1075/hop.m.soc2

Rommetveit, R. 1972. *Språk, Tanke og Kommunikation* [*Language, thought and communication*]. Oslo: Universitetsforlaget.

Rommetveit, R. 1979a. "Deep structure of sentences versus message structure." In *Studies of Language, Thought and Verbal Communication*, ed. by R. Rommetveit and R. M. Blakar, 17–34. New York: Academic Press.
Rommetveit, R. 1979b. "On the architecture of intersubjectivity." In *Studies of Language, Thought and Verbal Communication*, ed. by R. Rommetveit and R. M. Blakar, 93–107. New York: Academic Press.
Sacks, H. 1984. "Notes on methodology." In *Structures of Social Action: Studies in Conversation Analysis*, ed. by J. M. Atkinson and J. Heritage, 2–27. Cambridge: Cambridge University Press.
Sacks, H. 1992. *Lectures on Conversation*, vol. 2. Oxford: Blackwell.
Sacks, H., E. Schegloff and G. Jefferson. 1974. "A simplest systematics for the organization of turn-taking for conversation." *Language* 50(4): 696–735. https://doi.org/10.1353/lan.1974.0010
Sandra, D. 2010. "Psycholinguistics." In *Handbook of Pragmatics*, ed. by J-O. Östman and J. Verschueren. Amsterdam: John Benjamins. https://doi.org/10.1075/hop.14.psy1
de Saussure, F. 1976 [1916]. *Cours de Linguistique Générale*. Paris: Payot.
Schegloff, E. 1992. "Repair after next turn: The last structurally provided defense of intersubjectivity in conversation." *American Journal of Sociology* 97(5): 1295–1345. https://doi.org/10.1086/229903
Schegloff, E. 1993. "Reflections on quantification in the study of conversation." *Research on Language and Social Interaction* 26(1): 99–128. https://doi.org/10.1207/s15327973rlsi2601_5
Schegloff, E., G. Jefferson and H. Sacks. 1977. "The preference for self-correction in the organization of repair in conversation." *Language* 53(2): 361–382. https://doi.org/10.1353/lan.1977.0041
Schilbach, L. 2014. "On the relationship of *online* and *offline* social cognition." *Frontiers in Human Neuroscience*. https://doi.org/10.3389/fnhum.2014.00278
Schütz, A. 1967. *The Phenomenology of the Social World*. Evanston, Illinois: Northwestern University Press.
Takahashi, H., C. Saito, H. Okada and T. Omori. 2013. "An investigation of social factors related to online mentalizing in a human-robot competitive game." *Japanese Psychological Research* 55(2): 144–153. https://doi.org/10.1111/jpr.12007
Verschueren, J. 2010. "Interactional sociolinguistics." In *Handbook of Pragmatics*, ed. by J.-O. Östman and J. Verschueren. Amsterdam: John Benjamins. https://doi.org/10.1075/hop.14.int3
Voloshinov, V. N. 1973 [1930]. *Marxism and the Philosophy of Language*. New York: Seminar Press.
Wertsch, J. (ed.). 2003. *Ragnar Rommetveit: His work and influence*. Special issue of *Mind, Culture, and Activity* 10/3.
Wetherell, M. and J. Potter. 1992. *Mapping the Language of Racism: Discourse and the Legitimation of Exploitation*. New York: Columbia University Press.
Wodak, R. 2006. "Critical linguistics and critical discourse analysis." In *Handbook of Pragmatics*, ed. by J.-O. Östman and J. Verschueren. Amsterdam: John Benjamins. https://doi.org/10.1075/hop.10.cri1.
Wolf, G. and N. Love. 1997. *Linguistics Inside Out: Roy Harris and his Critics*. Amsterdam: John Benjamins. https://doi.org/10.1075/cilt.148
Wundt, W. 1900. *Völkerpsychologie, Eine Untersuchung der Entwicklungsgesetze von Sprache, Mythus und Sitte*, vol. 1–2. Leipzig: Engelmann.
Zahavi, D. 2008. "Simulation, projection and empathy." *Consciousness and Cognition* 17: 514–522. https://doi.org/10.1016/j.concog.2008.03.010

# Linear Unit Grammar

Anna Mauranen
University of Helsinki

## 1. Introduction

As we encounter speech in real life, it comes up as a continuous stream of sounds, which on paper might appear something like this:

(1) sothatwaythereisthecompositionalitybutfrommethodologicalpointofview wellIwouldsaythatfromamethodologicalpointofviewtheresultsarealsothat wehaveobtainedherearealsocompositionalinthesensethatwehaveamodelofthe behaviouroftheprotocolfromtheexternalpointofviewandwecanwecanusethis modelfurtherifwelikewecanuseitasacomponentinanothersystem

Looking at it in this way, and in view of the limits of our working memory, it seems little short of a miracle that we manage our everyday lives perfectly well with input of this kind – and respond in kind with no trouble at all. Linguists prefer clear units to messy representations like the above, and therefore perhaps would like to segment it into, say, words to begin with:

(2) so/ that/ way/ there/ is/ the/ compositionality/ but/ from/ methodological/ point/ of/ view/ well/ I/ would/ say/ that/ from/ a/ methodological/ point/ of/ view/ the/ results/ are/ also/ that/ we/ have/ obtained/ here/ are/ also/ compositional/ in/ the/ sense/ that/ we/ have/ a/ model/ of / the/ behaviour/ of/ the/ protocol/ from/ the/ external/ point/ of/ view/ and/ we/ can/ we/ can/ use/ this/ model/ further/ if/ we/ like/ we/ can/ use/ it/ as/ a/ component/ in/ another/ system

Such a procedure would seem to be in agreement with psychological research on perception, where it has been fairly well established that a good way towards understanding a phenomenon, whether an object or a sequence of events, is to break it up into parts (e.g. Gobet et al. 2001; Zacks & Swallow 2007). Similar cognitive processes have been proposed for language in cognitive research (Christiansen & Chater 2016) and in linguistics (Sinclair & Mauranen 2006). Segmenting language online as we encounter it in order to make sense of it would therefore appear to present a good point of departure for investigating the processes we employ as listeners. What we nevertheless tend to do in linguistics is to hold on to a tradition that looks analytically

https://doi.org/10.1075/hop.21.lin3

at whole extracts at a time, in a 'synoptic' manner, as it were, in the way we are used to approaching sentences or texts. In this way, we make speech look very much like writing, despite efforts to maintain speech-like qualities through often intricate transcription conventions and meticulous accounts of turn-taking in the unfolding of conversation. Most discourse analytical traditions assume a holistic approach to extracts of discourse and look at entire extracts at once. The fact that an extract is available to the analyst in its entirety constitutes a major problem if we seek to tease out the development of, say, a dialogue as it progresses. And monologue is no different in this respect. Such a view is never available to a listener in ordinary speaking environments: we encounter a continuous flow of speech that we need to make sense of very rapidly, as new material continues to fill our working memory – and we must make sense of the new material, too.

There are some linguistic traditions, like Conversation Analysis and Interactional Linguistics, which take on board the issue of conversation being constructed by participants in real time, and thus set great store on the temporal progression of speech events in their analyses (see, e.g. Auer 2005a; Couper-Kuhlen & Selting 2018). These traditions have been able to identify a wide array of linguistic devices that for instance contribute to interactants' ability to predict junctures at which a speaker's turn may be complete and another speaker may take the floor. Insights from this research are valuable for trying to come to grips with human speech processing, and indispensable for understanding speech in interaction. However, the primary goal of Interactional Linguistics research is to understand interaction and the roles of linguistic and other means of communication in making this happen; the present chapter, by contrast, focuses on looking at moment-to-moment processing of speech from the listener's perspective. It is therefore equally suited for dialogue and monologue, and it seeks to understand how the hearer perceives the speech stream as it unfolds.

This chapter suggests that a real-time perspective is vital for developing novel and more realistic models of language processing: we need to incorporate the online experience of language into accounts of its meaning and structure. It presents a model of language, *Linear Unit Grammar* (LUG; Sinclair & Mauranen 2006), which seeks to achieve precisely that. Linear Unit Grammar differs radically from other grammars in that it consists of two stages:

1. One that is based on the intuitive, spontaneous segmentation of ongoing speech, that is, how hearers chunk up speech as they hear it. This is independent of an analyst's view.
2. One that imposes an analytical, linguistic model on the chunks that the non-analytical first phase has produced. This is the analyst's perspective.

The two phases are very different: while the first is spontaneous and ideally based on the perceptions of segments in the speech stream by people with no linguistic training, the second is the linguist's domain and works as an analytical system, much in the way that grammars normally do. Linear Unit Grammar is basically a theoretical model for conceptualizing grammar. At the same time, it looks towards cognitive processes to understand how language works. Above all, it seeks to bridge the gap between the way language is experienced and the way it is depicted in grammars. Rather than presenting yet another grammatical system that could be applied to the description of a natural language such as English, it starts from the flow of language as it passes into our experience and shows how the experience connects to the complexities of grammars that traditionally have been based on static, frozen language. Moreover, in line with models depicting the search for understanding objects or events, it puts priority on the search for meaning in linguistic input.

## 2. Chunking ongoing speech

It is well established in cognitive and psychological research that in order to recognize or understand an object it is normal for people to segment their perception of it into spatial parts (e.g. Biederman 1987). More recently, it has also been discovered that in order to understand events and event sequences, we need to be able to segment those, too, as we observe them unfold in time (e.g. Zacks & Swallow 2007; Kurby & Zacks 2008). It is reasonable to assume that language is no exception to such general principles of processing and perception for making sense out of what is perceived.

Segmentation-based processes can be viewed in the light of a more general concept, 'chunking'. It has been established as a key mechanism in human cognition by perception, learning and cognition research. Initially proposed by De Groot (1946, 1978), the notion gained wide attention along with Miller's (1956) now famous suggestion of a general information measure based on it. Recent cognitive modelling of how we experience real-time language has moreover pointed out a dilemma in coping with the rapid rate of speech compared to the limited resources of working memory, which Christiansen & Chater (2016) identified as the 'now-or-never bottleneck' of processing: if linguistic information is not processed fast, that information is lost for good. What they suggest is that listeners (as well as speakers) engage in "Chunk-and-Pass"-processing, and incrementally chunk up speech as fast as possible, using all available information to process current input before new information arrives. For this, hearers make use of a wide array of information, such as different levels of linguistic structure, situational information, and prior knowledge. All this fast processing is carried out in a predictive manner, so that anticipation of what is to come next helps process the incoming input. These observations are well compatible with those made in models of incremental (Brazil 1995) and linear (Sinclair & Mauranen 2006), chunk-based approaches to language. Prediction to sequential processing has also been explored by authors like Schegloff (2013) and Auer (2005b).

Chunks, of course, are not in themselves alien to linguistics, quite the contrary; many researchers talk about chunks of language, by which they usually mean lexico-grammatical multi-word units of one kind or another. Linguists of different theoretical persuasions have identified numerous phraseological patterns and multi-word units over the last two or three decades: from corpus linguistic n-grams in their many variations, such as lexical bundles (Biber et al. 1999), fixed expressions (Moon 1998), phrase-frames (Fletcher 2002), concgrams (Greaves 2009), or PoS-grams (Stubbs 2007), and somewhat more diverse and complex patterns like collocational frameworks (Renouf & Sinclair 1991), units of meaning (Sinclair 1996), formulaic sequences (Wray 2002, 2008), collostructions (Stefanowitsch & Gries 2003), constructions (Goldberg 2006), and (lexicogrammatical) patterns (Hunston & Francis 2000). Such descriptions have also led to theoretical models, such as Pattern Grammar, Construction Grammar and usage-based models.

These various takes on phraseological patterning are nevertheless quite different from the process under discussion: they are concerned with repeated occurrences of the same phrasing – form and meaning pairings in recurrent multi-word units across different contexts. In effect, then, they reflect the output of large numbers of past language processes. By contrast, the chunks I am concerned with here are taking shape in the perception process of a hearer. The current approach thus assumes a process perspective: the ongoing processes people are engaged in with language as real-time input. These chunks are not fixed entities and may never repeat themselves in other contexts – although some undoubtedly do. They are therefore not stable, but always context-dependent. Assuming the hearer's perspective means shelving the speaker for the time being. I also prioritise speech to writing for most of the chapter, but return to their point of contact towards the end.

A forerunner in capturing the online nature of spoken language was David Brazil's *Grammar of Speech* (1995), which builds on the insight that meaning is made as utterances unfold, not after they are finished. A key component of Brazil's analysis is the incremental nature of ongoing speech. Brazil analysed elicited spoken narratives essentially in terms of 'telling increments', through which a speaker tells a story. Linear Unit Grammar shares Brazil's point of departure, constructing meaning in ongoing language and the incremental nature of utterances. It builds on this basis especially in its first part.

An important point of departure in connecting the experience of language with a model of grammar is the fundamental linearity of language. Speech is linear along the dimension of time, while writing is linear along the dimension of space. Linearity is probably more evident in speech than in writing, because the fleeting nature of speech and the difficulty of verbatim recall of what exactly was said a few minutes ago are part of our daily experience. Yet linearity is equally a property of the written text, organized as a sequence on the page or the screen. The reading process may be digressive and include interruptions, but to achieve meaning requires a modicum of linear reading: the predominant mode of reading for meaning follows the order of the text. Linearity is therefore at the heart of language. Nevertheless, conventional grammars are hierarchical. Thus, if language is seen as horizontal, descriptive grammars stand in a vertical relation to it. Grammars tend to incorporate meaning in a paradigmatic way, that is, as sets of mutually exclusive choices; meaning is seen as arising from the choice that was made in relation to alternatives that could have been selected but were not. By contrast, LUG takes meaning to arise from the co-selection of constituents. In this way, syntagmatic relations take precedence over paradigmatic ones, which leads to only minimal hierarchy. Interestingly, the primacy of sequential over hierarchical structure has been recently advocated by some cognitive linguists as well (see, Frank et al. 2012).

Dynamic models of syntax, such as *Dynamic Syntax* (Kempson, Meyer-Viol & Gabbay 2001) and *Syntactic Carpentry* (W. O'Grady 2005, 2008) also adopt a critical stance towards syntactic models which apply to sentences only as completed artefacts, not while still in progress. Their descriptions proceed from left to right and the analysis will not have to wait for sentence completion; in this sense they are dynamic. However, both utilize far more hierarchy than either LUG or Brazil's work, build their models on sentences rather than continuous speech, and use constructed rather than naturally-occurring language. Importantly, despite proceeding from 'left to right' (a consequence of operating only on (western) written text), the size of the units is predetermined by the analysts: the maximum unit is a sentence, isolated, and an artefact produced by the analyst. The lower-level items in the hierarchical models are similarly predetermined: clauses, determiners, words, etc. A development of Brazil's work that is not based on traditional syntax and addresses temporality is G. O'Grady (2010). Like Brazil, however, G. O'Grady does not really address spontaneous speech, as LUG does. On the other hand, it looks specifically at intonation patterns, which have only recently been addressed in LUG research (Vetchinnikova & Mauranen 2017), and thus it makes a contribution to incremental analyses. A linear model of discourse analysis has been developed by Smart (2016, 2017): Linear Unit Discourse Analysis (LUDA), which builds on LUG and discourse analysis. Smart's units of analysis are similar to the elements in LUG (Section 4 below), but in terms of length they bear more resemblance to combinations of LUG elements, that is, LUMs (Section 5). LUDA appears to work successfully for discourse interaction, both spoken and written, and by holding on to the principle of strict linearity brings to light insights that would remain hidden in more traditional analyses.

In contrast to other dynamic models, LUG does not prescribe the unit of analysis at the outset. The likely limits to chunk size are assumed to fit within the limits set in information theoretical and short-term memory research, above all Miller (1956), who concluded it to be seven units plus or minus two, and Cowan (2001), who posited four units as the more likely maximum to be held in working memory at any one time. In further distinction from the other models, LUG draws on only naturally-occurring data, whether speech or writing.

In the development stage of LUG, speech was represented by transcriptions only, which could be seen as a shortcoming. There were nevertheless reasons for it: the oldest speech extracts were only available in a transcribed form. They may look primitive to the contemporary eye, but they were among the first conversations that were recorded and transcribed for an electronic corpus (LEXIS). Transcription possibilities were scarce at the time, resulting in a text entirely in upper case letters, with spaces but no punctuation, and no indication of speaker changes. The attraction of a transcript of this kind is that it bears an astonishing resemblance to what we might expect a listener's experience to be. It offered a point of departure for modelling that was authentic but at the same time unfamiliar and alienating. The subsequent modelling used more ordinary transcripts, but for the sake of consistency were subjected to the same initial treatment: only letters and spaces. In later work, like in my analysis for this chapter, the sound track has been used.

Chunking up ongoing language to make sense of it, is, then, the perceptual basis for processing speech or writing, and I argue in this chapter that it should therefore constitute the point of departure for any theoretical account of language. The incremental processing of linguistic material does not determine a single descriptive model as the only possible one; most likely many alternative grammars can be compatible with what we know about cognitive processing. Clearly, however, a good model must be compatible with the way in which humans process natural language, and it must be able to account for natural speech in ordinary everyday circumstances – otherwise it remains a theoretical exercise in a self-invented game.

## 3. Perception of boundaries

In order to chunk up information, a hearer must be able to discern wholes that can be processed meaningfully. From the position of cognitive and information science, Gobet et al. (2001) define a chunk as follows: "a chunk is a collection of elements having strong associations with one another, but weak associations with elements in other chunks." (Gobet et al. 2001: 236). For language, a wealth of models is available for explaining such associations, but only if we speak of static 'synoptic' models as discussed in the previous section. If we want to account for chunks that are actually relevant to users' online perception of language, we must shift the perspective to active real-time chunking, the process through which hearers make sense. Only if we capture the chunks first is it tenable to tackle their internal associations in a way that is relevant to the listener perception. Moreover, in this way we can seek to avoid a linguist's a priori bias towards units we are most familiar with, like clauses, sentences, or recurrent phraseology.

The way to capture chunks is to pay attention to their boundaries, in line with research in event segmentation: as Kurby and Zacks (2008: 72) observe, "viewers tend to identify event boundaries at points of change in the stimulus". In a similar vein, we noted (Sinclair & Mauranen 2006) that if there is something in the flow of language that is incompatible with the ongoing chunk, a boundary is identified. Linear Unit Grammar takes 'chunk' as a pre-theoretical term: it refers to the segments that arise from the spontaneous process of making sense of unfolding speech. It is, eventually, an empirical question how long chunks are, and how far different individuals converge in their chunking, but we hypothesized that by and large they do converge. There is no reason to expect perfect agreement across listeners, as the contingencies of processing mean that the outcomes are more likely to be similar than identical. At this stage, the important point is that chunks are whatever we find between perceived boundaries in the speech stream.

What the size of a typical chunk might be is not possible to determine a priori, but the best guess would be to place them within the limits of working memory – with the upper limit somewhere around Miller's (1956) seven plus or minus two, and the average could be around four units (Cowan 2001). Distinguishing a boundary is likely to be holistic and come about by complex combinations of features that govern different layers of language: structural, semantic, phonological, prosodic – in addition to cognitive constraints. Any of these can trigger a sense of change, or incompatibility with continuation, and contribute to the sense of a 'natural' chunk boundary that we intuitively seem to respond to. All of them also contribute to meaning, which is the cornerstone of chunking. A reasonable prediction is, then, that when several factors converge, the likelihood of a boundary is strong. Support for the importance of coincident boundaries in processing is found in Monschau et al. (2004). However, different indicators or layers do not always work in unison, but some 'staggering' can be observed across the levels, as Mukherjee (2001) points out (cf. also Auer 2010). This would seem to account for the redundancy that we find in natural language, which serves to sustain its robustness despite noise in communication channels. It is also a language-based reason to expect a certain fuzziness in chunks, and probably in perception more generally.

LUG was first developed by the combined intuitions of its authors. Along the way a few workshops with other linguists working on chunking tasks contributed to the discussion. Some of the data samples were independently analysed for tone units (Cheng et al. 2008) with high intercorrelation. High correlations were similarly reported from small-scale inter-rater reliability analyses by Carey (2013) and Smart (2016), but all of these were, again, linguists' analyses. Mason (2008) criticized LUG for falling back on analyst's intuitions, but his alternative suggestion, to rely on multi-word units taken from corpus data instead, defeats the purpose: as already discussed in Section 2, this is not a viable alternative, because it skips processing altogether.

Empirical validation of the hypothesis that chunk boundary behaviour is largely convergent has recently started with experiments with non-linguist participants (Vetchinnikova & Mauranen 2017). The findings lend support to the hypothesis. The first experiment was run on a tablet application (Vetchinnikova, Mauranen & Mikusová 2017). Participants heard one extract at a time and were simultaneously shown its transcript, to which they were invited to respond when they felt a natural chunk boundary was due. Boundaries were indicated by tapping between words. The instructions did not specify what kinds of chunks to look for, but just asked participants to follow their intuition as they were listening, and simultaneously mark chunk boundaries in the transcript by tapping on a tablet. The 48 participants were university students fluent in English but had no linguistic training. There were altogether 66 test extracts, of about 30s each.

At the outset, then, chunking involves assigning boundaries, 'provisional unit boundaries' to ongoing speech. The example that we have already seen above (reproduced with speaker changes marked as Example 3) is drawn from the experiment. It is a 30-second excerpt from an authentic, non-scripted discussion dialogue, a doctoral thesis defence in the ELFA corpus (www.helsinki.fi/elfa/elfacorpus).

The rest of the presentation of the LUG model is based on boundaries empirically derived from the experiment (Vetchinnikova & Mauranen 2017). The boundaries taken into account in this extract were marked by a minimum of four participants (in merely three of the 18 cases by 4 to 6), so agreement was quite strong. The overall agreement rate varied across extracts, but remained high (65–91%) throughout. The extract starts with the end of S1's (the examiner) turn and comprises S2's (the doctoral candidate) whole turn.

(3) S1: ...so that way there is the compositionality but from methodological point of view.
S2: well I would say that from a methodological point of view the results are also that we have obtained here are also compositional in the sense that we have a model of the behaviour of the protocol from the external point of view and we can we can use this model further if we like we can use it as a component in another system.

Here is how the extract was segmented by study participants:

(4) S1: 1 so that way
2 there is the compositionality
3 but from methodological point of view
S2: 4 well
5 I would say that
6 from a methodological point of view

7 the results are also
8 that we have obtained
9 here are also compositional
10 in the sense
11 that we have a model of the behaviour
12 of the protocol
13 from the external point of view
14 and we can
15 we can use this model
16 further
17 if we like
18 we can use it as a component in another system

Chunk size seems to bear out the prediction fairly well: two are single-word units (lines 4 and 16), and only one is slightly longer than expected, ten words instead of the maximum of Miller's nine. By contrast, some of the chunk boundaries may appear slightly unusual: consider chunks in lines 7 to 9. Line 7 starts off a new chunk (*the results are also*), but the beginning of line 8 (*that we have obtained*) is incompatible with a continuation of 7, and seems to indicate the speaker's change of tack, which inserts a specification to what had already started. Between lines 8 and 9, *here* might have felt naturally to belong to the end of 8, rather than the beginning of 9, but this may result from a focus on meaning: *that we have obtained* works as a qualification to *results*, thus participants probably responded to it as a unit completing a sense. No-one placed a boundary after *here*. This suggests that boundary perception occurs where potential boundaries converge, like clausal and sense boundaries in this case. This, most likely together with additional clues facilitating predictability, occasionally leads to what might be called 'penultimate chunking': listeners segment just before the chunk would seem to end, when the whole sense is already apparent. This then manifests itself in two boundaries separated by one word where an anticipation of the end of a sense unit triggers a boundary mark in some listeners, while others mark the next item. The segmentation between lines 10 and 11 may also seem puzzling, but clearly, *in the sense* appeared as a 'chunkable' segment to the participants.

As the next step, a comparison was run between the perceived boundaries from the tablet experiment and an intonation analysis (Example 5), which was performed independently on the recordings by an external analyst. The intonation units came out like this:

(5) [S1>] 1 so that way there is
2 the
3 compositionality
4 but from methodological point of view
[S2>] 5 well
6 I would say that

7 from a methodological point of view
8 the
9 results are also
10 that we have obtained
11 here
12 are
13 also compositional
14 in the sense that we have a
15 model of the
16 behaviour
17 of the protocol
18 from the external point of view
19 and
20 we can
21 we can use this model
22 further if we like
23 we can use it as a component in another system

As we can see in (5), there were more intonation unit boundaries (IUBs) than perceived unit boundaries (PUBs): 23 vs.18, respectively. This reflects the whole data well, since out of all potential boundary places, that is, spaces between words, (4,824 in total) there were twice as many with an IUB alone (540, or 11.2%) than with a PUB alone (210, or 4.4%) More often, both coincided on a boundary (982, or 20.4%) – yet most frequently, no boundary was indicated by either: 64.1% (3,092) of all potential boundaries were unmarked, indicating agreement that a chunk was in progress, but not terminated.

Comparing the prosodic analysis to the empirical PUB markings, let us consider the stretch again that now occurs in lines 8 to 13 (corresponding to lines 7 to 9 in Example 4). We note that the prosodic analysis yields a more fine-grained result than the participants' perceived chunk boundary marking. The speaker pauses between certain items, as is indicated by the prosody analysis, which seems to explain why participants perceived a boundary before *here* (line 11). Prosody, in this case specifically pausing, thus contributes to a sense of boundary. This is no less than we might expect, of course. However, no perceived boundaries occurred after *here* (line 11) or *are* (line 12), which are also separated by noticeable pauses. This would then seem to lend support to the observation made above on Example (4) that converging indicators from different layers of language is likely to be what sets off a perception of a boundary in listeners.

The placement of boundaries, PUBs, concludes the first part of Linear Unit Grammar. The second part is analytical, looks inside boundaries, and is no longer intuitive but applies a set of principles to the elements obtained in the first, experimental phase.

## 4. Types of chunks

The analytical framework builds on the chunks arrived at independently of any system, in this case the outcome of a boundary-placing experiment. Analysing what is inside PUBs, that is, elements enclosed by chunk boundaries, is a cyclical process. Each cycle is based on a set of principles and works on the output of the previous one, applying a limited set of distinctions. The first cycle sets up a dichotomy between two main types: elements either update shared experience, or they help manage discourse. Elements of the first kind are concerned with what is being talked about (*we can use this model; there is the compositionality*), and elements of the second kind are concerned with discourse management (*I would say; well; so that way;*). The distinction is easily recognisable, although not easy to pin down in precise terms, and similar distinctions have indeed been made in systems that model spoken discourse (e.g. Chafe 1994) or in grammars with speech in a prominent position (e.g. Biber et al. 1999; Carter & McCarthy 2006).

Elements of the first type are called *message-oriented elements* ("M"). Similar units have been termed for instance 'topical matter', 'content', or 'message'. In LUG terms, M elements increment shared experience among interlocutors. They take forward the 'contents' that individuals contribute to the conversation. Elements of this kind need not always be complete, although in many cases they are. Their key characteristic is that they move the 'topic' forward. These are also the elements that seem to be best retained from conversations; if people summarise a conversation, it is on the basis of M elements that they tend to do it: this represents 'what was said'.

The second main element type focuses on discourse in the sense of interaction as well as in the sense of continuous, co-constructed text: these *organisation-oriented element* ("O") manage both. O elements help participants deal with various real-time aspects of conversation, with the fundamental task of maintaining cooperation: managing turn-taking, changing topic, shifting footing, manoeuvring situations. The decisive distinction between the O and the M elements lies in their basic orientation towards either *action* (O) or *message* (M). When this distinction is applied to our example we see a binary, sequential alternation of Os and Ms.

| | | | | |
|---|---|---|---|---|
| (5) | S1: | 1 | so that way | O |
| | | 2 | there is the compositionality | M |
| | | 3 | but from methodological point of view | M |
| | S2: | 4 | well | O |
| | | 5 | I would say that | O |
| | | 6 | from a methodological point of view | M |
| | | 7 | the results are also | M |
| | | 8 | that we have obtained | M |

| | | |
|---|---|---|
| 9 | here are also compositional | M |
| 10 | in the sense | O |
| 11 | that we have a model of the behaviour | M |
| 12 | of the protocol | M |
| 13 | from the external point of view | M |
| 14 | and we can | M |
| 15 | we can use this model | M |
| 16 | further | M |
| 17 | if we like | M |
| 18 | we can use it as a component in another system | M |

The assignment of M and O follows the principle of linearity in that it is implemented in the light of the discourse up to that point. Thus, each element value is assigned at the point of discourse that has been reached in a given chunk, without going beyond it. In this way, the elements are seen in the light of the context that lead up to it, which is vital for ensuring contextual relevance: we cannot assume that the same wording has the same value independent of its co-text. Take line 16 above: in many contexts, *further* might in other contexts be more naturally analysed as an O, but in view of what has immediately preceded, it must be an M. This illustrates the basic context-dependence of the meanings of language items, and the ensuing multifunctional potential of linguistic expressions, which can lead to flipping across categories. Even if items are used conventionally most of the time, speakers can choose to exploit their potential flexibility, which a robust grammar must accommodate. Given the real-time progression of language, an analysis that assigns functions with respect to what precedes is more realistic than one which can equally look at what follows and move back and forth.

### 4.1 Types of "O" elements

Once the basic element types, O and M, have been assigned, the order of performing the next analytical steps ceases to be a vital concern. Starting with the subtypes of O may be more natural since there are fewer of them, only two. As mentioned above, O elements attend to discourse as interaction and as text. We can thus draw a line between these two and note that one kind of O takes on the task of interactional management, such as controlling timing, managing turn-taking, holding or yielding the floor, framing or focusing moves, or maneouvring situations. Tasks of this kind play a major role in dialogic discourses, where competition for turns is common, sudden shifts are possible, people may join or leave a conversation – and cooperation needs to be maintained in all circumstances. This element type is labelled "OI", with "I" standing for 'interaction'. The other type, then, takes care of organising the discourse as text (whether spoken or written), which in effect means indicating interrelationships between M elements. These O elements are thus 'textually focused', or "OT".

They help establish textual relations such as contrast, continuation, or exemplification, and facilitate handling structures of smaller and larger sizes in text, including extended contexts like long discussions, meetings, or essays; they set up anticipation and help position sequences contextually. In brief, they achieve for discourse what Firth (1968) described as 'replacing sequence with order'. If we characterise the OT as 'text focused', because they look inwards to the text, we can contrast them with the 'situation focused' OI elements, which look outwards from the text. Again, if we relate these two types to M elements, we can speak of them in terms of first-level ordering (OT), organising the text itself, and second-level ordering (OI), going beyond the text to organise the interaction. Focusing on the O elements in our example text, we can now specify them further.

| | | | | |
|---|---|---|---|---|
| (6) | S1: | 1 | so that way | OT |
| | | 2 | there is the compositionality | |
| | | 3 | but from methodological point of view | |
| | S2: | 4 | well | OI |
| | | 5 | I would say that | OI |
| | | 6 | from a methodological point of view | |
| | | 7 | the results are also | |
| | | 8 | that we have obtained | |
| | | 9 | here are also compositional | |
| | | 10 | in the sense | OT |
| | | 11 | that we have a model of the behaviour | |
| | | 12 | of the protocol | |
| | | 13 | from the external point of view | |
| | | 14 | and we can | |
| | | 15 | we can use this model | |
| | | 16 | further | |
| | | 17 | if we like | |
| | | 18 | we can use it as a component in another system | |

Turn-taking in a doctoral defence extract is comparatively predictable, thus the extract may show fewer O elements than everyday conversations tend to (Sinclair & Mauranen 2006; Mauranen 2012). There are nevertheless two of both kinds: lines 1 and 10 are OT, lines 4 and 5 consist of an OI each. As we can see, O elements tend to be short, and here only the OI in line 5, *I would say that*, consists of four words. Neither of the OT in the example are very typical in the experimental data as a whole; more common OTs were *and, but, that, because*, and *for example*. Perhaps the unexpected one nevertheless is *in the sense* (line 10), which out of this context might not easily be seen as an O element, perhaps not even a chunk, but which here functions as a text organiser. The OI in the excerpt are not unusual, but most typical in the data were *okay, yeah, er*, and *you know*. However, although the O elements were tentatively all marked off in Sinclair & Mauranen (2006), and even thought of as candidates for a closed class (Carey 2013), the experimental results suggest that for hearers, they tend to be integrated with M elements more often than not. Listeners, then, take them into their stride, and appear to focus on the topic-incrementing elements as they segment ongoing text. The present example illustrates this tendency, too: *but* (line 3), *that* (lines 8,11), and *and* (line 14) each start a chunk, but none of them stand alone.

Even though many typical OI tend to just keep the floor (*er*), or show listenership (*yeah*), and generally assume a dialogically 'convergent' role, that is, orienting to a positive, consensual discourse, many are also 'divergent', like *well* here (line 4), or *I don't know; I don't think; not really*, which imply a clashing view, or shift the direction of the conversation by changing the topic, or making a new opening (Mauranen 2009a). Here lines 4 and 5 (*well, I would say*) illustrate divergent OI uses in a fairly typical way: *well* anticipates a contrasting position relative to the previous speaker, and *I would say* orients to the present speaker's stance, softening it with the conditional.

Even though this particular extract may play down the role of O elements somewhat, it needs to be emphasized that their role is indispensable in creating meaning, and in the whole that constitutes linguistic activity. Not only do they engender order in text, as both of the OT instances above do (lines 1 and 10) by picking up a specific sense in which the upcoming point applies, but they also mediate between textual and extra-textual contexts: the OI in our example set up a prospection (see, Sinclair 1993/2004), anticipating divergence (*well*). By also downtoning the divergence (*I would say*), the OI acts out conventional social relations between an examiner and a doctoral candidate.

### 4.2 Types of "M" elements

M elements increment the evolving topic. They vary in size and kind more than O elements do, and can be incomplete, even just fragments. This is particularly characteristic of spontaneous conversation: not all communicative elements are successful; many rephrase speaker's first formulations, or modify, clarify, or expand them. This does not mean that they play no role in constructing meaning; hearers (and analysts) can come up with interpretations of the import or meaning of chunks even if they do not seem to be complete, or even if they are fragments even smaller than a word (cf. Jefferson 1974). The resulting array of element types is more diverse than in the case of O.

The basic element is simply called "M". It is a straightforward, often 'grammatical' sequence that does not need anything else to complete it (*we can use this model; there is the compositionality; we have a model of this behaviour*). 'Grammaticality' is used here in a broad sense, by no means confined to standard written language. Although M elements often show full clause structure, they can also consist of nominal groups or even individual words. In our example, we can see clause type M elements in 2, 11, and 15. In 11, the chunk begins with a potential O type element, which has nevertheless been absorbed into the M in listeners' perception.

| | | | | |
|---|---|---|---|---|
| (7) | S1: | 1 | so that way | |
| | | 2 | there is the compositionality | M |
| | | 3 | but from methodological point of view | M |
| | S2: | 4 | well | |
| | | 5 | I would say that | |
| | | 6 | from a methodological point of view | MR– |
| | | 7 | the results are also | +M– |
| | | 8 | that we have obtained | MS |
| | | 9 | here are also compositional | +M |
| | | 10 | in the sense | |
| | | 11 | that we have a model of the behaviour | M |
| | | 12 | of the protocol | MS |
| | | 13 | from the external point of view | MS |
| | | 14 | and we can | MF |
| | | 15 | we can use this model | M |
| | | 16 | further | MS |
| | | 17 | if we like | MS |
| | | 18 | we can use it as a component in another system | MR |

Other kinds of M are not equally complete or independent. Some come after an M that is already complete and provide additional information or some specification to it. Such elements are 'message supplements' (MS). They can be clause-like (as in lines 8 and 17), or adjuncts (as in lines 12, 13, and 16). Line 8 (*that we have obtained*) shows how an MS can come as if an afterthought to a speaker; here he has already started talking about *the results*, and now clarifies which results, as if feeling that it might not be clear whether he is talking about their own results or something more general.

One subtype of an M element simply seems incomplete and expecting continuation. Like a 'plain' M, this is an M in its own right, yet raises a strong expectation of another, completing element. This is an 'incomplete M' symbolised by M– ("M dash"). An M– is thus not fully independent, but anticipates something else to follow, as in line 6 (*from a methodological point of view*). The anticipation is usually fulfilled, and the continuation follows immediately or without much delay. Where one follows, we have a 'completion M', called "plus M" (+M), like line 7 (*the results are also*). However, although line 7 evidently continues line 6, it does not complete what line 6 started, nor is it complete in itself. Neither does line 8 (*that we have obtained*) offer completion, but just provides additional specification, leaving the M– in line 6 without a satisfying end. It is only after the interruption of line 8 that completion is achieved in line 9 (*here are also compositional*). What about line 7 in this sequence? It accomplished some of the anticipation set up in line 6, but not all, and was thus caught between completion and incompletion. Elements of this kind have a place in the system: they are +M– ("plus M dash"), incomplete continuations of a previous M–. Such combinations are useful in accounting for the often seemingly fragmentary nature of speech, which nevertheless leads to coherent meanings.

To return once more to *from a methodological point of view*, we can see that it actually occurs twice: in lines 3 and 6, separated by a speaker change and two OI elements. While in this case a boundary is already prompted by speaker change, it seems that O elements more generally can intervene between types of M, and also between M– and +M sequences. In a similar vein, MS can intervene between an incomplete start and its completion, as we saw with lines 7, 8, and 9. But what does *a methodological point of view* do in line 6? It rephrases, if only slightly, a previous, nearly identical element, and is thus a 'message revision' (MR). It can rework an M by a slight reformulation like a small expansion, contraction, or rephrasing. In this case the repetition occurs despite a speaker change (thus showing interactional alignment), and is incomplete, thus marked as MR– ("incomplete message revision"). More often, speakers rephrase or repeat their own formulations, as in the MR in line 18 (*we can use it as a component in another system*), which expands on line 15 (*we can use this model*) together with its accompanying MSs (*further; if we like*) without really making a new contribution as an M in its own right.

There is one more M type in the extract that needs our attention: *and we can* (line 14). It is what is commonly known as a false start, or dysfluency, in LUG a "message fragment", MF. It makes a start, but instead of continuing, is replaced by a new start. In our present data such fragments were often not marked by experimental participants as separate chunks – they were simply incorporated in M chunks. Clearly, then, much of the time they seem not to be perceived as autonomous, and the fact that they tend to get absorbed into M elements tells on listeners' attention to meaning.

The principal M types have been illustrated here; some further minor types remain (see Sinclair & Mauranen 2006; Mauranen 2009a/ 2012, 2009b, 2016), and it is worth noting the possibility of combining the elements with + and – markings as the need arises (as above in line 6 with "MR–"), to capture continuity of meaning over boundaries which may be caused by intervening O elements, MFs, or MSs.

## 5. Linear units of meaning

The analysis of the extract is now complete. A value has been assigned to each element resulting from the boundaries marked by listeners. What we have here is a systematic description of ongoing spontaneous speech in terms of a limited set of elements. The model retains the incremental character of speech, with its occasionally fragmentary nature, while at the same time accounting for the progression as a 'shallow' process. Even in this short extract we can see that continuity between elements is possible even if listeners perceive chunk boundaries between them, and moreover, across intervening elements in some cases. So for example supplementary elements, MS, can insert themselves within one (line 8), and they can be interposed between an M and its rephrase (lines 16 and 17). In many of the other extracts drawn from the same data, O elements also interrupt two M segments without disrupting the flow of meaning between them.

| | | | |
|---|---|---|---|
| (8) | 1 | so that way | OT |
| | 2 | there is the compositionality | M |
| | 3 | but from methodological point of view | M |
| | 4 | well | OI |
| | 5 | I would say that | OI |
| | 6 | from a methodological point of view | MR– |
| | 7 | the results are also | +M– |
| | 8 | that we have obtained | MS |
| | 9 | here are also compositional | +M |
| | 10 | in the sense | OT |
| | 11 | that we have a model of the behaviour | M |
| | 12 | of the protocol | MS |
| | 13 | from the external point of view | MS |
| | 14 | and we can | MF |
| | 15 | we can use this model | M |
| | 16 | further | MS |
| | 17 | if we like | MS |
| | 18 | we can use it as a component in another system | MR |

The continuities noted across the short segments resulting from on-line processing points to the significance of interrelations between elements. Clearly, fluent speakers and listeners can process much larger meaning units than those that fill up the working memory at any given moment; this further processing must be fast and efficient, and able to extract meaning from small segments while integrating it into larger wholes that are continually updated as new material emerges in the course of a conversation, during extended listening to a monologue, or reading continuous text. Therefore, the immediate processing of chunks as encountered is likely to lead up to the processing of larger meanings, or possibly also towards more abstract structures, as Christiansen & Chater (2016) propose.

LUG set out to explore the possibilities of larger units as an optional continuation of its Stage Two. This final step consists of a synthesis, showing how individual elements that hearers perceive as segments in a speech extract can combine. The outcomes of such a synthesis are 'linear units of meaning' (LUM), or *topic increments* that update the virtual world of shared experience. LUMs also reveal affinities between speech and writing and throw light on LUG in relation to other grammars.

One point about the synthesis needs to be made before setting out: speaker changes are not taken note of. The extract is approached as one text, co-created by two speakers in dialogue, and the procedure applies to the elements irrespective of which speaker said what. This principle was already applied at the second stage (Section 4.2) where S2 repeated something that S1 had said; it was analysed as an MR in the same way as two formulations of something articulated by one speaker. It is of course common for conversationalists to repeat each other's expressions, with various interactional meanings. From a linear, incremental perspective, each increment contributes to the shared knowledge, even though conversationalists in the process alternate in the two available discourse roles of 'I' and 'you'.

The synthesis stage is again cyclical: first the OI elements are dealt with, then various types of M. In the case of the latter, the precise order in which each type is taken up is not crucial – it depends on the extract – but the process involves addressing one type at a time.

The OI are first shelved for later consideration. This means omitting lines 4 and 5 for the time being, leaving us with 16 elements, two of which are OT and the rest subtypes of M. One good way to start is with MR and combine the rephrased formulations into one in each case. Here we have two MR, in lines 6 and 18. Line 6 seems to add nothing to what was already there in line 3, so we can remove it altogether; what is then left from lines 3 through 7 after the first two alterations is: '*from a methodological point of view the results are also*'. Line 18 expands on line 15, and it would seem to make sense to leave the expansion in place but remove the redundant repetition (*we can use it*). Line 18 now reads *as a component in another system*.

Next, we can tackle the MS and join them up with the M they were supplementing: lines 12 and 13 supplement line 11, and by putting them together, we get '*that we have a model of the behaviour of the protocol from the external point of view*'. If we do the same in lines 15, 16 and 17, we get '*we can use this model further if we like*'. Now there is one MS left, and that is in line 8. As established earlier, this is an afterthought-like addition to the results in the previous line, so joining them up becomes '*the results are also that we have obtained*', which is not satisfactory, but it can wait a little, while we make the remaining combinatorial move, and join up the M– with their counterpart +M. In lines 3 through 9 this procedure gives us the following: '*from a methodological point of view the results are also we have obtained here are also compositional*'. By simply removing the repetition of '*are also*' (line 7 and again line 9), we get '*from a methodological point of view the results we have obtained here are also compositional*', which reads quite well.

Putting the results of these combinatorial operations together, we now have:

(9) *so that way there is the compositionality from a methodological point of view the results we have obtained here are also compositional in the sense that we have a model of the behaviour of the protocol from the external point of view we can use this model further if we like as a component in another system*

By restoring one OI (line 5, *I would say that*), which provides the relevant stance to the utterance, and one '*and*' from line 14, adding a dash (a semicolon of full stop would work too), a comma, the result is the following readable if somewhat long sentence:

(10) *So that way there is the compositionality – I would say that from a methodological point of view the results we have obtained here are also compositional in the sense that we have a model of the behaviour of the protocol from the external point of view, and we can use this model further if we like as a component in another system.*

This is now a LUM. The first thing that it suggests is a strong resemblance to written text, despite its starting point in speech. A similar relationship between speech and writing was suggested in Biber et al. (1999: 262). The outcome here may be slightly rambling as a sentence, but a tolerable text passage. As it stands, the extract illustrates an important facet of the co-constructive nature of spoken dialogue: the individual contributions of interlocutors in interaction increment shared knowledge and merge into one in the process. Co-construction has also been in focus in spoken discourse analysis traditions (e.g. McCarthy 2010; Clancy & McCarthy 2015) as well as Interactional Linguistics. We could also see this in terms of meanings or units distributed across speakers in collaborative speech (cf. Lerner 1991).

From a grammatical viewpoint a LUM's notable sentence-likeness means that it lends itself without difficulty to analyses based on units like clauses, phrases and words, which most grammars recognise. The outcome of the synthesis would thus arguably be analysable by most other grammars. What conventional grammars cannot deal with, though, are text increments as they appear in ongoing speech. The particular strength of LUG over more ordinary grammars is that it can handle the speech chunks as they appear in real speech, prior to any special procedures for making it more writing-like. Moreover, for anyone to judge whether the LUM that results from synthesising the O and M elements is a reasonable representation of the original transcript presupposes an understanding of the original form of the extract, whether it is perceived to be 'grammatical' or not. Anyone reasonably fluent in English can understand the extract. Grammarians, then, can intuitively handle more than their grammars. Of course, most grammars go into far more detail and precision than the LUG elements presented here – there is no evidence so far of any discrepancy between LUG and conventional grammars in this respect. Many categories, like nouns, verbs, prepositions, and so on go unchallenged by this approach, constituting a shared area. Others, again, like the status of conjunctions, subordination, or embedding, are seriously called to question.

## 6. Conclusion

The speech stream needs to be chunked up into small segments in order to make sense of it. This chapter has presented a model of analysing chunking, which captures both the cognitive process of perceiving chunks and a grammatical analysis of the same chunks. The recognition of the linearity of language is the key point: if we want to understand how language is experienced in real-time communication, we need to start from the fleeting nature of the spoken word, which occurs in temporal sequence, continually superseded by newer elements in the small window of our attentional resources at any point of time. The need to incorporate incrementality in speech (Brazil 1995) and 'left-to right' dynamic processing of writing (Kempson et al. 2001; W. O'Grady 2005) has been recognised by other linguists. Much has also been written about chunks in language from various angles (Section 2), but the various suggestions have contented themselves with a static point of view, observing repeated occurrences of the same chunks, and analysing their uses and characteristics. Linear Unit Grammar adopts a dynamic perspective and takes chunks as they appear along the temporal dimension.

It has been shown above that the fundamental assumption behind LUG holds: listeners tend to converge on chunking up online speech. Moreover, the system of analysis applied to the chunks works for empirically derived boundaries. Finally, the synthesis built on the analytical stage could conceivably work for more traditional grammatical models as well.

What makes Linear Unit Grammar unique is that it taps listeners' intuitions about language as they hear it in real time and takes that as a point of departure for its descriptive model. It thus bridges the gap between how we as humans experience language and how we as linguists describe it. LUG differs from any other model in its two-step approach: the initial, intuitive phase, and the descriptive phase, where a system of analysis is imposed on the outcome of the first one.

The initial stage of the model first came about by tapping the intuitions of its authors. Such an approach exposes itself to the criticism that linguists' intuitions may not be equivalent to those of ordinary listeners. The empirical work with non-linguist participants has therefore meant an important step forward. While it has reasonably well confirmed the linguists' intuitions, it has also brought to light new phenomena. Above all, the role of discourse organising elements ('O' elements), appears more marginal for boundary perception than was envisaged. This would seem to support the centrality of meaning, and possibly clause structure, in perceiving segments. However, the O also show a regularity worth noting: potential but not marked O elements seem to get integrated into beginnings of new M elements, not to the ends of finished ones. This would seem to support the observation that a boundary is perceived where an incompatibility arises with the continuation of the chunk so far; clearly, something like a discourse marker would be taken as a signal of change. This is in accordance with event segmentation research (Zacks & Swallow 2007) which finds that participants tend to segment events where movement features change. Finally, perceiving boundaries where potential O elements come up throws light on the role of the MS ('message supplement') elements. The MS account for the difference between a sequence being either 'complete' (not requiring anything more to follow) or 'finished' (when a speaker stops incrementing it further or something else takes its place). O elements tend to follow MS, not to come between M and MS.

Taking linearity on board in the temporal sense of speech segmentation fits in well with developments in cognitive research. Christiansen and Chater (2016) in particular make a strong case for addressing the dilemma of speech being remarkably ephemeral, while the capacity of the working memory is very limited; the processing mechanisms hearers engage to cope with this as envisioned by Christiansen & Chater are incremental and local, rely on prediction, and take place at multiple levels. Such processes are compliant with the picture painted in LUG. Similarly, recent research on event segmentation (e.g. Kurby & Zacks 2008; Zacks & Tversky 2001) shows that chunking mechanisms in making sense of continuous events bear distinct similarities to those that look like being involved in making sense of continuous speech.

Most cognitive language research and almost all cognitive neuroscience of language have hitherto been using stimuli that are carefully controlled, simulated or invented, and typically very short, isolated items like single words, sounds, or clauses. Some cognitive neuroscientists are nevertheless shifting towards more ecologically valid approaches, which involve more naturalistic language, that is, continuous language in context (see for instance papers in Willems 2015). It would be interesting to see if such research would be able to shed light processing larger units of meaning. Gobet et al. (2001) divide the cognitive and information science research literature on chunking into two broad categories: goal-oriented and perceptual chunking. The former assumes conscious control of the process, whereas the latter approaches it as an automatic, continuous process during perception. The 'goal-oriented' kind may be one way towards larger wholes of meaning – and units like LUMs (or perhaps LUDs; see Smart 2017) may benefit from insights from naturalistic cognitive research.

Finally, an important property of chunks as part of the Linear Unit Grammar that needs to be stressed is that they are fuzzy, because although listeners broadly agree on their boundaries on the whole, these are not exact but more or less strong in terms of hearer consensus. They leave room for variation. It is also important to note that these chunks are never stable or fixed but dynamic, because they are context-dependent.

## Primary data

ELFA. 2008. *The Corpus of English as a Lingua Franca in Academic Settings*. Director: Anna Mauranen. www.helsinki.fi/elfa/elfacorpus.

## References


Auer, P. 2005a. "Delayed self-repairs as a structuring device for complex conversation." In *Syntax and Lexis in Conversation*, ed. by A. Hakulinen and M. Selting, 75–102. Amsterdam: John Benjamins. https://doi.org/10.1075/sidag.17.06aue

Auer, P. 2005b. "Projection in interaction and projection in grammar." *Text* 25: 7–36. https://doi.org/10.1515/text.2005.25.1.7

Auer, P. 2010. "Zum Segmentierungsproblem in der Gesprrochenen Sprache." *InList* 49. www.inlist.unibayreuth.de/issues/49/inlist/49.pdf

Biber, D., S. Johansson, G. Leech, S. Conrad and E. Finegan. 1999. *The Longman Grammar of Spoken and Written English*. London: Pearson Education.

Biederman, I. 1987. "Recognition-by-components: A theory of human image understanding." *Psychological Review* 94: 115–117. https://doi.org/10.1037/0033-295X.94.2.115

Brazil, D. 1995. *A Grammar of Speech*. Oxford: Oxford University Press.

Carey, R. 2013. "'On the other side': Formulaic organizing chunks in spoken and written academic EFL." *Journal of English as a Lingua Franca* 2(2): 207–228. https://doi.org/10.1515/jelf-2013-0013

Carter, R. and M. McCarthy. 2006. *Cambridge Grammar of English*. Cambridge: Cambridge University Press.

Chafe, W. 1994. *Discourse, Consciousness, and Time*. Chicago: The University of Chicago Press.

Cheng, W., C. Greaves and M. Warren. 2008. *A Corpus-driven Study of Discourse Intonation*. Amsterdam: John Benjamins. https://doi.org/10.1075/scl.32

Christiansen, M. H. and N. Chater. 2016. "The now-or-never bottleneck: A fundamental constraint on language." *Behavioral and Brain Sciences* 39: 1–19. https://doi.org/10.1017/S0140525X1500031X

Clancy, B. and M. McCarthy. 2015. "Co-constructed turn-taking." In *Pragmatics: A Handbook*, ed. by K. Aijmer and C. Ruehlemann, 430–453. Cambridge: Cambridge University Press.

Couper-Kuhlen, E. and M. Selting. 2018. *Interactional Linguistics: An Introduction to Language in Social Interaction*. Cambridge: Cambridge University Press.

Cowan, N. 2001. "The magical number 4 in short-term memory: A reconsideration of mental storage capacity." *Behavioral and Brain Sciences* 24: 87–185. https://doi.org/10.1017/S0140525X01003922

De Groot, A. D. 1946. *Het Denken van den Schaker*. Hilversum: Noord Hollandsche

De Groot, A. D. 1978. *Thought and Choice in Chess*. Antwerp: Mouton Publishers.

Firth, J. 1968. "A synopsis of linguistic theory, 1930–1955." In *Selected papers of J. R. Firth*, ed. by F. Palmer, 168–205. London: Longman.

Fletcher, W. H. 2002. "Phrases in English." http://phrasesinenglish.org/ (accessed 23 April 2015).

Frank, S., R. Bod and M. H. Christiansen. 2012. "How hierarchical is language use?" *Proceedings of the Royal Society B* 279: 4522–4531. https://doi.org/10.1098/rspb.12.1741

Gobet, F., P. C. R. Lane, S. Croker, P.C-H. Cheng, G. Jones, I. Oliver and J. M. Pine. 2001. "Chunking mechanisms in human learning." *Trends in Cognitive Science* 5(6): 236–243. https://doi.org/10.1016/S1364-6613(00)01662-4

Goldberg, A. 2006. *Constructions at Work*. Oxford: Oxford University Press.

Greaves, C. 2009. *ConcGram 1.0: A phraseological search engine [Software]*. Amsterdam: John Benjamins.

Hunston, S. and G. Francis. 2000. *Pattern Grammar*. Amsterdam: John Benjamins. https://doi.org/10.1075/scl.4

Jefferson, G. 1974. "Error correction as an interactional resource." *Language in Society* 2: 181–199. https://doi.org/10.1017/S0047404500004334

Kempson, R., W. Meyer-Viol and D. Gabbay. 2001. *Dynamic Syntax: The Flow of Language Understanding*. London: Blackwell.

Kurby, C. and J. Zacks. 2008. "Segmentation in the perception and memory of events." *Trends in Cognitive Science* 12(2): 72–79. https://doi.org/10.1016/j.tics.2007.11.004
Lerner, G. H. 1991. "On the syntax of sentences-in-progress." *Language in Society* 20: 441–458. https://doi.org/10.1017/S0047404500016572
LEXIS. http://ota.ahds.ac.uk/texts/0173.html
Mason. O. 2008. "Stringing together a sentence: Linearity and the lexis-syntax interface." In *Language, People, Numbers: Corpus Linguistics and Society*, ed. by A. Gerbig and O. Mason, 231–248. Amsterdam: Rodopi. https://doi.org/10.1163/9789401205474_017
Mauranen, A. 2009a. "Chunking in ELF: Expressions for managing interaction." *Journal of Intercultural Pragmatics* 6(2): 217–233. Reprinted, 2012, in *Corpus Linguistics*, Volume 1, ed. by D. Biber & R. Reppen, 271-286. London: Sage.
Mauranen, A. 2009b. "Managing interaction: A linear perspective on interactive speech." In *Corpora and Discourse – and Stuff: Papers in Honour of Karin Aijmer*, ed. by R. Bower, M. Mobärg and S. Ohlander, 213–221. Göteborg: University of Gothenburg.
Mauranen, A. 2012. "Linear Unit Grammar." In *The Encyclopedia of Applied Linguistics*, ed. by C. A. Chapelle, 3409–3417. Oxford: Wiley-Blackwell.
Mauranen, A. 2016. "Temporality in speech - Linear Unit Grammar." *English Text Construction* 9(1): 77–98. https://doi.org/10.1075/etc.9.1.05mau
McCarthy, M. J. 2010. "Spoken fluency revisited." *English Profile Journal* 1(1). https://doi.org/10.1017/S2041536210000012
Miller, G. 1956. "The magical number seven, plus or minus two: Some limits on our capacity for processing information." *Psychological Review* 63: 81– 97. https://doi.org/10.1037/h0043158
Monschau, J., R. Kreyer and J. Mukherjee. 2004. "Syntax and semantics at tone unit boundaries." *Anglia-Zeitschrift für englische Philologie* 121(4): 581–609.
Moon, R. 1998. *Fixed Expressions and Idioms in English: A Corpus-based Approach*. Oxford: Clarendon Press.
Mukherjee, J. 2001. *Form and Function of Parasyntactic Presentation Structures: A Corpus-based Study of Talk Units in Spoken English*. Amsterdam: Rodopi.
O'Grady, G. 2010. *A Grammar of Spoken English Discourse: The Intonation of Increments*. London: Continuum.
O'Grady, W. 2005. *Syntactic Carpentry: An Emergentist Approach to Syntax*. Mahwah, N.J: Lawrence Erlbaum.
O'Grady, W. 2008. "Language without grammar." In *Handbook of Cognitive Linguistics and Second Language Acquisition*, ed. by P. Robinson and N. Ellis, 139–167. New York: Routledge.
Renouf, A. and J. McH. Sinclair. 1991. "Collocational frameworks in English." In *English Corpus Linguistics: Studies in Honour of Jan Svartvik*, ed. by Karin Aijmer and Bengt Altenberg, 128–143. London: Longman.
Schegloff, E. A. 2013. "Ten operations in self-initiated, same-turn repair." In *Conversational Repair and Human Understanding*, ed. by M. Hayashi, G. Raymond and J. Sidnell, 41–70. Cambridge: Cambridge University Press.
Sinclair, J. McH. 1993/2004. "Written Discourse Structure." In *Trust the Text: Language, Corpus and Discourse*, ed. by J. McH. Sinclair and R. Carter, 82–101. London: Routledge.
Sinclair, J. McH. 1996. "The search for units of meaning." *Textus* 9(1): 75–106.
Sinclair, J. McH. and A. Mauranen. 2006. *Linear Unit Grammar*. Amsterdam: John Benjamins. https://doi.org/10.1075/scl.25
Smart, C. 2016. *Discourse Reflexivity in Linear Unit Grammar: The Case of IMDb Message Boards*. Amsterdam: John Benjamins. https://doi.org/10.1075/scl.76

Smart, C. 2017. "Linear unit discourse analysis: The case of peer group interaction in the HKDSE public examination." *The Asian Journal of Applied Linguistics* 4(2): 148–160.

Stefanowitsch, A. and S. T. Gries. 2003. "Collostructions: Investigating the interaction of words and constructions." *International Journal of Corpus Linguistics* 8(2): 209–243. https://doi.org/10.1075/ijcl.8.1.02gri

Stubbs, M. 2007. "An example of frequent English phraseology: Distributions, structures and functions." In *Corpus Linguistics 25 years on*, ed. by R. Facchinetti, 89–106. Amsterdam: Rodopi.

Vetchinnikova, S. and A. Mauranen. 2017. "Chunking- the cognitive basis of a dynamic grammar." Paper presented at AAAL 2017 Conference, March 19, Portland, Oregon.

Vetchinnikova, S., A. Mauranen and N. Mikusová. 2017. "Investigating the relevant units of online speech processing." In *INTERSPEECH 2017 – 18th Annual Conference of the International Speech Communication Association, August 20–24, Stockholm, Sweden. Proceedings*, 811–812.

Willems, R. (ed.). 2015. *Cognitive Neuroscience and Natural Language Use*. Cambridge: Cambridge University Press. https://doi.org/10.1017/CBO9781107323667

Wray, A. 2002. *Formulaic Language and the Lexicon*. Cambridge: Cambridge University Press. https://doi.org/10.1017/CBO9780511519772

Wray, A. 2008. *Formulaic Language: Pushing the Boundaries*. Oxford: Oxford University Press.

Zacks, J. M. and B. Tversky. 2001. "Event structure in perception and conception." *Psychological Bulletin* 127: 3–21. https://doi.org/10.1037/0033-2909.127.1.3

Zacks, J. M. and K. M. Swallow. 2007. "Event segmentation." *Current Directions in Psychological Science* 16(2): 80–84. https://doi.org/10.1111/j.1467-8721.2007.00480.x

# Truth-conditional pragmatics

Jacques Moeschler
University of Geneva

## 1. Introduction

Pragmatics has been oriented, from its philosophical origins (Austin 1962; Grice 1975), in a direction which has made truth-conditional meaning either part of the semantic meaning (Gazdar 1979), or placed it outside the scope of pragmatics. Austin convincingly argued against the "descriptive illusion," proposing an analysis of the classical philosophical description of meaning (sense and reference) as "the act of 'saying something'," corresponding to what he calls the *locutionary* act (Austin 1962: 94), whereas the main meaning component of an utterance would be captured by the *illocutionary* act. Gazdar, an emblematic defender of a formal approach to pragmatics, popularized its scope by means of his famous equation: "PRAGMATICS = MEANING – TRUTH CONDITIONS" (Gazdar 1979: 2). This general agreement about the exclusion of truth-conditional meaning from the scope of pragmatics has been accepted as a common assumption of the developments of pragmatics following Grice (Gazdar 1979; Horn 1984, 1989), with as its main domain of investigation *implicatures*, and more specifically *generalized conversational* implicatures, even if things are less straightforward when we look at Levinson's (2000) approach to generalized conversational implicatures, as discussed in Huang (2014).

This division of labour between semantics (truth-conditional meaning) and pragmatics (non-truth-conditional meaning) has clearly been questioned since the publication of *Relevance* by Sperber and Wilson (1986), who introduced a notion between what is *said* (in the Gricean sense) and what is *implicated*, that is, what is explicated (*explicature*). As such, an explicature is the development of the logical form of the utterance, in other words, the full proposition taking truth-values as the result of an inferential and pragmatic process.

This new version of pragmatic meaning has given rise to full-grown pragmatic accounts, e.g. Carston (2002), who provided convincing arguments regarding the nature and function of explicit meaning. In parallel, but with other empirical and theoretical arguments, Recanati (2010) proposed a version of what truth-conditional pragmatics could be by distinguishing two types of pragmatic processes: primary ones which are mandatory, and secondary ones which are optional.

In this article, I will start by discussing the classical division of labour in Gricean and neo-Gricean pragmatics (Sections 2 and 3, respectively), then adding new

https://doi.org/10.1075/hop.21.tru3

pragmatic meaning as explicatures (Section 4) and primary pragmatic processes (Section 5). I will end by pointing out what are the consequences of this debate for the border between semantics and pragmatics (Section 6).

## 2. Gricean pragmatics and truth-conditional meaning

In Gricean pragmatics (Grice 1975, 1989), the main distinction is between what is *said* and what is *implicated*. What is said corresponds to truth-conditional meaning, whereas what is implicated is non-truth-conditional. Thus Grice would claim about examples (1) and (2)

(1) He is an Englishman: he is, therefore, brave.

(2) He is an Englishman: he is brave.

"I do not want to say that I have *said* (in the favoured sense) that it follows from his being an Englishman that he is brave, though I have certainly indicated, and so implicated, that this is so" (Grice 1975: 45). In (1), the implicit meaning belongs to the category of *conventional* implicature – "the conventional meaning of the words used [*therefore*] will determine what is implicated" (Grice 1975: 44). In (2), the implicature is conversational, that is, a "nonconventional implicature" triggered by the presumption of the speaker's respect for the Cooperative Principle – "Make you conversational contribution such as is required, at the stage at which it occurs, by the accepted purpose or direction of the talk exchange in which you are engaged" (Grice 1975: 45) – and respect for the maxim of relation (be relevant). The other conversational maxims, which can be used or exploited (ostensively violated) are placed under three other categories: (i) quantity (give enough but not too much information), (ii) quality (make your contribution true); and (iii) manner (be perspicuous).

The procedure of triggering a conversational implicature can be characterized as follows:

> A man who, by (in, when) saying (or making as if to say) that *p* has implicated that *q*, may be said to have conversationally implicated that *q*, provided that (1) he is to be presumed to be observing the conversational maxims, or at least the Cooperative Principle; (2) the supposition that he is aware that, or think that, *q* is required in order to make his saying or making as if to say *p* [...] consistent with this presumption; and (3) the speaker thinks (and would expect the hearer to think that the speaker thinks) that it is within the competence of the hearer to work out, or grasp intuitively, that the supposition mentioned in (2) is required. (Grice 1975: 49–50)

In other words, for a speaker to conversationally implicate a proposition *q* by asserting *p* requires (i) the presumption of the observance of the conversational maxims, (ii) the awareness of the speaker to do so, as well as (iii) the awareness of the hearer that the speaker is aware of doing so. This complex pragmatic process is directly commanded by Grice's definition of non-natural meaning:

> "*A* meant$_{NN}$ something by *x*" is (roughly) equivalent to "*A* intended the utterance of *x* to produce some effect in an audience by means of the recognition of this intention.
> (Grice 1989: 220)

The last relevant distinction proposed by Grice is the one between *generalized* and *particularized* conversational implicature. *Particularized* conversational implicatures are "cases in which an implicature is carried by saying that *p* on a particular occasion in virtue of special features of the context" (1975: 45). By contrast, a *generalized* conversational implicature is the case when "the use of a certain form of words in an utterance would normally (in the absence of special circumstances) carry such-and-such an implicature or type of implicature" (1975: 45). This is of great importance, because it shares some properties with conventional implicature, while nevertheless it is a conversational one.

So, we have now four categories of semantic and pragmatic meanings: what is *said*, *conventional implicature* (CI), *generalized conversational implicature* (GCI) and *particularized conversational implicature* (PCI). Using the criteria of conventional meaning, the presence or absence of a specific linguistic form, the use of conversational maxims, and the truth- vs. non-truth-conditional nature of meaning, we obtain the mapping in Table 1.

**Table 1.** Criteria for what is Said, CI, GCI, PCI

| | Said | CI | GCI | PCI |
|---|---|---|---|---|
| Conventional | + | + | – | – |
| Linguistic form | + | + | + | – |
| Conversational maxims | – | – | + | + |
| Truth-conditional | + | – | – | – |

As this table shows, CIs share only two properties with GCIs and one with PCIs, but three properties with what is said. Hence, the difference lies in the truth- vs. non-truth-conditional nature of meaning. As we shall see later, the CI category has been abandoned by most of the current pragmatic approaches, leaving it to formal approaches of meaning as dynamic semantics (see for instance Potts 2005, and, as a precursor, Karttunen & Peters 1979).

At the end of *Logic and Conversation*, Grice (1975) gives a list of six criteria distinguishing CI from GCI and PCI: calculability, cancellability, detachability, conventionality, the said/saying distinction, and indeterminacy:

i. Whereas CIs are not calculable, GCIs and PCIs are, as they require an inferential process, and the use of conversational maxims.
ii. Whereas CIs are not cancellable, GCIs and PCIs are, without exception, as the contrast between (3) and (4) shows (+> means 'implicates', # 'semantically odd'):

(3) a. Even Bill likes Mary.
+> others than Bill like Mary
b. # Even Bill likes Mary, but no one else does.

(4) a. Some students passed.
+> not all students passed
b. Some students passed; in fact, all passed.

iii. Whereas CIs are detachable – a detachable implicature is conveyed by the form and not by the content of what is said – GCIs and PCIs are not detachable, and simply determined by the content of what is said. For instance, a PCI (irony) as in (5) can be triggered by many utterances as in (6):

(5) Paul is an idiot.

(6) a. Paul is genius.
b. Paul is smart.
c. Paul has an exceptional IQ.

iv. Whereas CIs are (by definition) conventional, GCIs and PCIs are not conventional.
v. Whereas CIs are triggered by what is said (and the way it is said), GCIs and particularly PCIs are triggered by the saying of what is said (so that an implicature may be true without the truth of what is said).
vi. Finally, whereas CIs are determinate, PCIs are not determinate; GCIs, however, are triggered by a specific form, and thus determinate (*pace* Grice).

Table 2 summarizes these properties (leaving aside the difference between PCIs and GCIs in relation to (vi)).

**Table 2.** Grice's criteria for distinguishing types of implicatures

| | Conventional implicature | Conversational implicature |
|---|---|---|
| Calculable | – | + |
| Cancellable | – | + |
| Detachable | + | – |
| Conventional | + | – |
| Said/saying | said | saying |
| Determinate | + | – |

As Sadock (1978) has argued, these criteria are unfortunately not necessary and sufficient conditions: calculability is a necessary condition, but not a sufficient one for being a conversational implicature (it must be calculated using the maxims of conversation); cancellability is a necessary condition but not a sufficient one (the more an implicature is generalized, the less it is cancellable); detachability is not a necessary condition for being a conversational implicature (GCIs are triggered by a linguistic form, but are conversational – they are cancellable – and non-detachable); conventionality is circular; the said/saying contrast poses a problem as regards GCIs, which should be triggered only on the basis of the act of uttering, and not by lexical meaning; finally, (in)determinacy raises the problem of how determinate GCIs are (being triggered by a linguistic form, they are by definition determinate).

It seems that the opposition between conventional and conversational implicatures raises more issues than it could solve. As noted by Karttunen and Peters (1979: 48), "the distinction between generalized conversational implicatures and conventional implicature is sometimes hard to draw". The question whether two types of conversational implicatures are required raises different empirical questions, and some GCIs have been reinterpreted as *explicatures* (Wilson & Sperber 2012; Carston 2002). We shall see in Section 4 that whatever the type of conversational implicature (*generalized* vs. *particularized*), they are triggered by contextual assumptions and are not dependent on the way they are linguistically conveyed.

Before discussing this issue, let us examine how the category of GCI has been defined in the neo-Gricean approach. We will see that two models of the interaction between truth-conditional and non-truth-conditional meaning have been developed, one neo-Gricean departing from Gricean reasoning (Levinson 2000), and the second, more Gricean, coming back to what has been one central distinction in Gricean pragmatics, that is, the difference between what is *conveyed* (or *communicated*), *said* and *implicated* (Horn 2004).

## 3. Neo-Gricean pragmatics and the division of linguistic labour

In neo-Gricean approaches to meaning, two main issues have been put forward: first, a simplification of the nine Gricean maxims to a principled account of pragmatics; second, a clear definition of what is the semantics-pragmatics interface. In each solution (Horn's as well as Levinson's), the border between semantics and pragmatics has been maintained as truth-conditional: semantics bears the responsibility for computing truth-conditional meaning, whereas pragmatics is outside the domain of truth-conditional meaning. The main difference between these two contributors is that for Levinson some implicatures (I-implicatures) can contribute to semantic meaning (see 3.2).

### 3.1 Horn's Q and R principles

Horn's first simplification of the Gricean maxims leads him to reduce the maxims to two principles: the Q principle and the R principle (Horn 1984).

The Q principle resembles the first maxim of quantity ("Make your contribution as informative as is required", Grice 1975: 45) and the maxims of manner "Avoid ambiguity" and "Avoid obscurity of expression" (Grice 1975: 46). It states "Make your contribution sufficient. Say as much as you can (given R)" (Horn 1984: 13). The R Principle claims "Make your contribution necessary" and "Say no more than you must (given Q)". The R principle refers to the Gricean maxims of Relation ("Be relevant", Grice 1975: 46), the Q principle to the second maxim of Quantity ("Do not make your contribution more informative than is required", Grice 1975: 45) and the maxim of Manner ("Be brief (avoid prolixity)", Grice 1975: 46).

In Horn's perspective, there is a complementary relation between these two principles: the Q principle is hearer-based, because the sufficient nature of the speaker's contribution allows the hearer to draw the right implicature. On the other hand, the R principle is speaker-based: the speaker chooses the good quantity (as minimal as possible) of information to invite the hearer to draw the expected implicature. For instance, (7) has a Q-implicature, and (8) a R-implicature:

(7) It is possible that John solved the problem.
Q +> (For all the speaker knows) John didn't solve the problem.

(8) John was able to solve the problem.
R +> John solved the problem.

Moreover, the Q principle is a "lower-bounding principle, inducing upper-bounding implicata", whereas the R principle is an "upper-bounding principle, inducing lower-bounding implicata" (Horn 1984: 13). This means that the implicature of (7) is an upper-bounding implicatum (a lower-bounding predicate Q-implicates the negation of its upper-bounding correlate): for instance, *possible that p* Q-implicates *not-p*. Conversely, in (8), *to be able to p* R-implicates *p*, because there is a lower-bounding relation between *p* and *being able that p*: if John solved the problem, then he was able to solve it. But the other way around is not the case: being able to do *p* does not entail nor implicate *p*.

How does the interface between semantics and pragmatics work in Horn's perspective? Two main ideas must be put forward. The first is that Horn proposes a division of labour between linguistics and pragmatics, and this relates to how natural languages are shaped to convey special meanings, that is, *implicatures*. The second issue concerns the relation between what is *said* (as truth-conditional meaning) and what is *implicated* (as non-truth-conditional meaning).

### 3.1.1 *The division of linguistic labour*

Horn proposes the following principle:

> The use of a marked (relatively complex and/or prolix) expression when a corresponding unmarked (simpler, less 'effortful') alternate expression is available tends to be interpreted as conveying a marked message (one which the unmarked alternative would not or could not have conveyed). [...]
>
> The unmarked alternative [expression] E tends to become associated (by use or – through conventionalization – by meaning) with unmarked situation s, representing stereotype or salient member of extension of E/E'. (Horn 1984: 22)

In other words, by choosing an unmarked expression, the speaker R-implicates that the situation described by the utterance was normal. The contrast between (9) and (10) makes the difference clear (Horn 1984: 27):

(9) Lee stopped the car.

(10) Lee got the car to stop.

For instance, (9) R-implicated that Lee stopped the car in a usual way (by using the foot brake), whereas (10) R-implicates that he used a different way, for instance by using the hand brake.

### 3.1.2 *What is communicated*

The second outcome is Horn's proposal is linked to the general pattern of Grice's view of communication. The exact term used by Grice is *conveyed* meaning, which includes what is *said* and what is *implicated*, that is, semantic and pragmatic meanings. Horn (2004) uses a more common term instead of *conveyed*, that is, *communicated* (see also Levinson 2000).

The examples given in his article are about quantifiers, and more specifically particulars, that is, subcontraries such as *some* and *some not*. Whereas *some* Q-implicates 'not all', *some not* Q-implicates 'some', as (11) and (12) show:

(11) Some students passed.
Q +> Not all students passed/Some student didn't pass

(12) Some students did not pass.
Q +> Some students passed

Now, (11) and (12) *communicate* the same proposition, that is, 'some students passed and some students did not pass' (Horn 2004: 11). In other words, a subcontrary Q-implicates its opposite and communicates the conjunction of both. So, what is communicated (the sum of what is *said* and what is *implicated*) gives rise to a surprising conclusion: what is communicated is formally both a truth-conditional meaning and a non-truth-conditional meaning. From a semantic point of view, what is communicated by (11) and (12) – that is, the conjunction of the meaning of *some* and of *some not* – describes the whole set of students, that is, the subset of students who passed, and its complement set, the subset of students that did not. Thus, the combination of these two subsets gives a truth-conditional meaning. Both subcontraries are true, which corresponds to a situation where the one-sided reading of both subcontraries (13) is ruled out, since the only possible reading is the two-sided reading, that is, the reading where the implicature of each subcontrary is true (14):

(13) One-sided readings
 a. *some*: 'some if not all'
 b. *some not*: 'some not if not none'

(14) Two-sided readings
 a. *some*: 'not all'
 b. *some not*: 'some'

In other words, two subcontraries Q-implicating each other are in a disjunction relation: when both are true, each implicates the other. But as (13) shows, the one sided-reading is possible, implying that the other is false, as shown in Table 3.

**Table 3.** Truth-conditions for subcontraries

| *some* | *some not* | *some or some not* |
|---|---|---|
| 1 | 1 | 1 |
| 1 | 0 | 1 |
| 0 | 1 | 1 |
| 0 | 0 | 0 |

### 3.2 Levinson's heuristics

Levinson's (2000) theory of generalized conversational implicatures makes use of three heuristics: the Quantity, Informativeness and Manner heuristics.

The Q-heuristic corresponds to Grice's first maxim of conversation: "Make your contribution as informative as is required" (Grice 1975: 45). His formulation is "What isn't said, isn't", and is exemplified by scalar (15) and clausal (16) implicatures (Gazdar 1979):

(15) Some of the boys came.
 +> Not all of the boys came

(16) If there is life on Mars, the NASA budget will be spared.
 +> There may or may not be life on Mars

The I-heuristic states that "What is expressed simply is stereotypically exemplified". In other words, "minimal specification gets maximally informative or stereotypical interpretation" (Levinson 2000: 37). For instance, the "enrichment of conjunction by the assumption of temporal sequence or causality" (*conjunction buttressing* as in (17)), "the strengthening of conditionals to biconditionals" (*conditional perfection* as in (18)), "the assumption that conjoined subjects acted together" (*together-implication* as in (19)) are typical examples of the I-heuristic. It corresponds to Grice's second maxim of quantity "Do not make your contribution more informative than is required" (Grice 1975: 45):

(17) John turned the switch and the motor started.
I +> *p* and then *q*, *p* caused *q*, John intended *p* to cause *q*, etc.

(18) If you mow the lawn, I'll give you $5.
I +> if and only if you mow the lawn, will I give you $5

(19) John and Jenny bought a piano.
I +> John and Jenny bought a piano together

The M-heuristic – "What's said in an abnormal way isn't normal" – corresponds to Grice's maxim of Manner ("Be perspicuous"), more precisely the submaxims "avoid obscurity of expression" and "be brief (avoid unnecessary prolixity)" (Grice 1975: 46) and to Horn's division of labour. For instance, a complex formulation as well as the presence of a full NP in contrast to an anaphoric pronoun trigger M-implicatures as in (20) and (21):

(20) The corners of Sue's lips turned slightly upward.
M +> Sue didn't exactly smile

(21) John came in and the man laughed.
M +> *the man* and *John* denote two different individuals

These three heuristics describe three principles, labelled Q, I and M principles. These principles are elaborated versions of Horn's principles, but are not significantly more informative. What is more relevant is the implications that the three types of implicatures have for the interface between semantics and pragmatics. As we shall see, I- and M-implicatures occur at a very early stage of utterance interpretation, whereas Q-implicatures should be launched later after a full semantic interpretation. This two-step pragmatics is Levinson's solution to solve what he calls *Grice's circle*.

### 3.2.1 *Grice's circle and its solution*

Here is Levinson's definition of *Grice's circle*:

> Grice's account makes implicature dependent on a prior determination of "the said". The said in turn depends on disambiguation, indexical resolution, reference fixing, not to mention ellipsis unpacking and generality narrowing. But each of these processes,

> which are prerequisites to determining the proposition expressed, may themselves depend crucially on processes that look indistinguishable from implicatures. Thus what is said seems both to determine and to be determined by implicature. Let us call this *Grice's circle*. (Levinson 2000: 186)

In other words, Grice's circle shows that implicatures are dependent on what is said, but also determine what is said, that is, the proposition expressed. In Levinson's terms, Gricean inferences are needed for the determining the truth-conditional content, but also for obtaining postsemantic pragmatics. This implies that pragmatic processes – the computation of implicatures – intervene both before semantic interpretation and after it.

The first Gricean pragmatic process, which Levinson calls *presemantic pragmatics*, is about disambiguation, fixing reference, narrowing or broadening, and has as input compositional semantics and indexical pragmatics, as developed in a model-theoretic formalization in Montague (1970). The output of this process is the semantic interpretation, that is, a model-theoretic interpretation, producing as output the sentence meaning and giving rise to the proposition expressed. This is the starting point for the second Gricean pragmatic process (*postsemantic pragmatics*), yielding indirect meaning (as with indirect speech acts), irony and tropes. Finally, the output of this second pragmatic process is the speaker meaning, that is, the proposition meant by the speaker. Some arguments for a *double pragmatic computation* are given: *intrusive* constructions, such as comparatives, conditionals, metalinguistic negation, but also phenomena linked to reference assignment.

Let us examine one of Levinson's examples involving comparatives (see Reboul 2004 for experimental evidences). (22) should be contradictory, but it is not, because it I-implicates the 'and then' interpretation of *and*:

(22) Driving home and drinking three beers is better than drinking three beers and driving home
I +> Driving home *and then* drinking three beers is better than drinking three beers *and then* driving home

As Levinson (2000: 199) states, "what makes "*p* and *q* is better than *q* and *p*" non-contradictory is the inference from *and* to 'and then'". Now, the question is how can this be explained? In other words, where does the I-implicature take place, in Gricean Pragmatics 1 (GP1) or in Gricean Pragmatics 2 (GP2)? GP2 is excluded, because the sentence meaning, computed before, should be contradictory. So, the only possible solution is GP1: the 'and then' interpretation of *and* should occur before the model-theoretic interpretation. The main issue is whether this interpretation makes correct predictions (see Blochowiak & Castelain 2018 for experimental verification).

### 3.2.2 *Counter-examples*

Let us take the same issue, the 'and then' interpretation of *and*. As Cohen (1971) suggests, (23) presents a serious issue for the implicature explanation:

(23) a. If the old king has died of a heart attack and a republic has been declared, then Tom will be quite content.
b. If a republic has been declared and the old king has died of a heart attack, then Tom will be quite content.

In Levinson's proposal, (23a and b) do not have the same meanings (the propositions expressed), because the I-implicatures occur first, at the presemantic level. But this interpretation is difficult to accept, because the implicature is embedded, and occurs in the antecedent of the conditional. As Recanati claims,

> Uttering the antecedent therefore carries a conversational implicature which enriches the content of the supposition the hearer is invited to make; the implicature provides, as Walker puts it, 'a further condition on which the consequent is to be taken to depend'. (Recanati 2010: 160)

Now the question is whether this condition on the consequent (*Tom will be quite content*) can be achieved as an implicature. As Wilson and Sperber (2012:171) report, "Something which [...] is an implicature appears to be falling within the scope of logical operators and connectives [*if*]. That is, it appears to be contributing to the truth conditions of the utterance as a whole – in Grice's terms, not to what was implicated but to what was said". In other words, an implicature cannot contribute to the truth-conditions of an utterance as a whole, but only to the part of the sentence meaning which corresponds to what is said.

The puzzle is thus the following: How can an implicature be part of what is said, that is, of the sentence meaning defining the proposition expressed? In terms of Relevance Theory, this corresponds to the *explicature* of the utterance. In other words, whereas neo-Gricean theory has an enlarged vision of implicatures – including deixis, reference resolution, the minimal and enriched propositions – post-Gricean pragmatics limits the domain of implicature to additional propositions (Gricean Pragmatics 2 in Levinson's terms), explicatures including deixis and reference resolution, minimal and enriched propositions.

The next section presents the way Relevance Theory includes truth-conditional meaning of what is said at the explicature level.

## 4. Post-Gricean pragmatics, implicature and explicature

One strong contribution of Relevance Theory to pragmatics has been the reduction of the nine Gricean maxims to one principle, the Principle of Relevance: "Every act of ostensive communication communicates the presumption of its own optimal relevance" (Sperber & Wilson 1986: 158). The presumption of optimal relevance is defined as follows:

a. The set of assumptions {*I*} which the communicator intends to make manifest to the addressee is relevant enough to make it worth the addressee's while to process the ostensive stimulus.
b. The ostensive stimulus is the most relevant one the communicator could have used to communicate {*I*}. (Sperber & Wilson 1986: 158)

A second contribution is the new balance between what is explicitly and implicitly communicated. As defined in *Relevance* (Sperber & Wilson 1986: 182), "an assumption communicated by an utterance *U* is explicit if and only if it is a development of a logical form encoded by *U*". In other words, "logical forms are 'developed' into explicatures by inferential enrichment" (Wilson & Sperber 2012: 160).

This has several consequences. First, some cases defined in Gricean and neo-Gricean pragmatics as implicatures are re-analysed as cases of *explicatures*. Second, the domain of implicatures has been restricted: the category of generalized conversational implicature is abandoned, and reinterpreted as explicatures, whereas the domain of implicatures is limited to particularized conversational implicatures. As for conventional implicatures, they are generally defined as cases of *procedural meaning*, for instance in the case of connectives (Blakemore 1987; Wilson & Sperber 2012, Chapter 7). Third, if truth-conditional meaning is now defined as part of pragmatic meaning, this modifies the relation between semantics and pragmatics, not only the balance between what is said and what is implicated.

### 4.1 The domain of explicature

An explicature is a development of the logical form of the utterance, obtained by inference, but also by encoded information. Explicatures are of two types: basic and higher order. A basic explicature corresponds to the full proposition expressed, that is, a proposition receiving a truth value. Higher order explicatures correspond to the proposition plus its illocutionary force or its propositional attitude. For instance, an utterance like (24) receives the explicatures (25):

(24) I will be there.

(25) a. Basic: Jacques will be at Anne's home on Wednesday 18 January 2017.
b. Higher-order – illocutionary force: Jacques promises to Anne to be at Anne's home on Wednesday 18 January 2017.
c. Higher-order – propositional attitude: Jacques is willing to be at Anne's home on Wednesday 18 January 2017.

In what follows, I will concentrate on basic implicatures. To obtain a full and interpretable proposition in terms of truth value, explaining how a logical form can become a full proposition, two pragmatic processes intervene: (i) variable saturation and (ii) free pragmatic enrichment.

A. *Variable saturation*: What could be the logical form of (24)? Some variables are present, but some information, such as time, is a direct consequence of the act of uttering. Moreover, two demonstratives (*I, there*) are also interpreted *via* personal and spatial deixis. So, the logical form of (24) is something like (26):

(26) FUTURE [be(s, at l)]
where *s* = the speaker, *l* = a spatial variable

The saturation process interprets the future time from the moment of speaking (S), *s* referring to Jacques, *l* to Anne's home.

In some cases, even if the sentence is complete with respect to its arguments and time reference (Reichenbach 1947), a constituent is missing, because it does not need to be *articulated* and it is inferable from the context of speech. For instance, (27) does not have to be explicit about the place (noted as [where?]), because location is not an internal argument of the predicate, and is easily inferable as the place where the speaker is:

(27) It's raining [where?]

In other words, the full proposition, that is, the *basic explicature*, is obtained only if personal, spatial and temporal variables are saturated. However, contrary to Levinson's prediction that this contributes to GP1 and model-theoretical interpretation, this information is *inferred*. If in some examples, implying what Levinson calls I-implicature, the unarticulated constituents could be obtained at a presemantic level, as in (28).

(28) Abi and Fée climbed the Roche de Solutré [together].

What about examples such as (29) (Carston 2002: 22), implying non-conventional types of completion?

(29) a. Paracetamol is better [than what?].
b. It's the same [as what?].
c. She is leaving [from where?].
d. He is too young [for what?].

Clearly, these utterances are underdetermined as to linguistic meaning or sentence meaning, which leads Carston (2002: 19) to the conclusion that "linguistic meaning underdetermines what is said". The completion of *unarticulated constituents* (Recanati 2002; Korta & Perry 2011) is thus a requirement for the determination of *what is said*, that is, for the computation of a full proposition and the assignment of its truth value.

B. *Free pragmatic enrichment*: A second type of contribution to the determination of the explicature of an utterance is *free pragmatic enrichment* (Carston 2002). This process pertains to the determination of an inferred concept from the lexically encoded concept. Two main processes have been identified in *lexical pragmatics*: *narrowing* and *broadening* (Wilson & Carston 2007 and Wilson 2003).

In narrowing (or specification), the inferred CONCEPT* is more precise than the encoded CONCEPT, and narrowing occurs at the level of the encyclopaedic entry of the concept, as defined in Sperber and Wilson (1986: 86). For instance, in (30), the encoded concept BACHELOR preserves its logical entry – BACHELOR(x) → UNMARRIED(x) whereas the denotation of the *ad hoc* inferred concept BACHELOR* is only a subset of the individuals defining the denotation of the concept:

(30) Mary is happy: she finally met a bachelor.

By contrast, in broadening as in (31), the denotation of the inferred concept RAW* is a superset of the encoded concept RAW, and the logical entry RAW(x) → UNCOOKED(x) is ruled out.

(31) This steak is raw.

In some cases, as with *metaphors*, both narrowing and broadening work hand by hand. In (32), Sally does not belong to the set of ANGELS, because she is not a SUPERNATURAL BEING (as a logical property). However, some properties of the concept ANGEL will be activated, among them the one given in (33) (Wilson & Carston 2007: 247):

(32) Peter: Will Sally look after the children if we get ill?
Mary: Sally is an *angel*.

(33) Encyclopaedic properties of (GOOD) ANGEL
EXCEPTIONALLY GOOD AND KIND
WATCHES OVER HUMANS AND HELPS THEM WHEN NEEDED
VIRTUOUS IN THOUGHT AND DEED
MESSENGER OF GOD, etc.

So, the implicatures of Mary's utterance are of the kind given in (34) (Wilson & Carston 2007: 247).

(34) SALLY IS EXCEPTIONALLY GOOD AND KIND
SALLY IS WATCHFUL AND WILL HELP WHEN NEEDED
SALLY WILL LOOK AFTER THE CHILDREN IF PETER AND MARY GET ILL

In other words,

> lexical adjustment is a special case of a more general process of mutual parallel adjustment in which tentative hypotheses about contextual assumptions, explicatures and contextual implications are incrementally modified so as to yield an overall interpretation which satisfies the hearer's expectation of relevance.
> (Wilson & Carston 2007: 248)

Therefore, free lexical enrichment occurs to compensate for the semantic underdetermination, and is located at the levels of explicatures (narrowing, broadening) and implicature (metaphors). Explicature, being a development of the logical form, is therefore the locus of truth-conditional meaning.

## 4.2 The limits of implicatures

As we have seen previously, the scope of phenomena in the domain of *implicature* is strongly reduced because of *explicatures*. A prototypical example is the temporal and/or causal interpretation of *and*. In the Cohen's (1971) classical example, the 'and then' interpretation is no longer an implicature resulting from the submaxim of manner "be orderly" (Grice 1975: 46), nor an I-implicature (*conjunction buttressing*), but an explicature of the logical form of the utterance. So, Wilson and Sperber's example (2012: 171) is neither redundant nor uninformative, since '*p* and *q*' and '*q* and *p*' have to be interpreted at the explicature level as '*p* and then *q*' and '*q* and then *p*':

(35) It's always the same at parties: either I get drunk and no-one will talk to me or no-one will talk to me and I get drunk.

The question is how this interpretation can be obtained at the level of explicature. Recall that an explicature is the development of a logical form of the utterance. So, the logical form of '(*p* and *q*) or (*q* and *p*)' is made more specific at the explicature level, as '(*p* and then *q*) or (*q* and then *p*)'. In Relevance Theory, the specification process happens as a free enrichment: the concept AND, linguistically encoded as the linguistic conjunction *and*, can contain only information based on its truth-conditional meaning, represented by its elimination rules (Sperber & Wilson 1986: 86):

(36) *And*-elimination
a. Input: *p and q*
Output: *p*
b. Input: *p and q*
Output: *q*

So, we can make a more precise prediction: the *temporal* interpretation of the logical conjunction is a *specification* of its logical meaning. Conditionals are another example: the biconditional interpretation of *if* is a specification of its logical meaning. The biconditional interpretation restricts the truth-conditions of a conditional: a biconditional is true iff both propositions have the same truth-conditions (Moeschler 2017a). See Table 4.

**Table 4.** Truth tables for conditionals and biconditionals

| p | q | if p, then q | iff p, then q |
|---|---|---|---|
| 1 | 1 | 1 | 1 |
| 1 | 0 | 0 | 0 |
| 0 | 1 | 1 | 0 |
| 0 | 0 | 1 | 1 |

In a more general sense, the meaning of a specification process is a result of the general relevance-theoretic comprehension procedure (Wilson & Sperber 2004: 613):

*Relevance-theoretic comprehension procedure*

a. Follow a path of least effort in computing cognitive effects: test interpretive hypotheses (disambiguation, reference resolutions, implicatures, etc.) in order of accessibility.
b. Stop when your expectations of relevance are satisfied (or abandoned).

So, the explanation of the pragmatic meaning of logical connectives is given by the comprehension procedure: if we compare the two logical forms in (37), (a) is less relevant than (b) because it gives rise to an uninformative complex proposition ('*p* and *q*' and '*q* and *p*' are logically equivalent), whereas (b) is more relevant, since '*p* and then *q*' and '*q* and then *p*' are not truth-conditionally equivalent:

(37) a. (p and q) or (q and p)
b. (p and then q) or (q and then p)

In other words, '*p* and then *q*' and '*q* and then *p*' make an utterance like (35) relevant because it gives rise to positive cognitive effects. For instance, additional propositions, that is, *implicatures* as in (39), are easily triggered against the contextual assumptions in (38).

(38) *Contextual assumptions*
a. People at parties expect to be happy.
b. Being drunk at parties is not a good plan.
c. Being alone at parties is not a good plan.

(39) *Contextual effects*
a. Whatever the cause, the speaker gets drunk at parties.
b. Whatever the cause, the speaker does not meet any one at parties.
c. The speaker is unhappy at parties.

So, there is a strong connection between the computation of *explicatures* and *implicatures*. In the previous examples, the access to explicature is a condition for accessing implicatures, but this is not a general rule. In some cases, implicatures can be accessed first in order to reduce the domain of explicatures. For Examples (40) and (41), suppose that the question under discussion is whether the pragmatics exam was successful or not. Under these conditions, the positive particular *some* implicates a positive answer ('the speaker is happy'), whereas the negative *some not* implicates a negative one. So, in that case, these particularized conversational implicatures are necessary to access the quantitative or scalar implicature of *some* and *some not*. In other words, the contextual implications determine the generalized conversational implicature.

(40) Some students passed.
PCI: The exam was a success (because the speaker expected that no student passed)
GCI: Not all students passed

(41) Some students did not pass.
PCI: The exam was not a success (because the speaker expected that all students passed)
GCI: Some students passed

In Noveck and Sperber (2007), as well as in Moeschler (2017b), GCIs are reinterpreted as *explicatures*, that is, specifications of the logical meaning of quantifiers, blocking their logical meaning ('some if not all' and 'some not if not none'). So, in a framework where GCIs are reanalysed as explicatures – *some* explicating 'only some' and *some not* 'only some not' – implicatures can determine explicatures.

## 4.3 The relation between semantics and pragmatics

Does the opposition between explicature and implicature modify the relations between semantics and pragmatics? The Gricean perspective is straightforward, because what is said is equal to semantics. The Gricean perspective is popular enough to have inspired what is called *minimalism*, or *minimal semantics*. In this perspective, the main difference is made between "the literal meaning [...] – which is entirely *independent* of a context of utterance and another – the pragmatic speaker meaning – which is entirely *dependent* on the context of utterance" (Borg 2012: 513).

This view corresponds to the classical view of the semantics-pragmatics interface: *linguistics* includes *syntax* and *compositional semantics* yielding, thanks to the contribution of *indexical pragmatics*, the *semantic interpretation*, whose output is *literal meaning*; Gricean pragmatics intervenes then to yield as output utterance meaning, that is, speaker meaning (Levinson 2000: 173).

As we have seen, the neo- and post-Gricean perspectives make the picture less straightforward. In neo-Gricean pragmatics, at least in the theory of Generalized Conversational Implicatures (Levinson 2000), there is no clear-cut separation between linguistics (including syntax and semantics) and pragmatics, since pragmatics intervenes at a pre- and a post-semantic level. These entrenched layers of semantic and pragmatic meanings also impact the relation between *language* and *communication*, mainly because neo-Gricean approaches to language belong to the *social* vs. *cognitive* paradigm, as mainly 'functionalist' theories (Zufferey et al. forthcoming). The criterion is the *function* of language (Reboul & Moeschler 1998): Does natural language have a *social* or a *cognitive* function? Whereas the inferential model introduced by Grice is clearly an argument for the cognitive function – because of Grice's definition of non-natural meaning and the working out of implicatures – neo-Gricean approaches, even if they are inferential, represent social models of language. For instance, the place devoted in Levinson's work to politeness (Brown & Levinson 1987) clearly shows the social function of language in the neo-Gricean paradigm.

By contrast, post-Gricean pragmatics, mainly by making a strong difference between two models of communication (the code model and the inferential model), defines natural language as having a fundamentally cognitive function: natural languages are a way of externalising the language of thought (Fodor 1975, 2008; Reboul 2017). Communication, on the other hand, has not been introduced by natural language. The variety and complexity of animal communication (Hauser 1996) show that communication, defined as a transfer of information and a modification of the environment, is not specific to natural language. In Relevance Theory, following Grice's definition of non-natural meaning, linguistic communication is a special case of *ostensive-inferential communication*:

> The communicator produces a stimulus which makes it mutually manifest to communicator and audience that the communicator intends, by means of this stimulus, to make manifest or more manifest to the audience a set of assumptions {*I*}.
> (Sperber & Wilson 1986: 155)

So, even though natural languages are connected to thought as far as meaning is concerned, the linguistic use of natural language is mainly communicative. In linguistic communication, the speaker aims at changing her audience's representation of the world, and this is possible because her utterance is an ostensive stimulus that makes manifest her intentions. In ostensive communication, the speaker has two types of intention: an *informative* intention, defined as the speaker meaning, and a *communication* intention, which makes manifest that she has an informative intention:

> A communicator who produces an ostensive stimulus is trying to fulfil two intentions: first, the informative intention, to make manifest to her audience a set of assumptions {*I*}; and second, the communicative intention, to make her informative intention mutually manifest. (Sperber & Wilson 1986: 163)

By making her communicative intention manifest, the speaker thus invites her audience to infer her informative intention. Now, the main question is how linguistic meaning contributes to the computation of speaker meaning. Gricean Pragmatics is what has been defined as a radical approach to pragmatics (Cole 1981: xi):

> Radical pragmatics concerns itself with two possible subsystems: semantics, that system involved in the determination of conventional (or literal) meaning; and pragmatics, that system involved in the determination of nonconventional (or nonliteral) meaning.

However, Relevance Theory, as a post-Gricean tradition, departs from this definition on two main points: first, the computation of speaker meaning is not dependent on the computation of literal meaning; second, the logical form of the sentence is generally less informative than what conventional meaning should include. So, what is the type of meaning encoded by the linguistic system?

When examining free pragmatic enrichment, I gave a partial answer to that question. But this could be more specific, as far as lexical meaning is concerned. I would like to give two illustrations of this issue: the first comes from Carston's (2002: 65) discussion of Searle's (1983) thesis about *literal meaning* and *background*, and the second concerns so-called *procedural meaning* (Moeschler 2016a).

### 4.3.1 *Lexical meaning and pragmatics*

Carston gives examples such as (42), where the lexical meaning of *open* is determined by its internal argument:

(42) a. Jane opened the window.
b. Bill opened his mouth.
c. Sally opened her book to page 56.
d. Mike opened his briefcase.
e. The child opened the package.
f. The surgeon opened the wound.

As Carston noticed, the encoded meaning of *open* is the same, but varies with the sentential context. More precisely:

> Importantly, although it looks as if it is the meaning of the expressions we substitute for 'X' and 'Y' [in 'X opened Y'], particularly 'Y', that determines the interpretation of 'open', this is only so given a Background of assumptions concerning what is involved in an X opening a Y. (Carston 2002: 65)

Carston mainly argues for a *contextualist* approach to pragmatic meaning, even if she recognises that the internal argument plays a crucial role in determining the predicate meaning. This has been generalized as a semantic universal by Keenan (1978: 172):

> THE FUNCTIONAL DEPENDENCY PRINCIPLE (FDP)
>
> Given A and B distinct constituents of a SF [surface form] E, A may agree with B iff in the LF [logical form] of expressions of E, the LFs of expressions of A are interpreted as *functions* taking the interpretations of expressions of B as arguments.

So, whatever the nature of the encoded meaning, semantic compositionality is important for the linguistic contribution to the speaker meaning, because the specific meanings of *open* are determined by its internal arguments. One core common meaning of *open* can be determined by (43), the specific *states* being specified in (44), exemplifying the occurrences of *open* in (42).

(43) OPEN (x, y) → not-CLOSED(y)

(44) {outdoor connection, ready for speaking, readable, searchable, usable, cared…}

Even if the articulation between lexical semantics and pragmatic inference is still an open issue as regards lexical categories, it is clear that no pragmatic computation can be obtained without a minimal lexical contribution of semantic meaning. However, the question whether this contribution is constant (Borg 2012, 2004), before any contextual contribution, is ruled out by general semantic principles such as Keenan's FDP and compositionality.

#### 4.3.2 *Procedural meaning*

Procedural meaning was introduced by Diane Blakemore (1987) and Wilson and Sperber (1993), and has given rise to many recent contributions (Escandell-Vidall et al. 2011; Sasamoto & Wilson 2016). The question is now the following: How does procedural meaning make the interface between semantics and pragmatics efficient in natural languages?

Let us take the examples of French temporal *et* ('and'), causal *parce que* ('because'), and inferential *donc* ('therefore'), as in the following examples:

(45) a. Mary pushed John *et* he fell.
b. Mary pushed John, *donc* he fell.
c. John fell *parce que* Mary pushed him.

What is striking is that these causal relationships can be obtained without connectives (see Blochowiak 2014a for an analysis in terms of presuppositions):

(46) a. Mary pushed John. He fell.
b. John fell. Mary pushed him.

One hypothesis, developed in Moeschler (2011, 2016a), is that connectives such as *et, parce que, donc* do not differ from each other in terms of different meanings, but mainly by the type of meaning they encode or trigger. For instance, whereas both cause and consequence are entailed by *et* and the factive connective *parce que* (Moeschler 2016b; Blochowiak 2010), *donc*, as an inferential connective, does not entail the consequence. As a second property of these connectives, causality does not receive the same status: whereas it is not defeasible with *parce que*, it is defeasible with *et* and *donc* (Blochowiak 2014b), which leads to the conclusion that the causal relation is an explicature with *parce que*, and an implicature with *et* and *donc*. Third, whereas entailments and causality are clearly *conceptual* meaning (they are representational meanings), *procedural* meaning encoded by these connectives is about the direction of causality, that is, the direction in discourse between a cause and a consequence (see Blochowiak

2017 for an analysis of directionality beyond causality). In that sense, *parce que* is a backward connective, *et* and *donc* are forward connectives.

Examples (47) show the defeasible/non-defeasible property of these connectives, and Table 5 summarizes the nature of the meaning encoded by them.

(47) a. Mary pushed John, *et* he fell, but not because Mary pushed him, but because John slipped on a banana skin.
b. Mary pushed John, *donc* he should have fallen, but this is not certain.
c. # John fell *parce que* Mary pushed him, but there is no causal relation between these two events.

**Table 5.** Types of meaning for causal connectives (Moeschler 2016a: 134)

| **Meanings →** | **Conceptual** | | | | **Procedural** |
|---|---|---|---|---|---|
| **Connectives ↓** | Entailment | | Explicature | Implicature | Direction of CAUSE |
| *parce que* | P | Q | CAUSE (X,Y) | – | Q → P |
| *donc* | P | – | – | POSSIBLE_CAUSE (X,Y) | P → Q |
| *et* | P | Q | – | POSSIBLE_CAUSE (X,Y) | P → Q |

In a nutshell, all these connectives have a causal meaning, but this meaning is located at different layers: explicature for *parce que*, implicature for *et* and *donc*. They also differ in terms of their entailments and procedural meanings. So, the choice of a connective is directly dependent on these properties. First, the speaker has the choice between a factive implication or no implication (she has the choice between *et* and *parce que* vs. *donc*), she then has the choice between an iconic vs. non-iconic causal relation, and finally between a strong vs. weak causal relation (explicature vs. implicature). Figure 1 shows these different alternative.

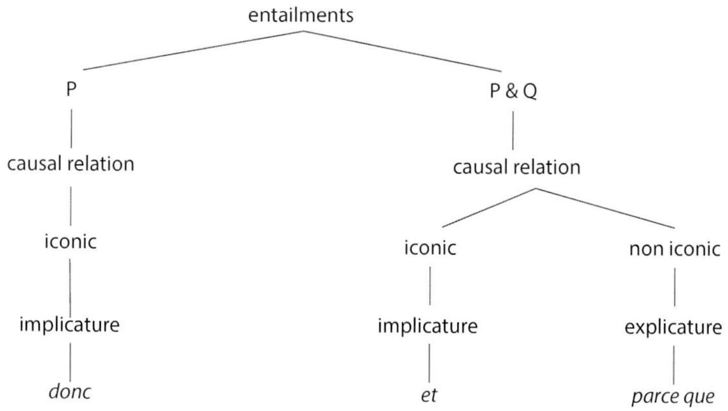


**Figure 1.** A decision tree for the choice of causal connectives

#### 4.3.3 *Synthesis*

In this section, I discussed post-Gricean pragmatics. The main outcomes of this discussion are threefold: first, the explicature/implicature distinction leads to the conclusion that pragmatics cannot be restricted to non-truth-conditional meaning; second, the domain of implicature has been seriously restricted, mainly because the majority of phenomena belonging to GCIs are reanalysed as cases of explicatures; and third, the main impact of the intrusion of truth-conditional meaning within the scope of pragmatics is a new type of relation between semantics and pragmatics. We have seen that even if contextualisation has an impact on the type of inferred concepts (see the role of narrowing and broadening), compositionality plays a role in the construction of explicatures, as the example of *open* showed. Finally, I demonstrated that connectives illustrate complex meaning including semantic entailment, explicature and implicature at the conceptual level, and procedural information restricted to causal directionality (see Section 6).

The question is now to see how truth-conditional pragmatics could be developed. The next section proposes an answer to this question.

## 5. Truth-conditional pragmatics

In his introduction to *Truth-Conditional Pragmatics* (TCP), Recanati (2010) opposes his pragmatic approach to minimalism, to Gricean theory and to post-Gricean theories such as Carston's. The concept of "'what is said' corresponds to the *intuitive truth-conditional content* of the utterance" (Recanati 2010: 12). The main contribution of TCP is that these truth-conditions "*are* affected by free pragmatic processes" (Recanati 2010: 12). What are these processes? Minimalism predicts that the intuitive truth-conditional content is only affected by bottom-up ones, such as *saturation*, but not by top-down processes (such as Gricean implicatures and free pragmatic enrichment). Now, the original contribution of TCP is that "such [top-down] processes may, in some cases, *interfere with semantic composition and take place locally*" (Recanati 2010: 15). These processes are called *modulation*, and they are *local* in the sense that "they interfere with semantic composition, despite their 'top-down' nature" (Recanati 2010: 16). They are also post-propositional and contribute to speaker meaning. These top-down pragmatic processes implied in modulation are called "*primary pragmatic processes*, rather than secondary processes presupposing the prior identification of what is said" (Recanati 2010: 16–17). Now, modulation is an optional process: "one may, but need not, modulate the sense of an expression, depending on the context" (Recanati 2010: 20). However, this process is under pragmatic control, as opposed to saturation: it is "a *pragmatically controlled* pragmatic process rather than a *linguistically controlled* pragmatic process (like saturation)" (Recanati 2004: 136). Now the opposition obligatory/

optional is not straightforward: even if modulation is optional, "we must go beyond linguistic meaning without being linguistically instructed to do so, if we are to make sense of the utterance" (Recanati 2004: 139). So, Recanati concludes that "modulation, though optional, often turns out to be mandatory" (Recanati 2010: 21). This leads to what Recanati (2004) has called *radical contextualism*.

This approach departs from minimalism, Gricean pragmatics, and post-Gricean pragmatics, but shares some properties with neo-Gricean pragmatics. This is linked to *pragmatic intrusion* (described in Section 3.2): "Without pragmatic intrusion of the optional (top-down) variety, no determinate proposition would be expressed" (Recanati 2004: 96). But his approach leaves open the question whether implicatures are *default* or *free enrichment* (see Recanati 2010: 170–180).

## 6. Conclusion: The semantics-pragmatics interface revisited

What can be the outcome of truth-conditional pragmatics? As we have shown, the main issue that should be solved for a truth-conditional pragmatics is the place of implicature, and its nature as non-truth-conditional meaning. For now, no complete theory of implicature is available, mainly because implicatures are at the crossroads of the interface between syntax and semantics on the one hand, and semantics and pragmatics on the other (see Chierchia 2013 for a robust contribution about the syntax-semantics interface).

In a programmatic contribution, Moeschler (2013a) proposed a new way of addressing the semantics-pragmatics interface from a truth-conditional pragmatic perspective. He discusses two main issues in this article: the first one is why semantic entailment and presupposition cannot be made explicit, whereas explicatures and implicatures can. (48) makes this difference explicit:

(48) a. entailment:
I bought a Chow, so I bought a dog.
b. presupposition:
My daughter is in Japan, so I have a daughter.
c. explicature:
Abi and Fée climbed the Roche de Solutré, and they did it together.
d. implicature:
Some of my students passed, so not all passed.

So, what makes the difference between semantic and pragmatic contents? Two criteria are responsible for this: *strength* and *accessibility*. First, semantic contents such as *entailment* and *presupposition* are *stronger* than pragmatic ones (explicatures and implicatures), because they are encoded and not left to free pragmatic enrichment (they are mandatory and not dependent on modulation):

(49) a. The more semantic the content, the stronger it is.
b. The more pragmatic the content, the weaker it is.

The test for deciding the *strength* of the contents is the speaker's *commitment*. In other words, by saying *I bought a Chow*, the speaker is committed to have bought a dog, just like by saying *My daughter is in Japan*, she commits herself to the truth of the proposition 'I have a daughter'. By contrast, it is only because of a free enrichment that [together] is inferred from *Abi and Fée climbed the Roche de Solutré*. Finally, the scalar implicature 'not all' is defeasible, and thus the pragmatic interpretation is not strongly communicated.

The second criterion is *accessibility*. Surprisingly, semantic contents such as entailments and presuppositions are not directly accessible, mainly because they are part of the conventional meaning. By contrast, pragmatic meaning, even if inferred, is highly accessible, explicatures being more accessible (as free enrichment) than implicatures (cf. Moeschler 2007 for an intercultural pragmatics explanation of the function of explicature). (50) makes these properties explicit:

(50) a. The more semantic the content, the less accessible it is.
b. The more pragmatic the content, the more accessible it is.

The picture given here is not complete, mainly because some semantic and pragmatic contents are truth-conditional (entailment and explicatures), whereas others are not (presupposition and implicature). In Moeschler (2013a), a general truth-conditional definition of semantic and pragmatic contents is given. The following truth table gives a precise picture of where the difference lies:

**Table 6.** Truth-conditions of semantic and pragmatic contents

| lines | p | q | Entailment | Presupposition | Explicature | Implicature |
|---|---|---|---|---|---|---|
| 1 | 1 | 1 | 1 | 1 | 1 | 1 |
| 2 | 1 | 0 | 0 | 0 | 0 | 1 |
| 3 | 0 | 1 | 1 | 1 | 0 | 0 |
| 4 | 0 | 0 | 1 | $1 \vee 0$ | 1 | 1 |

Entailment is a truth-conditional content, defined by the logical conditional connective. Explicature is also truth-conditional, and defined by the biconditional connective (equivalence). What about non-truth-conditional contents, that is, presuppositions and implicatures?

Presupposition is normally defined as a non-truth conditional relation, because both the assertion (*p*) and its negation (*not-p*) entail the same content (*q*). This is expressed in lines 1 and 3; line 2 states that if the presupposition *q* is false and the assertion *p* true, the presupposition relation does not hold; line 4 is more complex because, if the assertion and its negation, under descriptive negation, is false, then the presupposition relation is false, exactly as in line 2. In other words, it is not possible to assert (51) in a situation where there is no king of France, exactly for the same reason that the assertion (52) cannot be true when the presupposition is false:

(51) The king of France is not bald.

(52) The king of France is bald.

Now, a presupposition can be defeated by a metalinguistic negation, as in (53) (Moeschler 2013b):

(53) The king of France is not bald, since there is no king of France.

In this case, both the assertion (*p*) and the presupposition (*q*) are false. However, the speaker, by uttering (53), states something that is true. For instance, logical form (54) is true if *p* and *q* are false.

(54) $\neg$ [$\exists$x [King_of_France(x) $\wedge$ $\neg\exists$y[(x$\neq$y) $\wedge$ King_of_France (y)] $\wedge$ Bald(x)]

In other words, the presupposition relation can be true under metalinguistic negation, which explains the unorthodox truth value in line 4 (1 $\vee$ 0).

Now, what about implicature? *Implicature* is, as it has been argued in this chapter, a *non-truth-conditional content*. This is made explicit in line 2 of Table 6: the implicature is true even in case the assertion *p* is true and its implicatum *q* false (implicatures are defeasible). Line 3 is trivial because the implicature cannot be true if the assertion is false and the implicatum true (see Moeschler 2018, for a more complete explanation). This means that the implicature of a positive assertion cannot be true when the assertion is negated: in other words, negation does not preserve implicatures, contrary to presuppositions. Finally, what line 4 states is that when the assertion is false and the implicatum false, the implicature relation still holds, that is, is potentially active between *p* and *q*. For instance, if (55) implicates (56), then it is true that (57) does not implicate (56):

(55) Anne has three children.

(56) Anne does not have four children.

(57) Anne does not have three children.

Under metalinguistic negation, as in (58), the same result holds, because the corrective clause (*Anne has four children*) rules out the implicature of the positive assertion (55):

(58) Anne does not have three children, she has four.

What are the consequences of this truth-conditional reinterpretation of (non-) truth-conditional contents? The main conclusion is that a formal truth-conditional pragmatics is possible. The main advantage of this approach is that it uses the same tools to give a precise truth-conditional definition of semantic and pragmatic contents, and second, it allows addressing new issues on the semantics-pragmatics interface. For instance, the question of the conventional or semantic meaning is made explicit by making a clear distinction between conceptual and procedural contents. Such methods have been empirically tested (Grisot 2015 and Grisot & Moeschler 2014), with positive outcomes as regards the semantics and the pragmatics of verbal tenses.

## Acknowledgment

This article was written with the support of the Swiss National Science Foundation (project LogPrag n° 100012_146093 and VTS n° 100015_170008) and the Thematic Network Language & Communication (project ComplexVar, University of Geneva). Many thanks to Joanna Blochowiak and Cristina Grisot for their help and comments.

## References

Austin, John L. 1962. *How to Do Things with Words*. Cambridge, Mass.: Harvard University Press.

Blakemore, Diane. 1987. *Semantic Constraints on Relevance*. Oxford: Blackwell.

Blochowiak, Joanna. 2010. "Some formal properties of causal and inferential 'because' in different embedding contexts." *Generative Grammar@Geneva* 6: 191–202.

Blochowiak, Joanna. 2014a. "A presuppositional account of causal and temporal interpretations of and." *Topoi*. https://doi.org/10.1007/s11245-014-9289-9

Blochowiak, Joanna. 2014b. A Theoretical Approach to the Quest for Understanding. Semantics and Pragmatics of whys and becauses. PhD thesis, Department of Linguistics, University of Geneva.

Blochowiak, Joanna. 2017. "Connectives: Order, causality and beyond." In *Formal Models in the Study of Language*, ed. by Joanna Blochowiak, Cristina Grisot, Stéphanie Dürrlemann-Tame and Christopher Laenzlinger. Cham: Springer. https://doi.org/10.1007/978-3-319-48832-5

Blochowiak, Joanna and Thomas Castelain. 2018. "How logical is natural language conjunction? Am experimental investigation of the French conjunction *et*." In *Language, Evolution, and Mind: Essays in Honor of Anne Reboul*, ed. by Pierre Saint-Germier, 97–125. London: College Publications.

Borg, Emma. 2012. "Semantics without pragmatics?" In *The Cambridge Handbook of Pragmatics*, ed. by. Keith Allan and Kasia M. Jaszczolt, 513–528. Cambridge: Cambridge University Press. https://doi.org/10.1017/CBO9781139022453.028

Borg, Emma. 2004. *Minimal Semantics*. Oxford: Clarendon Press. https://doi.org/10.1093/0199270252.001.0001

Brown, Penelope and Stephen C. Levinson. 1987. *Politeness: Some Universals in Language Use*. Cambridge: Cambridge University Press. https://doi.org/10.1017/CBO9780511813085

Carston, Robyn. 2002. *Thoughts and Utterances: The Pragmatics of Explicit Communication*. Oxford: Blackwell. https://doi.org/10.1002/9780470754603

Chierchia, Gennaro. 2013. *Logic in Grammar: Polarity, Free Choice, and Intervention*. Oxford: Oxford University Press. https://doi.org/10.1093/acprof:oso/9780199697977.001.0001
Cohen, L. Jonathan. 1971. "Some remarks on Grice's view about the logical particles of natural language." In *Pragmatics of Natural Language*, ed. by Yoshua Bar-Hillel, 50–68. Dordrecht: Reidel. https://doi.org/10.1007/978-94-010-1713-8_3
Cole, Peter. 1981. "Preface". In *Radical Pragmatics*, ed. by Peter Cole, xi–xiv. New York: Academic Press.
Escandell-Vidal, Victoria, Manuel Leonetti and Aoife Ahern (eds). 2011. *Procedural Meaning: Problems and Perspectives*. Bingley: Emerald Brill. https://doi.org/10.1163/9780857240941
Fodor, Jerry A. 1975. *The Language of Thought. Cambridge*, MA: Harvard University Press.
Fodor, Jerry A. 2008. *LOT 2: The Language of Thought Revisited*. Oxford: Oxford University Press. https://doi.org/10.1093/acprof:oso/9780199548774.001.0001
Gazdar, Gerald. 1979. *Pragmatics: Implicature, Presupposition, and Logical Form*. New York: Academic Press.
Grice, H. Paul. 1975. "Logic and conversation." In *Syntax and Semantics 3: Speech Acts*, ed. by Peter Cole and Jerry L. Morgan, 41–58. New York: Academic Press.
Grice, H. Paul. 1989. *Studies in the Way of Words. Cambridge*, MA: Harvard University Press.
Grisot, Cristina. 2015. Temporal Reference: Empirical and Theoretical Perspectives. Converging Evidence from English and Romance. PhD thesis, Department of Linguistics, University of Geneva.
Grisot, Cristina and Jacques Moeschler. 2014. "How do empirical methods interact with theoretical pragmatics? The conceptual and procedural contents of the English Simple Past and its translation into French." In *Yearbook of Corpus Linguistics and Pragmatics 2014: New Empirical and Theoretical Paradigms*, ed. by Jesus Romero-Trillo, 7–33. Cham: Springer.
Hauser, Marc. 1996. *The Evolution of Communication*. Cambridge, MA: The MIT Press.
Horn, Laurence R. 1984. "Towards a new taxonomy for pragmatic inference: Q-based and R-based implicature." In *Meaning, Form and Use in Context. GURT 84*, ed. by Deborah Schiffrin, 11–42. Washington: Georgetown University Press.
Horn, Laurence R. 1989. *A Natural History of Negation*. Chicago. The University of Chicago Press.
Horn, Laurence R. 2004. "Implicature." In *The Handbook of Pragmatics*, ed. by Laurence Horn and Gregory Ward, 3–28. Oxford: Blackwell.
Huang, Yan. 2014. *Pragmatics*, 2nd edition. Oxford. Oxford University Press.
Karttunen, Lauri and Stanley Peters. 1979. "Conventional implicatures". In *Syntax and Semantics 11: Presupposition*, ed. by Choon-kyu Oh and David A. Dinneen, 1–56. New York: Academic Press.
Keenan, Edward.1978. "On surface form and logical form." In *Linguistics in the Seventies: Directions and Prospects*, ed. by Braj B. Kachru, 163–203. Special issue of*Studies in Linguistic Sciences* 8(2).
Korta, Kepa and John Perry. 2011. *Critical Pragmatics An Inquiry into Reference and Communication*. Cambridge: Cambridge University Press. https://doi.org/10.1017/CBO9780511994869
Levinson, Stephen C. 2000. *Presumptive Meanings: The Theory of Generalized Conversational Implicature. Cambridge*, MA: The MIT Press.
Montague, Richard. 1970. "Pragmatics and intensional logic". *Synthese* 22: 68–94. https://doi.org/10.1007/BF00413599
Moeschler, Jacques. 2007. "The role of explicature in communication and in intercultural communication". In *Explorations in Pragmatics: Linguistic, Cognitive and Intercultural Aspects*, ed. by Istvan Kecskes and Laurence R. Horn, 73–94. Berlin: Mouton de Gruyter.
Moeschler, Jacques. 2011. "Causal, inferential and temporal connectives: Why *parce que* is the only causal connective in French." In *Marqueurs discursifs et subjectivité*, ed. by Sylvie Hancil, 97–114. Rouen: Presses Universitaires de Rouen et du Havre.

Moeschler, Jacques. 2013a. "Is a speaker-based pragmatics possible? Or how can a hearer infer a speaker's commitment?" *Journal of Pragmatics* 43: 84–97. https://doi.org/10.1016/j.pragma.2012.11.019
Moeschler, Jacques. 2013b. "How 'logical' are logical words? Negation and its descriptive vs. metalinguistic uses." In *Nonveridicality and Evaluation. Theoretical, Computational and Corpus Approaches*, ed. by Maite Taboada and Radoslava Trnavac, 76–110. Leiden: Brill.
Moeschler, Jacques. 2016a. "Where is procedural meaning? Evidence from discourse connectives and tenses." *Lingua 175*-176: 122–138. https://doi.org/10.1016/j.lingua.2015.11.006
Moeschler, Jacques. 2016b. "Avec ou sans? Une approche pragmatique des discours causaux explicités et implicités" [With or without? A pragmatic approach of explicit and implicit causal discourses]. In *The Grammar of Causation*, ed. by Stéphane Viellard Irina Thomièresand, 36–51. Paris: CeliSo.
Moeschler, Jacques. 2017a. "Formal and natural languages: What does logic tell us about natural language?" In *The Routledge Handbook of Pragmatics*, ed. by Anne Barron A., Gerard Steen and Gu Yueguo, 241–256. London: Routledge.
Moeschler, Jacques. 2017b. "Back to negative particulars. A truth-conditional account." In *Pragmatics and its Interfaces*, ed. by Stavros Assimakopoulos, 9–31. Berlin: Mouton de Gruyter.
Moeschler, Jacques. 2018. "Representation and metarepresentation in negation." In *Relevance Theory: Pragmatics and Interpretation*, ed. by Robyn Carston, Kate Scott and Billy Clark. Cambridge: Cambridge University Press.
Noveck, Ira and Dan Sperber. 2007. "The why and how of experimental pragmatics: The case of 'scalar implicatures'." In *Pragmatics*, ed. by Noel Burton-Roberts, 184–212. Basingstoke: Palgrave. https://doi.org/10.1057/978-1-349-73908-0_10
Potts, Christopher. 2005. *The Logic of Conventional Implicatures*. Oxford: Oxford University Press.
Reboul, Anne. 2004. "Conversational Implicatures: Nonce or Generalized?" In *Experimental Pragmatics*, ed. by Ira Noveck and Dan Sperber, 322–333. Basingstoke: Palgrave Macmillan. https://doi.org/10.1057/9780230524125_15
Reboul, Anne. 2017. *Cognition and Communication in the Evolution of Language*. Oxford: Oxford University Press. https://doi.org/10.1093/acprof:oso/9780198747314.001.0001
Reboul, Anne and Jacques Moeschler. 1998. *La pragmatique aujourd'hui : Une nouvelle science de la communication* [*Pragmatics Today. A New Science of Communication*]. Paris: Seuil.
Recanati, François. 2002. "Unarticulated constituents." *Linguistics and Philosophy* 25: 299–345. https://doi.org/10.1023/A:1015267930510
Recanati, François. 2004. *Literal Meaning*. Cambridge: Cambridge University press.
Recanati, François. 2010. *Truth-Conditional Pragmatics*. Oxford: Oxford University Press. https://doi.org/10.1093/acprof:oso/9780199226993.001.0001
Reichenbach, Hans. 1947. *Elements of Symbolic Logic*. New York: Free Press.
Sasamoto, Ryoko and Deirdre Wilson (eds). 2016. *Little Words: Communication and Procedural Meaning*. Special issue of *Lingua* 175–176.
Searle, John R. 1983. *Intentionality*. Cambridge: Cambridge University Press. https://doi.org/10.1017/CBO9781139173452
Sperber, Dan and Deirdre Wilson. 1986. *Relevance. Communication and Cognition*. Oxford. Blackwell.
Sadock, Jerrold M. 1978. "On testing for conversational implicature." In *Syntax and Semantics 9: Pragmatics*, ed. by Peter Cole, 281–297. New York: Academic Press.
Wilson, Deirdre. 2003. "Relevance and lexical pragmatics." *Italian Journal of Linguistics* 15(2): 273–291.
Wilson, Deirdre and Robyn Carston. 2007. "A unitary approach to lexical pragmatics: Relevance, inference and ad hoc concepts." In *Pragmatics*, ed. by Noel Burton-Roberts, 230–259. Basingstoke: Palgrave Macmillan. https://doi.org/10.1057/978-1-349-73908-0_12

Wilson, Deirdre and Dan Sperber. 1993. "Linguistic form and relevance". *Lingua* 90(1–2): 1–25. https://doi.org/10.1016/0024-3841(93)90058-5

Wilson, Deirdre and Dan Sperber. 2004. "Relevance theory." In *The Handbook of Pragmatics*, ed. by Laurence R. Horn and Gregory Ward, 607–632. Oxford: Blackwell.

Wilson, Deirdre and Dan Sperber. 2012. *Meaning and Relevance*. Cambridge: Cambridge University Press. https://doi.org/10.1017/CBO9781139028370

Zufferey, Sandrine, Jacques Moeschler and Anne Reboul. Forthcoming. *Implicatures*. Cambridge: Cambridge University Press.

# Handbook A–Z

# Benedict Anderson's imagined communities

William O. Beeman
University of Minnesota, Minneapolis

## 1. Introduction

Benedict Anderson's great work, Imagined Communities: Reflections on the Origin and Spread of Nationalism (Anderson 1983; hereafter IC) has been hailed as the "best known single work in nationalism studies" (Breuilly 2016: 625). His work has had an enormous impact throughout the social sciences. Much of Anderson's formulation depends on observations about the importance of linguistics, communication, and standardization of language in community formation and identities. It is therefore paradoxical that few linguists have addressed Anderson's work. Even rarer are discussions of the implications of Anderson's work from the perspective of pragmatics. This essay is an attempt to begin an exploratory discussion of the many pragmatic issues raised by the concept of Imagined Communities as laid out in Anderson's important work.

Anderson's work deals with macro-social processes in which societies have changed from local collectives with allegiances to individuals, hierarchical political structures, economic interdependencies or religious affiliations to structures where individuals acquire a collective self-identification that is coterminous with a "nation," an abstraction that may or may not be enclosed within the political boundaries of a state.

Linguists, especially researchers concerned with pragmatics, are also concerned with generalizable behavior, sentiments and ideologies shared by large populations. However, they are also concerned with individual behavior and variability in communicational behavior. In the discussion that follows, I will try to "unpack" the linguistic aspects of Anderson's concept of the imagined community. I conclude that the idea of a "language" as a unifying principle for an imagined community is a widely accepted idealization of a linguistic reality. In fact, "imagined communities" may espouse and revere the idea that its members share a unified language, but in fact they must overlook remarkable linguistic diversity in order to maintain this belief. In short, "imagined communities" also embody "imagined linguistic unity."

## 2. Benedict Anderson's message

Benedict Anderson's theory of the development of nationalism encompasses the world's transition from small-scale to large-scale society. This human transition has been of interest to social scientists for many decades, with many theories as to the

https://doi.org/10.1075/hop.21.and1

origins of the "invention" of the nation state (Fallers 2011). Anthropologist Ernst Gellner (Gellner 1983) speculated that the origins of the nation-state and other large-scale societal formations lay in the industrial revolution and the economic and trade forces that were thereby unleashed. Gellner's study was only one of several writings that used a Eurocentric model for theories of the development of nationalism (Hobsbawm 1992; Hobsbawm & Ranger 1983; Baycroft & Hewitson 2006).

As anthropologists Thomas Hylland Eriksen and Ben Anderson point out, there is a common misconception about Anderson's work. The word "imagined" in Anderson's title is often read as "imaginary." Nothing could be more remote from Anderson's meaning. As they write, Anderson "links 'invention' not to fabrication and falsity, but to imagining and creation" (Breuilly 2016: 628). As Benedict Anderson states in *IC*:

> In an anthropological spirit, then, I propose the following [6] definition of the nation: it is an imagined political community – and imagined as both inherently limited and sovereign. It is imagined because the members of even the smallest nation will never know most of their fellow-members, meet them, or even hear of them, yet in the minds of each lives the image of their communion.
>
> (Anderson 1983: 5–6)

One of Anderson's primary focuses is on the role of language and linguistics in the formation of imagined communities and of nationalism. This is of great interest to research in pragmatics. As I stated above, this aspect of his work has not been sufficiently analyzed.

The transition between face-to-face encounter and broader ideologies of nationalism is mediated through language. Anderson's theory of national formation focuses on the commodification of language through the mechanism of "print-capitalism," whereby local communication varieties become standardized, and serve as the basis for the formation of national consciousness. Elliott Green summarizes the ways in which Anderson makes this connection:

> Anderson argues that print-capitalism allowed for the birth of national consciousness in three ways: (1) it created simple means of discourse and communication between members of a given 'language-field' thereby creating awareness of such fields as actual communities; (2) it standardised languages and thereby allowed future members of the language-field to identify with the past; and (3) it elevated certain languages to print form and not others, thereby prioritising certain language fields.
>
> (Elliott Green in Breuilly 2016: 645; Anderson 1983: 44–45)

Of interest to pragmatics is Anderson's designation of "creole pioneers," individuals who are instrumental in the creation of national consciousness through the conscious elevation of local language varieties to symbolic national status. (Anderson 1983: 47–66). This process occurs as communities transit to recognized nationhood. As a variety transits from being a "creole" to a recognized "language," there is no scientifically verifiable change in formal structure or communication behavior. It is the result of a political process. In short, a variety becomes a "language" serving as a hallmark of community or national identity when some politically recognized body has the authority to declare it so.

## 3. Language and identity

Although Anderson's focus was on the formation of nationalism, his work has far broader implications for pragmatic linguistics. In focusing on "communities," Anderson opens the discussion to the question of social identity, and for the purposes of this discussion, linguistic identity. As Tabouret-Keller aptly notes: "The language spoken by somebody and his or her identity as a speaker of this language are inseparable: This is surely a piece of knowledge as old as human speech itself. Language acts are acts of identity (Tabouret-Keller 1998: 349).

Certainly, nations qualify as imagined communities by Anderson's definition, but they are only one kind of imagined community. An unpacking of Anderson's insightful analysis presents an enormously complex panoply of human identity formation, only one aspect of which is nationality, and only one factor is the language variety or varieties which a person uses in the course of everyday life. Humans use many symbolic elements to assume a connection with others – even though they have no personal history with those individuals. As Tabouret-Keller staes:

> [E]mbedded identities ... rest on strictly symbolic means, such as family names, for example, [but] we must not forget that identities may also exploit scopic materials, sensory elements among which visual features seem to occupy a pre-eminent place. (Ibid: 350)

Identities can be thought of metaphorically as a series of Venn diagrams. One belongs to one broad ethnic or religious group that may transcend national boundaries. Then one is a citizen of a state (sometimes more than one). Within national boundaries, one may belong to a regional group, a local group and a vicinity. By refining this "identity map" even further, one's identity can be specified down to those with whom one has an actual face-to-face relationship, at which point the individuals so involved are no longer in an "imagined" relationship with each other.

Even within families there are potential overlapping community identities. One of my acquaintances laid this out for me in the following way:

> I have too many identities. My father is from Spain, my mother from France, both Roman Catholics. Her father was German Lutheran, and her mother from a Polish Jewish family. They met as students in Paris, where they married and made their home. My father's mother was also Spanish, but his father was Moroccan and a Muslim. I was

> born in Arizona, where my family attended a non-denominational Christian church. We spoke Spanish, French and English at home. I met my wife in Greece during a college semester abroad where her family, Assyrians from Iran, had migrated. They belong to the Syrian Orthodox Church. Our children were adopted as infants. One is African-American and the other is from China. We try to help our children understand their heritage but there are almost too many threads of heritage to follow.

The situation above is not atypical in today's world, and from this anecdotal account, it would be difficult to ascertain precisely what "imagined" community or communities to which my acquaintance belongs. But as Mary Bucholtz and Kira Hall (2004) point out, this is not a productive way to proceed. They suggest that identity is not something that can be easily determined by outside analysts. People who merely speak "the same language" or have "the same heritage" do not necessarily consider themselves to be part of the same community as everyone with whom they share some personal characteristic or history. As Bucholtz and Hall note:

> It is therefore crucial to attend closely to speakers' own understandings of their identities, as revealed through the ethnographic analysis of their pragmatic and metapragmatic actions. When individuals decide to organize themselves into a group, they are driven not by some pre-existing and recognizable similarity but by agency and power. (Bucholtz & Hall 2004: 371)

This is entirely in conformity with Anderson's ideas about the construction of the imagined community. Such communities do not arise *sui generis*, they are the result of the confluence of common social behaviors and symbols with political and social institutions that privilege those characteristics as a basis for forging a sense of community. Thus, in considering the imagined community, it is necessary to understand that the common identity that is the basis for the feeling of community is constructed by forces that are external to the members of the community.

This provides the crux of Anderson's argument – namely, that the content that forms the basis for imagination in an imagined community is an institutional construction. Without this institutional support the community and the things that constitute it may wither away and die. And the most essential element in the formation and preservation of identity is frequently institutionally supported linguistic communication systems. The institutional support can be formalized through political structures, or it can be provided by informal groups, educational or religious institutions or even extended family groups. Individuals may choose not to belong to one or more of the communities that claim their identity or identities, but the reverse is not true. If an individual wants to belong to an imagined community and claim that membership as part of their personal identity, they must embrace the characteristic behavior, attitudes, and activities of the community.

It is also true that one aspect of creating a national identity may be to create categories of individuals who are structurally excluded from full community membership.

These people cannot "choose" to be part of the imagined community. They are automatically excluded, even if they are otherwise perfectly qualified to join on the basis of birth, language skills and acculturation. One example are the *burakumin* of Japan, a caste group associated with polluting professions, who were excluded from the benefits of full community membership such as employment and education. Speaking of his experience growing up in the former Belgian Congo and later in Belgium, Jean Muteba Rahier speaks of the situation of the mulattos – the Métis – who were the children of European colonials and native spouses, who were socially categorized as neither black nor white, as well as other "mixed" groups in the Western hemisphere such as *mestizos* in Latin America. He writes:

> Too often, the scholars writing on nationalism have failed to recognize a contingent phenomenon of nationalism that elides a superficial reading and that contradicts the homogenizing ambition: the creation of one or various "Others" within and without the limits of the "national space." (Rahier 2003: 93)

Rahier points out that in this internationalized world, individuals may be categorized as part of one group at birth, and as he or she moves to other geographical areas may find him or herself re-categorized by the new community. I had a personal experience in Rhode Island and Southeastern Massachusetts with members of the Cape Verdean community before Cape Verde became an independent state. Cape Verdeans would immigrate to New England and expected to be part of the large Portuguese community already living there. To their great surprise they were categorized socially as "black" despite their Portuguese skills and personal cultural identification.

That said, there is no one way in which this takes place. The variations in the construction of personal identities within imagined communities are extensive. Since this discussion is focused on pragmatics, and particularly linguistic pragmatics, in the sections to follow, I will try to provide some account of the extraordinary variety of the ways that language and language behavior is incorporated within communities to contribute to, and sometimes qualify a person for acceptance in a community.

As with all elements of culture, these are points of orientation, not hard and fast rules. One can be Italian and not like pasta, but an Italian will never be surprised as a guest when pasta appears on the dinner table. One can be Japanese and not observe the intricate rules of politeness and deference that constitute the communicational practice of *keigo*. But a member of the Japanese "imagined community," will definitely know what *keigo* is, and if he or she chooses to ignore this practice, will also have an excellent idea of the social consequences that will ensue.

Language instruction is one important way in which children develop community (and national) identity. Language instruction is, of course, unavoidable in contemporary society. Written and oral communication are necessary for the functions of civic life. Nevertheless, prescriptive language instruction creates models of idealized language that vary considerably from individuals' personal sense of identity, and more importantly one's sense of identity in different contexts. This includes personal choices concerning stylistic levels, choice of one variety over another. As Bourdieu notes

> What is problematic is not the possibility of producing an infinite number of grammatically coherent sentences but the possibility of using an infinite number of sentences in an infinite number of situations, coherently and pertinently. Practical mastery of grammar is nothing without mastery of the conditions for adequate use of the infinite possibilities offered by grammar.
>
> (Bourdieu 1977: 646)

As will be seen below, the palate of variation of language use within a single community is enormous. True competence within a community requires command of a full set of skills. Moreover, as one conceives of one's self as having different personal identities, linguistic behavior will conform to the requirements of those identities.

## 4. States need languages

The need for a common national language in the era of the modern nation-state (some of which are states with very weak national identity) is so strongly felt that nations have devised artificially constructed varieties to serve as the national vernacular. There is a practical reason for this, due to the need for uniformity in official communication, record keeping, public signage and education. However, as Van der Jeught notes, practicality is frequently overshadowed by symbolic identification with the state:

> "L'État, c'est la langue," an expression attributed to the French King Louis XIV, concisely conveys the idea that language is one of the most important features of national identity. In Europe, and not only there, this belief has led to the concept of linguistic hegemony (cuius regio, eius lingua), namely that a State should have only one national language. The tendency to establish a monolingual State has a long tradition. Already in 1380, Geoffrey Chaucer wrote: "God save the king, that is lord of this language," identifying thus the king's language with that of the nation.
>
> (Van der Jeught 2015: 9)

The drive to create standardized languages in the era of the nation-state is both an ideological and a practical matter. It is ideological when states feel that they must have their own "unique" language to underscore national identity. Blommaert and Verschueren have identified the imperative in modern times that states be uniform throughout as a dogma, the dogma of *homogeneism:*

> [Homogeneism is] a view of society in which differences are seen as dangerous and centrifugal, and in which the 'best' society is suggested to be one without intergroup differences. In other words, the ideal model of society is mono-lingual, mono-ethnic, mono-religious, mono-ideological. Nationalism, interpreted as the struggle to keep groups as 'pure' and homogeneous as possible, is considered to be a positive attitude within the dogma of homogeneism. Pluri-ethnic or pluri-lingual societies are seen as problem-prone, because they require forms of state organization that run counter to the 'natural' characteristics of groupings of people.
>
> (Blommaert & Verschueren 1991; Blommaert & Verschueren 1992: 362)

In many modern nations, the expectations that individuals will conform to the forms of standardized languages can be coercive. The standards may be established by elite arbiters, such as the Académie Française, or the editors of the German Duden. These bodies frequently have actual governmental enforcement power, for example, the Académie Française is the official recognized arbiter of standard French. Its power derives from the Toubon Law of 1994 mandating the use of French in most public and private communications (van der Jeught 2016a). The Académie vets every governmentally sponsored publication, such as academic articles published by French universities in their official academic journals as well as academic seminars and conventions (van der Jeught 2016a: 148). The Académie is also a political actor. It intervened with "furious opposition" in a parliamentary debate to protest constitutional protection for the legal status of regional "tongues" recognized as languages by their communities of speakers such as Alsatian, Basque, Breton, Catalan, Corsican, Occetan and Francoprovençal. Despite the Académie's disapproval, the measure passed Parliament (Allen 2008).

Official governmental movements to standardize and control language are numerous. Some of the most famous are the Turkish language reform of 1928; the Chinese character simplification reform starting in the 1950's, ongoing today; the German spelling reform of 1996; the Romanization of Azerbaijani beginning in 1929, ongoing today; and the Cyrillization of many Central Asian Languages during the Soviet Union, are all examples of state-imposed language standardization. A number of nations require command of the national standard language for immigrants to qualify for citizenship.

However, even official language arbitration bodies must change over time, yielding to trends in common usage. Spelling reforms are among the most common revisions. Inevitably, these organizations may create state-imposed limitations on communicative behavior that can meet with social resistance. The public has often resisted these reforms. The Turkish language reform was enforced with drastic measures. Schoolteachers who did not adopt the reformed language were reportedly arrested and even executed (Eminov 2001; Lewis 2002). Modern social opposition to even mild reforms can be seen frequently. Germany tried to impose spelling reform several times in the 20th Century with mixed results, as the citizenry resisted. The latest attempt in 1996 had mixed success with public protests, as seen in the image of the t-shirt in Figure 1 decrying the reduction of the β character in German spelling. The t-shirt further uses Gothic script, largely abandoned after World War II.

**Figure 1.** "Save the β"

The felt need for a single national language has extended beyond Europe to relatively new nations, who themselves have felt that if such an obvious national language does not already exist, it needs to be constructed for their nation to be thought of as fully legitimate. Some of the most prominent recently constructed national languages are Hindi, Bhasa Indonesia, Modern Hebrew and Modern Standard Arabic. Of these four, only Modern Hebrew, which began to be developed in the 19th Century, has been successful in becoming a first language – a "mother tongue" – for a large segment of the population of the State of Israel. However, in 2013, although 90% of Israelis were considered "proficient" in Hebrew, only 49% of Israelis over the age of 20 had Hebrew as their "mother tongue." The other 51% of Israelis were raised speaking Russian, Arabic, French, English, Yiddish, and Ladino, and frequently used these for primary communication with family and close friends (Druckman 2013).

The homogeneism imperative has driven many "language revival" projects. Many communities see "language revival" or "language revitalization" as essential for preserving a sense of identity, and also gaining respect among other polities as "real" communities. These efforts have increased as feelings of nationalism have grown starting in the 19th Century to the point that every community must have its own standard language. Preserving these linguistic varieties is dependent on political and other social processes, since the work involved is arduous and expensive. Nevertheless, the fervor with which many community members have pursued these enterprises is remarkable and unprecedented in human history.

One of the most successful efforts has been the revitalization of Irish in the Irish Republic. Irish instruction is mandatory in schools in Ireland, but English medium schools do not produce fluent Irish speakers. Schools with instruction entirely in Irish, known as Gaelscoileanna, have increased the number of Irish speakers (Gaelscoileanna – Irish Medium Education 2018). More than 60,000 students are regularly receiving their education through Irish immersion. One result has been the increase in popular Irish language media, including Irish television (Loftus 2016).

In the United States language revival in American Indian communities has been highly active. The economic situation of many American Indian tribes has improved, largely through income from casinos. As a result, many tribes have, over the last decades, developed an increased sense of their own identity and sovereignty – identifying themselves proudly as "nations." Consequently, local tribal funding for school, college and community instruction in native languages has increased. Ojibwe is the most widely taught American Indian language. Others with regular instruction are Navajo, Lakota/Dakota, Cherokee, and Creek. The popularity of American Indian language instruction is high enough that commercial language instruction programs have been developed for the more popular languages. Since the number of native speakers is still small, these instructional efforts may be said to have higher symbolic value than functional communicative value. Simple phrases, such as greetings and social niceties, have become symbolic markers of community membership even if the speaker doesn't know much more than these.

Today there are few nations on earth that do not have their own "language." The official standardized language in Yugoslavia was Serbo-Croatian, with Serbian written in Cyrillic characters and Croatian in Roman characters. After the breakup of Yugoslavia in 1992, the successor states – Bosnia and Herzegovina, Croatia, Montenegro, Macedonia, Serbia and Slovenia all developed standardized official languages.

The case of Montenegro, where the standardization process is still underway, is a particularly interesting one in the light of Anderson's work. "Montenegrin" is fully mutually intelligible with Serbian. Indeed, Montenegro was part of Serbia until its declared independence in 2007. The nation's new constitution declared Montenegrin as the official language of the new nation, recognizing Albanian, Bosnian, Croatian and Serbian. The Montenegrins established a Council for the Codification of the Montenegrin language, which is still wrangling over the official letters for the Montenegrin alphabet and many other features of the official language.

Some feel that the establishment of an official Montenegrin language is more political than linguistic. The Montenegrin P.E.N. Center, part of the P.E.N. international literary organization, wrote a declaration stating:

> Montenegrin language does not mean a systemically separate language, but just one of four names (Montenegrin, Serbian, Croatian and Bosnian) by which Montenegrins name their part of [the] Shtokavian system, commonly inherited with Muslims, Serbs and Croats. (Declaration of Montenegrin P.E.N. Centre 1997)

## 5. Old languages, new models

In Chapter 5 of *Imagined Communities*, titled "Old Languages, New Models," Anderson provides examples of well-recognized languages that have been codified and standardized long before "nationhood" or he Nation State became an organizational principle in the modern world. Languages such as Greek or French are examples of languages that were concretized by scholars and learned by elites in nations where literacy was highly restricted. The chart and table below show illiteracy in England from 1500–1900 and comparative literacy in European nations in 1700. It is paradoxical that, although French was universally acquired by European elites in 1700 and before, actual literacy in France at this time was extremely low.

**Table 1.** Illiteracy in Europe 1500–1900 (Mitch 2004: 244)

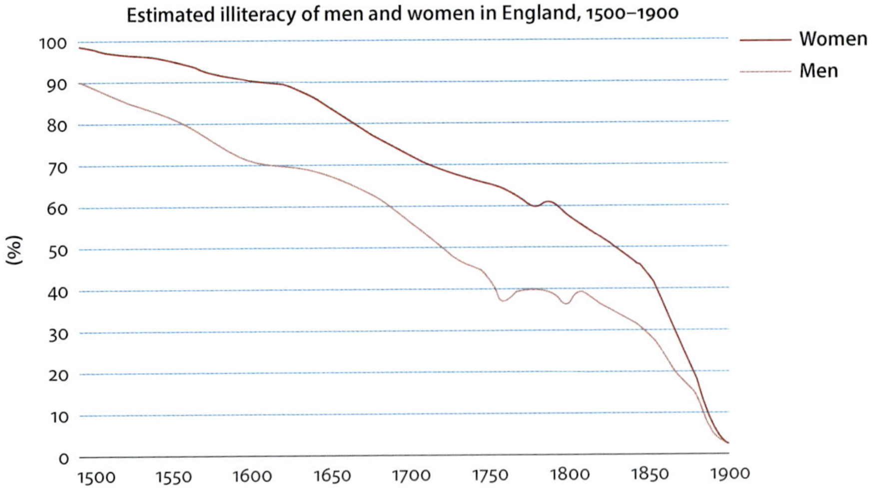

Literacy for selected areas in Europe and North America c.1700

| Region | Male literacy rate | Female literacy rate |
|---|---|---|
| England | 40% | 25% |
| France | 29% | 14% |
| Amsterdam | 70% | 44% |
| Moklinta, Sweden | 89% | 89% |
| Iceland | Almost 50% | Almost 50% |
| New England | 70% | |

*Note*: Literacy rates for England, France and Amsterdam based on signature rates at marriage

Despite the unusually high literacy rates in the Netherlands and Sweden shown in these tables, it seems that, however desirable, there was little practical need for extensive literacy in the general European population before and at the beginning of the Industrial Revolution. We see in the English of Shakespeare and Elizabethan correspondence enormous variation in spelling and grammatical construction from person to person and institution to institution, and the same is true about all written languages during this period. Being "literate" in pre-modern times meant principally being able to use written language with little attention to standardization. The models for standardized language were first beginning to be seen already in the Renaissance. Dante's *Divine Comedy* (1320); the first modern European grammar, Antonio de Nebrija's Spanish Grammar (1492); Martin Luther's German bible translation (1534), the King James Bible (1611), Cervantes' Don Quixote (1615) are some works that laid the foundations for standardization of their respective languages.

Anderson views the development of literacy in the 17th–19th Centuries as driven by and reinforcing of a new sense of community identity. Latin, Greek and Hebrew were worthy of study and semi-standardization, since they were the languages of scripture, which had to be treated with exactitude for religious reasons. There might be practical reasons for learning a vernacular for trade, diplomacy or interpersonal communication, but scholarly attention was decidedly of secondary importance until the advent of print-capitalism.

> From this point on the old sacred languages – Latin, Greek, and Hebrew – were forced to mingle on equal ontological footing with a motley plebeian crowd of vernacular rivals. … If all languages now shared a common (intra-)mundane status, then all were in principle equally worthy of study and admiration. But by who? Logically, since now none belonged to God, by their new owners: each language's native speakers-and readers.
> (Anderson 1983: 70–71)

Anderson then points out that print-capitalism resulted in a new industry of lexicography, grammar, and philology. The "lexicographic revolution" (Ibid: 72) concretized languages in written form and thereby contributed to the creation of national identities. Every vernacular group was keen on having its own concretized standard language as a mark of identity. Emblematic of this movement was the "split" between Danish and Norwegian. The two varieties were mutually intelligible and virtually indistinguishable. Norwegian Patriot-lexicographer, Ivar Aasen wrote a new Norwegian grammar and dictionary in 1848 and 1850 respectively, thus creating a distinctive Norwegian print language.

*Imagined Communities* provides many examples of the ways in which the rise of national consciousness articulated with the rise of national sensibilities – a process that continues down to the present day as witnessed by the standardization of modern "creoles." Indeed, in times recent to this writing we have seen linguistic varieties that were once dismissed as "inferior" communication media, standardized and developed as national languages as former colonial territories became independent nations. Some examples are Tak Pisin in New Guinea, Cape Verdean Creole (Kabuverdianu), Papiamento and Haitian Creole (Kreyòl Ayisyen).

## 6. Standard languages and non-standard speakers

Because Anderson's work is focused on the drive toward unified national consciousness, he does not go into detail about the behavioral reality on the ground for speakers in all but the smallest "nationalities." The normal human situation is one where every separate face-to-face community exhibits a unique communicational form. It is for this reason that anthropologists and linguists find it difficult to even use the word "language" to describe the communicational structures of a community. The term "variety" is widely used, though the more vernacular "dialect" also reflects the variation found in "imagined communities." It also gives rise to the quip attributed to sociolinguist Max Weinrich: "A language is a dialect with an army and navy."

Because standard languages are artificial constructions, there is good reason to claim that their very existence is a kind of fiction – part of the "imagination" that underlies imagined communities. Language education specialist Timothy Reagan exemplifies this position:

> I want to offer a fairly simple and straightforward proposition: there is, or at least there may well be, no such thing as English. Indeed, my claim is even a bit stronger than this – not only is there arguably no such thing as English, but there is also arguably no such thing as Russian, French, Spanish, Chinese, Hindi, or any other language.
> (Reagan 2004: 42)

Reagan may be correct in an objective sense, though his position is not universally shared (Makoni & Pennycook 2005), but Anderson would broadly agree. Notwithstanding the artificial nature of standard languages, Anderson sees them as one of a range of symbolic elements contributing to the state construction of nationalism, and concomitantly the imagined community. He provides an excellent historical example of the contrast between local communities and broad national standardized languages regarding Japanese.

> While the Japanese spoken in Kyushu was largely incomprehensible in Honshu, and even Edo-Tokyo and Kyoto-Osaka found verbal communication problematic, the half-Sinified ideographic reading-system was long in place throughout the islands, and thus the development of mass literacy through schools and print was easy and uncontroversial. (Anderson 1983: 95–96)

For researchers in pragmatics, this raises the fascinating question of how to assess the linguistic behavioral balance between the use of a variety which a person has learned from birth and the standard "language" that serves as the hallmark of national or community identity – a linguistic form that may be said not to exist as the result of any natural human communication processes, but rather as the result of a political process. In a sense, then, humans in modern times have learned a new linguistic skill. They have learned to speak more than one variety – the variety of their immediate face-to-face community and the overarching constructed variety that constitutes a standardized language. As a practical matter, if a community is to exist, its members must be able to communicate with each other in a mutually intelligible manner. Nevertheless, the formalized standard languages of mass communication which have evolved nearly everywhere as necessary artificial constructs, constitute one of the building blocks of Anderson's imagined communities. In short, to belong to a "nation," one must comprehend the standardized language of that nation.

The tension between local and national communication forms results in everyday communication dilemmas for individuals. Children in school are criticized when using their local vernacular. At the same time, they may be encouraged to use that vernacular in creative writing. Use of local vernacular forms is an effective rhetorical tool for politicians trying to appeal to voters in face-to-face encounters. However, that same rhetorical style is avoided in formal speeches addressed to a whole nation. Official communication in government and business often involves a struggle between overly formal adherence to official standards, and casual and direct expression that has strong personal and emotional impact (cf. Bailey 1997).

It is easy to dismiss the importance of local varieties in the context of national culture. However, local community identity becomes important in many situations. The most common example is the use of the shibboleth. The shibboleth constitutes a particularly apt example in the context of Anderson's writings, since it is a linguistic method for ascertaining community belonging. Persons who can produce the shibboleth accurately through correct pronunciation of a difficult characteristic word or phrase are presumed to belong to the community, whether they are personally known to the person executing the test or not. Shibboleths date back to Roman times and likely long before. Indeed, the word shibboleth itself is a Hebrew word meaning the part of a plant that contains grains, such as a stalk on a wheat plant. In the Biblical Book of Judges, the tribe of Ephraim tried to invade the town of Gilead and was defeated. After the battle the Ephraimites tried to retreat to their home by crossing the River Jordan at public fords and were stopped by the people of Gilead. To distinguish the Gileadites from the Ephraimites those crossing the river were asked to pronounce the word *shibboleth.* The Ephraimites would pronounce the word [sibboleth] and were killed. The Bible gives the following account:

> And the Gileadites took the passages of Jordan before the Ephraimites: and it was so, that when those Ephraimites which were escaped said, Let me go over; that the men of Gilead said unto him, Art thou an Ephraimite? If he said, Nay;
>
> Then said they unto him, Say now Shibboleth: and he said Sibboleth: for he could not frame to pronounce it right. Then they took him, and slew him at the passages of Jordan: and there fell at that time of the Ephraimites forty and two thousand.
>
> (Judges 12: 5–6, Holy Bible, King James Version)

There are many examples of shibboleths being used as a mark of community membership. One night in 1302 the citizens of Bruges went out hunting Frenchmen: if they pronounced "Schild ende vriend" with initial 'sk' and 'fr' instead of 'sχ' and 'vr', they were killed (Ryckbosch & Vrijders 2005). The Frisian rebel leader, Pier Gerlofs Donia used the phrase: *Bûter, brea, en griene tsiis; wa't dat net sizze kin, is gjin oprjochte Fries*, which means "Butter, rye bread and green cheese, whoever cannot say that is not a genuine Frisian," during a Frisian rebellion (1515–1523). Sailors who couldn't say this had their ships plundered and were thrown overboard; soldiers who couldn't say the phrase were beheaded (Ritsema 2008: 10). This shibboleth continues today as a popular Frisian iconic phrase.

**Figure 2.** Frisian Shibboleth

In more modern times, the shibboleth "lollapalooza" was used by American soldiers during World War II to trap Japanese, for whom /l/ and /r/ were allophones. Filipinos could say the word; Japanese could not, thus revealing them as the enemy (Owuor 2015: 144). During World War II the Dutch resistance identified German infiltrators by letting them pronounce "Scheveningen," the seaside district of The Hague. For the Germans the bad news came if the initial 'sχ' was replaced by 'ʃ.' During the Bosnian conflict in the 1990s shibboleths were used to identify members of local communities (see Senior 2004 for this and many other shibboleths). Those without the ability to use the correct pronunciation were detained or killed. The use of shibboleths in Bosnia had long currency dating back perhaps centuries due perhaps to the extraordinary numbers of recognizable varieties of Slavic, Greek and Albanian there (Evans 2013: 96).

Shibboleths would be a mere curiosity if one doesn't understand their more profound meaning. The ability to pronounce things without a detectable accent is the ultimate sign of community belonging. Even in sub-national community units, it is a touchstone for the "imagined" aspect of community belonging. If people sound the same, they must be part of the same community.

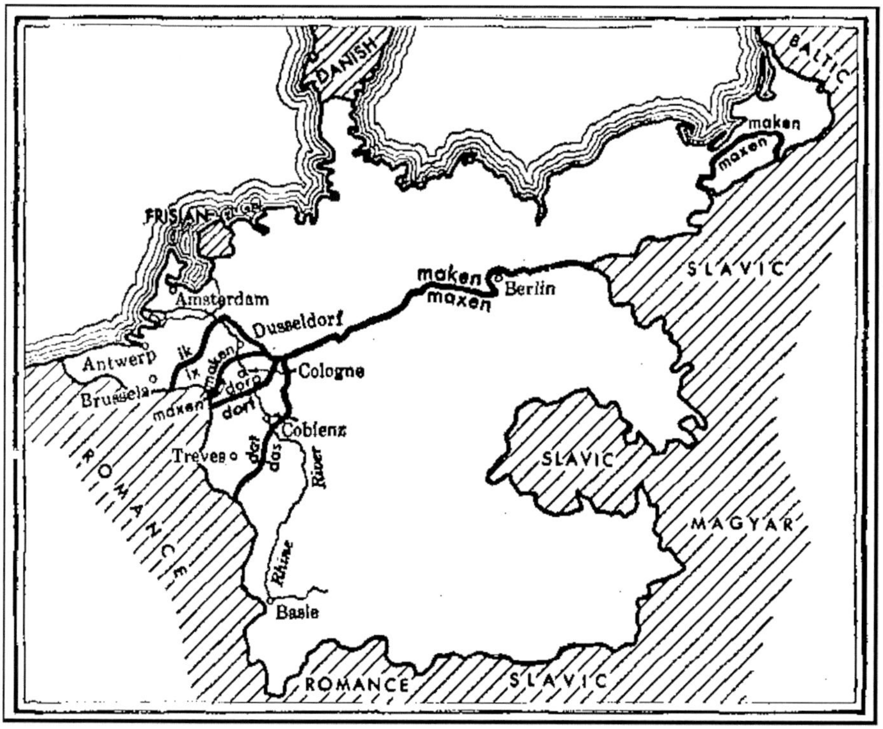


Figure 3. German isoglosses (from Bloomfield 1935: 344)

However, forms of speech judged to be "neutral" often do not correspond to standardized varieties. The most "neutral" form of spoken German is generally felt to be the variety spoken in Hanover, not coincidentally the place where Luther accomplished his Bible translation. The most "neutral" form of Italian is centered in Tuscany, where Dante wrote the Divine Comedy. The standard form of Swahili is the variety spoken in Zanzibar. The "best" Mandarin Chinese is spoken in the Donbei/Northeast region. However, in all of these "neutral" areas, the spoken and written vernacular still may fall far short of the standardized ideal.

When we examine actual speech in nations that seem to have monolithic standards, we find that there is considerable variation in the realization of that standard on all levels: phonological, morphological, syntactical and discourse. The linguistic analytic unit, the *isogloss* is used to delineate some of these differences geographically. In Figure 3, one can see some of the isoglosses for Standard German (pre-World War II). These isoglosses correspond with shifting political boundaries over many centuries, the most pronounced differences occurring in the "Rhenish fan" in the far Western part of the country where differences in pronunciation can divide communities.

## 7. Bi- and multi-lingual nations

In modern sociolinguistic and linguistic anthropological research, "speech communities" are a more viable analytic unit than "language communities." One "speech community" often consists of many "language communities" (Silverstein 1998: 407). A "speech community" may be localized, coterminous with state boundaries or transcend national boundaries. Despite the ideological drive to establish "one language – one nation" in many countries, this may be better thought of as an aspirational goal than an accomplished fact. At an even more fine-grained level, there are regional or local varieties that are acknowledged in many nations. These local varieties may have official status at a provincial level and may exist in written or legal form for court proceedings, official documents, media broadcasts and government communications.

The simple practicalities of achieving this can be enormous. One obvious reason is that post-colonial states often have been left with political boundaries that are not coterminous with linguistic or ethnic boundaries. This was occasionally done on purpose. The Durand Line dividing Afghanistan from British India (later Pakistan) was specifically designed to split the troublesome Pushtun community and their Pashto language in half, with the idea that they could thus be better controlled by the British colonial army (Kaura 2017). The Kurdish population was split among five separate states after World War II – a situation that continues to generate violence today.

Pre-nation-state Europe, where royal marriages and political alliances generated unusual combinations of ethnic groups within state boundaries has created a legacy of enormous legal problems for many states (Van der Jeught 2015; Van der Jeught

2016b). The Catalan language community spans four nations (France, Andorra, Spain and Italy). The Basque community is divided between France and Spain.

Outside of Europe, Iran has numerous language communities, many of which also transcend national boundaries (Beeman 1986). India has 22 officially recognized languages, including Tamil, Bengali, Punjabi, Kashmiri. Anderson's own area of specialization, Indonesia, has approximately 50 recognized languages. The most intense concentration of local varieties is in Papua New Guinea. In addition to the three "official" languages, there are 836 recognized local languages used in this nation. The official language of Nigeria is English, but Yoruba, Hausa and Igbo are recognized languages of the parliament and there are 529 other languages spoken in that nation as well as a local Pidgin. Zambia recognizes 72 languages within its borders. Even the small Pacific island nation, Vanuatu houses 110 distinct local varieties. Each of the states cited above can be considered to be "speech communities" despite the multiple varieties spoken there, largely due to the imposition of a *lingua franca* in each state, assuring some form of communality of communication.

This linguistic complexity pervades most, if not all of the world's nations, where many "national" languages are recognized along with the "official" language or languages in which government business is conducted and which are mandatory as media of education.

The existence of these overarching common languages did not arise automatically. Most exist because the long colonial period in human history resulted in a kind of linguistic hegemony, where the language of the colonizer became *de facto* the language of colonial administration. Local individuals who wished to be employed in an official capacity had to learn the official language, though it might not be in any way their mother tongue. In the post-colonial period, these linguistic policies continued – partly due to the enormous difficulty in shifting from the colonial language to local varieties.

As a result, there are many nations that recognize more than one official language as part of their national identity. These nations are well known as seen in the chart below:

**Table 2.** Multi-lingual states

| Nation/State | Languages |
|---|---|
| Abkhazia | Abkhazian and Georgian |
| Afghanistan | Pashto and Dari (Afghan Persian) |
| Aruba | Papiamento and Dutch |
| Belarus | Belarusian and Russian |
| Belgium | Dutch, French and German |
| Brunei | Malay and English |

(*Continued*)

**Table 2.** (*Continued*)

| | |
|---|---|
| Cameroon | English and French |
| Canada | English and French |
| Central African Republic | French and Sango |
| Curaçao | Papiamento, Dutch and English |
| Cyprus | Greek and Turkish |
| Djibouti | Arabic and French |
| East Timor | Tetum and Portuguese |
| Faroe Islands | Faroese and Danish |
| Fiji | Fijian, English and Hindi |
| Finland | Finnish and Swedish |
| Hong Kong | English and Chinese |
| India | Hindi and English (and 22 official regional languages) |
| Ireland | Irish and English |
| Israel | Hebrew and Arabic |
| Kazakhstan | Kazakh and Russian |
| Kiribati | Kiribati and English |
| Kyrgyzstan | Kyrgyz and Russian |
| Luxembourg | Luxembourgish, French and German |
| Macau | Chinese and Portuguese |
| Malta | Maltese and English |
| Marshall Islands | Marshalese and English |
| Morocco | Arabic and Berber |
| New Caledonia | French and Kanak languages |
| New Zealand | English, New Zealand Sign Language and Maori |
| Palau | Palauan and English |
| Papua New Guinea | Tok Pisin, English and Hiri Motu |
| Paraguay | Guarani and Spanish |
| Philippines | Filipino and English |
| Rapa Nui (Easter Island) | Rapa Nui, Chilean Spanish |
| Samoa | Samoan and English |
| Singapore | English, Mandaran Chinese, Malay and Tamil |
| South Africa | isiZulu, isiXhosa, Afrikaans, Sepedi, Setswana, English, Sesotho, Xitsonga, Siswati, Tshivenda, and isiNdebele. |
| South Sudan | Arabic and English |
| Sri Lanka | Sinhala and Tamil |
| Sudan | Arabic and English |
| Switzerland | German, French, Italian and Romansh |

Table 2. (*Continued*)

| | |
|---|---|
| Tonga | Tongan and English |
| Tuvalu | Tuvaluan and English |
| Vanuatu | Bislama, English and French |

An inspection of the list above shows a fascinating pattern. The majority of bilingual or multilingual nations have as at least one of their official languages the language of their colonial past. English, French, Spanish, Russian, Chinese and Portuguese predominate. The second "official" language is likely to be the predominant pre-colonial local language or languages. South Africa is a particularly apt illustration of this tendency. The most widely spoken first language in South Africa is Zulu (isi-Zulu) followed by Xhosa (isiXhosa), Afrikaans and English. Even though Afrikaans and English, the languages of the colonial era, are the third and fourth largest "first languages," they still are the predominant languages of government, education, and commerce. Even for English, however, several distinctly South African varieties have emerged that are gaining acceptance in official circles (Hibbert 2003). As mentioned above, India recognizes 22 "official" languages, but aside from English and Hindi, these are "official" only at the local level. All Indians are expected to learn English, Hindi and one of the other official languages appropriate to their region of residency.

There are four significant exceptions to the single standard language dominance pattern. Belgium, Canada, Luxembourg, and Switzerland. These four nations have their own unique histories in which different language groups have been enclosed within a state boundary and have been relatively successful in fostering official language equality for two or more varieties. Even so, perfect bilingualism or multilingualism does not exist in any of these states except for Luxembourg, which will be discussed below. Belgium has three official languages, but few Belgians are perfectly bilingual. Only around 20% of Belgians living in the French or German speaking sections of the country speak Dutch with perfect fluency. The proportion of citizens in the Dutch speaking area who speak French is somewhat higher, but citizens in the Dutch and French speaking areas generally do not speak German. The preponderant language in Switzerland is overwhelmingly German, with smaller proportions of the population speaking French, Italian or Romansh. There are monolingual French speakers in Canada, and many English speakers in Canada who do not speak French, although its instruction is mandatory in schools.

Luxembourg, then, is almost the only nation in the world for which complete multilingualism is an aspirational hallmark of national identity. For this reason, it merits special attention considering Anderson's important work. Luxembourgish (Lëtzebuergesch) is the historical "national language" – it is a variety of Franconian-Moselle German (Gilles 1999; Gilles & Moulin 2003). There is a prevailing "doctrine" in the

European union of "one nation – one language"(Van der Jeught 2015: 24), although in recent years protection for linguistic minorities has grown in member states. In this regard Luxembourg represents a departure, as it is officially a tri-lingual nation. Luxembourgish as the recognized "national language" is commonly spoken and also written, but Standardized German and French are fully recognized as official administrative languages. Newspapers are published in all three languages – occasionally in the same paper. Literary writers are as likely to author books and stories in any of the three languages, and all are present in broadcast media. The education system is rigorous in its efforts to promote perfect trilingual competence (Fehlen 2002; Horner & Weber 2008).

Even with this official policy in place, there is still social differentiation in terms of language use. Individuals may have the ability to work with all three languages, but each language may have a slightly different functionality in everyday life. Indeed, proficiency English may also be necessary as a practical matter.

> Proficiency in Luxembourgish alone does not lead to success on the job market: knowledge of the standard varieties of French and English are often necessary in the private sector, whereas the standard varieties of French and German – together with Luxembourgish – are normally required in the public sector. It is access to combinations of the standard varieties of French, English and, to a lesser extent, German that creates opportunities in various spheres of employment, whereas knowledge of Luxembourgish continues to serve as a gate-keeping device with regard to civil service positions. (Horner & Weber 2008: 119)

So, in the example of Luxembourg, perhaps the most explicitly tri-lingual nation on earth, we see that the different languages that are hallmarks of this national identity are still differentiated according to function and context. Ethnographic studies of language use in many countries that espouse more than one "official" language reveal similar patterns. One language may be used for official communication, whereas an historical vernacular is used for everyday communication. Moreover, the languages, despite all efforts, are not equal even in the education system resulting not in trilingual fluency, but a situation where students are not fully competent in any of the three languages. The strain on students is a factor in less than ideal school outcomes. This is particularly true of recent immigrants, which now constitute nearly half of the population.

> Luxembourgish plays a subordinate role as a written language [in school education], German is replaced by French only after a few years of school and pupils do not have the necessary prerequisites for French as a native language. It appears that most pupils have in fact a triglossic deficit.
>
> In a 2006 Report on the Luxembourgish school system, a group of Council of Europe experts was particularly harsh. It concluded that the system cannot achieve its goals, such as social cohesion, integration of newcomers, individual success and a competitive economy.

> The high drop-out rate of students is of particular concern in this regard. Moreover, as early as primary school, 17,9% of pupils have an educational delay of one year or more. This figure rises to 62,6% for secondary school students. Besides, only 38,4% of students make it to the classical school (as opposed to vocational training).
>
> (Van der Jeught 2015: 119–120)

Delving into the linguistic history of the state reveals that the current day situation is the result of a complex historical process over many centuries. French was at one time the prestige language of the upper classes, German held sway during times of German political (and military) influence, and Luxembourgish emerged in the post-World War II period as a symbolic mark of national identity. So, even this paragon tri-lingual nation reveals that a great deal of social and cultural fluctuation took place before arriving at the present situation, which is still highly dynamic (Van der Jeught 2015: 109–126; Horner & Weber 2008; Fehlen 2002).

## 8. Linguistic habitus and speaker strategies

Looking at the situation in Luxembourg, one can conclude that expecting the population of any nation to maintain perfect bilingual or multi-lingual skills, and for the state to function with using different language varieties equally may be an idealistic desirable goal, but it is extremely difficult to accomplish. The more natural pattern is one where co-existing varieties become culturally and functionally differentiated. In short, speaker behavior is a kind of "linguistic *habitus*" – a concept deriving from Bourdieu who defines the general concept of habitus as follows:

> […] the structures characterizing a determinate class of conditions of existence produce the structures of the habitus, which in their turn are the basis of the perception and appreciation of all subsequent experiences. The habitus, product of history, produces individual and collective practices – more history – in accordance with the schemes generated by history.
>
> (Bourdieu 1990: 54; Blommaert 2015)

This linguistic habitus encompasses a situation where all speakers develop a routine where they are switching on a regular observable basis between varieties during the course of their daily lives. Indeed, it is difficult not to conclude that variety switching is the natural universal pattern of human language use. Indeed, it is the ability to acquire this linguistic habitus that may be the most salient component of membership in an imagined community. If one can switch readily between varieties under the proper contextual circumstances, one can claim membership in the community of others who can do this as part of their own identity.

This pattern of alternation of varieties on the part of individual speakers, when applying to different variants of the "same language" has been understood for decades under the general term *diglossia* as articulated by Charles Ferguson (Ferguson 1959; see also Daniëls 2018 for a recent approach to Arabic diglossia). Ferguson's original designation covered usages such as the alternation between Katharévousa and Dhimotikí in Greek or Swiss German and Standard German in Switzerland.

Fishman accounted for this alternation based on a variety of factors as shown in Table 3.

**Table 3.** Factors governing diglossic alternation

| DIFFERENCES | |
|---|---|
| **Alternation parameter** | **Description** |
| Specialization | One variety is used for specialized purposes, the other for general use |
| Prestige | One variety has higher social prestige |
| Context of use | One variety is acquired under special circumstances, such as in formal school instruction, or in special usage contexts such as in a court or religious establishment. |
| Standardization | One variety is highly standardized with formal grammar and orthography |
| Complexity | One variety is more complex and/or highly inflected |
| SIMILARITIES | |
| **Description** | **Diglossic communalities** |
| Vocabulary | The two varieties share the bulk of their vocabulary, though there may be some distribution of terms according to formality |
| Phonology | The two varieties share overall phonological structures |

Fishman and Gumperz extended this concept to include situations such as in Paraguay, Belgium or in the example of Luxembourg when two standardized languages were used interchangeably (Gumperz 1971; Fishman 1972). In this case the same criteria apply for the variation in use of the different varieties and styles that are components of every communication system (Beeman 1977; Jakobson 1960; Hymes 1974)

Fishman continued to elaborate on his exploration of bilingualism. In an important paper in 1980 he posited that speakers not only shift varieties, they also undergo a shift in identity when they change. He called this shift "di-ethnia," to designate the ability to alter cultural identity in not only bilingual, but also bicultural situations. He points out that the societal compartmentalization and functional specificity that facilitates this ability to switch is difficult to establish and maintain, but that some societies "have developed a talent for exactly such arrangements" (Fishman 1980: 3).

Ethnographic studies of language variation, including diglossia, bilingualism and biculturalism have shown that speakers in communities that have multiple linguistic varieties officially or unofficially available to them have challenges in maintaining equal competence in all of these varieties. The universal existence of non-standard varieties competing with formal standard varieties might not be problematic, except for the fact that the non-standard varieties are not socially neutral, as Fishman noted in his original formulation of diglossia. Taking one of Fishman's criteria, different varieties frequently are either seen as "prestige" varieties or as "stigmatized" varieties (Labov 1973; Labov 2006). Prestige forms may be just as deviant from standardized forms as stigmatized forms (Ross 1954), so there is no particular measurable correspondence of features that would suggest that prestige forms are "closer" to standardized varieties. Nor are stigmatized forms necessarily "less logical" or "deficient" compared to standardized varieties (Labov 1969).The prestige factor may have to do with regional origin, economic status, educational status or professional occupation.

Whole languages may be stigmatized. In Pakistan, the "official" language is Urdu. Paradoxically few people in Pakistan speak Urdu as their "mother tongue," the exception being Mohajirs, individuals who migrated to Pakistan after the partition of the state from British India, a group who are stigmatized in Pakistan today. The principal languages of pre-independence Pakistan were Punjabi in the North, Sindhi in the South, Baluchi in the Southwest and Pashto in the Northwest. Several other smaller languages are also spoken.

Today in Pakistan the "prestige" language is English. In Lahore, the large metropolis in the North, Punjabi is the vernacular language everyone learns at home. Punjabi, Urdu and English are also taught in school, but Urdu is only used in limited formal situations. There is a hierarchy of prestige. English is the most prestigious language. Urdu is next and Punjabi is the least prestigious. Persons who speak Urdu or English with a strong Punjabi accent are disadvantaged socially and professionally (Sullivan 2005). Speaking with a research colleague working in Pakistan, I was surprised to find that when he addressed professional level people in Lahore in Punjabi they were insulted. It was as if he was talking down to them, implying that they didn't know English, and were therefore "lower class."

The same dynamic applies in Central Asia where Russian is the prestige language despite the ubiquitous presence of local varieties such as Tajik, Uzbek, Kyrgyz, Kazakh and Turkman. An official, scholar or high-level business person would expect to speak Russian in most public situations. Even in the Middle East, where Arabic is so dominant, European languages – predominantly French and English – are used to indicate status. Not knowing these languages is professionally untenable for those who aspire to middle and upper-class careers.

But at the same time, Rudyard Kipling's admonition that one must be able to "walk with kings, nor lose the common touch" is essential to function in social life in any nation. In the United States, middle-class African Americans, many of whom have grown up using African-American Vernacular English (AAVE) (Rickford 2003) often feel challenged adjusting to different social contexts in managing the speech varieties in which they are proficient. African-American arts and culture journalist Joshua Adams writes:

> Growing up, my Black friends said I talked "white" and my non-Black friends said I talked "ghetto." When I'm with non-Black friends, in the classroom, or at a job interview, I automatically turn on the "talking white" switch. When I'm with my Black friends, I reset to my normal south-side Chicago diasporic slur. Pretty soon, I was both the accuser and the accused in the racial speech witch trials. (Adams 2015)

Adams' story can be repeated all over the world by people in different nations, since the human reality is that humans are continually managing different speech modalities. Some systems are extremely complex. Iranian *ta'ārof* (Beeman 2017; Beeman 1986), Japanese *keigo* (Wetzel 2004; Pizziconi 2003; Shibamoto-Smith & Cook 2011; Shibamoto-Smith 2011), and Javanese *krama iggil* (Errington 1988) all embody substitutions of semantically equivalent verbs, pronouns and other speech elements according to social rules of politeness, respect and formality. Thus, even when speaking a "foreign" language, native speakers of languages such as these still embody the same linguistic habitus in their linguistic and social behavior toward others (Bahmani 2004; Wijayanto 2013; Iwasaki 2011).

One group that is particularly challenged are immigrants. In the Netherlands and Belgium in speaking about communities who have immigrated from different regions, a geological metaphor has been used for such groups for some time – perhaps as an alternative to the term "(im)migrant," a category which is often seen in a negative light. In this terminology, original residents of a nation are "autochthonous" and immigrants are "allochthonous." (In geological terms, an autochthonous stratum is an original geological formation, over which an allochthonous layer is deposited through water, plate movement or other means. Autochthonous is also used to mean "native people" in English). The Dutch terms are *autochtoon* and *allochtoon* (Yanow & Haar 2013; Zienkowski 2017).

Immigrants, or allochthonous people are frequently required to learn the standard language of the countries to which they migrate. This is especially true in Europe. Germany, Sweden and other states establish language classes specifically for these people. The states that welcome these people view learning the standardized language of the state as proof of the desire of the allochthonous people to join the nation. Of course the practical need to communicate for work, official business and education is usually cited as the reason for the (semi-)compulsory language instruction.

Despite the efforts of the new home state, however, these communities often maintain a separate communication community that uses the vernacular of the community of origin for everyday interpersonal and often commercial dealings. Their communication medium may be a standard language of their homeland, or it may be an indigenous variety. Initially the allochthonous community may truly be a face-to-face community when numbers are small, but as their numbers grow, they transform into an Andersonian imagined community. Frequently new members gain admission through their ability to speak the vernacular variety that unites the community.

Even when individuals are speaking "the same language" to each other, they may still view themselves as being part of different communities. These differences may be understood in pragmatic terms. Discourse frames, issues of discussion and rhetorical practice may divide communities from each other. One such community comprises Moroccans and their descendants living in Belgium. Pragmatic linguist Jan Zienkowski has published a detailed research monograph dealing with the Morroccan allochthonous community in the Flemish speaking area of Belgium and the communication strategies they and their hosts employ to carry out day-to-day interaction, particularly in the realm of political activity. Zienkowski's study is particularly timely given the risk of stigmatization due to violent activities on the part of terrorists in Belgium in recent years (Zienkowski 2017)

The United States is full of such communities. The largest language community in the United States aside from "native English" speakers are Spanish speakers – but even here there are many varieties of Spanish depending on the geographic origin of speakers. The same is true of Chinese, Portuguese, and French speakers, to name some of the most prominent linguistic groups. These communities have their own news publications, radio and television broadcasts, social clubs, and sports teams. Even when speaking English, in contrast to earlier waves of immigrants, many retain the cultural identities of their regions of origin – and thus their membership in "imagined" allochthonous communities. The presence of so many – actually hundreds – of "allochthonous" communities in the United States has become a major political issue. One of the most frequent complaints is that the allochthonous communities "don't learn English." Of course, this is not true, but such judgements are indicative of the highly symbolic importance of language as an indicator of community membership.

## 9. Conclusion – imagined communities, imagined languages

Benedict Anderson's concept of the imagined community has rightfully sparked the interest and attention of social scientists in many disciplines. The symbolic touchstones used by members of imagined communities to cement their community identities are highly varied. However, having a "common language" is one element that is privileged.

Community members believe that they belong to X community because they speak X language, and if someone else whom they have never met also speaks X language, they are accepted as belonging to the same X community. Examined from the perspective of pragmatics, however, this syllogism quickly breaks down.

First, I have suggested that the idea that members of an imagined community speak a common language is a fiction. Given the enormous variation in speech varieties in all communities, members of an imagined community only "imagine" that they are speaking a common language. We may thus conclude that they embrace an "imagined language" to accord with the imagined community. By no means do I wish to suggest that the feeling of community is unreal. It is, however, essentially a political construct.

Second, I have tried to show that the idea of a unitary standard language, though the result of extensive scholarly work, is also a fictional construct. Indeed, as Reagan stated above: "There is no English … etc." (Reagan 2004: 41). Given its important functionality in the operations of states, as industrialized and communicative interconnectivity has grown in human society, it would be absurd to say that standard languages are therefore invalid or useless. They are an essential social and administrative institution in all communities. Therefore, it is not surprising that acquisition of a standard language is a requirement for belonging to a community. Proficiency in this standard language is frequently a requirement for a successful life – as a major factor governing personal and romantic relations, educational advancement, and career achievement.

Third, there is no community on earth where only one communicational variety is used in everyday life. All states and all nations are multi-varietal, often with varieties that originate in different historical language families.

Fourth, creolization because of social and linguistic contact between communities is a normal, fluid and ongoing process. At some point when communities' common identities coalesce, and they develop a political and social structural infrastructure, what was once seen as a "creole" or "pidgin" is standardized and becomes a "language" that becomes a touchstone component of community identity.

Fifth, language acquisition and language use can be politically or socially coercive through community regulation. This regulation is often justified as a measure to preserve the community and to ensure the welfare of its members. As a practical matter, for community members to reject or be unable to acquire a standard language is to endanger their ability to advance in life. Deficiency in this language acquisition can even be dangerous. In the case of the imposition of a shibboleth test, not being able to "pass" can get a person killed. Similarly, using standard language as a hallmark of education or breeding can significantly inhibit progress in life. In many states acquisition of the standardized language associated with the state is a legal requirement for citizenship. It is a test of competency in decisions affecting admission to higher education programs. Acquisition of a standard ritual language may also be required to be considered a member of a religious community.

There is a central paradox in the language-community relationship: Standard languages are essential qualifications for community membership, but no one actually speaks any standard language with consistent uniform perfection and precision. Not only do even the most erudite users of language regularly lapse into non-standard discourse, they do so with pragmatic competence. They act in conformity with a linguistic habitus that requires adjustment to physical and social context, participants, rhetorical purpose, discourse standards and communicational effectiveness. So, when two people who do not know each other declare that they speak the "same language," it is a certainty that they do not. They only imagine that they do.

In modern post-colonial times we also see that individuals may belong to more than one imagined community. Fishman's concept of *di-ethnia* in which persons may activate more than one language as a way of identifying themselves with more than one community is now a standard feature of modern society throughout the world (Fishman 1980)

From a linguistic and pragmatic standpoint, Anderson's views of the relationship between language and community are highly useful, but perhaps not in the ways that he himself envisioned. He raised wonderful questions for linguistic analysts, and for research in pragmatics. Certainly, the cultural and social-psychological persistence of "imagined languages" as components of identity for members of imagined communities even though they do not exist in observable reality is something pragmatic researchers must strive to understand more fully.

## References

Adams, Joshua. 2015. "Confessions of a code-switcher: 'Talking White' as an accent." *Huffington Post*. https://www.huffingtonpost.com/joshua-adams/confessions-of-a-code-switcher-talking-white-as-an-accent_b_7288956.html (accessed March 25, 2018).

Allen, Peter. 2008. "France's L'Académie Française upset by rule to recognise regional tongues." *The Telegraph*, August 16, 2008. https://www.telegraph.co.uk/news/worldnews/europe/france/2569651/Frances-LAcadmie-Franaise-upset-by-rule-to-recognise-regional-tongues.html (accessed March 10, 2018).

Anderson, Benedict Richard O'Gorman. 1983. *Imagined Communities: Reflections on the Origin and Spread of Nationalism*. London: Verso.

Bahmani, Behrouz. 2004. "The martial art of Taarof." *Iranian.Com*, April 2004. http://iranian.com/BruceBahmani/2004/April/Taarof/index.html

Bailey, Edward P. 1997. *The Plain English Approach to Business Writing*, Revised edition. New York: Oxford University Press.

Baycroft, Timothy and Mark Hewitson. 2006. *What Is a Nation?: Europe 1789–1914*. Oxford: Oxford University Press.

Beeman, William O. 1977. "Hows and whys of Persian style: A pragmatic approach." In *Studies in Language Variation*, ed. by Ralph W. Fasold and Roger W. Shuy, 269–282. Washington: Georgetown Univertsity Press.

Beeman, William O. 1986. *Language, Status, and Power in Iran*. Bloomington: Indiana University Press.

Beeman, William O. 2017. "TA'ĀROF." *Encyclopedia Iranica*. http://www.iranicaonline.org/articles/taarof (accessed March 28, 2018).

Blommaert, Jan. 2015. "Pierre Bourdieu – Perspectives on anguage in society". In *Handbook of Pragmatics*, ed. by Jan-Ola Östman and Jef Verschueren, 1–16. Amsterdam: John Benjamins Publishing Company. https://benjamins.com/online/hop/articles/bou1 (accessed March 28, 2018).
Blommaert, Jan and Jef Verschueren. 1991. "The pragmatics of minority politics in Belgium." *Language in Society* 20(4): 503–531. https://doi.org/10.1017/S0047404500016705
Blommaert, Jan and Jef Verschueren. 1992. "The role of language in European nationalist ideologies." *Pragmatics* 2(3): 355–375. https://doi.org/10.1075/prag.2.3.13blo
Bloomfield, Leonard. 1935. *Language*. London: George Allen & Unwin. http://arrow.latrobe.edu.au:8080/vital/access/manager/Repository/latrobe:34348 (accessed May 18, 2018).
Bourdieu, Pierre. 1977. "The economics of linguistic exchanges." *Social Science Information* 16(6): 645–668. https://doi.org/10.1177/053901847701600601
Bourdieu, Pierre. 1990. *The Logic of Practice*. Stanford: Stanford University Press.
Breuilly, John. 2016. "Benedict Anderson's imagined communities: A symposium." *Nations and Nationalism* 22(4): 625–659. https://doi.org/10.1111/nana.12236
Bucholtz, Mary and Kira Hall. 2004. "Language and identity." In *A Companion to Linguistic Anthropology*, ed. by Alessandro Duranti, 369–394. Oxford: Blackwell.
Daniëls, Helge. 2018. "Diglossia: A language ideological approach." *Pragmatics* 28(2): 185–216. https://doi.org/10.1075/prag.00006.dan
Druckmann, Yaron. 2013. "CBS: 27% of Israelis struggle with Hebrew." *Ynetnews* (https://www.ynetnews.com/articles/0.7340.L-4335235.00.html)
Eminov, Ali. 2001. "Review of *The Turkish Language Reform: A Catastrophic Success*." *Language* 77(2):384–86. https://doi.org/10.1353/lan.2001.00.78
Errington, James Joseph. 1988. *Structure and Style in Javanese: A Semiotic View of Linguistic Etiquette*. Philadelphia: University of Pennsylvania Press.
Evans, Arthur. 2013. *Through Bosnia and the Herzegovina on Foot during the Insurrection, August and September 1875: With an Historical Review of Bosnia, and a Glimpse at the Croats, Slavonians, and the Ancient Republic of Ragusa*. (accessed March 13, 2018). https://doi.org/10.1017/CBO9781139794947
Fallers, Lloyd A. 2011. *The Social Anthropology of the Nation-State*. New Brunswick, N.J: Transaction Publishers.
Fehlen, Fernand. 2002. "Luxembourg, a multilingual society at the Romance/Germanic language border." *Journal of Multilingual and Multicultural Development* 23(1–2): 80–97. https://doi.org/10.1080/01434630208666456
Ferguson, Charles Albert. 1959. "Diglossia." *Word* 15: 325–340. https://doi.org/10.1080/00437956.1959.11659702
Fishman, Joshua A. 1972. *The Sociology of Language: An Interdisciplinary Social Science Approach to the Study of Language in Society*. Rowley, Mass.: Newbury House Publishers.
Fishman, Joshua A. 1980. "Bilingualism and biculturism as individual and as societal phenomena." *Journal of Multilingual and Multicultural Development* 1(1): 3–15. https://doi.org/10.1080/01434632.1980.9993995
Gaelscoileanna - Irish Medium Education. 2018. http://www.gaelscoileanna.ie/en/
Gellner, Ernest. 1983. *Nations and Nationalism. New Perspectives on the Past*. Ithaca: Cornell University Press.
Gilles, Peter. 1999. *Dialektausgleich Im Lëtzebuergeschen: Zur Phonetisch-Phonologischen Fokussierung Einer Nationalsprache* [*Dialect Levelling in Luxembourgish: About the Phonetic- Phonological Focussing of a National Language*]. Tübingen: Niemeyer. https://doi.org/10.1515/9783110935066
Gilles, Peter and Claudine Moulin. 2003. "Luxembourgish." In *IMPACT: Studies in Language and Society*, ed. by Ana Deumert and Wim Vandenbussche, 303–329. Amsterdam: John Benjamins Publishing Company. https://benjamins.com/catalog/impact.18.12gil (accessed March 23, 2018).

Gumperz, John Joseph. 1971. *Language in Social Groups*. Stanford: Stanford University Press.
Hibbert, Liesel. 2003. "Changing Language Practices in Parliament in South Africa." *Southern African Linguistics and Applied Language Studies* 21(3): 103–117. https://doi.org/10.2989/16073610309486334
Hobsbawm, Eric J. 1992. *Nations and Nationalism since 1780: Programme, Myth, Reality*, 2nd edition. Cambridge: Cambridge University Press.
Hobsbawm, Eric J. and Terence O. Ranger. 1983. *The Invention of Tradition*. Cambridge: Cambridge University Press.
Horner, Kristine and Jean Jacques Weber. 2008. "The Language Situation in Luxembourg." *Current Issues in Language Planning* 9(1): 69–128. https://doi.org/10.2167/cilp130.0
Hymes, Dell H. 1974. *Foundations in Sociolinguistics: An Ethnographic Approach*. Philadelphia: University of Pennsylvania Press.
Iwasaki, Noriko. 2011. "Learning L2 Japanese 'politeness' and 'impoliteness': Young American men's dilemmas during study abroad. *Japanese Language and Literature* 45: 67–106.
Jakobson, Roman. 1960. "Closing statement: Linguistics and poetics." In *Style in Language*, ed. by Thomas Sebeok, 350–377. Cambridge, MA: MIT Press.
Kaura, Vinay. 2017. *The Durand Line: A British Legacy Plaguing Afghan-Pakistani Relations*. Middle East Institute. https://www.mei.edu/content/article/durand-line-british-legacy-plaguing-afghan-pakistani-relations (accessed March 28, 2018).
Labov, William. 1969. "The logic of non-standard English." *Florida F L Rep* 7(1): 60–74.
Labov, William. 1973. *Sociolinguistic Patterns*. Philadelphia: University of Pennsylvania Press.
Labov, William. 2006. *The Social Stratification of English in New York City*, 2nd edition. Cambridge: Cambridge University Press. https://doi.org/10.1017/CBO9780511618208
Lewis, Geoffrey. 2002. *The Turkish Language Reform: A Catastrophic Success*. Oxford: Oxford University Press.
Loftus, Valerie. 2016. "11 reasons why TG4 is actually the best channel on Irish television." *The Daily Edge* (http://www.dailyedge.ie/tg4-is-the-best-3127497/)
Makoni, Sinfree and Alastair Pennycook. 2005. "Disinventing and (re)constituting languages." *Critical Inquiry in Language Studies* 2(3): 137–156. https://doi.org/10.1207/s15427595cils0203_1
Mitch, David. 2004. "Education and skill of the British labour force." In *The Cambridge Economic History of Modern Britain*, ed. by Roderick Floud and Paul Johnson, 332–356. Cambridge: Cambridge University Press. https://doi.org/10.1017/CHOL9780521820363.013
Owuor, Yvonne Adhiambo. 2015. "O-Swahili: Language and liminality." *Matatu* 46(1): 141–152. https://doi.org/10.1163/9789004298071_009
Pizziconi, Barbara. 2003. "Re-examining politeness, face and the Japanese language." *Journal of Pragmatics* 35(10–11): 1471–1506. https://doi.org/10.1016/S0378-2166(02)00200-X
Rahier, Jean Muteba. 2003. "Métis/mulâtre, mulato, mulatto, negro, moreno, mundele kaki, black, …: The wanderings and meanderings of identities." In *Problematizing Blackness: Self-Ethnographies by Black Immigrants to the United States*, ed. by Percy C. Hintzen, Jean Muteba Rahier, and Florida International University, 85–112. New York: Routledge.
Reagan, Timothy. 2004. "Objectification, positivism and language studies: A reconsideration." *Critical Inquiry in Language Studies* 1(1): 41–60. https://doi.org/10.1207/s15427595cils0101_3
Rickford, John R. 2003. "African American Vernacular English (AAVE)." In *International Encyclopedia of Linguistics*, 41–44. Oxford: Oxford University Press. http://www.oxfordreference.com.ezp2.lib.umn.edu/view/10.1093/acref/9780195139778.001.0001/acref-9780195139778-e-0023 (accessed March 25, 2018).
Ritsema, Alex. 2008. *Pirates and Privateers from the Low Countries, C.1500-C.1810*. Alex Ritsema.

Ross, Alan S.C. 1954. *Linguistic Class-Indicators in Present-Day English*. Modern Language Society of Helsinki. https://books.google.com/books?id=2-SWmAEACAAJ.

Ryckbosch, Wouter and Dries Vrijders. 2005. "Schild ende Vriend." *Schamper* http://www.schamper.ugent.be/431/schild-ende-vriend (accessed May 19, 2018).

Senior, Andrew. 2004. "Shibboleths." http://www.andrewsenior.com/shibboleth/list.html (accessed May 19, 2018).

Shibamoto-Smith, Janet S. 2011. "Honorifics, 'politeness', and power in Japanese political debate." *Journal of Pragmatics* 43(15): 3707–3719. https://doi.org/10.1016/j.pragma.2011.09.003

Shibamoto-Smith, Janet S. and Haruko Minegishi Cook. 2011. "Negotiating linguistic politeness in Japanese interaction: A critical examination of honorifics." *Journal of Pragmatics* 43(15): 3639–3642. https://doi.org/10.1016/j.pragma.2011.08.008

Silverstein, Michael. 1998. "Contemporary transformations of local linguistic communities." *Annual Review of Anthropology* 27(1): 401–26. https://doi.org/10.1146/annurev.anthro.27.1.401

Sullivan, Celeste M. 2005. Language Use in Lahore: The Role of Culture, Social Structure, and Economics in Shaping Communication Patterns and Language Form in a Pakistani Multilingual Community. Ph.D. dissertation, Brown University.

Tabouret-Keller, Andree. 1998. "Language and identity." In *The Handbook of Sociolinguistics*, ed. by Florian Coulmas, 327–343. Oxford: Blackwell Publishing Ltd. http://doi.wiley.com/ (accessed March 20, 2018). https://doi.org/10.1111/b.9780631211938.1998.00021.x

Van der Jeught, Stefaan. 2015. *Conflicting Language Policies in the EU and Member States*. Brussels: Vrije Universiteit Brussel.

Van der Jeught, Stefaan. 2016a. "The Loi Toubon and EU law: A happy or a mismatched couple?" *European Journal of Language Policy* 8(2): 139–152. https://doi.org/10.3828/ejlp.2016.9

Van der Jeught, Stefaan. 2016b. "The protection of ethnic minorities in Italy: A clean break with the past." *Journal on Ethnopolitics and Minority Issues in Europe (JEMIE)* 15(3): 57–81.

Wetzel, Patricia Jean. 2004. *Keigo in Modern Japan: Polite Language from Meiji to the Present*. Honolulu: University of Hawaii Press.

Wijayanto, Agus. 2013. "The emergence of the Javanese sopan and santun (politeness) on the Refisa: Strategies issued by Javanese learners of English." *Language, Culture and Society* (36): 34–47.

Yanow, Dvora and Marleen van der Haar. 2013. "People out of place: Allochthony and autochthony in Netherlands Identity Discourse – Metaphors and categories in action." *Journal of International Relations and Development* 16: 227–261. https://doi.org/10.1057/jird.2012.13

Zienkowski, Jan. 2017. *Articulations of the Self and Politics in Activist Discourse*. Cham: Springer International Publishing. http://link.springer.com/10.1007/978-3-319-40703-6 (accessed March 19, 2018). https://doi.org/10.1007/978-3-319-40703-6

# Emotions
## A philosophical and cognitive perspective

Claudia Strey
Escola Superior de Propaganda e Marketing, São Paulo

*There can be no knowledge without emotion. We may be aware of a truth, yet until we have felt its force, it is not ours. To the cognition of the brain must be added the experience of the soul.* (Arnold Bennett)

### 1. Overview

The relationship between language and emotions is quite ordinarily addressed in everyday communication – we feel something and we speak about it; we speak about something and we feel it. Friends gather to talk about their lives; family meet to celebrate and to discuss problems; strangers hold polite conversations on elevators. Most everyday encounters seem to be grounded in some kind of emotional phenomenon – whether it is to share happiness, to bicker over something, or to establish hierarchy.

Linguists sometimes may face theoretical problems when emotions are involved in communication. The relationship is neither easy to describe nor to explain. How do some people get crossed after speaking to each other and others do not? How do we explain that language arouses emotional, chemical feelings? If a theory is successfully able to explain that, some other questions have to be clarified: What are emotions? What is language? Is an emotional state able to trigger inferences or alter the cognitive environment? Is language strictly rational? Is a linguist theory able to investigate emotions?

According to Popper (1963: 88), "We are not students of some subject matter, but students of problems. And problems may cut right across the borders of any subject matter or discipline". That seems to be the case of language and emotions – the relationship between them is not an object of one discipline, but rather of many. In this sense, how we set the boundaries of research is sometimes more important than the work itself. If we can state exactly from where we are looking upon a problem, we have more chances of grasping its properties.

For the purposes of this Handbook article, we have decided not to try and cover the full complexity of the relationships between language and emotions. Let me try to clarify the perspective to which this contribution will restrict itself. Firstly, it is

https://doi.org/10.1075/hop.21.emo2

necessary to clarify the notion of 'emotion'. Although Wierzbicka (1995) points out that if you intend to study a concept, you should not start with a clear definition of it – or you will end up with something very rigorous – still it seems important to adopt a clearly linguistic notion of emotions. A linguist may not be interested exactly in how they work at a chemical level, but in how they are expressed in language. Even so, a further restriction seems to be called for. If the question is "What are emotions?" the answer should be: it depends on the theoretical perspective. Within language studies, for instance, emotions can be looked at from the perspective of linguistics and cognitive psychology, or linguistics and philosophy, for example. When looking at the pragmatics of emotions, the same is true for the question "What is Pragmatics?" The answer depends on the perspective taken, as there are different theories, for instance, to explain how we imply more than we say. This paper will refrain from taking the perspective of discursive psychology or from taking a conversation-analytical point of view. Rather, it assumes the cognitive perspective that people communicate in order to establish connections and to convey intentions. In this line of reasoning, people also communicate to convey their emotions, and they may do that by means of linguistic marks, weak implicatures, and the like. If one assumes a cognitive perspective on communication, we must also explain how cognition[1] and communication are bound together.

Accepting the intrinsic complexity of the topic, this article only aims to shed some light on the basis of its investigation, covering philosophical and neurological aspects of emotion studies in order to extend it towards a pragmatic theory, more specifically towards relevance theory.

## 2. A philosophical perspective on emotion and language

Defining emotions has always been a challenge for scientists and philosophers. First, the word itself is problematic, as it can cover sentiments, feelings, passion, and instinct (its original sense in English, from the mid-sixteenth century, is *mental agitation;* cf. the Oxford English Dictionary). As Schmitter (2014) posits, even trying to recognise theories of emotion in early modern writing is hard, because there are different vocabularies for talking about the same phenomenon: For example, philosophers of the seventeenth century talked about 'passion' and 'affect', while eighteenth century thinkers would use 'sentiment'. She adds, "None of these terms (or their French and

1. Nowadays, cognition is a term used loosely, relating to processes such as memory, attention, language, problem solving and planning – in other words, processing information, applying knowledge and changing preferences.

Latin cognates) carried the meaning they now do or that 'emotion' has come to bear (which did not have a primarily psychological sense until the nineteenth century)" (Schmitter 2014).

It is also important to understand that there is a strong rationalist tradition to treat emotion as something of minor importance, a property of the body, not of the soul. For Socratic-Platonic philosophy, emotion is different from reason, as the first brings limitations to the latter – senses interfere with the clarity with which reason is perceived. Socrates was a rationalist in terms of his theory of knowledge, as he believed that truth comes from the mind and not from the senses. For him, our mind is limited by emotions, so humans should use rational thought to understand the truths about the world. Plato also believed that we should not trust sensory information, as they can 'confuse' reality with imagination. This philosopher argued that things are not always what they seem, and that we are not always able to perceive we are making mistakes. Through his dialogues, especially *Phaedo*, he sustained a belief in an immutable reality (independent of what is perceived by the senses), and in the immortality of the soul – the subject of his Theory of Form. In proposing the use of reason instead of observation, Plato laid the foundations of rationality that would influence many other philosophers afterwards.

Like Plato, Aristotle assumed that there is a special and interactive communication between body, mind, and emotions. However, he took Plato's main theory and fleshed it out into a more empirical one, with ideas and observations that seem to appeal to the common sense. Rejecting the Platonic dualism between mind and matter, he indicated that one is part of the other – and that senses could help give evidence to the theories. Prior to Aristotle's treatment of emotion, senses were only viewed as irrational, as something that completely escaped reason (Menezes e Silva 2010). In both his *Rethoric* and his *Nichomachean Ethics*, emotions (or *pathos*) are treated as susceptible to rational influence and voluntary action, although not directly subject to choice.

The different positions of Plato and Aristotle on the perception of the world – empirical or rational – build the foundations for the organization of Western thought. In the seventeenth century, the debate reached its culmination after Descartes published his *Discourse on Method*. Descartes was part of the so-called Scientific Revolution, and he wondered about the possibility of expanding the knowledge and understanding of the world. He defended pure research, freeing science from scepticism. At the same time, he sought to show that we could not trust our senses as a secure basis for knowledge, because they are able to deceive us. Descartes is frequently described as the father of Modern Philosophy, because he pursued certainty in Philosophy, as it exists in Mathematics, but without subscribing to dogmas or considering arguments from authority, and establishing a firm and rational basis for knowledge.

Whilst Descartes believed that, in order to practice science, one should put one's passions aside since they can tempt us to understand the properties of the world inappropriately, he argued that it is necessary to define bodily-based perceptions in order to know them better and avoid those interferences (see Descartes' *Principles of Philosophy*). Commentators on the philosopher always assume that he did not think passions should be completely eradicated, because they are functional – they are meant to inform which things are helpful and which are not damaging (Schmitter 2014). Similarly, Brassfield (2012) affirms that we should not understand *passions* as guides to evaluate our experiences, because they can exaggerate what is good and what is bad.

Descartes believed that the division between reason and emotion was methodological, so that knowledge could be obtained without being sensitive to the passions of the soul. This split inspired other philosophers and scientists, who developed a tendency to neglect emotions – perhaps because of the great variety of phenomena covered by the word (De Souza 2010). This methodological separation between emotions and reason assumes "a negative view of emotions", looking at emotions as negatively affecting reasoning.

Antonio Damasio's book *Descartes' Error*(1994) changed this paradigm. He claimed that patients who suffered serious brain damage in the prefrontal cortex had their ability to experience emotions diminished and had difficulties making practical decisions, such as choosing the better day for a medical appointment between two available dates. Damasio's ideas marked a revolution in scientific studies, where a more complex approach to the human mind is established, and emotions become the focus of interdisciplinary study. This paradigm change reflected on cognition studies – from neuroscience to cognitive psychology – and in the last decades a positive connection between emotion and reasoning has become the object of study.

## 3. A neuroscience perspective

Prior to the paradigm shift in the late twentieth century, the relationship between emotion and reasoning was not treated as a favourable phenomenon, as emotions were seen to interfere negatively in reasoning. Nowadays, by contrast, emotion is understood as a label to talk about different aspects of the brain and the mind: there are approaches that assume a relation between drive and motivation; others focus on conscious/unconscious processes; some discuss a possible distinction between basic and extended emotions (Pessoa 2008). This loose use of the term does not facilitate a clear definition.

In search of clarity, Pham (2007) groups series of neuroscience studies that show how emotional states affect rational processes, as well as humans' logical ability. Intense emotional states such as anxiety influence the capacity of the working memory, carrying a vast number of consequences, such as a lower ability to recall information and organise this information in memory; a longer time to verify the validity of logical inferences; the selection of an option without considering alternatives; a tendency to make more mistakes in geometric and semantic analogical problem solving; less thorough processing of persuasion arguments (Pham 2007: 157).

Pham also presents evidence that lighter emotional states also influence the rational process. Compared with neutral emotional states, some emotions lead people to categorise objects more widely, to generate more creative and interesting responses, to come out better in solving problems involving ingenuity, and to solve problems involving multiple tasks more efficiently. According to Pham (2007: 158), these findings demonstrate that positive emotions bring positive results to decision-making, as well as reasoning and problem-solving. Likewise, Pham states that positive emotions may also negatively influence people, who may have their performances on deduction tasks decreased. What is clear is that whether the emotions are positive or not, they do affect logical reasoning.

Damasio (1994) points out that, on the one hand, rationality and decision-making implies a logical strategy to produce valid inferences supported by attention and working memory. On the other hand, emotions play an essential role in decision and reasoning processes, functioning as a kind of alarm to the premises completed – a device that the author calls the *somatic marker hypothesis*.

Emotion would thus have a crucial role in reasoning and decision-making, something that is only possible because all of our life experiences, whether personal or social, are accompanied by some kind of emotion. Damasio also states that, whether emotions respond to stimuli chosen by evolution, as in the case of sympathy, or to individually learned stimuli, as in fear, the fact is that emotions and feelings – positive or negative – become inevitable components of our social experiences. In other words, emotions (whether learned or determined by evolution) form a basis to help in predicting the future consequences of a decision. It is important to note, as Damasio (2003) points out, that this feature of emotions may be something that occurs partially or completely, consciously or unconsciously. The author shows that, regardless of this variability, the mechanism will focus attention on certain aspects of the problem in order to improve its analysis.[2]

If we change the perspective to the relationship between language and emotion, there are many neuroscience studies that explain emotional communication. According to Gazzaniga et al. (2002), emotional communication is an important tool to understand how the brain works. The authors state that not just structural or neural systems should be studied, but we should also understand how the right and the left

2. There is some criticism on Damasio's position about how emotion and reason relate to each other (see Greenspan 2003). But for him, emotions can guide reasoning, and they regulate rational responses.

hemispheres interact and contribute to emotional experiences – such as the perception, production, and conscious experience of emotion.

It has been widely assumed that the right hemisphere is more important for emotions than the left one – and there is evidence from damaged-brain patients. Apparently, the main representation of language use is in the right hemisphere, because dysfunctions on this side of the brain are often associated with the inability to perceive (and sometimes produce) figurative meaning, inferences, indirect requests, and humour – pragmatic operations by definition. For Van Lancker Sidtis,

> Given these facts – a longer processing window, pattern recognition, and complex pitch perception – it is not surprising that most elements of the pragmatics of communication, including recognition of paralinguistic material such as emotions, sarcasm, irony, and humour; response to conversational cues; and discernment of nonliteral and inferential meanings in speech are often impaired in right-hemisphere damage. (Van Lancker Sidtis 2008: 205–206)

Gazzaniga et al. (2002) state that there are two types of emotional stimuli that are studied within emotional communication: emotional prosody and facial expressions. Van Lancker Sidtis (2008) says that prosody and gesture are universals of emotional expression across languages[3] – which implies that the difference does not seem to be in language itself, but at a paralinguistic level. It is important, however, to make a remark about the use of 'paralanguage'. According to Wharton (2009), the term is problematic, because

> Some people treat 'paralanguage' as including only those vocal aspects of language use that are not strictly speaking part of language: intonation, stress, affective tone of voice, rate of speech, hesitation (if that can be considered vocal) etc. On this construal, facial expression and gesture are non-linguistic. Others treat the paralinguistic as including most or all of those aspects of linguistic communication that are not part of language *per se*, but are nonetheless somehow involved with the message or meaning a communicator conveys. On the first construal, while the set of paralinguistic phenomena intersects with the set of natural phenomena I am concerned with, there exist both paralinguistic phenomena that are not natural – deliberate frowns or fake smiles – and natural phenomena which might be co-opted for communicative use that I would not want to call paralinguistic on any conception – a bruise or a pale complexion, for example. (Wharton 2009: 5–7)

Despite this problem of definition, neuropsychological studies show that disorders of emotion affect communicative competence, and language disorders interfere in the efficient communication of emotional and attitudinal information (Van Lancker

3. Prosody and gestures expressing emotions can be assumed to be universal phenomena. Different cultures may use the same prosody and gestures to communicate different emotional states.

Sidtis 2008). For the author, there is plenty of evidence that emotions, moods, and affect underlie and inform nearly every normal expression. Therefore, we could assume that pragmatics should be the natural place to study the relationship between emotion and language.

Assuming a positive view of emotions, if reasoning is related to emotions, and if cognition and emotions should be seen as a unitary system, how should language studies be carried on? Does the presence of emotion alter language production and comprehension? If so, how? For LeDoux (1996), we often categorize and label our experiences in linguist terms, as well as store experiences in ways that can be accessed linguistically. All that should be taken into consideration when future studies involving emotions are developed, since many experiments involve some kind of linguistic or paralinguistic exposure (Van Lancker Sidtis 2008). For linguists to contribute to the debate, it is also also important to know how language is understood by neuroscience.

## 4. Linguistics and emotions: A cognitive perspective under construction

When trying to create an adequate basis for investigating how emotions and language correlate in communication, it is important to understand how linguists have already indirectly studied the relationship between human language and human emotion. Cognitive linguistics, discourse analysis, and rating studies are some of the areas that have somehow approached the topic. There are also topics related to utterance reception/appraisal and production, to the limits of politeness and impoliteness, as well as to how media is shaping the discourse and relying on emotions to affect their target audience. In psycholinguistics, priming studies have examined the role of emotion in word storage and retrieval (Van Lancker Sidtis 2008; Scherer 2003).

Leaving aside interaction-based research, which is beyond the scope of this article, there are different possible perspectives to understand the relationship between language and emotion. The first one assumes that there is no necessary relationship at all, as language can verbalise different things – a mathematical formula, a personal feeling or a scientific claim. This is true, but it neglects the underlying mechanisms of language. Another perspective accepts that language has roots in emotional expression – a view that is supported by evolutionism. For Darwin, emotional expression is an important way of establishing communication between individuals, either humans or animals.

> The movements of expression in the face and body, whatever their origin may have been, are in themselves of much importance for our welfare. They serve as the first means of communication between the mother and her infant; she smiles approval, and thus encourages her child on the right path, or frowns disapproval. We readily perceive sympathy in others by their expression; our sufferings are thus mitigated and

> our pleasures increased; and mutual good feeling is thus strengthened. The movements of expression give vividness and energy to our spoken words. They reveal the thoughts and intentions of others more truly than do words, which may be falsified.
> (Darwin 1872: 364)

One of the psychologists who rely on Darwin's comments on emotion in humans is Steven Pinker. For Pinker (2008: 28), the relations of words and emotions are in "the way in which words don't just point to things but are saturated with feelings, which can endow the words with a sense of magic, taboo, and sin". In his perspective, words connect to thoughts, feelings, relationships and reality itself. In order to understand the language system, one should not only care about semantics, but about the relations of the words to community, to the act of conversation. Nevertheless, the most important idea comes from the notion of "language as a window into human nature", where Pinker argues that, if a Martian linguist would describe our species, he would say that grammar is a window into thoughts, swearing into emotions, and indirect speech into social relationships. If we assume that language is the window into the mind, we can hence assume that it is also the gateway for complex investigations of thinking and feeling in their reciprocal interactions.

In earlier linguistic studies, some ideas on this relationship are linked up with language functions, especially related to Jakobson's (1960) theory. Based on Bühler, his theory represents one of the most important moments of the interface between language and emotion, as he approached the emotional effect of an utterance in the audience. His model of language functions is based on the mathematical model of communication, which presupposes the existence of the following factors: context, addresser, addressee, contact, common code and message. Each function operates between the message and these factors.

The emotive function "aims a direct expression of the speaker's attitude toward what he is speaking about. *It tends to produce an impression of a certain emotion whether true or feigned*" (Jakobson 1980: 81 – italics mine). The author explains further that emotive impressions are purely presented by interjections, which differ from referential language by sound pattern and syntactic role, but can be extended to phonic, grammatical and lexical levels. Furthemore, he posits that expressiveness can be coded in language through differences between short and long vowels, for example, and that those expressive features convey ostensive information about the speaker's attitude. However, according to Klinkenberg (1996: 53), emotive function, which could be called '*expressive* function', should not be understood as referring to human affect, because it has nothing to do with emotion. In his view, any message, including the most neutral, reveals the condition of its sender.

One of the limitations of Jakobson's theory is that it relies on Shannon and Weaver's (1949) Code Hypothesis Model. In this model, human communication is understood as a process of transmitting messages through encoding and decoding. The main objective of the model was to develop a mathematical theory of communication in order to assist telecommunication. For this reason, some other phenomena were left out, such as differences in cultural assumptions and in communication preferences. In the code model, a simple statement such as *This lovely British winter!*, where the speaker expected the hearer to understand irony, would probably not be interpreted as ironic or would not imply emotional responses. When applied to Natural Language, this model simplifies and reduces human communication, as semantic and pragmatic aspects are disregarded.

According to Strey (2016), the notion that humans are social beings leads to the idea that there is some property that causes things to be said in a certain way and not another – and this property seems to be emotional states. As Pinker (1997) posits, when choosing between a more neutral and a more emotional tone of voice, the literal meaning of words is not modified, but the emotional sense is. Tannen (2001) says that we must understand that people are emotionally involved with each other and we talk in order to establish contact, keep it and monitor it. In general, more than just to inform, communication involves intentions and emotions.

## 5. The pragmatic path: Beyond meaning

Pragmatics can be defined as the study of the relationship between sentence meaning and speaker's meaning, including topics such as presupposition, anaphora, speech acts, intentions, inferences. In general, pragmatic theories explain how we understand utterances, and how we use language to imply more than what we say. What falls inside the concept of what is not said differs depending on the theory, according to the perspective assumed. The phenomena covered also vary: it is possible to study how an utterance threatens someone's face, or how strong or weak implicatures, such as those expressed by metaphors, are conveyed. However, it seems that emotional effects are not a classical locus of study, especially in theories that follow from the Gricean tradition. They are not fully absent from pragmatic theories, but they are rarely clearly approached and explained (again, leaving aside the more interaction-based approaches).

Many theories have been developed since Grice's seminal work. However, even if it was the place for what is not explicitly said, much has been left aside in pragmatic studies. According to Carston (2002), pragmatics is concerned with ostensive stimuli, especially with verbal utterances, although "they themselves are frequently accompanied by other ostensive gestures of the face, hands, voice etc, all of which have to be interpreted together if one is to correctly infer what is being communicated" (2002: 129). Wharton (2016) states that "any pragmatic theory worth its salt simply must have a view on non-verbal communicative behaviours and how they contribute to speakers' meanings".

In the 1980s, Mehrabian identified the '7%-38%-55% Rule' (Mehrabian 1981), that posits that 55% of communication is facial/body language, 38% tone of voice and inflection, and only 7% the words themselves. Even if the proportion is not exactly this one, the fact is that language communication is defined both by linguistic and non-linguistic properties, such as intonation and gestures (Wharton 2009). This shed light on a really simple question: why is nonverbal communication not systematically part of a theory of pragmatics? If words are only 7% of what is being conveyed, it seems linguists are still bound to the logical tradition of propositions and to the logical form.

To understand how non-verbal communication can be part of pragmatics in a Gricean tradition, it is first necessary to discuss the difference between natural and non-natural meaning. Grice, in his famous paper *Meaning* (1957), raises an important question about the difference between 'deliberately and openly letting someone know' and 'telling', or between natural meaning (meaning$_{N}$) and non-natural meaning (meaning$_{NN}$). While natural meaning is defined as when you are able to infer *p* from *x means p* (e.g. *smoke means fire*), non-natural meaning involves the existence of a particular kind of intention. Grice's definition of meaning$_{NN}$ is: "'A meant$_{NN}$ something by X' is (roughly) equivalent to 'A intended the utterance of x to produce some effect in the audience by means of recognition of its intention'" (Grice 1989: 219). He adds that, if you ask *A* what he meant, the answer would be a specification of the intended effect.

Wharton (2009) discusses Grice's clear-cut division between showing and telling. Assuming a cognitively-oriented pragmatics, he advocates a natural pragmatics, which deals with the interpretation of non-verbal behaviours, and how they contribute to overt communication or to more covert/accidental forms of communication. He posits that natural and deliberately shown behaviours that may be seen as cases of natural meaning can be used in overt intentional communication.

Relevance theorists have argued for the existence of a continuum of cases between showing and meaning$_{NN}$, and that all of them fall within the domain of pragmatics (Sperber & Wilson 1995, 2015). Wharton (2003b) argues that there is a continuum of showing-meaning$_{NN}$, and he claims that natural behaviours are somewhere along this continuum. He proposes a difference between natural signs, which carry information by providing evidence for it, and signals, which carry information by encoding it. Wilson and Wharton (2005: 430) affirm that human communication is a combination of decoding and inference making, and it has three types of inputs: natural signs (interpreted inferentially), natural signals (sometimes interpreted only by decoding), and linguistic signals (combination of decoding and inference).

Wharton argues that natural behaviours may carry information for the hearer/observer by betraying one's thoughts and feelings without intentionally communicating them; by deliberately producing them to be intentional, or by involuntarily producing them (resulting in their being overtly shown). "Intentional verbal communication, then, involves a mixture of natural and non-natural meaning, and an adequate pragmatic theory should take account of both" (Wharton 2009: 11). If speakers conveys how bored, frustrated or angry they are by their tone of voice or facial expression, they may not be deliberately providing evidences about their state of mind. However, the hearer may pick up those inputs in a relevance-driven heuristic and operate with them to understand the speaker's meaning.

Nonverbal inputs should not simply be ignored by any holistic theory of communication: to understand an utterance means to interpret natural behaviours that often "show us more about a person's mental/physical state than the words they accompany; sometimes, they replace words rather than merely accompany them" (Wharton, 2003a: 109). Going beyond traditional meaning should be one of the aims of all pragmatic theories, because we should not overlook the fact that they are part of communication. So far, this insight has been restricted too much to interaction-based pragmatic approaches.

## 6. Final thoughts

We are used to talking about things we can see or describe. We look at the sky at night and we see stars, some planets, and the shining moon. If we look at that with a powerful telescope, we may be able to see other stars and galaxies that are not to be seen with the naked eye. This is the so-called bright matter, and it is one of the main topics in astronomy and physics. However, scientists do not only try to explain bright matter (like stars), they wonder about what they cannot see but know to be there: dark matter. They know it is there because they can infer this from its gravitational effects on bright matter.

Why discuss dark/bright matter? I think it is possible to make a parallel with language and communication by creating a metaphor to explain emotional communication. Informational communication is the bright matter: we can see it, and certainly it has been studied a lot by linguists. Emotional communication, on the other hand, is the dark matter: we know it is there, we kind of know how to describe it, and we know it interferes with the bright matter. The problem of emotions in communication is that they cannot be exactly described; they cannot be laid down on a surgical table and dissected. We can infer some of their properties based on how they behave and interplay with propositional communication.

What falls inside the concept of what is not said, of what emotions are conveyed and why, may differ depending on the theory adopted and the perspective taken. Any definition may change the phenomena covered: it is possible to study how an utterance threatens someone's face, or how metaphors convey the embodiment of the mind. As assumed in this paper, it seems necessary for a cognitive perspective on pragmatics to cover nonverbal inputs, such as gestures, facial expressions, and prosody.

There is already a considerable amount of work changing the rationalist paradigm and moving towards a more emotion-integrated one (e.g. Wharton 2016; Yus 2018;

Dezecache, Mercier & Scott-Phillips 2013). But there is ample scope for (neo-, post-) Gricean pragmatics to take further steps beyond propositional meaning and thus to contribute to efforts that have been developed from a different perspective in fields such as discursive psychology and other interaction-based approached to communication.

## Acknowledgment

Research for this paper was undertaken while I was working on my dissertation, where I developed a pragmatic approach to emotion within relevance theory (Strey 2016). I would like to thank professors Dr. Jorge Campos da Costa and Dr. Tim Wharton for their insights during my PhD trajectory.

### References

Brassfield, S. 2012. "Never let the passions be your guide: Descartes and the role of the passions." *British Journal for the History of Philosophy* 20(3): 459–477. https://doi.org/10.1080/09608788.2012.670839

Carston, R. 2002. *Thoughts and Utterances: The Pragmatics of Explicit Communication*. Oxford: Blackwell. https://doi.org/10.1002/9780470754603

Damasio, A. 1994. *Descartes' Error: Emotion, Reason, and the Human Brain*. New York: Grosset/Putnam.

Damasio, A. 2003. *Looking for Spinoza: Joy, Sorrow, and the Feeling Brain*. Orlando: Harcourt.

Darwin, C. 1872. *The Expression of the Emotions in Man and Animals*. New York: D. Appleton and Company. https://doi.org/10.1037/10001-000

De Souza, R. 2010. "Emotion." In *The Stanford Encyclopedia of Philosophy*, ed. by E. N. Zalta. Stanford: Stanford University Press. <http://plato.stanford.edu/archives/spr2010/entries/emotion/> (accessed 8 October 2014).

Dezecache, G., H. Mercier and T. C. Scott-Phillips. 2013. "An evolutionary approach to emotional communication." *Journal of Pragmatics* 59: 221–233. https://doi.org/10.1016/j.pragma.2013.06.007

Gazzaniga, M. S., R. B. Ivry and G. R. Mangun. 2002. *Cognitive Neuroscience*. New York: Norton & Company.

Greenspan, P. 2003. "Emotions, rationality, and mind/body." *Royal Institute of Philosophy Supplement* 52: 113–125. https://doi.org/10.1017/S135824610000792X

Grice, P. 1957. "Meaning." *Philosophical Review* 66: 377–388. https://doi.org/10.2307/2182440

Grice, P. 1989. *Studies in the Way of Words*. Cambridge, Mass.: Harvard University Press.

Jakobson, R. 1960. "Closing statement: Linguistics and poetics." In *Style in Language*, ed. by T. Sebeok, 350–377. Cambridge, Mass.: MIT Press.

Jakobson, R. 1980. "Metalanguage as a linguistic problem." In *The Framework of Language*, ed. by R. Jakobson. Ann Arbor: University of Michigan.

Klinkenberg, J. M. 1996. *Précis de sémiotique générale*. Paris: Seuill.

LeDoux, J. 1996. *The Emotional Brain*. New York: Touchstone.

Mehrabian, A. 1981. *Silent Messages: Implicit Communication of Emotions and Attitudes*. Belmont: Wadsworth

Menezes e Silva, C. M. 2010. "O papel das emoções na Retórica de Aristóteles." *AISTHE* 5.

Pessoa, L. 2008. "On the relationship between emotion and cognition." *Nature (Reviews Neuroscience)* 9: 148–158. https://doi.org/10.1038/nrn2317
Pham, M. T. 2007. "Emotion and rationality: A critical review and interpretations of empirical evidence." *Review of General Psychology* 11(2): 155–178. https://doi.org/10.1037/1089-2680.11.2.155
Pinker, S. 1997. *How the Mind Works*. New York: Norton.
Pinker, S. 2008. *The Stuff of Thought: Language as a Window into Human Nature*. New York: Penguin Books.
Popper, K. R. 1963. *Conjectures and Refutations: The Growth of Scientific Knowledge*. New York: Routledge and Kegan Paul.
Scherer, K. R. 2003. "Vocal communication of emotion: A review of research pragmatics." *Speech Communication* 40: 227–256. https://doi.org/10.1016/S0167-6393(02)00084-5
Schmitter, A. M. 2014. "17th and 18th century theories of emotions." In *The Stanford Encyclopedia of Philosophy*, ed. by E. N. Zalta. Stanford: Stanford University Press. <https://plato.stanford.edu/entries/emotions-17th18th/>
Shannon, C. and W. Weaver. 1949. *The Mathematical Theory of Communication*. Urbana: University of Illinois Press.
Sperber, D. and D. Wilson. 1995 [1986]. *Relevance: Communication and Cognition* (2nd. ed.). Oxford: Blackwell.
Sperber, D. and D. Wilson. 2015. "Beyond speaker's meaning." *Croatian Journal of Philosophy* XV(44): 117–149.
Strey, C. 2016. *The Language of Emotions: An Ostensive-Inferential Study*. PhD dissertation. Porto Alegre: Faculdade de Letras, PUCRS.
Tannen, D. 2001. *You Just Don't Understand: Women and Men in Conversation*. New York: Paperback Ballantine.
Van Lancker Sidtis, D. 2008. "The relation of human language to human emotion." In *Handbook of the Neuroscience of Language*, ed. by B. Stemmer and H. Whitaker, 199–208. San Diego: Elsevier. https://doi.org/10.1016/B978-0-08-045352-1.00019-7
Wharton, T. 2003a. "Natural pragmatics and natural codes." *Mind & Languages* 18: 109–161.
Wharton, T. 2003b. "Interjections, language, and the 'showing/saying' continuum." *Pragmatics & Cognition* 11: 39–91. https://doi.org/10.1075/pc.11.1.04wha
Wharton, T. 2009. *Pragmatics and Non-Verbal Communication*. Cambridge: Cambridge University Press. https://doi.org/10.1017/CBO9780511635649
Wharton, T. 2016. "Paralanguage." In *The Routledge Handbook of Pragmatics*, ed by G. J. Steen, A. Barron and G. Yueguo. Abingdon: Routledge
Wierzbicka, A. 1995. "Everyday conceptions of emotion: A semantic perspective." In *Everyday Conceptions of Emotion*, ed. by J. A. Russell, J.-M. Fernández-Dols, A. S. Manstead and J. Wellenkamp, 17–47. Dordrecht: Kluwer Academic Publishers. https://doi.org/10.1007/978-94-015-8484-5_2
Wilson, D. and Wharton, T. 2005. "Relevance and prosody." *UCL Working Papers in Linguistics* 17: 427–454
Yus, F. 2018. "Attaching feelings and emotions to propositions: Some insights on irony and Internet communication." *Russian Journal of Linguistics* 22(1): 94–107. https://doi.org/10.22363/2312-9182-2018-22-1-94-107

# Language maintenance and shift

Louisa Willoughby
Monash University, Melbourne

## 1. Introduction

Language maintenance and shift research forms a sub-field of linguistics with a complex history. Inspired at least in part by the Germanic research tradition into *Sprachinseln* (language enclaves that resist shift to the language of the surrounding society for generations; see Pauwels 2016) from the mid-1960s onwards we see an increasing movement of scholars documenting language practices among migrant families and communities – especially in the US (e.g. Clyne 1968; Fishman 1966; Lopez 1978; Skrabanek 1970). At the same time we see a parallel growth in research with indigenous communities around issues of language endangerment and reclamation (for an overview see Pauwels 2016). While the terms 'language maintenance and shift' have historically been used much more in reference to research on migrants, rather than indigenous groups, it is clear that many of the issues and theories are applicable in both contexts, and thus this entry will discuss both where relevant.

Language maintenance and shift are generally understood as describing patterns around a person or group's habitual language practices (with terms like code-switching and translanguaging being used to describe elements of language mixing in specific utterances – see Auer & Eastman 2010). However, researchers use the terms in slightly different ways. Clyne (2003: 20) reminds us that what a researcher means by 'language shift' might encompass changes in any of the following:

- language use at the community or individual level
- the main language used
- the dominant language or individuals or groups
- the language used in one or more specified domains
- the ability of people to read, write, speak or understand the heritage language

There is also a parallel issue that some researchers prefer to avoid a term like shift, as it has connotations of finality that are seen as unhelpful – particularly in the language reclamation context. Thus for example terms like *survivance* (Wyman 2012) might be used to describe practices in communities that are undergoing shift to English, but where people are still deliberately and habitually making use of words, phrases or discourse patterns from the heritage language in certain contexts.

https://doi.org/10.1075/hop.21.lan12

The driving concern of language maintenance and shift research has been to understand the factors that lead some individuals and/or communities to be much more successful at ongoing transmission and use of a heritage language in minority contexts than others. This question has been approached from a variety of angles, with major sections of this article devoted to outlining statistical studies of language maintenance and shift and domain-based approaches. Most 20th century research on language maintenance and shift started from the assumption that its subjects were people who had a single heritage language and migrated once in their life to a place where they remained, and where only one national language was widely spoken. These assumptions do not adequately describe the conditions of many 21st century migrants' lives, and in the final section this article explores how contemporary scholars are responding to these developments.

## 2. Statistical studies of factors influencing language maintenance and shift

In many countries, the national census asks people questions around some combination of their ethnicity, country of birth, knowledge or use of the national language and knowledge or use of any heritage languages.[1] Scholars of language maintenance and shift have used this data to draw a number of insights around how language shift normally unfolds in immigrant contexts; as well as the demographic factors that may hasten or retard it. In very general terms we can say that language shift among migrants in modern industrial societies is a three generation process, whereby those who initially migrate maintain a strong preference for speaking their heritage language, their children are bilingual in the heritage language and the national language (and feel they have a better command of the latter due to the influence of school) and the grandchildren have little to no knowledge of the heritage language, having shifted to the language of the host society (Clyne 1982; Clyne 1991; Veltman 1983). However exactly how this process unfolds, and the degree to which it is indeed complete by the third generation has been shown to vary widely: not only between individuals but also between ethnolinguistic groups as a whole. For example looking at the 1996 Australian Census, Clyne and Kipp (1997) found that 62% of Dutch-born migrants reported speaking English only at home, but only 4% of Chinese-born migrants did

1. Kertzer and Arel (2002) provide an excellent book-length discussion of the ways these questions are asked in different national censuses and the merits and pitfalls of each approach. The topic is also addressed more concisely in Chapter 3 of Pauwels (2016) and, with a particular focus on European Censuses in Extra (2010).

so. Similarly for the second generation (i.e. Australia born children of migrants) 95% of those with Dutch-born parents spoke only English at home, while for Korean and Turkish the comparable figures were 16% and 18%.

Census data, and other large-scale population surveys, has shown us that a number of demographic factors influence the likelihood that an individual will maintain a heritage language. While this kind of 'demolinguistic' work has been conducted in a variety of national contexts (see e.g. de Vries 1994; Extra & Yağmur 2004; Soehl 2016; Stevens 1999; Veltman 1983) the most extensive work in the area has been conducted in Australia by Michael Clyne and colleagues. This data demonstrates that language shift increase with length of residency for the first generation and with age for members of the second generation (Clyne 1991). Exogamous marriage in the first generation decreases the rate of language maintenance in the second (Clyne 1991; Clyne & Kipp 1997a), while living in a municipality or state with a comparatively high concentration of co-ethnics strengthens language maintenance for both generations (Clyne 1991; Kipp & Clyne 2003). What all of these factors have in common is that they effect the amount of exposure speakers have to the language of the host society, with increased exposure unsurprisingly hastening language shift. Stevens (1999) provides a slightly different take on these issues by considering the relationship between demographic variables and migrant's self-reported English proficiency in the US census. In line with Clyne's findings reported above, she finds highly significant positive correlations between young age of arrival and long length of residence and self-reported English proficiency, with high proficiency also correlating with at least some US education, marriage to a US-born spouse and not being of Hispanic background (which arguably relates to Clyne's point above around living in communities where there are large numbers of people who share the same heritage language).

In Clyne's work gender also emerges as a variable of interest: there is a reasonably consistent trend in Australian census data of women showing lower rates of language shift than men, albeit with wide variation between language groups on the strength of this trend (Clyne & Kipp 1997). (Stevens (1986) also reports a similar trend in US census data). As with more general work in sociolinguistics, the reasons behind this observation remain a matter of debate, but it may be related to women's traditional role of caregivers, which may mean both that they spend less time outside the home interacting with English speakers than men and that they feel they have a responsibility to pass on the language to the next generation (Pauwels 2016). However, it is important to note here that a number of small-scale studies of minority communities show a tendency of women adopting the nation standard in place of the local vernacular at a higher rate than men (e.g. Aikio 1992; Cavanaugh 2006; Gal 1979). The relationship between gender and language maintenance is clearly complex and dependent on a number of social factors, including the status of men and women in the minority community and the wider society as well as the degree to which gender norms are in flux.

Thus, rather than being a clear predictor of language maintenance or shift behaviour, gender is arguably better thought of as an important variable that affects opportunities and expectations a person will have to use the heritage and national language in their everyday lives.

While demographic factors play an important role in ascertaining the likelihood that language maintenance or shift will take place within a community, they are not the only relevant factors. Positive attitudes towards the heritage language also play a very important role in ensuring ongoing maintenance. As Clyne explains "tests of attitudes to language do not necessarily predict language behaviour, since the latter involves a more active component. However, where there is a choice of languages, a positive attitude may be one prerequisite of language maintenance" (1991:31). Giles et al.'s concept of ethnolinguistic vitality and associated questionnaire (Bourhis, Giles & Rosenthal 1981; Giles, Bourhis & Taylor 1977) is arguably the most popular method for measuring attitudes and comparing the degree to which members of different ethnolinguistic groups orient to language maintenance and in-group identity. However, Kipp Clyne and Pauwels (1995) sound a note of caution in measuring attitudes across a community as a whole, since there may be major cleaves in the community (for example around when/ why they migrated) that influence how they perceive vitality or the relationship between language and other aspects of their culture and identity (see also Perera 2015). For all of these reasons it is important for language maintenance researchers to look at the details of everyday life that influence participants' code choices, to which we now turn.

## 3. Domains of use

Researchers examining if, how and why people continue to use a heritage language in daily life have approached the question from a variety of different angles. Some studies focus on language shift throughout an individual's lifetime, asking participants to reflect on how their (and/or their children's) language use patterns have changed over time (e.g. Garcia & Diaz 1992; Shin 2002), in order to say something about the order in which the language of the host society enters various contexts and what key life events might prompt or mitigate language shift. A more common approach, however, is to compare the current language use patterns of a number of speakers (usually, but not always, from the same ethnic group), in order to see how differences in individual circumstances might lead to different levels of ethnic language retention or use in certain settings (cf. Gibbons & Ramirez 2004; Ninnes 1996; Starks 2005). Research in this vein has been heavily influenced by Fishman's (e.g. 1965) famous formulation "Who speaks what language to whom and when?", as well as his approach of exploring language use in different domains, such as the family, neighbourhood, work and religion (see e.g.

Holmes et al. 1993; Ninnes 1996; Pütz 1991). Since the 1990s there has also been a rise in so-called ego-focussed studies that focus on participant's habitual language use with particular people, rather than in particular settings (a social network approach, as in Li Wei 1994; Stoessel 2002); as well as work such as Gibbons and Ramirez's study of Hispanic teens in Sydney (2004) which takes a hybrid social network and domain based approach.

From this research tradition arguably the two areas that have received the most attention are language practices within the family and in institutional settings. We also see a subtle shift taking place in language maintenance and shift research over the years. While many 20th century studies focus on documenting how and why some people or contexts shift faster than others, much of the more recent research takes an activist or applied stance and seeks to understand how best to support individuals and communities in transmitting heritage languages to their children.

## 4. Family language policy

One of the most consistent findings from language maintenance research is that using the heritage language for parent-child communication in the home is a necessary, but not always sufficient condition for language transmission to the next generation (Fishman 1965; Pauwels 2005; Soehl 2016). In the preschool years, parental talk – and particularly talk from mothers – plays a vital role in establishing the developing child's knowledge of the heritage language. As the child matures parents may well be the only HL interlocutors the child has contact with on a daily basis or with whom they discuss a wide variety of topics (Heller 1994). However, continued language maintenance within a household can become difficult down the years: as children age they may become self-conscious about being 'different' and refuse to speak the heritage language at home, or simply find it easier to express themselves in the minority language. Older siblings also often bring the national language home from school, meaning that second and subsequent siblings may receive substantially less heritage language input than first-born children even in the preschool years (Shin 2002).

As a result of these and other pressures, researchers have shown keen interest in exploring aspects of family language policy – the explicit and overt planning in relation to language use taking place in bilingual households (King, Fogle & Logan-Terry 2008). King el al see research in this vein as connecting "what families actually do with language in day-to-day interactions; their beliefs and ideologies about language and language use; and their goals and efforts to shape language use and learning outcomes" (2008: 909). When parents themselves have minimal competence in the language of the host society, this acts as a constraint on the degree to which language shift can take place in parent-child interaction. However when parents themselves are bi/multilingual, those who do not have explicit family language policies (or strategies for addressing breaches of these policies by children keen to use the national language) often find family interactions shifting to the national language over time, regardless of their overarching attitudes towards the value of language maintenance (King, Fogle & Logan-Terry 2008; see also Lambert 2008; Schüpbach 2009).

Two of the most studied specific strategies that parents may draw on for language transmission are the One Parent One Language (OPOL) approach (i.e. each parent uses/receives a different language from the child) and minority/heritage language at home; where all family members speak the minority language at home and exposure to the national language comes through interactions with wider society (school, media etc). King et al. (2008) and Guardado (2016) both review research on each strategy, noting either can prove successful, but OPOL can be vulnerable if the quality or quantity of interaction with one parent is limited (for example when the minority language speaking parent is also a non-primary caregiver who works long hours away from home). As with all areas of language policy, there is also the issue of how effectively/consistently these overarching strategies are translated into everyday interactions – for example in how parents respond if children address them in the 'wrong' language (Lanza 1997). Family members may also show different degrees of buy-in to a particular language policy. This is shown particularly clearly in Smith-Christmas' (2014) study of language shift on the Isle of Skye. In the family under discussion the mother and paternal grandmother show a strong commitment to speaking Gaelic only with the child generation. However, other family members (their father, aunt and uncle) rarely instigate interactions in Gaelic with the children and in fact model language shift by frequently replying in English if adult family members address them in Gaelic. The complexity of how family language policy and practices are negotiated in minority language communities undergoing language shift has been a topic of increasing interest in language endangerment and language contact research in recent years (see e.g. Vaughan et al. 2015; Wyman 2012) and family language policy seems to be an area of increasing convergence and cross-fertilisation between scholars who investigate language maintenance in immigrant contexts and those who do so in indigenous contexts.

Attempts to pass heritage languages on to the next generation are not simply nostalgic. Studies of psychological adjustment among second-generation migrant teens have consistently found that adolescents who report high levels of language maintenance also score higher on measures of family cohesion, self-esteem and secure attachment patterns than those with lower language maintenance scores (Luo & Wiseman 2000; Portes & Rumbaut 2001; Tannenbaum & Howie 2002). Similarly, a number of qualitative studies of the migrant adaptation process provide anecdotal evidence of the rift that can occur between parents and children when they do not share fluency in a common language (cf. Cho & Krashen 1998; Wong-Fillmore 1991). While it remains unclear whether increased language maintenance is generally cause or consequence of better relationships with the parents (Tannenbaum & Howie 2002), we can conclude that it plays an important role in building relationships between parents and their children, and that this is an important reason for promoting and supporting language maintenance efforts in migrant and indigenous communities.

## 5. Institutional support for heritage language learning and use

While family language practices are key for initial transmission of heritage languages, opportunities and support for people to use the heritage language outside the home are vitally important for ensuring ongoing use and development. This is taken up by Fishman (1991) at the whole-of-community level with the development of his Graded Intergenerational Disruption Scale (GIDS); which charts the extent to which a community as a whole is undergoing language shift. Note that in Fishman's parlance Xish/Xmen refers the minority language and its speakers, while Ymen are members of the wider society.

- Stage 8: most vestigial users of Xish are socially isolated old folks and Xish needs to be re-assembled from their mouths and memories and taught to demographically unconcentrated adults
- Stage 7: most users of Xish are a socially integrated and ethnolinguistically active population but they are beyond child-bearing age
- Stage 6: the attainment of intergenerational informal oralcy and its demographic concentration and institutional reinforcement [i.e. the language is widely used as a natural language of communication across the generations and there are a number of potential interlocutors and institutions where the language can be used]
- State 5: Xish literacy in home, school and community, but without taking on extra-communal reinforcement of such literacy
- Stage 4: Xish in lower education (types a and b) that meets the requirements of compulsory education laws
- Stage 3: use of Xish in the lower work sphere (outside of the Xish neighborhood/community) involving interaction between Xmen and Ymen
- Stage 2: Xish in lower governmental services and mass media but not in the higher spheres of either
- Stage 1: some use of Xish in higher level educational, occupational, governmental and media efforts (but without the additional safety provided by political independence) (Fishman 1991: 87–111)

Fishman (1991: 92) notes that a great many languages continue to survive and thrive at stage 6 without further development to higher stages; and thus that stage 6 is a crucial stage for language maintenance and shift. He also nominates stage 4 (the appearance of the heritage language as a medium of instruction in primary education) as a key stage for communities looking to develop greater autonomy, but notes that this (and subsequent stages) can be very challenging to achieve politically.

Fishman's GIDS provides a useful taxonomy for understanding the different positions heritage langauges can occupy in society, however it tends to assume that the communities in question are relatively homogenous – i.e. that there is one local heritage language ('Xish') and one dominant language ('Yish'). In multilingual societies stages 6 and up will require a much more complex constellation of language practices, with individuals using a complex mix of local/tribal/heritage languages and regional/dominant/lingua franca languages depending on the context of their interaction and the language proficiency and preferences of their addressee(s). Some of these complexities are explored in the following section. This also raises questions around how community institutions should respond if they have (potential) members who do not share the heritage language proficiency required to take full part in the life of the institution. For religious organisations in the diaspora, for example, there often comes a (potentially traumatic) point where they must decide whether to make changes to the language of worship and/or pastoral care to cater to members of the second generation (or interested members from other ethnic backgrounds) who are not fluent in the heritage language, or reconcile themselves to the death of the organisation with the passing of the older generation (Perera 2016; Woods 2004)

Because of the complexities Fishman notes in establishing formal education in minority languages, many migrant groups rely on informal after-hours schools to transmit literacy skills in the heritage language to children and consolidate heritage language skills taught in the home. As generally volunteer-run enterprises these schools may face issues with teacher quality, availability of appropriate teaching materials, substandard teaching facilities and highly heterogeneous proficiencies within the one class (Willoughby 2014; Willoughby 2016a). Never-the-less they provide a much-valued safe-space – not only to impart language skills, but to bring children together to develop social networks, cultural knowledge and a shared sense of ethnic identity (García, Zakharia & Otcu 2012; Lytra & Martin 2010; Bryant & Mascitelli 2016).Within indigenous contexts, after-hours schools appear to be less popular and there is a greater emphasis on bilingual/immersion schooling. Here the 'language nest' model of immersion preschool has proven highly popular for language reclamation in New Zealand and the US (and is spreading to other countries), notwithstanding issues in finding suitably qualified teachers (Hermes, Bang & Marin 2012; May 2005). However an issue faced by heritage language education in both the migrant and indigenous context is that opportunities tend to contract once children finish primary education, and even when classes remain available teens often do not have the time or interest to continue formal study during the busy senior high-school years (Willoughby 2016b). How best to mitigate these issues is an area of increasing scholarly interest, as evidenced by the publication of several major handbooks on the topic of heritage language education in recent years (Kagan, Carreira & Chik 2017; Trifonas & Aravossitas 2016; Seals & Shah 2017). The interested reader is referred to these texts for a more wide-ranging discussion of the issues than is possible in this short chapter.

## 6. Challenges for language maintenance and shift research

As alluded to in the previous section, a significant challenge facing language maintenance and shift research in the 21st century is the complex reality of multilingualism in many societies. While it is a point of some debate in contemporary sociolinguistics whether diversity has itself increased or whether we are simply more aware of diversity that has always been in our midst (Pennycook 2016), the upshot is that many of the underlying assumptions of Fishmanian language maintenance research do not hold in contemporary communities. Chief among them is the idea that migrants or indigenous people orient to a single host or heritage language or society. Duarte and Gogolin note (2013: 4) that contemporary migration is not a linear, once in a lifetime process. For increasing numbers of people migration is a temporary or multistep process, involving periods of residence in one or more countries and potential return to the country of origin, dependent on factors as varied as resolutions of conflict situations, availability of (legal or illegal) work opportunities and types of transnational connections. When migrants themselves are from multilingual societies – such as exist in much of Africa – these complexities grow, as becomes apparent in Hatoss' (2013) and Ndhlovu's (2014) work on language practices in emerging African communities in Australia. For many members of these communities, the journey to Australia involved years of waiting in third country refugee camps, where children were born and schooled and a variety of local languages and lingua francas were often added to the refugee's linguistic repertoire. On resettlement in Australia, many of these languages picked up on the migration journey are being maintained and used to form and mark communities. This is especially so if the family's original language has a small speaker base in Australia. For example, Ndhlovu (2014) discusses how Kirundi speakers living in regional Australia formed a network with other locals African refugees who could speak Swahili (a language the parents had learnt in refugee camps) and prioritised the transmission of Swahili to their children.

The communities that migrants move into on arrival in the host society are themselves linguistically and culturally heterogeneous. In their book *Metrolingualism* (2015) Pennycook and Otsuji argue that the use of a complex admixture of different languages and other communicative resources is a natural part of communicative exchange for many residence of multilingual cities, and thus that there is a need to focus on examples of actual language in use (rather than reported language practices) if we are to understand the nature of contemporary multilingual practices (a point also raised by Blommaert 2010). However, they also discuss the immense methodological complexity of undertaking such analysis (including, but not limited to finding research assistants who can work with the different languages that occur in an interaction and working out what is actually being said in highly multilingual utterances).

Willoughby (2018) argues that continuing a focus on specific heritage languages can remain methodological justified as long as one is cautious around several points. The first is to be clear about the different relationships participants may have to their heritage languages and the ways in which different biographies (for example different patterns of migration) may influence language practices. This also entails a very cautious use of census or other large-scale data to map community profiles, since this data invariably fails to capture much of the complexity outlined above (see Ndhlovu & Willoughby 2017 for more on this point). The second is to be conscious of the fact that self-reported data on language practices may tell us more about how the participant views themselves than their 'actual' practices, but also that moving from broad-sweeping questions about habitual language practices to more focused, contextualised and probing questions (e.g. questions about practices with particular people in particular settings) does produce results that better match observed reality (see also Gibbons & Ramirez 2004). Finally, Willoughby argues that it is important that practices be studied within the context of a particular community that is meaningful for participants. In these contexts the question need not be (a la Pennycook & Otsuji 2015) to unpack the detail of what is said in a particular interaction and why, but to understand the motivations and social meanings participants attach to their different language practices – for example why some heritage languages but not others might have cache as 'cool' within the group. Such a view of language maintenance and shift is necessarily qualitative and – like research in family language policy – tends to focus on the process of how languages are used and social meanings attached to them, rather than the outcome of changes in habitual practices over time.

Another important challenge for engaged scholarship around language maintenance and shift is in assisting communities to better understand their own aspirations for language maintenance and the ways in which to best achieve these goals. At a simple level this involves supporting community members to unpack the sorts of skills they have in mind in maintaining or reclaiming a heritage language, or their reasons for wanting to maintain or develop skills in the language. These can be surprisingly disparate. Florey (2004) noted that at a single workshop organised to support Mulukan language reclamation in the diaspora, the aspirations of participants ranged from wanting to learn about the languages in general or learning a few words to use as identity markers in conversation, to becoming fluent enough to write songs, poetry or literature or converse on a range of matters in ancestral languages. Clearly, in these sorts of contexts participants need to be clear about the objectives of any training sessions that they attend, but also may benefit from guidance from linguists and other speakers about setting realistic goals for language learning, or the obstacles that they might encounter along the way (and strategies to navigate them). King and Hermes (2014) raise the additional point that in revitalisation contexts many of the methods students commonly use to learn indigenous languages (such as respectfully listening at ceremonies, reciting traditional greetings/ genealogies and memorising vocabulary and grammatical patterns) are not particularly effective, as they do not involve opportunities for the negotiation of meaning. Similar concerns occur in the literature on heritage language education in the migration context, where volunteer teachers frequently rely on rote learning and the traditional teaching methods they were exposed to at school themselves to teach the next generation (García, Zakharia & Otcu 2012). There is thus rich opportunity for collaboration between applied linguists and those involved in heritage language education in developing pedagogical strategies that are effective, but that also suit the unique cultural and learning contexts of these learners and their communities.

Finally, language maintenance and shift scholarship arguably has a responsibility to educate communities around the ways in which certain attitudes or behaviours may be counter-productive for arresting language shift. Terborg and Ryan (2002) note that in communities undergoing language shift older, fluent speakers are often desirous of preserving the traditional (and complex) forms of the heritage language and will thus correct or ridicule 'semi-speakers' (members of the group who have only partial command of the heritage language; Dorian 1981); when they make errors. This criticism however has the unintended consequence of discouraging semi-speakers from using the language (either in the presence of elders, or simply full stop), hastening language shift. Terborg and Ryan thus forcefully conclude that "language maintenance cannot be successful when the promoters of the minority language are trying to preserve [grammatical] competence" (2002: 63). For indigenous groups this can raise painful questions around authenticity, change and loss as the resulting languages that emerge when younger/less fluent speakers adapt a traditional language can look very different indeed to the original (see e.g. McConvell & Meakins 2005; O'Shannessy 2005). In the migrant diaspora context language shift to the dominant language seems overwhelmingly more common than the development of a hybridised variant of the heritage language, although the latter occur in some specialised contexts. Most notably, Burridge (2017) argues that a major factor behind the survival of Pennsylvania German down the centuries has been the total absence of purist discourse within the community and acceptance of language change and contact as natural processes.

## 7. Conclusion

Language maintenance and shift is an area of linguistic research that has its underpinnings in a particular 20th century sociological view of migration, and associated interest in charting migrant assimilation down the generations. In the 21st century, the complexities of back-and-forth migration, shifting identities and scepticism of the value of sociological 'grand narratives' has led some to question the ongoing relevance of this sub-field. As I hope this entry has shown, many of these concerns are highly justified and require a re-thinking of what it means to research language maintenance and shift. However, the field clearly still has a lot to offer in exploring not just factors that promote or hinder heritage language use, but the dynamics of contexts and personal relationships that support language maintenance, and the ways in which heritage language use interpolates with other cultural practices and signals of identity.

## References


Aikio, Marjut. 1992. "Are women innovators in the shift to a second language? A case study of Reindeer Sámi women and men." *International Journal of the Sociology of Language* 94(1): 43–62. https://doi.org/10.1515/ijsl.1992.94.43

Auer, Peter and Carol Eastman. 2010. "Code-switching." In *Handbook of Pragmatics*, ed. by J.-O. Östman and J. Verschueren. Amsterdam: John Benjamins. https://doi.org/10.1075/hop.14

Blommaert, Jan. 2010. *The Sociolinguistics of Globalization*. Cambridge: Cambridge University Press. https://doi.org/10.1017/CBO9780511845307

Bourhis, Richard Yvon, Howard Giles and Doreen Rosenthal. 1981. "Notes on the construction of a 'subjective vitality questionnaire' for ethnolinguistic groups." *Journal of Multilingual and Multicultural Development* 2(2): 145–155. https://doi.org/10.1080/01434632.1981.9994047

Bryant, Catherine and Bruno Mascitelli. 2016. *From Small Beginnings: The Victorian School of Languages*. North Melbourne: Victoria Australian Scholarly.

Burridge, Kate. 2017. *Linguistic Cleanliness is Next to Godliness — But not for Conservative Anabaptists*. Park City, Utah: Brigham Young University.

Cavanaugh, Jillian R. 2006. "Little women and vital champions: Gendered language shift in a northern Italian town." *Journal of Linguistic Anthropology* 16(2): 194–210. https://doi.org/10.1525/jlin.2006.16.2.194

Cho, Grace and Stephen Krashen. 1998. "The negative consequences of heritage language loss and why we should care." In *Heritage language development*, ed. by Stephen Krashen, Lucy Tse and Jeff McQuillan, 31–40. Culver City, CA: Language Education Associates.

Clyne, Michael. 1968. "The maintenance of bilingualism." *Australian Journal of Education* 12(2): 125–130. https://doi.org/10.1177/000494416801200202

Clyne, Michael. 1982. *Multilingual Australia: Resources, Needs, Policies*. Melbourne: River Seine Publications.

Clyne, Michael. 1991. *Community Languages: The Australian Experience*. Cambridge: Cambridge University Press. https://doi.org/10.1017/CBO9780511597084

Clyne, Michael.2003. *Dynamics of Language Contact: English and Immigrant Languages*. Cambridge: Cambridge University Press. https://doi.org/10.1017/CBO9780511606526

Clyne, Michael and Sandra Kipp. 1997. "Trends and changes in home language use and shift in Australia, 1986–1996." *Journal of Multilingual and Multicultural Development* 18(6): 451–473. https://doi.org/10.1080/01434639708666334

Dorian, Nancy. 1981. *Language Death: The Life Cycle of a Scottish Gaelic Dialect*. Philadelphia: University of Pennsylvania Press. https://doi.org/10.9783/9781512815580

Duarte, Joana and Ingrid Gogolin. 2013. "Introduction: Linguistic superdiversity in educational institutions." In *Linguistic Superdiversity in Urban Areas: Research Approaches*, ed. by Joana Duarte and Ingrid Gogolin, 1–24. Amsterdam: John Benjamins. https://doi.org/10.1075/hsld.2

Extra, Guus. 2010. "Mapping linguistic diversity in multicultural contexts: Demolinguistic perspectives." In *Handbook of Language and Ethnic Identity*, 2nd edition, ed. by Joshua A. Fishman and Ofelia García, 107–122. Oxford: Oxford University Press.

Extra, Guus and Kutlay Yağmur. 2004. *Urban Multilingualism in Europe: Immigrant Minority Languages at Home and at School*. Clevedon: Multilingual Matters.

Fishman, Joshua A. 1965. "Who speaks what language to whom and when?" *La linguistique* 1(2): 67–88.

Fishman, Joshua A. 1966. *Language Loyalty in the United States: The Maintenance and Perpetuation of Non-English Mother Tongues by American Ethnic and Religious Groups*. The Hague: Mouton.

Fishman, Joshua A. 1991. *Reversing Language Shift: Theoretical and Empirical Foundations of Assistance to Threatened Languages*. Clevedon: Multilingual Matters.

Florey, Margaret. 2004. "Countering purism: Confronting the emergence of new varieties in a training program for community language workers." In *Language Documentation and Description*, vol. 2, ed. by Peter Austin, 9–27. London: SOAS.

Gal, Susan. 1979. *Language Shift: Social Determinants of Linguistic Change in Bilingual Austria*. New York: Academic Press.

García, Ofelia, Zeena Zakharia and Bahar Otcu (eds). 2012. *Bilingual Community Education and Multilingualism: Beyond Heritage Languages in a Global City*. Clevedon: Multilingual Matters. https://doi.org/10.21832/9781847698018

Garcia, R. and C. Diaz. 1992. "The status and use of Spanish and English among Hispanic youth in Dade County (Miami) Florida: A sociolinguistic study." *Language and Education* 6: 13–32. https://doi.org/10.1080/09500789209541322

Gibbons, John and Elizabeth Ramirez. 2004. *Maintaining a Minority Language: A Case Study of Hispanic Teenagers*. Clevedon: Multilingual Matters.

Giles, Howard, Richard Bourhis and Donald Taylor. 1977. "Towards a theory of language in ethnic group relations." In *Language and Ethnicity in Intergroup Relations*, ed. by Howard Giles, 307–48. New York: Academic Press.

Guardado, Martin. 2016. "Heritage language development in interlingual families." In *Handbook of Research and Practice in Heritage Language Education*, ed. by Peter Pericles Trifonas and Themistoklis Aravossitas, 17: 1–17. Cham: Springer International Publishing. <https://link.springer.com/content/pdf/10.1007/978-3-319-38893-9_17-1.pdf>.

Hatoss, Anikó. 2013. *Displacement, Language Maintenance and Identity: Sudanese Refugees in Australia*. Amsterdam: John Benjamins. https://doi.org/10.1075/impact.34

Heller, Monica. 1994. *Crosswords: Language, Education, and Ethnicity in French Ontario*. Berlin: Mouton de Gruyter.

Hermes, Mary, Megan Bang and Ananda Marin. 2012. "Designing Indigenous language revitalization." *Harvard Educational Review* 82(3): 381–402. https://doi.org/10.17763/haer.82.3.q8117w861241871j

Holmes, Janet, Mary Roberts, Maria Verivaki and 'Anahina 'Aipolo. 1993. "Language maintenance and shift in three New Zealand speech communities." *Applied Linguistics* 14(1): 1–24. https://doi.org/10.1093/applin/14.1.1

Kagan, Olga, Mary Carreira and Claire Chik (eds). 2017. *The Routledge Handbook of Heritage Language Education: From Innovation to Program Building*. New York: Routledge.

Kertzer, David I. and Dominique Arel. 2002. *Census and Identity: The Politics of Race, Ethnicity, and Language in National Censuses*. Cambridge: Cambridge University Press.

King, Kendall A., Lyn Fogle and Aubrey Logan-Terry. 2008. "Family language policy." *Language and Linguistics Compass* 2(5): 907–922. https://doi.org/10.1111/j.1749-818X.2008.00076.x

King, Kendall A. and Mary Hermes. 2014. "Why Is This So Hard?: Ideologies of Endangerment, Passive Language Learning Approaches, and Ojibwe in the United States." *Journal of Language, Identity & Education* 13(4): 268–282. https://doi.org/10.1080/15348458.2014.939029

Kipp, Sandra and Michael Clyne. 2003. "Trends in the shift from community languages: Insights from the 2001 census." *People and Place* 11: 33–41.

Kipp, Sandra, Michael Clyne and Anne Pauwels. 1995. *Immigration and Australia's Language Resources*. Canberra: Australian Government Publishing Service.

Lambert, Brigitte E. 2008. *Family Language Transmission: Actors, Issues, Outcomes*. Frankfurt: Peter Lang.

Lanza, Elizabeth. 1997. *Language Mixing in Infant Bilingualism: A Sociolinguistic Perspective*. Oxford: Oxford University Press.

Li Wei. 1994. *Three Generations, Two Languages, One Family: Language Choice and Language Shift in a Chinese Community in Britain*. Clevedon: Multilingual Matters.

Lopez, David E. 1978. "Chicano language loyalty in an urban setting." *Sociology and Social Research* 62(2): 267–78.

Luo, Shiow-Huey and Richard Wiseman. 2000. "Ethnic language maintenance among Chinese immigrant children in the United States." *International Journal of Intercultural Communication* 24(3): 307–324. https://doi.org/10.1016/S0147-1767(00)00003-1

Lytra, Valy and Peter Martin. 2010. *Sites of Multilingualism: Complementary Schools in Britain Today*. Stoke-on-Trent: Trentham.

May, Stephen. 2005. "Bilingual/immersion education in Aotearoa/New Zealand: Setting the context." *International Journal of Bilingual Education and Bilingualism* 8(5): 365–376. https://doi.org/10.1080/13670050508668620

McConvell, Patrick and Felicity Meakins. 2005. "Gurindji Kriol: A mixed language emerges from code-switching." *Australian Journal of Linguistics* 25(1): 9–30. https://doi.org/10.1080/07268600500110456

Ndhlovu, Finex. 2014. *Becoming an African diaspora in Australia: Language, Culture, Identity. Houndsmill*, Basingstoke: Palgrave Macmillan.

Ndhlovu, Finex and Louisa Willoughby. 2017. "Migration, heritage languages, and changing demographics in Australia." In *The Routledge Handbook of Heritage Language Education: From Innovation to Program Building*, ed. by Olga Kagan, Mary Carreira and Claire Chik, 22–32. New York: Routledge.

Ninnes, Peter. 1996. "Language maintenance among Vietnamese-Australian students." *Australian Review of Applied Linguistics* 19(2): 115–138. https://doi.org/10.1075/aral.19.2.06nin

O'Shannessy, Carmel. 2005. "Light Warlpiri: A new language." *Australian Journal of Linguistics* 25(1): 31–57. https://doi.org/10.1080/07268600500110472

Pauwels, Anne. 2005. "Maintaining the community language in Australia: Challenges and roles for families." *The International Journal of Bilingual Education and Bilingualism* 8(2–3): 124–31. https://doi.org/10.1080/13670050508668601

Pauwels, Anne. 2016. *Language Maintenance and Shift*. Cambridge: Cambridge University Press. /core/books/language-maintenance-and-shift/FC511EF9CB53FEFD72E159A7FB808ADB (3 August, 2017). https://doi.org/10.1017/CBO9781107338869

Pennycook, Alastair. 2016. "Mobile times, mobile terms: The trans-super-poly-metro movement." In *Sociolinguistics: Theoretical Debates*, ed. by Nikolas Coupland, 201–216. Cambridge: Cambridge University Press. https://www.cambridge.org/core/books/sociolinguistics/mobile-times-mobile-terms-the-transsuperpolymetro-movement/E38C40B40CF48BE9E6D73B78156BB4E8. https://doi.org/10.1017/CBO9781107449787.010
Pennycook, Alastair and Emi Otsuji. 2015. *Metrolingualism: Language in the City*. Abingdon, Oxon: Routledge.
Perera, Nirukshi. 2015. "The maintenance of Sri Lankan languages in Australia–comparing the experience of the Sinhalese and Tamils in the homeland." *Journal of Multilingual and Multicultural Development* 36(3): 297–312. https://doi.org/10.1080/01434632.2014.921185
Perera, Nirukshi. 2016. "Tamil in the temples – Language and religious maintenance beyond the first generation." *Multilingua* 35(5): 535–559. https://doi.org/10.1515/multi-2015-0059
Portes, Alejandro and Ruben Rumbaut. 2001. *Legacies: The Story of the Immigrant Second Generation*. Berkeley: University of California Press.
Pütz, Martin. 1991. "Language maintenance & language shift in the speech behaviour of German-Australian migrants in Canberra." *Journal of Multilingual and Multicultural Development* 12(6): 477–492. https://doi.org/10.1080/01434632.1991.9994477
Schüpbach, Doris. 2009. "Language transmission revisited: Family type, linguistic environment and language attitudes." *Journal of Bilingual Education and Bilingualism* 12(1): 15–30. https://doi.org/10.1080/13670050802149499
Seals, Corinne and Seena Shah. 2017. *Heritage Language Policies around the World*. London: Routledge.
Shin, Sarah. 2002. "Birth order and the language experience of bilingual children." *TESOL Quarterly* 36(1): 103–113. https://doi.org/10.2307/3588366
Skrabanek, Robert L. 1970. "Language maintenance among Mexican-Americans." *International Journal of Comparative Sociology* 11: 272–282. https://doi.org/10.1177/002071527001100402
Smith-Christmas, Cassie. 2014. "Being socialised into language shift: The impact of extended family members on family language policy." *Journal of Multilingual and Multicultural Development* 35(5): 511–526. https://doi.org/10.1080/01434632.2014.882930
Soehl, Thomas. 2016. "But do they speak it? The intergenerational transmission of home-country language in migrant families in France." *Journal of Ethnic and Migration Studies* 42(9): 1513–1535. https://doi.org/10.1080/1369183X.2015.1126171
Starks, Donna. 2005. "The effects of self-confidence in bilingual abilities on Pasifika langauge use in South Auckland." *Journal of Multilingual and Multicultural Development* 26: 533–50. https://doi.org/10.1080/01434630508668424
Stevens, Christine A. 1999. "Selection and settlement of citizens: English language proficiency among immigrant groups in Australia." *Journal of Multilingual and Multicultural Development* 20(2): 107–133. https://doi.org/10.1080/01434639908666372
Stevens, Gillian. 1986. "Sex differences in language shift in the United States." *Social Science Research* 71(1): 31–6.
Stoessel, Saskia. 2002. "Investigating the role of social networks in language maintenance and shift." *International Journal of the Sociology of Language* 153: 93–131. https://doi.org/10.1515/ijsl.2002.006
Tannenbaum, Michal and Pauline Howie. 2002. "The association between language maintenance and family relations: Chinese immigrant children in Australia." *Journal of Multilingual and Multicultural Development* 23(5): 408–424. https://doi.org/10.1080/01434630208666477

Terborg, Roland and Phyllis Ryan. 2002. "The inadequacy of the concept of competence." In *Methodological and Analytical Issues in Language Maintenance and Language Shift Studies*, ed. by Maya Khemlani David, 57–64. Frankfurt am Main: Peter Lang.

Trifonas, Peter Pericles and Themistoklis Aravossitas (eds). 2016. *Handbook of Research and Practice in Heritage Language Education*. Cham: Springer International Publishing.

Vaughan, Jill, Gillian Wigglesworth, Deborah Loakes, Samantha Disbray and Karin Moses. 2015. "Child-caregiver interaction in two remote Indigenous Australian communities." *Frontiers in Psychology* 6 (4 September, 2017). https://doi.org/10.3389/fpsyg.2015.00514

Veltman, Calvin. 1983. *Language Shift in the United States*. Berlin: Mouton. https://doi.org/10.1515/9783110824001

Vries, John de. 1994. "Canada's official language communities: An overview of the current demolinguistic situation." *International Journal of the Sociology of Language* 105–106: 37–68. https://doi.org/10.1515/ijsl.1994.105-106.37

Willoughby, Louisa. 2014. "Meeting the challenges of heritage language education: Lessons from one school community." *Current Issues in Language Planning* 15(3): 265–281. https://doi.org/10.1080/14664208.2014.915457

Willoughby, Louisa. 2016a. "The Victorian School of Languages as a model for heritage language education." In *Handbook of Research and Practice in Heritage Language Education*, ed. by Peter Pericles Trifonas and Themistoklis Aravossitas, 39: 1–13. Cham: Springer International Publishing. https://doi.org/10.1007/978-3-319-38893-9_39-1

Willoughby, Louisa. 2016b. "High stakes assessment of heritage languages: The case of the Victorian Certificate of Education." In *Handbook of Research and Practice in Heritage Language Education*, ed. by Peter Pericles Trifonas

Willoughby, Louisa. 2018. *Language Practices of Migrant Youth: From School to Home*. Abingdon, Oxon: Routledge.

Wong-Fillmore, Lily. 1991. "When learning a second language means losing the first." *Early Childhood Research Quarterly* 6(3): 323–346. https://doi.org/10.1016/s0885-2006(05)80059-6

Woods, Anya. 2004. *Medium or Message? Language and Faith in Ethnic Churches*. Clevedon: Multilingual Matters.

Wyman, Leisy Thornton. 2012. *Youth Culture, Language Endangerment and Linguistic Survivance*. Clevedon: Multilingual Matters. https://doi.org/10.21832/9781847697417

# *Mianzi/lian*

## Chinese notions of face

Ling Zhou & Shaojie Zhang
Northeast Normal University, Changchun

## 1. Introduction

Face in Chinese is semantically and pragmatically different from its counterpart in English. Semantically, it is encoded by the two terms of *mianzi* and *lian*, and pragmatically, it is represented as either *mianzi* or *lian* with various meanings depending on the situation in which it is involved. In Chinese, there are a great variety of explicit expressions of *mianzi* and *lian*, for example, "have *mianzi/lian*", "lose *mianzi/lian*", "don't want *mianzi/lian*", or "give *mianzi/lian*", which are often used in social interaction, just to mention a few. Apart from *mianzi* and *lian* as the primary terms, there are a good many secondary terms used for face in Chinese, such as *guangcai*, *zhengqi*, *diuren* and the like, which can be equivalents of *mianzi* or *lian* in specific situations.

This chapter presents how Chinese notions of *mianzi* and *lian* have been conceptualized in historical literature and how these two notions differ from or relate to the findings in the mostly English-based literature on face and politeness. And finally, it focuses on how they resemble and differ from each other by taking the perspective of self-other interaction.

## 2. Conceptualizations of *mianzi/lian* in historical literature

The term *mianzi* is known to be utilized in the long Chinese history much earlier than *lian* (Hu 1944). *Mianzi* is originally derived from *mian*, the whole of one's face, by adding the particle *zi* to it.[1] Nowadays both *mian* and *lian* literally refer to the forepart of one's face. When used in contrast to each other, however, *mianzi* and *lian* always mean 'face' non-literally. In the non-literal sense, *mianzi* and *lian* can be substituted for each other on some occasions of use, but they cannot on other occasions. Although the concept of *mianzi/lian* is deeply rooted in ancient Chinese history, it became a

1. The particle *zi* means 'infant' or 'son' by itself, but it is merely a morpheme when it is combined with *mian* as grammaticalized *mianzi*.

https://doi.org/10.1075/hop.21.mia1

topic of scholarly attention quite late in modern times. In this section, we first present the socio-cultural understanding of *mianzi/lian* by drawing on the historical literature available, and then focus on the culture-specific approach to *mianzi/lian* in more recent research.

## 2.1 Socio-cultural interpretations of *mianzi/lian*

Face issues did not arouse attention from Chinese scholars until after Arthur Henderson Smith, an American missionary, published his book entitled *Chinese Characteristics* in 1894. Smith was the first foreigner who let the Western world begin to know about Chinese culture and Chinese people by writing this book. From then on right through the 1930s, face became an important topic of considerable discussion among Chinese scholars. Lin Yutang was said to be the first Chinese scholar who was aware of the importance of *mianzi/lian* in Chinese culture. Another Chinese scholar, Lu Xun, began to comment on *mianzi/lian* at the same time. We are not sure about who was the first to be aware of *mianzi/lian* as an issue in Chinese culture, but the fact was that both of them shed light on the concept of *mianzi/lian* in Chinese culture earlier in history.

In 1934, Lu Xun wrote a short essay "A Talk about '*Mianzi*'", in which he made a sarcastic comment on those who would rather want "*mianzi*" than "*lian*".[2] In order to explain what *mianzi* was, Lu Xun told a story at the very beginning of his essay. The story goes like this: "In the time of the former Qing Dynasty, a foreign messenger went to see the Prime Minister in his mansion to ask for more interests from China. Under the messenger's threat, the high-ranking officials were forced to give their promises. Nonetheless, the messenger was told to go through the back door when he left. This indicated he had no *mianzi* at all without going through the front door, and as a result of this, the Chinese had *mianzi* instead." By telling the story, Lu Xun did have the intention to say that *mianzi* is, spiritually, a guiding principle in Chinese culture, and to foreigners, it seemed hard to grasp the concept of Chinese *mianzi*. As shown in this case, the Chinese lost *mianzi*, but they found it back at least spiritually by letting the messenger go through the back door. According to Lu Xun, *mianzi* and *lian* are interrelated with an individual's identity or status in society. Every identity goes with a kind of *mianzi*, or a kind of *lian*. But the concepts differ to a certain extent in that *lian* is seriously constrained, referring to a person's individual character. In some cases, if a person wants to have *mianzi* stubbornly, he or she might become a laughingstock so as to lose his or her *lian* even without being aware of it. Generally speaking, upper-class people have more *mianzi* than lower-class people. Just because of this, in many cases,

2. What remains unsaid in Lu Xun's essay is that some people cared so much about their *mianzi* that they were not ashamed of losing their personal character – a kind of *lian* – by sacrificing the common interests.

the former would have more opportunities to lose *mianzi*, and perhaps *lian* too. In addition, Lu Xun (1934: 128–129) pointed out that Chinese *mianzi* is "a kind of tactics for adapting oneself to changeable circumstances". Lu Xun's interpretation lets us understand that *mianzi/lian* is in essence a socio-cultural pair of notions.

Although we are not so sure about who was the first Chinese scholar, Lin Yutang or Lu Xun, to catch sight of the importance of face, there is no doubt that Lin Yutang was the first one to offer an in-depth account of Chinese *mianzi* in his book *My Country, My People* published in 1936. LinYutang also offered a socio-cultural understanding of *mianzi* underlying Chinese society. According to Lin Yutang, some dominant ideas such as *mianzi*, favor, privilege, thankfulness, etc, all originated from the family system which laid a solid foundation for Chinese society, and the social hierarchical ideas derived from Confucianism as the social philosophy that dominated the family system (1936: 180–181). Hidden inside the family system were *mianzi*, *fate*, and *favor* interweaving as a trinity (1936: 199). Fate determinism and thankfulness together with *mianzi* are the three elements dominating people's lives. *Mianzi*, in this context, is a social-psychological notion. It can be gained or lost, and even given as a commodity to others. To give *mianzi* means to give favor and not to give *mianzi* sometimes means humiliating others. Consider a policeman who catches a car violating the traffic law. If the person in the car reminds him/her that s/he knows his/her boss very well, and the policeman lets the driver go without being fined, then the driver has gained *mianzi*. If the person said s/he knows the policeman's boss's boss, s/he would gain even bigger *mianzi*. This kind of *mianzi*, which obviously represents hierarchical social relations, is considered to be the negative part of the notion of *mianzi* in Chinese culture.[3]

From the historical literature, *mianzi/lian* was mainly interpreted from the socio-cultural point of view. It shows that mainzi/*lian*, interweaving with a person's identity and social status, is a dominant element of Chinese culture.

## 2.2 Culture-specific accounts of *mianzi/lian*

Research on Chinese face in a sense directly relevant to present-day pragmatics began in the 1940s with Hu's academic endeavors. In 1944, Hu published an article "The Chinese concept of 'Face'" in *American Anthropologist*, which is regarded as a pioneering research on Chinese culture-specific *mianzi* and *lian*. In Hu's account, *mianzi* "stands for the kind of prestige that is emphasized in this country: a reputation achieved through getting on in life, through success and ostentation" (1944: 45). In contrast, *lian* is defined as "the respect of the group for a man with a good moral reputation".

3. It should be pointed out that *mianzi* by itself is one of the positive elements in Chinese culture, but it may be taken advantage of as a kind of tactics for doing something negative.

Besides, it "represents the confidence of society in the integrity of the ego's moral character, the loss of which makes it impossible for him to function properly within the community" (Hu 1944: 45). Thus, *mianzi* is conceptualized as social reputation in contrast to *lian* as moral reputation.

Following Hu's research till the present day, Chinese scholars have provided different but related accounts of *mianzi* and *lian*. Ho (1976: 874–879) offered a substantial account in which he generally agrees with Hu's interpretation of *mianzi* and *lian*, but disagrees with her on *mianzi* as being "altogether devoid of moral content", because the two terms can be substituted for each other on some occasions. In his account, "*mianzi* is the respectability and/or deference which a person can claim for himself from others..." It is not identical to identity, status and honor, but "ties together a number of separate sociological concepts, such as status, authority, prestige, and standards of behavior" (1976: 883), whereas *lian* is something more innate than *mianzi* (Ho 1976: 870). Furthermore, *mianzi* is what is gained from others owing to one's achievement in society, and such social values as reputation, fame, identity, social status, wealth and the like all contribute greatly to one's achievement. Ho's interpretation of *mianzi* is strongly supported by the findings in He and Zhang's research (2011).

Mao (1994) quite agrees about Hu's (1944) distinction between *mianzi* and *lian* by defining *mianzi* as a reputable image, which is ascribed to someone by members of one's community, and *lian* mainly as the moral reputation one possesses. Yu (2001) preserves the distinction between *mianzi* and *lian* as counterparts by utilizing other terms such as *Mian* Face and *Lian* Face, emphasizing their metonymic and metaphoric basis and thus helping us to understand the interaction between our physical and social faces. Based on Hu's account, however, Jin (2006: 254–257) coined two other terms, Social *Mianzi* and Moral *Mianzi*, in his research. He defines Social *Mianzi* as being highly dependent on others' judgment and closely associated with one's social status, identity, and academic quality. Therefore, *mianzi* is not static but dynamically constructed in social interaction. It can be negotiated, gained or lost, depending on whether one abides by the social norms or not. He affirms Hu's moral interpretation of *lian* by naming it Moral *Mianzi*. Attempts to distinguish between *mianzi* and *lian* are also attributed to other scholars, among whom Cheng (2006: 34–47), who categorizes *mianzi* into Subjective *Mianzi* for self-identity in society, and Objective *Mianzi* for social recognition, and Zhu (2006: 192–193) who elaborates on his Capability *Mianzi* and Morality *Lian* for the internal and external functioning of face, as well as Zhai (2011: 93) who defines *mianzi* as a person's engagement in impression management for the purposes of being accepted and identified as a member of a given social group, and who also stresses (in Zhai 2004) the moral characteristics of *lian* as claimed by Hu. Christopher Earley (1997) as a non-native Chinese speaker contributes his initial ideas to the understanding of *mianzi* and *lian*, which are identified as two forms of face analyzed as organizational behavior within a cross-cultural context. In his analysis, *mianzi* is understood as being a target person's behavior involved in both personal and external social judgments (1997: 68), and *lian* as being innate moral conduct evaluated on the basis of the rules of a given society (1997: 80). However, face as organizational behavior in his analysis seems too broad a concept.

The historical literature and recent research seem to indicate that *mianzi* and *lian*, as the dominant elements of Chinese culture, are culture-specific to a great extent if compared to the notion of face in the English-based literature. Thus, the next section is intended to illustrate how the concept of face in Chinese differs from that in English. Where necessary, the relation of face to politeness will also be considered.

## 3. Differentiation of Chinese face from English-based face and politeness

As mentioned at the outset, Chinese face is realized by the two terms *mianzi* and *lian*, which normally occur in explicit expressions or collocations. This fact already makes it characteristically different from face in English. However, it is often claimed that face, like politeness, is a universal phenomenon that exists in or underlies all languages and cultures. Rather than asking what a universal notion of face might look like, let's focus on how the concept of Chinese face differs, in general, from the English-based notion of face.

### 3.1 Differences between generalized concepts of face in Chinese and English

The term *mianzi* can be used both in a specific sense and in a general sense. For instance, "He was so mean that he didn't give me *mianzi* at all." Here, the term *mianzi* is used in a specific sense and its meaning depends on specific situations. On the other hand, if someone claims "Chinese culture is a *mianzi* culture," the term *mianzi* is used in a general sense. It must be pointed out, however, that the term *lian* is not used in the same way as *mianzi*. Therefore, a grasp of the generalized unitary concept of Chinese face should start from considering how *mianzi* and *lian* coexist and interrelate with each other (see Figure 1).[4]

4. This figure is quoted from Zhou and Zhang (2017).

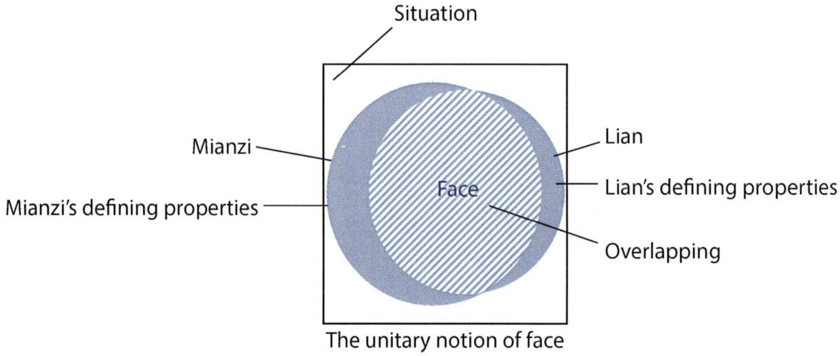


**Figure 1.** The unitary notion of face in Chinese

The figure represents the fact that face in Chinese is primarily covered by the two terms *mianzi* and *lian*, which coexist, being dependent on each other and forming an interface in Chinese culture. The bigger circle and the smaller circle stand for *mianzi* and *lian*, respectively. The interface formed across the two circles indicates that there is a large proportion of overlap between them, and the crescent-shaped areas of non-overlap show that *mianzi* and *lian* have their own defining properties. The two circles put together stand for face as a whole. Briefly, the generalized concept of Chinese face requires understanding *mianzi* and *lian* as the two forms of the high-level unitary face. They coexist and depend on each other, functioning as a unitary system in Chinese culture.

When looking back at the conceptualizations of *mianzi* and *lian* in the literature, it is not difficult to find that Chinese face is associated with social status in Lu Xun's interpretation, with favor in particular in Lin Yutang's interpretation, reputation in Hu's account, or respectability or deference in Ho's account, just to mention a few ingredients. As a matter of fact, such ingredients that constitute the concept of Chinese face represent commonly recognized values, which can fall into individual, socio-cultural, and cognitive categories.[5] In oneword, Chinese face represents a cluster of such values as public self- image, morality, capability, social status, favor, dignity, self-esteem, etc. which are manifested from the interplay of *mianzi* and *lian* in social interaction.

Compared with the concept of Chinese face, two generalized definitions of English-based face have been widely accepted: one is Goffman's and the other is Brown and Levinson's. According to Goffman, face is "the positive social value a person effectively

5. In Zhou and Zhang's (2017) article "How face as a system of value-constructs operates through the interplay of *mianzi* and *lian* in Chinese: A corpus-based study", it is proposed that there are different face-sensitive factors which can be considered as the internal value-constructs of face. Thus, three categories of individual, socio-cultural, and cognitive values are offered.

claims for himself by the line others assume he has taken during a particular contact" (1967: 5). On the one hand, Goffman's interpretation seems similar to the general sense of face in Chinese, representing social values. On the other hand, it is characteristically different. Face in English is often claimed by a person for himself/herself, while face in Chinese is often claimed not only by a person for himself/herself, but also by others for a target person who wants to have face through the third party not involved in the interaction. In addition, face in Chinese can be claimed by a group or institution, or it can be given to a group or institution to which a person belongs. Furthermore, Goffman was not able to explain how face as a social value on the whole is possibly decomposed into various conceptual ingredients recognized by people in the same community.

Following Goffman, Brown and Levinson clearly defined the folk notion of face as "the public self-image that everyone wants to claim for himself" (1987: 61). This definition, to a great extent, is similar to Goffman's in the way that it is self-centered and value-oriented. By self-centered we mean that from both Goffman's and Brown and Levinson's definition, face in English language and culture is a subject matter related to oneself, and it seems that others have no right to step on one's territory. Otherwise, one's face would be in danger of getting hurt. By value-oriented we mean that Brown and Levinson also take a view of face as a kind of social value – public self-image, which is widely recognized in the English-based culture. In comparison, the public self-image is only one of the value constructs that face represents in Chinese (Zhou & Zhang 2017).

### 3.2 Differences in how face relates to politeness in Chinese and English

The Chinese concept of face differs from that of English-based face also in the understanding of how face is correlated with politeness in interpersonal communication. It is true that in Chinese culture, face and politeness are related but different phenomena prevailing in interpersonal communication. First, face issues tend to emerge whenever interpersonal relations are involved, while politeness issues tend to arise when a person's behavior, verbal or non-verbal, is improperly conducted. For instance, if a person asks his/her friend to do a favor, giving the favor or not will involve the person's face, and even his/her friend's face. This has nothing to do with politeness between the person and his/her friend. Second, face pertains more to goal-oriented behavior than politeness, which is rule-governed or maxim-regulated behavior. This means that behind face claims, whether a person claims face for himself/herself, or face is claimed by others, there is often an action plan for certain purposes. In contrast, a person's behavior, polite or not, will be measured or constrained by the politeness principle and its maxims (Gu 1990).[6] On the other hand, the two notions of face and politeness

6. In 1990, Gu formulated the Chinese politeness principle and its maxims in the light of the theoretical framework proposed by Leech. Despite the fact that his formulation is based on Chinese

are sometimes correlated with each other. For some speech acts like invitations, if an invitee who occupies a high position accepts the invitation issued by an inviter who is less privileged, then the inviter will have face (*mianzi*). In the same case, if the invitee promised to come to dinner on time, but failed for some reason to be present on time, s/he would feel very impolite for his/her not being punctual. This example illustrates how face is possibly correlated with politeness. However, face and politeness remain essentially different notions in Chinese.

Comparatively, face and politeness are inherently interrelated notions as described in the English-based literature. According to the face-politeness model proposed by Brown and Levinson, face as the public self-image is what everyone wants, but face claims always involve a risk of threatening the other's face. In order to meet face needs, politeness is called for. To be specific, when someone's face is felt to be threatened or hurt in the performance of a speech act, the claimant will utilize politeness strategies to save the addressee's face from being hurt, or in other words, to lessen the risk of threatening the other's face or to mitigate the imposition on the addressee (Brown & Levinson 1987). Thus, face is a psychologically recognizable end and politeness is the face-saving means in English. The ends-means relation of face and politeness has been largely accepted by English native speakers, but it does not fit in with the psychological reality of Chinese native speakers, though the face-politeness model may be applied to the analysis of some Chinese data at a superficial level.

## 3.3 Differences of positive and negative face in Chinese and English

It is well known that face is further sub-divided into positive face and negative face within Brown and Levinson's model. Briefly, positive face is the individual desire of

---

data, some of the maxims, for instance his Address Maxim, remain questionable. The maxim means to "address your interlocutor with an appropriate address term". There are two possible interpretations: (a) to address with an appropriate term means to show respect or admiration to others, and (b) to address appropriately means to show respectfulness and attitudinal warmth. It seems that this maxim fits the first interpretation because the author clearly explicated that "a failure to use an appropriate address term is a sign of rudeness or a signal of breakdown of established social order" (1990: 239). This line implies that to address your interlocutor with an appropriate address term means to address according to the social status or position of the addressee. Yet by addressing in such a way, it seems impossible to guarantee what the appropriate address term to choose is, due to the fact that the interlocutor plays different roles in different situations. For instance, a school dean would like to be addressed as "Teacher" in the classroom, or as "Professor" at a seminar or conference, or as "Dean" on public occasions outside the school. Therefore, politeness involves appropriateness in addressing, which in turn means respectfulness and attitudinal warmth. If our observation is right, then the Address Maxim is questionable as a separate maxim, which could be revised into a "Respectfulness Maxim", owing to the fact that addressing with appropriate address terms is oriented to respectfulness to others in Chinese. Furthermore, this maxim fails to reveal the essence of politeness.

being appreciated or approved by others, and negative face is the individual freedom or freedom of action, of not being imposed upon or neglected by others (Brown & Levinson 1987). Positive face, defined in terms of face needs, seems to have been largely accepted, but negative face has been extensively criticized in culture-specific studies based on diverse language data (Matsumoto 1989; Mao 1994; Ide 1989; O'Driscoll 1996, 2017).

Recent research on Chinese face (Zhou & Zhang 2013, 2016; Wang & Spencer-Oatey 2015) demonstrates that the distinction between positive and negative face is not applicable to the analysis of Chinese data. In a typically Chinese context, face works like a game that involves gain or loss. Face gain is similar to the notion of positive face with regard to the individual desire of being appreciated. In contrast, face loss is fundamentally different from the notion of negative face conceived in terms of the individual freedom of not being imposed upon. For example, "Can you help me to carry this heavy box to the third floor?" On most occasions, the addressee will offer help without feeling his/her freedom is imposed upon or his/her negative face is threatened. Hence, face needs are largely appreciated, but face threats are counterintuitive for Chinese speakers. Instead of the distinction between positive and negative face, there is a contrastive notion of positively and negatively evaluated face in Chinese (Zhou & Zhang 2016). The former refers to a kind of face targeted at a person apt to be approved or recognized by others, while the latter concerns a kind of face targeted at a person liable to be criticized or rejected by others. These two kinds of face interweave to bring about face gain or face loss. Thus the negative face defined by Brown and Levinson does not really fit the picture.

As Lim (1994: 210) points out, the claim for face relates to positive social values, because "people do not claim face for what they think is negative." Perhaps, it is right to say that face is never negative by itself, but the judgment or evaluation of face can be positive or negative. To solve the problem regarding positive and negative face, Spencer-Oatey (2000: 12) offers an alternative. She believes that face is a universal phenomenon: everyone has the same face concerns; however, culture can affect the relative sensitivity to different aspects of people's face, as well as the strategies which are most appropriate for managing face. Therefore, she (2000: 14) proposes the distinction between "quality face", a fundamental desire for people to evaluate someone positively in terms of one's personal qualities, and "identity face", a fundamental desire for people to acknowledge and uphold their social identities or roles. Here it is not the right place to comment on this alternative view, but at least it shows that the classic distinction between positive and negative face requires theoretical reconsideration.

The foregoing elaboration indicates that the Chinese concept of face differs from that of face in the English-based literature in a number of ways. The differences illustrated above may be considered central.

## 4. Reinterpreting Chinese *mianzi/lian* in interaction

So far we first have presented the socio-cultural interpretations of *mianzi* and *lian* in the historical literature, followed by the culture-specific accounts of the two notions in more recent studies, and then we have provided a comparative understanding of Chinese face in opposition to an English-based notion of face. This section will concentrate on how the two notions of *mianzi* and *lian* resemble and differ from each other in actual usage.

### 4.1 Similarities and differences in *mianzi/lian* representations

As shown in 3.1, understanding the generalized unitary face in Chinese depends on a holistic grasp of the coexistence and interdependence of *mianzi* and *lian* in social interaction. In the light of the corpus-based research on face in Chinese (Zhou & Zhang 2017), face is defined as a system of value constructs which are represented through the interplay of *mianzi* and *lian* in interactions. The two notions clearly resemble each other in their representations, while they also differ significantly from each other.

The similarities and differences between *mianzi* and *lian* are to be found at three levels of representation. First, the two terms form a variety of V+*mianzi/lian* collocations or explicit set expressions with different verbs, which are commonly used to represent face in Chinese. Some of these common collocations are given in the order of high-to-low frequency in Table 1.

**Table 1.** Predominant V+*mianzi/lian* collocations[7]

| V+*mianzi* collocations | V+*lian* collocations |
|---|---|
| have no *mianzi* | lose *lian* |
| have *mianzi* | don't want *lian* |
| don't give *mianzi* | have no *lian* |
| lose *mianzi* | rip open *lian* |
| give *mianzi* | turn over *lian* |

In addition to these predominant collocations, there are other lexical and syntactical variations. The expression "give *mianzi*", for example, may vary between "give *le*

7. Our corpus-based study (Zhou & Zhang 2017) finds that 9 types of V+*mianzi* collocations and 5 types of V+*lian* collocations were predominantly used in Chinese face-representations.

*mianzi*" and "give *mianzi le*", with the particle *le* inserted after the verb or after *mianzi*.[8] Observing the V+*mianzi* and V+*lian* expressions, the difference between them can be easily found. The most striking distinction is that most *mianzi* expressions are conventionalized in a positive sense, and in contrast, *lian* expressions are mostly in a negative sense. In keeping with the occurrence of these expressions, *mianzi* tends to be positively evaluated, while *lian* is liable to be negatively evaluated in terms of their representations in specific situations. This observation further confirms that the Chinese concept of face is different when compared with the distinction between positive face and negative face by Brown and Levinson (see 3.3).

Secondly, *mianzi* and *lian* share a good number of values in face-representations. Face-representations in specific situations (Spencer-Oatey 2005, 2007; He & Zhang 2011) are sensitive to value-based factors, which means that people generally make judgments or evaluations about a person's behavior or conduct according to such values. In other words, underlying Chinese culture exists a set of commonly recognized values which put constraints on a person's face behavior.

**Table 2.** Primary values shared by mianzi and lian

| |
|---|
| public self-image, self-esteem, dignity, capability, success, integrity, wealth, social status, social power, social role, reputation, favor, trust, honor, harmony |

The values listed in Table 2 are not exhaustive but primary. This suggests that there is a large overlap between *mianzi* and *lian* in behavior representations. Two examples can be given for illustration.

(1) [In a wedding ceremony, the bride is dressed so well. Many friends have come to congratulate her on her marriage and one of them, A, makes a remark on the way she looks.]

A: jīn tiān nǐ zhēn měi, zhēn yǒu miànzi.
Today you really beautiful, really have *mianzi*
(You look very beautiful today and you really have *mianzi*!)

The Bride: zhēn de a! xièxiè nǐ, Lǐ Bīng.
Really (sentence-final particle)! Thank you, Li Bing.
(Really! Thank you, Li Bing)

The friend, by saying she has *mianzi*, is actually making a comment on her dress. It is the value-based sensitive factor of *public self-image* that triggers this *mianzi*-representation. In the Chinese context, such *mianzi* can be enhanced by inviting as

8. The particle *le* does have grammatical meaning as a tense marker. It indicates past tense or perfect aspect depending on the specific situation in which its expression is used.

many leaders, friends and relatives as possible to join in the wedding ceremony. The more guests one is able to bring in, the more *mianzi* one will have. Another example:

(2) [A female student has decided to go back to the village where her parents live after graduation from college. Her mother is strongly against her decision.]

| | | | | | | | | |
|---|---|---|---|---|---|---|---|---|
| wǒ | jìu | bù | míngbái | wèi shén me | bìyè | hòu | yào | huí |
| I | just | not | understand | why | graduation | after | want | come |

| | | | | | | | |
|---|---|---|---|---|---|---|---|
| laí | dāng | zhūguān, | nǐ | zhēn | ràng | wǒ | dīu liǎn! |
| back | become | swineherd, | you | really | make | me | lose *lian*! |

(Mother: I don't understand why you want to come back to be a swineherd. You really make me lose *lian*!)

In the rural areas of China, it is hard for young people to go to college. So once a child has the chance to go to college, he/she is expected to find a good job in a city after graduation. The girl does not live up to her parents' expectations, which makes her mother feel ashamed and causes her to lose *lian*. The concept of *lian* for this example can be understood at two levels. At the speech level, by saying she is caused to lose *lian*, the mother indicates that she feels loss of her *public self-image* before the villagers. At a deeper level, however, it is the value-based sensitive factor of *social status* that triggers this *lian*-representation, because being a swineherd is considered to be a job for people who occupy no social status.

The above two cases are among the innumerable examples that can be found to illustrate face as a system of value constructs. To be specific, what *mianzi* and *lian* represent is a set of generally recognized values in social interaction.

Although *mianzi* and *lian* representations are associated with values underlying Chinese culture, the values they tend to represent are different to various degrees. According to a corpus-based analysis (Zhou & Zhang 2017), *mianzi* represents public self-image, capability, dignity, and reputation as the salient components of its internal value-constructs. In contrast, *lian* represents the public self-image, capability, dignity, and morality as the salient components of its internal value-constructs. It is apparent that the defining feature of *mianzi* is the representation of *reputation*, which distinguishes it from *lian* with the defining feature of *morality*. This is probably the essential distinction. Further research, however, is needed to provide more evidence for this claim or to offer new findings based on new data.

Thirdly, both *mianzi* and *lian* occur at three levels of face-representations, namely, individual, relational, and collective. At the individual level, *mianzi* or *lian* has the speaker as target. For instance, when a student was asked to comment on plagiarism, he said: "I just cannot do plagiarism, that dirty thing, in examinations. Otherwise I would lose my *lian*." At the relational level, *mianzi* or *lian* is targeted not at the speaker but at others related to the speaker, as in "These girls are so different that they just didn't give *mianzi* to those super stars." At the collective level, the *mianzi* or *lian* target is a group of people of which the speaker is a member. This third level of face-representation often occurs in interactions, as in the example below:

(3) [The head of the village felt excited when he heard that Yongqiang, a young man from the village, had been admitted to college.]
Yǒng qiáng, nǐ shì wǒmen cūn de jiāoào, nǐ wèi wǒmen
Yǒng qiáng, you are our village's pride, you for us
zhèng le miànzi.
earn (particle) *mianzi*.
(Head: Yongqiang, you are the pride of our village. You've gained *mianzi* for us.)
Xièxiè nǐ de kuājiǎng, dàshū
Thank your praising, uncle.
(Yongqiang: Thank you for praising me, uncle.)

In this example, *mianzi* is not targeted at the speaker, the head of the village, but it is directed at the whole village, a typical collective *mianzi* or group *mianzi* highly appreciated in the Chinese context.

The three levels of face-representation show that there are three types of face: individual face, relational face, and collective face in Chinese. Therefore, a grasp of the Chinese concept of face should start from the interrelated representations of *mianzi* and *lian* in interpersonal communication. This explains our use of terminology that may sound unfamiliar in relation to 'face' in English: unlike 'face' in English, *mianzi/lian* is not primarily a property of interactants, but it is literally *targeted* interactively at interactants, their relationships, and the communities to which they belong.

In relation to the three levels of representation, *mianzi* and *lian* are distinctive. *Mianzi*-representations are nearly evenly distributed across the three levels., while *lian*-representations are unevenly distributed, with a high frequency of occurrence at the individual level and a low frequency at the collective level (for details, see Zhou & Zhang 2017). This distinction seems to suggest that the concept of *lian* is more related to individual qualities of a person at which his/her face is targeted. This finding echoes the claim of earlier research about *lian* as more morality-oriented to a person's character (see 2.2).

### 4.2 Similarities and differences in orientation to the self and others

More recent research indicates that face can be accounted for by drawing insights from self-presentation theory in social psychology (Simon 2004; Brewer & Gardner 1996; Spencer-Oatey 2007). However, in the light of studies on Chinese face conducted by Chinese scholars (Gao 1998; Huang 2006; Yu & Gu 1990; Li 2017), it seems more suitable to understand Chinese face from the perspective of the relation between self and other in interaction (Zhou & Zhang 2017). In what follows, some central ideas of an alternative analysis will be recapitulated and adapted to the purposes of this chapter.

From a holistic point of view, Chinese face which is internally constructed by *mianzi* and *lian* operates as an inseparable whole. From an interactive perspective, it operates as a dual unity of other-related *mianzi* and self-oriented *lian*. This means that an understanding of the concept of Chinese face should start from considering how *mianzi* and *lian* interact with each other.

By other-relatedness, we mean that *mianzi* tends to be triggered or activated in the representation of potential values used when others pass judgments on or make evaluations of a person's behavior. In other words, the potential values that *mianzi* represents exert constraints on a person's behavior mainly through other-judgments. So *mianzi* is other-related in a social sense. In contrast, by self-orientedness, we mean that *lian* is apt to be triggered or activated in the representation of potential values used when a person passes a judgment on or makes an evaluation of his or her own behavior. Or rather, the potential values that *lian* represents put constraints on a person's behavior specifically through self-judgments. So *lian* is more self-oriented in a personal sense.

At the interactive level, *mianzi* and *lian* representations tend to move in opposite directions The other-related *mianzi* is always appreciated or desired by every individual, and the self-oriented *lian* is always watched or scrutinized by the community to which the person belongs. The following example can be used for illustration.

(4) [Neighbors A and B are gossiping about a young girl.]

A:

| | | | | | | | |
|---|---|---|---|---|---|---|---|
| kàn | lǎo | wáng de | guīnǖ, | yí gè | nián qīng | rén | zǒng shì |
| Look | old | wang's | daughter, | one | young | person | always |

| | | | | | | | | |
|---|---|---|---|---|---|---|---|---|
| hé | nánhái er | zài wài miàn | xián | guàng | dào | bàn yè | zhēn | bú |
| with | boys | outside | hang | out | till | mid-night | really | not |

| | |
|---|---|
| yào | liǎn! |
| want | face! |

(Look at Lao Wang's daughter! A young girl always hangs outside late till midnight with boys. She doesn't want her *lian* at all!)

B:

| | | | | | | |
|---|---|---|---|---|---|---|
| Shì | a, | zhēn | shì | bú | jiǎn | diǎn |
| Yes | (particle), | really | is | not | behave | herself! |

(Yeah. What a shameful girl!)

In the above example, A and B are neighbors of Lao Wang, members of the same community. In their view, Wang's daughter is not well behaved and therefore they bother to deliver their value judgment on his daughter's behavior by saying the girl does not want her *lian*. Normally, the self-oriented *lian* does not have to be evaluated by others, due to the fact that it is more related to personal moral character.[9] In Chinese society,

9. The literature indicates that there is general agreement on the essence of *lian* among scholars who are interested in the Chinese concept of face. It is commonly claimed that *lian* is related to the moral character of a target person, though there are different terms used to define it.

however, a person's *lian* seems to be a vulnerable object, always at risk of being judged, evaluated, or criticized by others. In contrast, the other-related *mianzi* is what everyone wants, for no one wants to be a weak link in the social relations. Therefore, we conclude that it is the internal and external interaction between the other-related *mianzi* and the self-oriented *lian* that determines face gain and face loss. As Lim (1994: 210) points out, "...face is not what one thinks of oneself, but what one thinks others should think of one's worth". In addition, the interaction between *mianzi* and *lian* explains how individuals depend on society and in turn how social forces may affect an individual's behavior in Chinese culture. On the whole, people typically act or are acted upon in accordance with the common values in interpersonal communication in order to mediate or adjust social relationships through face gain or face loss.

## 5. Concluding remarks

In this chapter, we have focused on the Chinese notions of *mianzi/lian* which have been appealing to both native and non-native Chinese speakers ever since the end of the 19th century. The Chinese concept of face clearly appears to be different, with its own culture-specific characteristics, in comparison with the English-based notion of face. Rooted in the long Chinese history, face in Chinese is like one coin with two sides, of which the true essence is hard to define. As Lin Yutang commented in his life time: Chinese face is almost impossible to define. So what we can do with it, perhaps, is to approach it step by step, and finally to reach it. We hope the bird's-eye view of *mianzi/lian* provided in this chapter may be of some help to the readers.

## References

Brewer, Marilynn B. and Wendi Gardner. 1996. "Who is this 'we'? Levels of collective and self-representations." *Journal of Personality and Social Psychology* 71(1): 83–93. https://doi.org/10.1037/0022-3514.71.1.83

Brown, Penelope and Stephen Levinson. 1987. *Politeness: Some Universals in Language Usage*. Cambridge: Cambridge University Press. https://doi.org/10.1017/CBO9780511813085

Cheng, Zhongying. 2006. "脸面观念及其儒学根源 [The conceptualization of lian & mian and its Confucian root]." In 中国社会心理学评论（第二版） [*The Critics on Chinese Socio-psychology*], 2nd edition, ed. by Xuewei Zhai, 34–47. Beijing: Social Sciences Academic Press.

Earley, P. Christopher. 1997. *Face, Harmony, and Social Structure: An Analysis of Organizational Behavior across Culture*. New York: Oxford University Press.

Gao, Ge. 1998. "An initial analysis of the effects of face and concern for other in Chinese interpersonal communication." *International Journal of Intercultural Relations* 22(4): 467–482. https://doi.org/10.1016/S0147-1767(98)00019-4

Goffman, Erving. 1967. *Interaction Ritual: Essays in Face to Face Behavior*. New York: Pantheon Books.

Gu, Yueguo. 1990. "Politeness phenomena in modern Chinese." *Journal of Pragmatics* 14(2): 237–257. https://doi.org/10.1016/0378-2166(90)90082-O

He, Ming and Shaojie Zhang. 2011. "Re-conceptualizing the Chinese concept of face from a face-sensitive perspective: A case study of a modern Chinese TV drama." *Journal of Pragmatics* 43(9): 2360–2372. https://doi.org/10.1016/j.pragma.2011.07.003

Ho, David Yau-fai. 1976. "On the concept of face." *The American Journal of Sociology* 81(4): 867–884. https://doi.org/10.1086/226145

Hu, Hsien Chin. 1944. "The Chinese concept of 'Face'." *American Anthropologist* 46(1): 45–64. https://doi.org/10.1525/aa.1944.46.1.02a00040

Huang, Guangguo. 2006. "人情与面子:中国人的权力游戏 [Favor and face: The power game of the Chinese]". In 中国人的心理 [*The Psychology of the Chinese*], ed. by Yang Guoshu, 226–248. Nanjing: Jiang Su Education Publisher.

Ide, Sachiko. 1989. "Formal forms and discernment: Two neglected aspects of universals of linguistic politeness." *Journal of Cross-Cultural and Interlanguage Communication* 8(2/3): 223–248. https://doi.org/10.1515/mult.1989.8.2-3.223

Jin, Yaoji. 2006. "'面'、'耻'与中国人行为之分析 [An analysis of *mian*, shame and the behavior of Chinese people]." In 中国人的心理 [*The Psychology of the Chinese*], ed. by Yang Guoshu, 249–269. Nanjing: Jiang Su Education Publisher.

Li, Qing Kinnison. 2017. "Power, integrity, and mask - An attempt to disentangle the Chinese face concept." *Journal of Pragmatics* 114: 32–48. https://doi.org/10.1016/j.pragma.2017.03.015

Lim, Tae-Seop. 1994. "Facework and interpersonal relationships." In *The Challenge of Facework*, ed. by S. Ting-Toomey, 209–229. New York: State University of New York Press.

Lin, Yutang. 1936[2010]. 吾国与吾民 [*My Country and My People*]. Nanjing: Jiang Su Literature & Arts Publisher.

Lu, Xun. 1934. "说'面子' [On 'face']." In 且介亭杂文 [*Essays of qie jie ting*], ed. by Xun Lu, 128–131. Beijing: People's Literature Publisher.

Mao, LuMing Robert. 1994. "Beyond politeness theory: 'Face' revisited and renewed." *Journal of Pragmatics* 21(5): 451–486. https://doi.org/10.1016/0378-2166(94)90025-6

Matsumoto, Yoshiko. 1989. "Politeness and conversational universals: Observations from Japanese." *Multilingua: Journal of Cross-Cultural and Interlanguage Communication* 8: 207–221. https://doi.org/10.1515/mult.1989.8.2-3.207

O'Driscoll, Jim. 1996. "About face: A defence and elaboration of universal dualism." *Journal of Pragmatics* 25(1): 1–32. https://doi.org/10.1016/0378-2166(94)00069-X

O'Driscoll, Jim. 2017. "Face and (im)politeness." In *The Palgrave Handbook of Linguistic (Im) politeness*, ed. by J. Culpeper, M. Haugh and D. Z. Kádár, 89–117. London: Palgrave Macmillan. https://doi.org/10.1057/978-1-137-37508-7_5

Simon, Bernd. 2004. *Identity in Modern Society: A Social Psychological Perspective*. Oxford: Blackwell.

Spencer-Oatey, Helen (eds). 2000. *Culturally Speaking: Managing Rapport Through Talk Across Cultures*. London: Continuum.

Spencer-Oatey, Helen. 2005. "(Im)politeness, face and perceptions of rapport: Unpackaging their bases and interrelationships." *Journal of Politeness Research* 1(1): 95–120. https://doi.org/10.1515/jplr.2005.1.1.95

Spencer-Oatey, Helen. 2007. "Theories of identity and the analysis of face." *Journal of Pragmatics* 39(4): 639–656. https://doi.org/10.1016/j.pragma.2006.12.004

Wang Jiayi and Helen Spencer-Oatey. 2015. "The gains and losses of face in ongoing intercultural interaction: A case study of Chinese participant perspectives." *Journal of Pragmatics* 89: 50–65. https://doi.org/10.1016/j.pragma.2015.09.007

Yu, D. H. and B. L. Gu. 1990."中国人的情面焦虑 [The Chinese people's concerns over *mianzi* and favor]." In 中国人的人情与面子 [*Favor and mianzi of the Chinese People*], ed. by The Editor Office of Dr. Zhang's Monthly Journal, 55–93. Beijing: China Friendship Publishing Co.

Yu, Ning. 2001. "What does our face mean to us?" *Pragmatics & Cognition* 9(1): 1–36. https://doi.org/10.1075/pc.9.1.02yu

Zhai, Xuewei. 2004. "人情，面子与权力的再生产 [Favor, Face and Reproduction of the Power: A way of social exchange in an reasonableness society]." *Sociological Research* 5(4): 48–57.

Zhai, Xuewei. 2011. 中国人的脸面观: 形式主义的心理动因与社会表征 [*Perspectives on Chinese "face": Psychological Motives and Social Representations*]. Beijing: Peking University Press.

Zhou, Ling and Shaojie Zhang. 2013. "表达的明示性: 汉语言文化特性的'面子' [The explicitness of '*mianzi*' in Chinese]." *Foreign Language Education* 34(3): 22–26.

Zhou, Ling and Shaojie Zhang. 2016. "汉语文化特性的'积极评价面子'与'消极评价面子'概念建构:基于身份理论的视角 [Constructing Positively-evaluated Face and Negatively-evaluated Face in Chinese Culture:An Identity Theory-based Approach]." *Foreign Languages and Their Teaching* 5: 41–49.

Zhou, Ling and Shaojie Zhang. 2017. "How face as a system of value-constructs operates through the interplay of mianzi and lian in Chinese: A corpus-based study." *Language Sciences* 64: 152–166. https://doi.org/10.1016/j.langsci.2017.08.001

Zhu, Ruiling. 2006. "中国人的社会互动：论面子的问题 [The social interaction of Chinese: On face]." In 中国人的心理 [*The Psychology of the Chinese*], ed. by Yang Guoshu, 189–225. Nanjing: Jiang Su Education Publisher.

Smith, Arthur. 1894. 中国人的素质 [*Chinese Characteristics*] 秦悦(译) [translated by Yue Qin]. Shanghai: Shanghai Xuelin Publisher.

Denkzettel

amnesty international
FÜR DIE MENSCHENRECHTE

# Roman Jakobson

Manfred Bierwisch
Humboldt University, Berlin

Jakobson was one of the dominant figures representing the theory of language in the 20th century. Together with Trubetzkoy, he developed a new orientation in dealing with the problems of natural language, especially its sound structure, essentially by enriching the conceptual framework of phonology. Jakobson's particular emphasis in this endeavour concerned the nature of distinctive features as the minimal elements of phonological structure. Extending the structuralist approach to problems of the linguistic content, Jakobson made ground-breaking contributions to morphology as the framework of grammatical structure, notably with regard to the theory of Case, and by rethinking the traditional verbal categories. A further breakthrough resulted from his application of basic linguistic principles to the analysis of data from aphasia. Linguistic insights were also the guideline in his fascinating analyses of poetry, taking the poetic function of language as one of its integrated aspects. Arguing against Saussure's principle of arbitrariness of the sound-meaning relation of language, Jakobson finally came very close to establishing the combinatorial principle as the essence of language.

## 1. Biography

It was a remarkable intellectual career, that began on October 23, 1896, in Moscow. Roman Osipowich Jakobson was the first of two sons of a prominent Jewish industrialist of Austrian origin. At the age of fifteen, he had resolutely decided that language and poetry would be the object of his fascination and study. In 1914 he obtained his B.A. at the Lazarov Institute of Oriental Languages in Moscow and studied linguistics and literature at Moscow University from 1914 to 1918. As early as 1915, while still a student, he was a founding member of the Moscow Linguistic Circle, whose president he was from 1915 to 1920. During these years, he supported Russian Formalism and became close friends with futurist poets such as Chlebnikov, Majakovskij, and Pasternak, while experimenting with poems himself under the pseudonym Aliagrov. A fundamental concern for poetry and art remained with him all his life, stimulating also his core linguistic interests. Thus he participated in the St. Petersburg/Petrograd-based Society for the Study of Poetic Language (usually referred to by its Russian acronym OPOJAZ) and eventually secured a promising position at Moscow University in 1918. In 1920, however, he left Moscow for Prague, serving as an interpreter for the Red Cross mission the new Soviet government was operating for taking care of soldiers of

https://doi.org/10.1075/hop.21.jak1

World War I. He left this position fairly soon, to return to linguistic and literary studies at the German university of Prague, where he finally earned his PhD in 1930 with a dissertation on the verse structure of the Serbo-Croatian epic poetry.

Earlier, in 1926, Jakobson had been a leading participant in an event that became very influential for the development of linguistics as a systematic research program: A group of ten young linguists founded the Prague Linguistic Circle, which soon became one of the main centers of structural linguistics in Europe (Jakobson was its vice-president from 1927 until 1939). Other influential members of the group were, the circle's president, Vilém Mathesius, and Nikolaj S.Trubetzkoy (who was visiting from Vienna). In 1933, Jakobson became Assistant Professor, and in 1937 Full Pofessor of Russian Philology at the newly founded Masaryk University in Brno; also in 1937, Jakobson and his wife Sonja were granted Czechoslovak citizenship. These were the years when some of Jakobson's most important papers on phonology, morphology, and poetics were written and published, and when he made programmatic contributions to the many important international congresses taking place during this period: 1928 Linguistics in The Hague, 1929 Slavistics in Prague, 1930 Phonology in Prague, 1932 Phonetics I in Amsterdam, and 1938 Phonetics III in Ghent. This extremely stimulating time ended abruptly with the German dismantling and later occupation of Czechoslovakia in 1938–1939. Jakobson and his wife left Brno in March 1939, hid in Prague, waiting for visas, and arrived (on April 21, through Germany!) in Copenhagen. Here, he interacted with the colleagues of the Cercle Linguistique de Copenhague, the other European center of linguistics, until September, 1939 when he left for Norway, to lecture at the university of Oslo. In April 1940, the Nazi occupation of Denmark and Norway forced the Jakobsons once again to flee, this time crossing on foot into Sweden via the Norwegian-Swedish nature reserve to reach Särna in Swedish Dalarna. Upon arriving in Stockholm, he was made a Visiting Professor at the university of Uppsala; in face of further German aggression in much of Europe, Jakobson used his connections with workers at the local hospital to pursue his original and quite unusual research on linguistics and aphasia, thereby opening up entirely new perspectives in an important field of interdisciplinary research. Due to its adjacency to Nazi-occupied Scandinavian territory, however, Sweden was not a safe place for a Russian Jew to stay, so Jakobson and his wife left Sweden in May 1941 on a cargo ship, arriving in June 1941 in New York harbor.

Jakobson's first position in the United States was at the École Libre des Hautes Études in New York, founded by French emigrants with the aid of the Rockefeller Foundation. There he got in touch very intensely with Claude Lévi-Strauss, who extended the structuralist principles for the analysis of language and poetry to problems of culture, social organization, and anthropology. In 1943, Jakobson changed to Columbia University, where he became a founding member of the Linguistic Circle of New York, founded in 1943 mainly by emigrants from Europe. At the end of the war, he briefly considered a return to Prague, but as he did not trust the new political situation, he stayed in the USA. In 1949, he was appointed to the chair of Russian philology at Harvard University, which he held until his retirement in 1965. Early in this period, together with Gunnar Fant and Morris Halle, he worked out the essential details of what was going to be his theory of phonetic features. On account of his far-ranging contributions to all fields of linguistics (and beyond), Jakobson was appointed Institute Professor at MIT, the Massachusetts Institute of Technology, in 1957, while still teaching at Harvard – a rather unusual professional situation, which however reflected the important role he had established for himself during his years in the United States. He retired from MIT in 1970, but went on lecturing as visiting professor at universities such as Yale, Princeton, Brandeis, the Salk Institute, and the Collège de France. Roman Jakobson died at the age of 86 in Cambridge, Mass. on July 18, 1982.

## 2. Phonology: Phonemes and distinctive features

Soon after settling in Prague, and clearly in continuation of the new and radical orientation he had experienced in the Moscow and St. Petersburg linguistic circles, Jakobson began to develop, together with Nikolaj Trubetzkoy, the programmatic principles of Phonology; this was right from the beginning one of the major contributions of the Prague Circle to the burgeoning field of structural linguistics. The program was stimulated by the earlier work of Ferdinand de Saussure and Jan Baudouin de Courtenay; it was conceived in contrast to the still dominating trend of historical linguistics due to the so-called 'Young Grammarians'. Jakobson and his co-workers conceived of phonology as a new, systematic approach to the nature of language and to the methods of investigating it. The theory's major tenets are due to Saussure (1916) and his students Bally and Sechehaye; in outline it is characterized by the following concepts, distinctions, and principles:

1. A fundamental difference to be recognized is that between the *knowledge* and the *use* of language (or *langue* and *parole*); the actual instances of linguistic utterances have concrete spatio-temporal properties, produced and perceived by the language user on the basis of a system of (tacit) linguistic knowledge.
2. This difference corresponds to the relation between *invariants* and *variation* of linguistic expressions: utterances have varying properties of realization that are compatible with the underlying linguistic elements. Thus, spoken words may differ in actual realization and interpretation, but are still acknowledged as instances of the same words.
3. This leads to the distinction between linguistic *structure* and *change* of language, the basis of what is called *synchrony* and *diachrony*: The structure of language is

the system of invariants characterized by synchrony. Differences of language use over time, resulting in different structural invariants, are captured by diachrony.
4. The invariant *elements* are determined by their distinctness within the *system*: the elements of the whole are nothing but values functioning by their relations within the system, due to the difference from other elements, rather than by the (phonetic or meaning-related) substance which they consist of (although their use necessarily relies on those substances). In this sense, the parts depend on the whole, rather than the whole depending exclusively on the parts.
5. The elements of the system are related along two dimensions, viz. *combination* and *alternation*. Combined elements are *syntagmatically* related, building a syntagm, alternative elements are *paradigmatically* related, constituting a paradigm.
6. The elements making up linguistic knowledge are signs connecting a sound structure (or *signifiant*) and a conceptual structure (or *signifié*, roughly: the meaning). The relation between *signifiant* and *signifé* constitutes the linguistic sign; the relation is conventional, but necessary, and it exists through the *habits* of the language user, without which the sign would not exist.

Jakobson and Trubetzkoy developed Phonology as the theory of the sound structure of language, with the phoneme as its smallest, indivisible segment, not determined by any acoustic or articulatory properties, but only by the element's relations in the system, notably the syntagmatic relations of syllable structure and the paradigmatic relations of the vowel and consonant systems. What Trubetzkoy and Jakobson called a *correlation* or *privative opposition*, is of particular interest: It holds for otherwise identical segments which are paradigmatically related by the asymmetrical contrast between a marked and an opposite, unmarked or neutral, term. An obvious case in point are the voiced consonants and their corresponding unvoiced counterparts. In German, e.g., the voiceless stops /p, t, k/ are unmarked because they can appear in positions where their voiced counterparts /b, d, g/ are excluded: syllable final obstruents cannot be voiced. More generally, the marked term of a correlation comes with a specific property, while the unmarked term may, but need not, show the opposite property, including asymmetrical combinatorial possibilities. A fair range of characteristic conditions of this sort, interrelating paradigmatic and syntagmatic aspects of phonological structure, have been identified i.a. by Trubetzkoy (1939) and Jakobson (1971).

Jakobson's specific contribution was the observation that the properties of phonemes do not just serve to classify segments as vowels, consonants, nasals, labials, etc., but are basic components in their own right. They turn phonemes into bundles of more elementary components, called distinctive features. These features are – like all components of linguistic structure – purely structural entities of relational character, yet systematically bound to their articulatory, auditory, and acoustic interpretation, as it was convincingly demonstrated by Jakobson, Fant, and Halle (1952). Their groundbreaking studies established a general theory of presumably universal phonetic features and their physiological, sensory, and acoustic realizations.

One crucial implication of this, by now widely accepted, view is the recognition of a basic structural dimension, viz. the sequential, basically temporal organization of the sound shape. Here, all the elements are assigned a position in strictly linear order, in accordance with their potential temporal realization, which results in an additional dimension where the segmental features are arranged simultaneously. For Jakobson, this observation contradicts the linearity of the *signifiant* (the one of the two basic principles of the Saussurean framework, along with that of the arbitrariness of the linguistic sign). Jakobson claims repeatedly that the principle of linearity is falsified by the discovery of features arranged in simultaneous bundles, which requires the sound pattern to be two-dimensional. Although his observation is accurate, Jakobson somehow misses the point: simultaneous features do not deprive the *signifiant* of its sequential organization, they merely add an additional dimension. Thus, the temporal axis is fully preserved, even for the components of different phonemes (the feature 'labial' of the first /p/ in /papa/ clearly precedes that of the second /p/). Linear ordering does not preclude simultaneity of different elements; as pointed out by Saussure (1916, p. 180), a syllable's vowel and stress are different, but simultaneous elements. In contrast to the linear nature of even two-dimensional *signifiants*, there is no possible linearity with respect to their *signifié*. While the words and their segments in a simple sentence like "John loves music" are sequentially ordered, there is just no sequential relation between the pertinent concepts. And even within single words such as "unreadable", the components "un", "read", and "able" are ordered by their *signifiant*, while there is no linear ordering of their *signifié*. In short, while the two-dimensionality of sound structure is one of Jakobson's important discoveries, it does not void Saussure's principle of linearity. As for Jakobson's concern with the principle of arbitrariness, we will return to it in Section 6, below.

## 3. Morphology

Keeping to the Saussurean framework, Jakobson successfully applied several of the concepts and principles of phonology to problems of morphology. By exploring mainly grammatical categories such as Case and Number in (primarily Russian) nouns and verbs, he gained important insights by means of the crucial assumption that morphemes, just like phonemes, consist of asymmetrical, binary features. In Jakobson (1936), he showed that the eight Russian Cases are characterized by three binary features, making up three oppositions, in much the same way as do correlations in phonology: Nominative is the unmarked Case, in opposition to Accusative, Accusative is unmarked with respect to Dative, etc. Similarly for the category of Number: Singular is unmarked in opposition to Plural. Similarly for the Russian verb,

Jakobson (1932 and 1948) analyzes the unmarked Present as opposed to the marked Past, the unmarked Singular as opposed to marked Plural, etc. More generally, a marked morpheme has the more specific content and the more complex phonological shape (exhibiting more segments or features than does its unmarked counterpart).

Even though Jakobson shows that interesting generalizations carry over from phonology to morphology with regard to features and categories, there still are some fundamental differences that must be recognized.

First, whereas phonological features like Dental, Voiced etc. are assumed to make up segments of the *signifiant*, morphological features like Past, Plural, or Location are elements of the conceptual and grammatical organization of the *signifié*, and thus their interpretation is of a rather different kind.

Second, and more intricately, marked morphemes are usually more complex than unmarked ones (at least in part) also by their sound structure (as e.g. in "kid*s*" vs. "kid" or "work*ed*" vs. "work"); however, morphemes are essentially two-sided entities, relating specified configurations of the *signifiant* to their functional or conceptual purport in the *signifié* by language specific rules and principles. Hence the complexity of morphological elelents pertains to both the *signifiant* and *signifié*. Here, the simplest relation is a direct correspondence of sound and meaning, as in /-ed/ – Past, or /-s/ – Plural, where morphemes are just minimal signs. But fairly complex conditions show up already in regular cases like German "buch" vs. "b*ü*ch-*er*", "kopf" vs. "k*ö*pfe" or in exceptional cases like English "child" vs. "child-*ren*", with vowel alternation plus suffix addition associated to one feature, Plural, in all cases. For the same reason it is unclear how features of morphemes combine: in German "kind-<u>er</u>-*n*", Plural and Dative belong to different morphemes, while in "menš-*en*" they seem to be assigned to one morpheme.

Even more complex problems show up under conditions like concord, as in German "manch-*en* klug-*en* büch-*er*-*n*", raising the question, how many instances of Case and Number features show up in congruent suffixes und must be interpreted conceptually in the construction as a whole. Issues like these were taken up later, e.g. by Halle and Marantz (1993) in their "Distributed Morphology", where they deal with the conditions for splitting and fusing morphological components in syntactic constructions. The basic concepts, however, originate in Jakobson's approach to morphological features; his overall theoretical framework constituted a new and very advanced stage of linguistic theorizing.

## 4. Child language, aphasia, language universals

Jakobson typically pursued the problems of his field not only with a keen eye on surrounding disciplines – he also brought his own questions and concepts into the neighbouring domains. While fleeing Nazi aggression from one country to the next, he held on to his research program – now turning to the nature, development, and loss of language knowledge. The fascinating result of this endeavour was the slim volume "Kindersprache, Aphasie und allgemeine Lautgesetze" (1941). Impressive data on children's acquisition of language and on its disturbance in aphasia led Jakobson to postulate that such observations should no longer be considered as a collection of isolated facts, but had to be analyzed in relation to their inherent linguistic structure. The steps in language acquisition as well as the phenomena of its disturbance can be seen as directly determined by the distinctive features and the laws of markedness. More marked feature-configurations are acquired later than less marked ones; they are also easier lost in cases of aphasic disturbance.

Child language and aphasia thus ought to be integrated into the domain of linguistic research. Moreover the principles of sound structure are seen to dominate differences between typologically different languages, which leads to the interesting, albeit speculative, conjecture that not only ontogenetic, but also phylogenetic patterns are subject to the sound laws in question.. Thus, a large range of so far unconnected facts could be explained by universal principles of mental organization determining the growth and loss of knowledge. However, aphasic disturbances are not the inverse of language development, as one might be tempted to suppose; in fact, considering, even implicitly, this contrary relation as a kind of inverse process would be a perhaps interesting and productive, but still) erroneous assumption.

This linguistic approach to aphasia, which relied essentially on the theory of phonology and the concept of markedness, was extended in Jakobson (1963) to other aspects of linguistic theory, as well as to the more general problems of aphasia. First, Jakobson applies the layers of the markedness hierarchy to morphological categories and their dependency on the combinatorial principles within words, phrases, and sentences. Second, he connects the two fundamental aspects of linguistic organization (syntagmatic and paradigmatic structure), which provide the combinatorial and selectional relations, with two types of aphasia and their respective syndromes: disturbances in combination of lexical items and their grammatical properties are seen as syntagmatic deficits, while failures to select and recognize items are considered paradigmatic deficits. Based on analyses by Luria (1962) and on related observations, Jakobson argues that lesions in different brain areas are related to the linguistically characterized types of deficit. Ramifications within the complex syndroms of aphasia are still subject to ongoing debate and analysis, but Jakobson's pioneering ideas and results have created new fields of research in language development and deficit.

## 5. The model of communication

Jakobson's ultimate goal was an overall picture covering all aspects of language. Among his stimuli was his intense interest in the poetic function of language, which he considered one of its intrinsic aspects, as becomes obvious from his model of human communication. To Bühler's (1934) Organon model of language, which assigns three functional relations to the linguistic Message: *expression* for the *Sender*, *appeal* for the *Addressee*, and *representation* for *Things* and *Situation*, Jakobson (1960) adds two elements, which he calls *Contact* and *Code*. Contact comes with the channel or medium by which a Message connects Sender and Recipient (or Addresser and Addressee), and Code is the sign system through which the Message is understood as referring to Things and States of Affairs in its Context. The relations between these six factors are schematized (not very perspicuously) by Jakobson as follows:

Context

Message

Addresser ← → Addressee

Contact

Code

The Message has a specific functional relation to each factor in this schema, including the Message itself: for the Addresser, the function is EMOTIVE, for the Addressee, it is CONATIVE, with respect to the Context, it is REFERENTIAL, and for the Code, it is METALINGUAL (this latter expression representing a somewhat special sense of the term). Less obviously, the function of the Message with respect to the Contact, i.e. the channel, is called PHATIC, turning on the mere connectedness. Most surprising is Jakobson's idea that the Message has a functional relation to and by itself, and that this is what makes it POETIC. Poetry focuses attention, so to speak, on the verbalization as such. This unusual, yet perhaps particularly revealing move shows that for Jakobson, poetry had always a central place in language (as it is also documented by his extensive and careful analyses of literary works in various languages, from the old Russian epic poetry, through Puškin and Chlebnikov, to Hölderlin and Brecht).

Two additional points must be made in this connection. First, the schema's functions, as bound to the six factors, are not mutually exclusive, but allow for various combinations. Thus, a CONATIVE asking does not exclude the EMOTIVE function, REFERENCE can imply EMOTION, and so on. Second, the different functions of a Message are in each case hierarchically ordered, such that one function can dominate over the others: a question is primarily CONATIVE with respect to the Addressee, but has usually a Context to which it is REFERENTIAL; likewise, the POETIC function can be subordinate to the CONATIVE function in an invitation, but it may also dominate all other functions (poetry does not exclude the other functions, but its primary, dominating function concerns the message itself).

In a later work, Jakobson (1970) outlines an even larger view, in which he contrasts language with other sign systems, comparing different conditions the factors of the above schema are subject to. Thus, proper symptoms originating in a source that lacks intention have no Addresser sending the signal – which results in a condition called 'information' (as distinct from communication). More specifically, Jakobson compares different types of Contact bound to different media, leading to spatial (as opposed to temporal) *signifiants*. Thus, language and music are systems with time-dependent, sequential *signifiants*, as opposed to pictures and sculptures, with their two- or three-dimensional signs. Various other, often hybrid systems are found, such as film, dance, theatre, and even writing, all of which need to be analyzed as specific sign systems. Here, by the way, Saussure's principle of the linear *signifiant* of language is no longer controversial for Jakobson, since language now is seen as time-structured.

As to music, which is commonly considered not to have a conceptual meaning, Jakobson thinks of a sign-structure where the *signifiant* is its own *signifié*, i.e. the 'meaning' of music is simply the structure of its form. Given the varying sorts of intense attitudes and emotional values that characteristically are conveyed by music, Jakobson considers an interesting alternative, which relates to the two dichotomies – natural vs. imputed and similar vs. contiguous – by which Peirce (1894) distinguishes three fundamental types of signs: ***icons***, based on natural similarity between *signifiant* and *signifié*; ***indexes***, based on their natural contiguity; and ***symbols***, based on imputed contiguity of *signifiant* and *signifié*. Peirce's typology does not have signs based on imputed similarity. This could neatly account for the imputed similarity, characteristically experienced (and often culturally modulated) as emotional attitudes and processes associated with musical structures. While it is a matter of debate whether this proposal accounts adequately for the place of music among the sign systems, there are numerous artistic phenomena that integrate different types of signs, as in singing, which combines music and language, or dancing, which integrates music and body-movement. Abstract painting, on the other hand, is (much like music) devoid of conceptual meaning.

Further ramifications are easily adduced and again, as Jakobson emphasizes, the different possibilities are subject to hierarchical dependencies among the conditions in question, with natural language always as their ultimate foundation.

## 6. The essence of language: Combination

The organization of linguistic signs, notably the nature of the sound-meaning relation, was Jakobson's central concern right from the beginning. While he vigorously supported Sausssure's view that *signifiant* and *signifié* are different structures, with separate, autonomous conditions, he could not accept Saussure's first principle, according to which the connection of the two sides, and hence the sign as a whole, is arbitrary. Saussure had, of course, noted cases of onomatopoeia (like *cuckoo* or *babble*) and exclamations like *oh!*, where the sound-meaning relation is motivated by similarity or natural contiguity; but for him, these were marginal cases which did not invalidate the basic arbitrariness of the sign. More importantly, signs like *nineteen* or *rainbow* (which combine the arbitrary *nine* and *ten*, or *rain* and *bow*) are themselves only arbitrary to a degree. Again, this partial motivatedness does not abolish the combined signs' basic arbitrariness, especially since the ways in which the combining contributes to the meaning of an expression may also be arbitrary (as in *nineteen* versus *rainbow*). Saussure emphasizes, however, that such arbitrariness is not a matter of individual choice, but of common agreement in the speech community.

In any case, Saussure's idea of taking pure arbitrariness as the nature of language provoked Jakobson's search for principles and generalizations. He pursued two strategies to refute Saussure's first principle. First, he emphasized that according to Saussure's own observation, words (and linguistic expressions generally) are indissoluble sound-meaning connections, completely dependent on their being connected. While the sound-meaning relation thus is the opposite of arbitrariness, its necessary connection does not prevent the community's free choice; it does not determine a particular *signifié*, but merely states that a *signifiant* needs its *signifié* (and vice versa). Here, the decisive point is that the absence of any constraints gives language access to any conceptual domain whatsoever.

Jakobson's second strategy is to carefully analyze a wide range of different regularities that show up in the sound-meaning correspondence and reveal surprising phenomena (in addition to the similarities of onomatopoeia). The morphological patterns mentioned above, with marked categories corresponding to more complex affixes than do unmarked ones, are an important case in point. Lexical oppositions like *vie/mort* with bright vs. dark vowels, or the phonemic similarity of Russian items like *devjat'* (for '9') and *desjat'* (for '10'), or of items with similar meanings like English *mash smash crash splash flash* are examples from a wide range of different phenomena. Thus Jakobson identifies an impressive variety of sound-meaning correspondences which are by no means purely incidental, but subject to various systematic conditions.

Even so, connections of this type merely testify to important tendencies; they are not laws or principles, hence counterexamples are easily adduced. For instance, the English 3rd Person Sing Present, as in *sings*, is an anomaly with regard to the principle of morphological markedness: despite belonging to the least marked verbal category, it is the only Present form with an inflectional suffix. Moreover, lexical items are unsystematic in principle, thus *lash, rash* and others do not fit into the *smash*-group, etc. More generally, the effect of additional, accidental motivation does not abolish the validity of general convention, based on arbitrary choice – just as e.g. gravity would not lose its dominating effect in the presence of additional forces influencing the path of a falling body. The principles of morphology do not remove the fundamental conventionality of signs, as the contrast of e.g. *sang* vs. *talked* easily shows (even *thunder* is conventional, its sound similarity notwithstanding).

Acknowledging this possible overlay of different types of relation, Jakobson (1965) pleads for signs with mixed motivations and again considers a ranking of possibilities. He reconciles Saussure's dichotomy of arbitrariness vs. motivation with Peirce's (1894) distinction of icon, index, and symbol (cf. Section 5, above), where 'symbol' is based on *imputed contiguity* and defines the arbitrary sign. Imputed contiguity of symbols plausibly admits also the natural similarity in icons like *cuckoo, thunder*, etc. And Jakobson agrees with Saussure and Peirce that linguistic signs are basically symbols, with all their characteristic consequences.

A highly specific type of integration that conflates symbols and indexes, on the basis of their imputed natural contiguity, is essential for natural languages; typical cases are pronouns like "you", "we", "they", or adverbials like "now", "here". Jakobson (1957) elucidates their nature and importance using Jespersen's term *shifter*, indicating that their interpretation regularly switches with their use. Shifters are *symbols* because of their imputed contiguity of e.g. the Addressee with "you", or of Location with "here"; but they are at the same time *indexes* depending on their natural contiguity with the very Message they belong to. In other words, their meaning (or reference) changes with their actual use. According to Jakobson, the twofold semiotic character of e.g. pronominals applies also to verbal categories like tense or mood. It makes the situatedness of language possible.

The most important proposal made in Jakobson (1965) concerns the motivated combination of symbols – which is in some sense the very essence of natural language. The proposal draws on Peirce's distinction between two types of icons, called ***image*** and ***diagram***. An image relates the structure of the *signifiant* by natural similarity to that of the *signifié*, while the components of a diagram have imputed relations to parts of its *signifié*, with natural similarity being reduced to these relations, such that e.g. the size of the segments of a circle corresponds to the size of the political parties represented in a certain parliament. In other words, diagrams function in two steps: components of the form (segments of the circle) have imputed relations to parts of the meaning (parties in the parliament), and their size obeys similarity (the parties' relative size). Thus, a diagram applies one type of form-meaning relation (imputed contiguity) to another type of form-meaning relation (natural similarity). Jakobson's stimulating idea was to take Peirce's diagram theory as an explanation of the way in which syntax determines the combination of symbols: Syntactic patterns are like diagrams by which linguistic constituents are combined and interpreted.

However, Jakobson's fascinating idea raises at least three serious problems. First, the components combined in a diagram are necessarily homogeneous and preserve their similarity relations under the imputed correspondence (the parties of the parliament differ only in size). But the constituents combined in syntax usually have no similarity that could be preserved. Except for special cases (like in "veni, vidi, vici"), syntax does not hinge on form-meaning similarity.

Second, and more importantly, syntactic combination usually depends on the combining parts' properties, such as categorization or argument structure (e.g. in *see* vs. *show*, where the combination turns on the presence of two vs. three arguments). But no such dependency is possible among parts of diagrams.

Third, and most importantly, the combinatorial possibilities of syntax have no analogy in diagrams. Although phrase structure hierarchies suggest a certain analogy to diagrammatic structures, with the meaning of symbols integrated according to imputed tree structures, but there are no diagrammatic counterparts to syntactic phenomena like quantifier raising or verb movement. More generally, the difference between merging and moving constituents in syntactic structures, a topic extensively discussed in the most recent syntactic literature, completely escapes the scope of diagrams. Syntax simply goes beyond the diagram-based similarity of imputed correspondents.

In conclusion, one can only admire Jakobson's ingenious intuitions, not least in regard to the combinatorial structure of language, and even with the above reservations. His initial linguistic work was within the framework of Saussurean linguistics, where syntax (in the later sense of Generative Grammar and related approaches) was simply not a recognized topic. Jakobson therefore never had to deal with strongly syntactic phenomena like raising, verb shift, question formation, or quantifier movement. Nevertheless, he specifically realized that the combinatorial nature of language is not merely an indispensable aspect of its syntagmatic structure, but in principle transcends the sequential and hierarchical combination of constituents. Syntax (along with morphology) formally indicates how the *signifiés* of the parts are to be integrated according to their own features, in order to build a common *signifié* of the linguistic-semiotic whole. Jakobson's proposal to use Peirce's theory of diagrams as a way to model syntactic combination opened up a perspective that extended further than did most attempts of his generation to come to grips with the combinatorial structure of symbols and its problems.

## References

[SW = Selected Writings of Roman Jakobson, Volumes I–III – see below]

Bühler, Karl. 1934. *Sprachtheorie*. Jena: Gustav Fischer

Halle, Morris and Alec Marantz. 1993. "Distributed morphology and the pieces of Inflection." In *The View from Building 20*. Cambridge, Mass.: MIT Press.

Jakobson, Roman. 1932. "Zur Struktur des russischen Verbums." In *Charisteria Gulielmo Mathesio quinquagenario*. Reprinted in SW II.

Jakobson, Roman. 1936. "Beitrag zur allgemeinen Kasuslehre." *TCLP* VI. Reprinted in SW II.

Jakobson, Roman. 1941. "Kindersprache, Aphasie und allgemeine Lautgesetze." Reprinted in SW I.

Jakobson, Roman. 1948. "Russian conjugation." *Word* 4. Reprinted in SW II. https://doi.org/10.1080/00437956.1948.11659338

Jakobson, Roman. 1957. "Shifters, verbal categories, and the Russian verb." Reprinted in SW II.

Jakobson, Roman. 1960. "Closing statement: Linguistics and poetics." In *Style in Language*, ed. by Thomas Sebeok, 350–377. Cambridge, Mass.: MIT Press. Reprinted in SW III.

Jakobson, Roman. 1962. *Selected Writings*, Volume I. The Hague: Mouton.

Jakobson, Roman. 1963. "Toward a linguistic classification of aphasic impairments." In *Ciba Foundation Symposium on Disorders of Language*, London. Reprinted in SW II.

Jakobson, Roman. 1965. "Quest for the essence of language." *Diogenes* 13(51): 21–37. Reprinted in SW II. https://doi.org/10.1177/039219216501305103

Jakobson, Roman.1970. "Language in relation to other communication systems." In *Linguaggi nella società e nella tecnica*. Milan: Communità. Reprinted in SW II.

Jakobson, Roman.1971. *Selected Writings*, Volume II. The Hague: Mouton.

Jakobson, Roman. 1981. *Selected Writings*, Volume III. The Hague: Mouton.

Jakobson, Roman, Gunnar Fant and Morris Halle. 1952. *Preliminaries to Speech Analysis*. Cambridge, Mass.: MIT Press.

Luria, Aleksandr R. 1962. *Vysšie korkovye funcii čeloveka*. Moscow: University Publishing House.

Peirce, Charles S. 1894. "Grand logic, the art of reasoning, Chapter II: What is a Sign." Reprinted 1974–1979, in *Collected Papers* (2.281), Cambridge, Mass.: Harvard University Press.

Saussure, Ferdinand de. 1916. *Cours de Linguistique Générale*. Paris : Payot.

Trubetzkoy, Nikolaj S. 1939. *Grundzüge der Phonologie*. TCLP VII. Reprinted 1962, Göttingen: Vandenhoeck & Ruprecht.

# Stance

Hiroko Takanashi
Japan Women's University, Tokyo

## 1. General overview

We take stances in every aspect of social life: we evaluate an entity, express our attitude or viewpoint toward it, coordinate our subjectivity in relation to other parties, and so on. We may say that every act entails *stancetaking* because even taking a neutral stance is a form of stancetaking (Jaffe 2009b). Stancetaking, broadly understood as "personal belief/attitude/evaluation" (Englebretson 2007b: 14), needs to be studied with respect to its form and function in the matrix of social contexts. It deploys a broad array of semiotic resources that carry certain functions and indexical meanings. Since stancetakers are social actors with identity and agency, the act of stancetaking is embedded in meaningful social contexts and its expressions are in this respect reconciled with the social indexical field. That is to say, it presupposes and indexes social values such as morality, ideology, and identity, simultaneously bringing about consequences to social life.

Due to the crucial role stance plays in social life, it has been extensively investigated, especially since around the 1980s, in various approaches of linguistics and related disciplines with focus on language and other semiotic devices (see Athanasiadou, Canakis & Cornillie 2006a, and Englebretson 2007b for detailed overviews of the literature, and Jaffe 2009b, particularly for studies in sociolinguistics and linguistic anthropology). Several volumes and special issues directly address stance as their research agenda (Englebretson ed. 2007, for discourse and interaction; Hunston & Thompson 2000, for authorial stance; Jaffe 2009c, for sociolinguistic and linguistic anthropological studies; Kärkkäinen & Du Bois 2012, for affective stance in discourse analysis from a conversation analytic standpoint, focusing on the sequential dimension of stancetaking).

It should be noted that different labels may be used both within a single approach and across disciplines to refer to the concept of "stance" as treated in this article. Furthermore, different terms imply different concepts. Acknowledging the potential discrepancy among different paradigms with regard to the conceptualization of "stance," however subtle it may be, and respecting their own theoretical, methodological, and terminological particularities, this article makes reference to various relevant studies for the present purpose of formulating a comprehensive picture of stance.

https://doi.org/10.1075/hop.21.sta2

*Evaluation* is seemingly the most prevalent and general term for stance (Hunston & Thompson 2000; Labov & Waletzky 1967; Lemke 1998; Linde 1997; Macken-Horarik & Martin 2003). Other frequently used terms include: *subjectivity* (Benveniste 1971; Langacker 1985; Lyons 1994; Scheibman 2002), *evidentiality* (Biber & Finegan 1989; Chafe 1986), *assessment* (C. Goodwin & M. H. Goodwin 1992; Heritage 2002; Pomerantz 1984), *attitude* (Biber & Finnegan 1989), *appraisal* (Macken-Horarik & Martin 2003; Martin 2000; Martin & White 2005), *point of view* or *viewpoint* (Chafe 1994; Dancygier & Sweetser 2012; DeLancey 1981; Scheibman 2002), and *perspective* or *perspectivization* (Chafe 1994; Ensink & Sauer 2003b; Fillmore 1977; Langacker 1987; MacWhinney 1977).

In what follows, we will delineate the research contributions to stance, and its closely related concepts under different labels as presented above, in an attempt to clarify the implications of these studies for the scholarship of pragmatics and other related paradigms that investigate language use and its meanings. For, as Englebretson argues, the study of stance "represents an ongoing trend toward understanding the full social and pragmatic nature of language, as it is used by actual speakers or writers to act and interact in the real world" (2007b: 1).

## 2. Forms and functions of stance

The expression of stance takes various forms that carry different functions. Since stancetaking is pervasive in language practice, the function of stance is naturally variegated; moreover, a particular occasion of a stance act may have multiple functions. For this reason, it is quite challenging to identify the functions of stance, although attempts have been made to propose a typology (Wu 2004, as discussed in Du Bois & Kärkkäinen 2012).

The study of stance has a complex nomenclature due to the diverse scholastic disciplines from which it has been approached. For instance, Thompson and Hunston (2000) use the term *evaluation* for expressions of attitude (certainty, obligation, desirability, and other sets of values), stance, viewpoint, and feelings, whereas Biber and Finegan (1989) regard *stance* as expressions of attitude, feelings, judgment, or commitment. The three types of stance Englebretson (2007b: 17) suggests are evaluation (value judgment, assessment, attitude), affect (personal feelings), and epistemicity (commitment).

As the descriptions above show, stance is often claimed to have epistemic and emotional functions. C. Goodwin (1986) considers "epistemological stance" as both commitment to and feelings about the propositional content, utterance or text. By the same token, Haviland (1989) posits that evidentials are not only about truth value but also about feelings and commitments. Additionally, Sarangi (2003) argues for the integrity of stance as comprising "informational" (i.e., descriptive) and "affective" (i.e., evaluative) levels of language functions, stating that "it makes sense to see these functions not as two separate entities but as intricately intertwined along a communication continuum, very much like a double helix" (p. 166). For a theoretical foundation, Sarangi refers to Bateson (1972) and Jakobson (1960): Bateson maintains the inseparability of "thought/cognition" and "feeling/emotion" (cf. Sarangi 2003: 166), and Jakobson's six functions of language (referential, poetic, emotive, conative, phatic, and metalinguistic) can be understood as continuous configurations between the two poles of "informational" and "affective" functions of stance (cf. Sarangi 2003: 167).

Martin (2000, 2003) considers judgment, appreciation, and affect as the three aspects of *appraisal* (a term which can be viewed as a subtype of stance), in which each aspect is described as "attitudes about character, designed to sanction or proscribe behavior" (i.e., judgment, e.g., 'It was *kind* of him to do that'), "attitudes about texts, performances and natural phenomena" (i.e., appreciation, e.g., 'I consider it *innovative*'), and "emotion" (i.e., affect, e.g., 'I feel very *happy*') (2003: 173). It is interesting that Martin considers the former two aspects (i.e., judgment and appreciation) as "institutionalized" affect, suggesting that emotion or feelings are fundamentally inherent in any enactment of stance. Du Bois and Kärkkäinen (2012: 442) corroborate this view, arguing that affect exhibits "a pervasive presence in the field of stance, constituting an always-imminent potential."

Du Bois and Kärkkäinen take the position that the ultimate goal for scholars should not be to identify and classify types of stance (Du Bois 2007; Du Bois & Kärkkäinen 2012); instead of such "disjunctive" definitions of stance, what we need is a "prototype" definition of stance (Du Bois & Kärkkäinen 2012), and this is what stance theory as integrated in the stance triangle (see Section 3) is aimed at.

Acknowledging the above-mentioned complexity of the functions of stance, we can roughly divide stance types into *epistemic* and *affective* (Du Bois 2007; Jaffe 2009b; Ochs 1996). Biber and Finegan (1989: 93) espouse this classification as they note "(t)he linguistic expression of attitude has been studied under two main topics: evidentiality and affect," where "attitude" and "evidentiality" could be paraphrased as "stance" and "epistemicity," respectively. In addition, as they further argue that stance should be conceived of as "the lexical and grammatical expression of attitudes, feelings, judgments, or commitment concerning the propositional content of a message" (p. 93), such "lexical and grammatical" displays of stance will be presented in the next two subsections for epistemic stance (2.1) and affective stance (2.2), followed by another subsection that presents the prosodic, paralinguistic, and bodily devices of stance display (2.3).

## 2.1 Epistemic stance

Epistemic stance concerns speakers' knowledge about and commitment to the stance object. Jaffe (2009b: 7) describes it as "speakers' degree of certainty about their propositions." Since stance is a public act whose representations are observable and interpretable to speech participants as well as to analysts (Du Bois 2007; Englebretson 2007b), one primary concern of stance researchers is the way stance is publicly displayed, in conjunction with how stance forms are encoded in a language system (Stubbs 1986).

Linguistic resources for epistemic stance are analyzed in a variety of lexical and grammatical forms for evaluation, subjectivity, evidentiality, discourse modality, *discourse stance* (Berman 2004, 2008; Berman, Ragnarsdóttir & Strömqvist 2002), and *interactive stance* (Ginzburg 2012). Studies examine stance indexes of nouns and adjectives (Hunston & Sinclair 2000), adverbials (Biber & Finegan 1988, 1989; Conrad & Biber 2000; Downing 2002), and mood/modality markers (Fairclough 2003; Halliday 1994; Hodge & Kress 1988). Hodge and Kress (1988) survey speakers' modality with respect to the propositional truth value (see Thompson & Hunston 2000, for a detailed review of the studies of English modals).

Epistemic stance has been examined with respect to its forms and function, not only for English (Field 1997; Hyland & Tse 2005; Kärkkäinen 2003, 2006, 2007, 2012a, 2012b; Keisanen 2007; Precht 2003; Scheibman 2002; Thompson & Mulac 1991), but also for other languages, including Finnish (Rauniomaa 2007), Italian (Rocci 2012), Dutch and French (Berman, Ragnarsdóttir & Strömqvist 2002), Indonesian (Englebretson 2007a), Japanese (Hayano 2011; Maynard 1993), Mandarin Chinese (Endo 2013; Wu 2004), Western Samoan (Ochs 1986, 1988, 1992), Tzotzil (Haviland 1989), Sakapultek (Shoaps 2007), and cross-linguistically (Clancy, Akatsuka & Strauss 1997). Furthermore, epistemic stance has been investigated in various discourse contexts: narrative discourse (Mushin 2001), argumentative discourse (C. Goodwin 2006; Haviland 1989; Lempert 2008; Rocci 2012), assessment sequences of agreement (Heritage & Raymond 2005), reported speech (Clift 2006), political discourse (Lempert 2009), jurisdictional discourse (Matoesian 2005), wedding counseling discourse (Shoaps 2004), authorial discourse (Hunston & Thompson 2000), and interactional academic discourse (Hyland 2005).

Linguistic resources for expressing epistemic stance are not limited to lexical items such as adjectives and adverbs; they may take the form of grammaticized or conventionalized constructions or *fragments* (Kärkkäinen 2003, 2007, 2012a; Rauniomaa 2007). Such epistemic constructions are examined for the English expressions 'I don't know' (Scheibman 2000), 'I think' (Kärkkäinen 2003), 'I thought' (Kärkkäinen 2012a), 'I guess' (Kärkkäinen 2007), 'that' constructions (Hyland & Tse 2005), the Finnish expressions *minun mielestä* ('in my opinion') and *minusta* ('I think') (Rauniomaa 2007) and extraposition (Laury 2012). In addition, analyzing what is generally treated as complement constructions in English conversation, Thompson (2002: 136) argues that these grammatical constructions "are not biclausal constructions with matrix assertive predicates and their clausal complements, but are rather best seen as monoclausal utterances." That is, what are generally analyzed as subordinate clauses should be regarded as "epistemic/evidential/evaluative formulaic fragments" which display speakers' stance toward the content of a clause. This argument attributes the pervasiveness of "the subjective nature of ordinary conversation" (p. 140) to the driving force for grammaticization of formulaic expressions, implying that local stance acts have consequences for change in the language system, which conforms to the aforementioned usage-based approaches to grammar (Bybee 2006, 2007, 2010; Scheibman 2000).

From the perspective of the organization of conversation, the second speaker's epistemic stance has been analyzed as *listener stance*, as displayed in response tokens (Gardner 2001), as resistance to the first speaker's *epistemic authority* in assessment sequences (Heritage & Raymond 2005), as congruent alignment display in assessment sequences (M. H. Goodwin 1998, 2006), and as challenge toward the prior speaker's turn (Keisanen 2007).

### 2.2 Affective stance

Affective stance concerns speakers' "emotional states" (Jaffe 2009b: 7), or more specifically, "a mood, attitude, feeling and disposition, as well as degrees of emotional intensity vis-à-vis some focus of concern" (Ochs 1996: 410). Affect is sometimes referred to as *empathy* (Kuno 1987), *emotion* (Bolinger 1986; M. H. Goodwin, Cekaite & C. Goodwin 2012; M. H. Goodwin & C. Goodwin 2000; Peräkylä & Sorjonen 2012), and *feelings* (Besnier 1989; Ochs 1986). Research on affect reveals how participants align their affect with their co-participants to organize interaction in social life (Besnier 1990, 1992; C. Goodwin 2007b; Haviland 1989; Kärkkäinen & Du Bois 2012; Ochs 1989; Park 2011). Since "evaluation is tied to affect" (Du Bois & Kärkkäinen 2012: 437), affective stance is often investigated in conjunction with epistemic stance (Biber & Finegan 1989; Ochs 1996; Precht 2003).

Affective stance is explored in mother-child interaction in language socialization (Clancy 1999; Ochs 1996; Ochs & Schieffelin 1989; Painter 2003). For instance, in line with Ochs and Schieffelin (1989), who argue for *social referencing*, whereby affective information is gathered, Clancy (1999) analyzes how a child's socialization of affect is constituted by focusing on the Japanese affective lexical item *kowai* ('be scary/be afraid (of)'). Painter (2003) takes the appraisal approach of systemic-functional linguistics to examine a child's affective language and argues that this *protolanguage* stage of language development is to be understood as a system where affect is semioticized.

### 2.3 Stance-displaying devices beyond lexis and grammar

Since stance can be "a physical act," exemplified with a judo posture as it is explained by a judo master (Englebretson 2007b: 7–8), it is natural that semiotic devices of stance-display extend beyond lexical and grammatical forms to multimodal resources of embodied movements and positioning (C. Goodwin 2006, 2007a, 2007b; M. H. Goodwin 1998, 2006; M. H. Goodwin & Alim 2010), to acoustic and prosodic features

(Couper-Kuhlen 2012; Macken-Horarik & Martin 2003), and even to *resonance* (Du Bois 2014), a relational configuration across utterances.

M. H. Goodwin (2006: 206) claims that "(n)ot only what one says, but also how one positions the body, can display a participant's terms of engagement." M. H. Goodwin (2006) examines how adolescent girls engaged in gossip display their feelings of disdain and ridicule by embodied affective stance resources such as handclaps, hand movements, and gestures, in addition to linguistic resources. Conversely, when the girls show their *united stance* to emotionally align with their co-participants, they use handclaps and overlapping speech as affective stance displays. Here, the use of the same resource of handclaps used for opposite affective stances (i.e., convergent and divergent) suggests an *indirect indexicality* between symbolic form and social meaning, which has been claimed as well for identity display (Eckert 2008; Silverstein 1985). Similarly, M. H. Goodwin & Alim (2010) analyze neck rolls, eye rolls, and teeth sucks performed by preadolescent girls as resources for the affective display of a mocking stance. Matoesian (2005) also demonstrates a series of physical devices for the expression of *embodied stance* in his analysis of jurisdictional discourse.

Prosody is another significant multimodal resource for conveying stance. Drawing on Halliday (1981), who argues for the significance of prosody for expressing interpersonal meanings, studies of appraisal seek to describe the prosodic displays of evaluation (Macken-Horarik & Martin 2003). Couper-Kuhlen (2012) and Reber (2012) both focus on *affectivity*, the affective aspect of stance, as conveyed through the prosodic features in English conversation. Along this line are works by Kärkkäinen (2012b) on conversational digressions, and Tainio (2012) on taking an emotionally charged critical stance in classroom interaction.

Furthermore, stance may be displayed by (*dialogic*) *resonance*, defined as "the catalytic activation of affinities across utterances" (Du Bois 2014: 360). Resonance as a form of signaling the intersubjective alignment in dialogic interaction has been investigated as indexing a second story (Siromaa 2012). From a sociocognitive point of view, Du Bois, Hobson & Hobson (2014) analyze the capacity for producing *frame resonance* (one type of dialogic resonance which particularly concerns interactional framing) by adolescents with autism in interview speech. This sort of framing function of stance is also examined as *humorous stance* in the telling of humorous personal anecdotes (Norrick 1993), *joking stance* (Oropeza-Escobar 2011), and *play stance* (Takanashi 2004, 2011). The stance that shapes the contextual organization of humor, joking, and play is better understood as both epistemic and affective: epistemic for the cognitive apprehension of the contextual orientation, and affective for the pleasant emotional states, as represented by *affect keys* (Gumperz 1977; Ochs & Schieffelin 1989). In these works, signals of stance typically go beyond the lexis and grammar to include multimodal devices such as laughter, dramatic prosody, smiling voice quality, and embodied movements.

## 3. The stance triangle

What exactly does it mean to take a stance? Here we introduce Du Bois' (2007) definition of stance, as it captures an overall theoretical conceptualization of stance:

> Stance is a public act by a social actor, achieved dialogically through overt communicative means, of simultaneously evaluating objects, positioning subjects (self and others), and aligning with other subjects, with respect to any salient dimension of the sociocultural field. (Du Bois 2007: 163)

For Du Bois, stancetaking in its simplest sense encompasses a set of three entities: *first subject*, *second subject*, and *stance object*. Additionally, stancetaking comprises a set of three simultaneous co-acts (or sub-acts) of the overarching act of stancetaking: ***evaluation***, ***positioning***, and ***alignment***. Each co-act can be characterized as ***objective*** (evaluation), ***subjective*** (positioning), and ***intersubjective*** (alignment). Du Bois notes that these three co-acts are not isolated from each other. Rather they are to be construed as closely interconnected and operationalized together, representing "simply different aspects of a single stance act" (p. 163). In other words, they are "the three-in-one subsidiary acts" (p. 164) of stancetaking, which is "a triune act, or tri-act" (p. 162). Stancetaking should be regarded as a social action situated and contextualized in the real world that carries actual social values, processes, and consequences (Du Bois 2007; Englebretson 2007b; Jaffe 2009b).

The dynamics of stancetaking can be represented by a diagram called the *stance triangle* (see Figure 1).

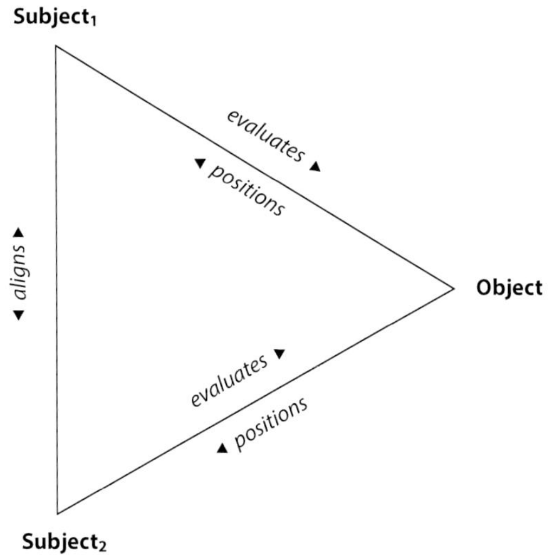


**Figure 1.** The stance triangle. (Du Bois 2007: 163)

Du Bois' stance triangle provides scholars an analytical tool for grasping the entire picture of the stancetaking act, calling attention to the necessity of the co-act of *alignment*, whereby intersubjectivity is achieved. The alignment aspect of stancetaking has often been either neglected or merely assumed without being explicitly pointed out. Without alignment, and in turn, intersubjectivity, no stance act is complete. The stance triangle is noteworthy in adding the ***intersubjective*** dimension of stancetaking to stance research, which had been primarily concerned with the evaluative and ***subjective*** aspects of stance. In the following subsections, each co-act will be explained in order with reference to the relevant literature on stance. There are two points that call for attention: (1) the distribution of the literature into each stancetaking dimension of evaluation, positioning, or alignment, is not intended to be rigid, and nor should it be; for, as mentioned earlier, the three dimensions of stancetaking are inextricably intertwined, and therefore, it is often the case that the literature introduced under one dimension also pertains to (an)other dimension(s), and (2) as addressed earlier in Section 1, much of the research introduced in this article should be considered as relevant to the present conceptualization of "stance" rather than "stance research" per se; each study should be fundamentally regarded in light of the original term and concept as meant by each scholar.

### 3.1 Evaluation

The first co-act of stancetaking is *evaluation*, which refers to "the process whereby a stancetaker orients to an object of stance and characterizes it as having some specific quality or value" (Du Bois 2007: 143). In the stance triangle (Figure 1), this act is illustrated on the two sides that connect either first or second subject to an object, filling one direction of the vector oriented to the object. Evaluation serves as the basis of stancetaking; without this objective act, no subjective act, and in turn, no intersubjective act can occur. In performing this act, stancetakers evaluate the *stance object*, which encompasses a range of entities including not only things but also persons (stancetakers, co-participants, third parties, etc.), propositions, speech acts (including stances), and so on. Examples (1) and (2) illustrate that the speaker evaluates the object of stance ('that') as 'horrible' and 'nasty,' respectively.

(1) PETE; That's horrible.

(2) KEVIN; @that's @nasty.

(Du Bois 2007: 142, the symbol "@" denotes laughter)

Although the objective aspect of stancetaking is singled out here under the label of evaluation for analytical convenience, evaluation as used in previous research is often entailed in the (inter)subjective properties of stance, as will be presented in the next two subsections. This is simply because "subjectivity takes an object" (Du Bois 2007:

156). Accordingly, it may be appropriate here to introduce the literature on subjectivity, as it is often called, which particularly focuses on the evaluative dimension of the stance triangle.

Subjectivity lies at the foundation of the concept of language in use (Benveniste 1971; Lyons 1981, 1994, as discussed in Englebretson 2007b). Lyons (1994: 13) suggests that *locutionary subjectivity* is immanent in any locutional act performed by a *locutionary agent. Point of view/viewpoint* and *perspective/perspectivization* are often used as well to refer to the omnipresent subjective nature of language practice. Chafe (1994: 132) argues, for instance, that a conversational topic is "verbalized from some point of view." Likewise, Ensink & Sauer (2003a: 2) claim that "'(p)erspective' refers to the fact that the content of a discourse necessarily is 'displayed' from some point of view" (emphasis in original).

Taken this way, the area of subjectivity is quite broad; therefore, studies have become more attuned to precisely what subjectivity is taken to be, and terms other than subjectivity, such as *evaluation* and *stance*, have been often employed to refer to a more specific kind of subjectivity oriented toward a more specific stance object, i.e., subjectivity "with a focus" (Englebretson 2007b: 16). The research on evaluation (Biber & Finegan 1988, 1989) and *appraisal*, as it is termed in systemic-functional linguistics (Macken-Horarik & Martin 2003; Martin 2000; Martin & White 2005), is particularly concerned with the evaluative aspect of subjectivity, although it naturally pertains to the positioning aspect of subjectivity for the reasons presented above.

## 3.2 Positioning

The second co-act of stancetaking is *positioning*, which may be construed as the subjective dimension of the stancetaking act. It is defined as "the act of situating a social actor with respect to responsibility for stance and for invoking sociocultural value" (Du Bois 2007: 143). Positioning is enacted as stancetakers take up their position vis-à-vis the stance object, thereby committing themselves to the social action of stancetaking. This co-act is located on each side of the stance triangle (Figure 1) that connects the object back to either first or second subject, proceeding along the opposite vector to that of evaluation on the same side. In the examples below, the use of the first person pronoun 'I' makes it explicit that the speaker is locating his position as to his evaluation of the stance object, either epistemically (3) or affectively (4).

(3) DAN; ... I don't know.

(4) LANCE; I'm glad.

(Du Bois 2007: 143)

Since the 1970s and 1980s, the understanding of "subjectivity with a focus" (whose evaluative aspect has been mentioned in 3.1), or stance, has been attracting much attention from linguists, in discourse-functional linguistics (Cornillie 2008; Field 1997; Scheibman 2002), cognitive linguistics (Athanasiadou, Canakis & Cornillie 2006b; Fillmore 1977; Langacker 1985; MacWhinney 1977), social psychology (Davies & Harré 1990), semantics (Lemke 1998), historical linguistics (Traugott 1989), linguistic anthropology (Kockelman 2004), and conversation analysis (C. Goodwin 2006; C. Goodwin & M. H. Goodwin 1992; Heritage 2002; Heritage & Raymond 2005; Pomerantz 1984).

In Langacker's work on cognitive grammar (1985, 1987, 1999; *inter alia*), subjectivity is a key element for the *scene construal* processed in human cognition, and is thus attributed to the cognitive organization of language structure (discussed in Englebretson 2007b). The attempt to shed light on the cognitive motivation for the formation of language expressions of stance is also observed in the research on historical linguistics or grammaticization (Hopper & Traugott 2003; Traugott 1989; Traugott & Heine 1991).

Examining discourse data, studies in discourse-functional, systemic-functional, and corpus linguistics grapple with subjectivity to elucidate its lexical, grammatical, and textual patterning in language use (Athanasiadou 2007; Bednarek 2006; Chafe 1986, 1994; Channell 2000; Cornillie 2008; Downing 2002; Englebretson ed. 2007; Field 1997; Fitzmaurice 2004; Gardner 2001; Hunston 2007; Hunston & Thompson 2000; Hyland & Tse 2005; Iwasaki & Yap 2015; Kärkkäinen 2003; Labov & Waletzky 1967; Linde 1997; Martin & White 2005; Maynard 1993; Onodera & Suzuki 2007; Page 2003; Precht 2003; Scheibman 2002, 2007; Wu 2004). These studies are generally concerned with how subjectivity is encoded in the language system. Typically taking the approach of grammaticization, they examine a wide range of language forms from modals/modality to lexis such as adjectives and adverbials, and to syntactic and discourse structures.

To take an example, Scheibman (2002) analyzes a corpus of American English conversation and demonstrates that language forms which involve speaker's subjectivity (or point of view) are subject to frequent use, contributing to the formation of conventionalized expressions. Frequency is particularly an important factor for language patterning in corpus linguistics and usage-based linguistics (Bybee 2006, 2007, 2010; Scheibman 2000), which often take a quantitative as well as a qualitative approach to examine the function of language form in context.

Many of these studies of subjectivity are implicitly or explicitly related to intersubjectivity. For instance, within the scope of systemic-functional linguistics, Martin (2003) foregrounds the intersubjective property of social evaluation. In the same special issue, White (2003) presents a dialogic view of *intersubjective stance* displayed by modality markers in his corpus of written journalistic commentary.

Another strand of work on stance includes sociocultural and interactional linguistics, linguistic anthropology, and conversation analysis. Since these disciplines attend to the interactional and social aspects of language use, intersubjectivity is naturally assumed, even though it may not be directly addressed (Englebretson ed. 2007; Jaffe 2009c; Kockelman 2004). As an example, Jaffe (2009b: 3) defines stancetaking as "taking up a position with respect to the form or the content of one's utterance." Jaffe further elaborates on positionality that it is taken toward not only "words and texts" but also "interlocutors and audiences" (p. 4). In a sociocultural context, one's positionality takes another party's positionality to be adequately located in the social field. This phenomenon depicts the co-act of alignment coordinated between multiple social actors' subjectivity, i.e., intersubjectivity.

## 3.3 Alignment

The third co-act of stancetaking is *alignment*, "the act of calibrating the relationship between two stances, and by implication between two stancetakers" (Du Bois 2007: 144). In the stance triangle (Figure 1), this co-act is indicated in the mutual orientations of the vector on the vertical side which connects first and second subjects. Alignment represents the stance property of intersubjectivity, that is, "the relation between one actor's subjectivity and another's" (Du Bois 2007: 140). In other words, intersubjectivity enacted by alignment links subjectivities taken by individual subjects, thereby accomplishing the act of stancetaking.

Alignment allows social actors to situate themselves in relation to each other in the matrix of socially meaningful contexts. The intersubjective, and therefore, interactional and relational, nature of stancetaking is also underscored in Englebretson (2007b), M. H. Goodwin (2006), and Scheibman (2007). M. H. Goodwin (2006: 191) notes: "A first speaker offers an assessment, which establishes a field for agreement, disagreement, or adjustment in next utterances." In this quote, assessment may be construed as stance.

Consider (5), which exemplifies how the second subject in a dialogic engagement aligns her subjectivity in relation to the first subject (line 3).

| | | | |
|---|---|---|---|
| (5) | 1 | SAM; | I don't like those; |
| | 2 | | (0.2) |
| | 3 | ANGELA; | I don't either. |

(Du Bois 2007: 159)

In (5), the two interlocutors are taking stances toward their common stance object, namely, the *shared stance object*, which "becomes the cornerstone of the dialogic construction of intersubjectivity" (Du Bois 2007: 159). Although the shared stance object 'those' (line 1), in addition to the stance predicate 'like' (line 1), is linguistically omitted in Angela's utterance (which constitutes what Du Bois (2007: 161) terms a *stance follow*, a counterpart to a *stance lead*, as realized in Sam's utterance in line 1, in the dynamics of dialogic and intersubjective stance pairing), it is understood that the two stancetakers are expressing their stances toward the shared stance object referred to as 'those' in Sam's stance lead. Resonating with Sam's stance lead, as we see in the linguistic representation of the parallel syntactic structure, and adding an adverbial 'either,' Angela's stance follow utterance (line 3) indicates her convergent stance with Sam's toward the shared stance object. Angela's stance alignment clearly reveals intersubjectivity, as achieved by way of interactional positioning of subjectivity in coordination with the previously displayed stance by a dialogic partner.

Linguists who investigate stance phenomena have primarily devoted themselves to demonstrating the linguistic markers of stance. As an example of a stance marker, the adverbial 'either,' as we saw in (5), is used almost obligatorily in English stance follow, in parallel with its preceding stance lead (Du Bois 2007). This becomes evident when we compare (5) with (6), which lacks a linguistic marker of intersubjectivity.

(6) is an excerpt drawn from a conversation in an interview context between speaker I (interviewer) and speaker P (interviewee, an adolescent with autism). In this example, the adverbial 'too' (instead of 'either,' due to its affirmative syntactic structure) that indexes the intersubjective convergent stance alignment is absent in speaker P's stance follow: P says 'I do,' instead of the normally expected 'I do too.' The lack of a conventionalized English intersubjective stance marker makes this utterance sound somewhat awkward.

(6) I: I like the Burglar Bill one.
P: I do. (Du Bois, Hobson & Hobson 2014: 434)

Du Bois, Hobson and Hobson argue that, although in this case the interview setting between strangers might have caused uneasiness to speaker P, speakers with autism "often failed to assimilate this [= some kind of linguistic frame they pick up from the interviewer] to their own stance in order to provide a coherent expansion of their own" (Du Bois, Hobson & Hobson 2014: 434). That is to say, they often failed to engage with their co-participant intersubjectively within the *interactive frame* (Tannen & Wallat 1993) at hand. This point suggests the significance of alignment and its linguistic representation for a successful stancetaking interaction.

Alignment in Du Bois' discussion of stancetaking should be regarded as encompassing different orientations, i.e., parallel, opposed, or orthogonal (Du Bois 2014: 360), as well as various degrees with respect to intersubjective positionality between stancetakers. Therefore, alignment does not merely mean the speakers' convergent, congruent, or assimilating positioning. Rather, it should be understood as constituting a scalar continuum from convergent to divergent at the oppositional poles, with many points in between, including the (ostensibly) neutral point. From this perspective, what is often distinguished as "disalignment" is considered one point on the alignment continuum.

### 3.4 Previous research on stance alignment

What follows is a cursory overview of research on stance whose approach is primarily intersubjective and interactional. In the contemporary literature, the intersubjective dimension of stance is highlighted in discourse-functional linguistics (Cornillie 2008; Du Bois, Hobson & Hobson 2014; Fitzmaurice 2004; Kärkkäinen 2006; Kärkkäinen & Du Bois 2012; Onodera & Suzuki 2007; Scheibman 2007; Verhagen 2005), systemic-functional linguistics (White 2003), sociocultural linguistics (M. H. Goodwin 1998, 2006; M. H. Goodwin & Alim 2010; Johnstone 2007, 2009; Oropeza-Escobar 2011; Park 2011, 2013; Shoaps 2009), and conversation analysis (C. Goodwin & M. H. Goodwin 1992; Heritage & Raymond 2005). These studies describe the semiotic resources and operationalization of stance for the organization of conversation and sociocognitive/sociocultural life.

The above-illustrated upsurge of stance research since the beginning of the 21st century, especially in discourse-functional and sociocultural linguistics, is evident in edited books (Englebretson ed. 2007; Hunston & Thompson 2000; Jaffe 2009c) and special issues of journals (Berman 2004; Iwasaki & Yap 2015; Kärkkäinen & Du Bois 2012; Macken-Horarik & Martin 2003) on stance. In addition, a special issue of *Pragmatics* (Takanashi & Park 2011) regards stance as one key concept for understanding *frame* (Bateson 1972; Goffman 1974, 1981; Gumperz 1982; Tannen 1993), combined with Goffman's notion of *footing* (1974, 1979, 1981). The notion of footing in conjunction with intersubjectivity is also explored in Szatrowski (2007).

Despite the fact that the explosion of studies on the intersubjectivity of stance is relatively recent, scholars were aware of the prominence of intersubjectivity for the study of language before the turn of the 21st century (Bruner 1986; Bühler 1934; Schutz 1962; Vygotsky 1986). Such burgeoning of the research inquiry into intersubjectivity is observed in a variety of research paradigms such as cognitive linguistics (Tomasello 1999), language acquisition and socialization (Clancy 1999; Ochs 1988), referentiality (Hanks 1990), reflexivity (Lucy 1993), and affect (Besnier 1990; Ochs 1986, 1989; *inter alia*).

## 4. Contextualization of stance: The local-global nexus

While the fundamental mechanisms of stancetaking can be modeled in the stance triangle (Du Bois 2007), the operationalization of stance in the dynamics of social interaction can be complex. For instance, there may be an act of stancetaking which involves more than two subjects. Yet the stance triangle is still serviceable to accommodate such variability. The stance triangle is designed to be "deployed" for the analysis of actual interaction to "clarify the array of entities and sociocognitive relations that are activated, constituted, and brought into relation to each other by a particular stance action" (Du Bois 2007: 170).

Research on stance in natural discourse has blossomed in the last couple of decades, showing that stance is not only pivotal to local contextualization but also to global contextualization, both of which, hand in hand, constitute the value systems of a given *community of practice* (Eckert and McConnell-Ginet 2011).

### 4.1 The local context: Dialogicality and sequentiality

We have seen in 3.3 that the alignment co-act of stancetaking is crucial to the enactment of intersubjectivity. From the local contextual point of view, this form of engagement is intimately linked with dialogicality and sequentiality, both of which are the interactional dimensions of contextualization achieved in part by stancetaking. Of the two, sequentiality is particularly salient in conversation and other forms of natural discourse which unfold in real time.

Dialogicality is a major characteristic of stance because stance typically occurs in "pairs" in dialogic relations. In other words, "the stance utterance of a subsequent speaker is constituted as carrying a close analogy to the stance utterance of a prior speaker" (Du Bois 2007: 140). Bakhtin (1981) suggests that dialogicality is immanent in any utterance that potentially inhabits *heteroglossia* or *multivocality*, in which multiple *voices* are dialogically layered. The issue of heteroglossia is pursued in Macken-Horarik and Martin (2003) from the perspective of stance (or what they term appraisal/evaluation). Although Bakhtin formulates the idea of dialogicality primarily through his analysis of literary texts, Voloshinov considers dialogicality in the context of speech:

> In point of fact, word is a two-sided act. It is determined equally by whose word it is and for whom it is meant. As word, it is precisely the product of the reciprocal relationship between speaker and listener, addresser and addressee. Each and every word expresses the 'one' in relation to the "other" [emphasis in original].
>
> (Voloshinov 1973: 85–86, quoted in Sarangi 2003: 166)

Goffman (1974, 1979, 1981) relates the notion of dialogicality to *footing* (and its related notions of *participant roles/performance roles/participation frameworks*) or *frame* (also Bateson 1972), that is, the way speech participants organize the speech activity at hand as joint work by *keying* (or displaying) their alignment with one another. Ahearn (2017: 37) posits that *shifts/changes in footing* (Goffman 1981) often index changes in speakers' stance. C. Goodwin (2007a, 2007b), M. H. Goodwin (1998), and Damari (2010) offer insights as to how stance is deployed for the organization of footing in interaction. For contextual or discourse framing (Tannen 1993), the dynamic and intersubjective alignment of speakers' stance in the on-going context is essential (Jaffe 2009b), despite the fact that many studies along this line only imply the notion of stance without making it explicit. Takanashi (2004, 2011) and Takanashi &

Park (2011) exemplify framing and articulate the fundamental link between framing and stance. Takanashi (2004, 2011) argues that stancetaking in conversational play is indispensable for *play framing* and is indexed by a set of *play stance indices* (Takanashi 2004), reminiscent of *contextualization cues* (Gumperz 1982, 1992) that specifically index a play context. Similarly, Park & Takanashi (2011) regard stance as one of the primary ingredients of interactional framing.

Sequentiality is another key concept that is illuminated in the analyses of local contextualization of stance. Research on stance and related notions that deals with language interaction seeks to reveal the process whereby participants' stance is sequentially negotiated for the collaborative construction of talk (C. Goodwin & M. H. Goodwin 1992; Haddington 2007; Heritage 2002; Kärkkäinen 2007; Keisanen 2007; Rauniomaa 2007; Takanashi 2004).

Dialogicality and sequentiality are separate but interconnected notions necessary for the local contextualization of stancetaking. Because of the linear nature of conversation, each local dialogic engagement of stancetaking accrues to formulate a stretch of interactional stance sequence, generating *stance accretion* (Du Bois 2002; Rauniomaa 2003), which is consequential to social life (Du Bois 2007; Englebretson 2007b; Haddington 2007; Jaffe 2009b; Keisanen 2007; Rauniomaa 2007; Takanashi 2011).

As for dialogicality and sequentiality, dialogicality may be construed as a broader notion because it involves contextual relations or intertextuality between two contexts that are not only immediate but also remote, within a single text or across multiple texts in which the prior utterance may have occurred some days or even years ago. Regardless of such specific properties of each, however, dialogicality and sequentiality are both key to the local contextualization of stance, which is embedded in, and thus closely tied to, the global contexts of stance.

## 4.2 The global context: Indexicality and consequences

From a global point of view, stancetaking can elucidate how social reality is constructed through linguistic practices, especially in sociolinguistics and linguistic anthropology, where indexicality and consequences are of special interest.

The importance of context for stancetaking, among other socially salient linguistic performance, presupposes an indexical field (Jakobson 1971; Peirce 1933; Silverstein 1976) charged with sociocultural values. These sociocultural values are indexed and reproduced by the use of stance displays (Clift 2006; Du Bois 2007; Englebretson 2007b; Jaffe 2009b; Kockelman 2004; Lempert 2008, 2009, 2012).

Since a stancetaker is a social actor who manipulates socially situated agency (Ahearn 2001), taking a stance means to perform a social action which attributes accountability, responsibility, or "ownership" to the stancetaker (Du Bois 2007: 173). Social agents have the capacity to negotiate, recreate, and constitute any social values that are invoked by stance resources by virtue of indexicality.

Language ideology is a system of such social values shared in a given community of practice. Jaffe (2009a) examines the construction of bilingual ideologies in classroom interaction between teachers and students in a Corsican school. Jaworski and Thurlow (2009) demonstrate how the ideology of elitism is shaped as elite tourists take an *elitist stance* thus differentiating themselves from "lay tourists." This case represents a particular case of *stance differential*, which highlights the difference between stances (Du Bois 2007: 166; Takanashi 2001) in a dramatic way. The notion of stance differential encompasses various degrees of differential between stances, on a scalar continuum from convergent to divergent. We can see stance differential even between considerably convergent stances as long as the two stances are exhibited by distinct agents, or by the same agent at different moments on the linear scale of temporality. In the case of Jaworski and Thurlow (2009), the stance differential is maximized to index the two contrastive ideological groups of people, i.e., elitists and laypeople.

Social morality is one dimension of language ideologies enacted via stancetaking. Shoaps (2007) observes modal particles in Sakapultek discourse where moral personhood is portrayed and ideologically formulated. Although not directly attending to stance Harrison (2011), adopting Goffman's (1974) notion of *performance roles*, analyzes social morality by studying how "culturally ideal personhood" is framed in Fulfulde personal narratives.

Identity is another central dimension of language ideology indexed and constructed in the course of stancetaking. Thus, "speakers position themselves and others as particular kinds of people" (Bucholtz & Hall 2005: 595) as they perform *tactics of intersubjectivity* (Bucholtz & Hall 2004). Drawing on Ochs (1992, 1993), Bucholtz and Hall (2005: 595) further argue that the context in which stancetaking takes place is the very site where identity is constructed, as speakers negotiate and (re)produce their identity by associating it to interactional stances by virtue of *indirect indexicality* between a given symbolic form and a certain identity (Eckert 2008; Silverstein 1985). Ochs directly calls attention to the significant role stance plays for identity construction, and in turn, for "the constitution of social life", when she writes:

> ----- linguistic structures that index epistemic and affective stances are the basic linguistic resources for constructing/realizing social acts and social identities. Epistemic and affective stance has, then, an especially privileged role in the constitution of social life.
>
> (Ochs 1996: 420)

A number of sociocultural studies endeavor to illuminate this connection between stancetaking and construction of identity: regional identity indexed by local dialect (Johnstone 2007), racial identity of "the white" and its associated power (Bucholtz 2010; Kiesling 2001), national identity (Damari 2010, 2012), and a community of special interests based on their activity (Stockburger 2015). Damari (2010) demonstrates how a binational couple displays *constructed stance* as they produce constructed dialogue to manipulate intertextuality, which builds their distinct identities from each other. As a way of presenting and reproducing identity, *style* or *stylization* is also explored from the perspective of stancetaking (Bucholtz 2009; M. H. Goodwin & Alim 2010; Johnstone 2009; Kiesling 2009; Park 2013). Such studies are particularly insightful for understanding the local-global nexus of contextualization through stancetaking, since they reveal how stylistic forms (linguistic and embodied) enacted in local contexts shape more enduring configurations of identity. The local alignment potentially expanding to a global patterning over time is also at the heart of *enregisterment* discussed by Agha (2005).

## 5. Summary and implications of stance

Taking a stance, then, is a social action interactionally achieved through overt symbolic displays (linguistic, prosodic, paralinguistic, and bodily) of evaluations (epistemic and affective) that are dialogically positioned between stancetakers. The stance triangle models how the stancetaking act intertwines three simultaneous co-acts (i.e., evaluation, positioning, and alignment, Du Bois 2007), each of which further represents the objective, subjective, and intersubjective property of a unified act of stancetaking.

Stance takes various forms and it is operationalized with certain functions in situated contexts, as we have seen for epistemic and affective stance. Nonetheless, we should bear in mind that stance is not always displayed explicitly. In fact, it is often the case that stance is left implicit where dialogic participants arrive at the comprehension of the implicit stance by conversational inferences (Gumperz 1977, 1982, 1992) and analogies "based on comparing the relevant stances" available either in the immediate context or in the repertoire of their sociocultural knowledge (Du Bois 2007: 144). Meanings thus conveyed, interpreted, and further reproduced through the linguistic practice of stancetaking are subject to negotiation between speech participants. This in turn suggests that it is a researchers' task to describe and elucidate what meanings, or more precisely, what kind and degree of stances, are conveyed in what manner in natural discourse, in conjunction with what consequences they bring to social life.

Stancetaking may be considered as one of the essential behaviors that are entextualized (Agha 2005; Bauman & Briggs 1990; Enfield & Levinson 2006; Silverstein 2003) through decontextualization, recontextualization, and precontextualization (Bauman & Briggs 1990; Du Bois 1986; Günthner 1999; Ochs 1992) because contextualization transcends time, connecting the present to the past and the future (Ochs 1992: 345). These aspects pertain to the intersubjective, dialogic, sequential, and indexical properties of stancetaking. Ultimately, stancetaking involves actual speakers (i.e., social actors) engaged in actual linguistic performances (i.e., social acts) in a given context which is intimately connected to larger sociocultural contexts via indexical relations. This is what makes stance research an important area in the study of language in use.

## References


Agha, Asif. 2005. "Voice, footing, enregisterment." *Journal of LinguisticAnthropology* 15(1): 38–59.

Ahearn, Laura M. 2001. "Language and agency." *Annual Review of Anthropology* 30: 109–137. https://doi.org/10.1146/annurev.anthro.30.1.109

Ahearn, Laura M. 2017. *Living Language: An Introduction to Linguistic Anthropology*, 2nd edition. Malden, MA: Blackwell.

Athanasiadou, Angeliki. 2007. "On the subjectivity of intensifiers." *Language Sciences* 29(4): 554–565. https://doi.org/10.1016/j.langsci.2007.01.009

Athanasiadou, Angeliki, Costas Canakis and Bert Cornillie. 2006a."Introduction." In *Subjectification: Various Paths to Subjectivity*, ed. by Angeliki Athanasiadou, Costas Canakis and Bert Cornillie, 1–13. Berlin: Mouton de Gruyter. https://doi.org/10.1515/9783110892970

Athanasiadou, Angeliki, Costas Canakis and Bert Cornillie (eds). 2006b. *Subjectification: Various Paths to Subjectivity*. Berlin: Mouton de Gruyter. https://doi.org/10.1515/9783110892970

Bakhtin, Mikhail M. 1981. *The Dialogic Imagination: Four Essays*, ed. by Michael Holquist, trans. by Caryl Emerson and Michael Holquist. Austin, TX: University of Texas Press.

Bateson, Gregory. 1972. *Steps to an Ecology of Mind: Collected Essays in Anthropology, Psychiatry, Evolution, and Epistemology*. San Francisco: Chandler.

Bauman, Richard and Charles L. Briggs. 1990. "Poetics and performance as critical perspectives on language and social life." *Annual Review of Anthropology* 19: 59–88. https://doi.org/10.1146/annurev.an.19.100190.000423

Bednarek, Monika. 2006. *Evaluation in Media Discourse: Analysis of a Newspaper Corpus*. New York: Continuum.

Benveniste, Émile. 1971. "Subjectivity in language." In *Problems in General Linguistics*, trans. by Mary E. Meek, 223–230. Coral Gables, FL:University of Miami Press.

Berman, Ruth A. 2008. "The psycholinguistics of developing text construction." *Journal of Child Language* 35(4): 735–771. https://doi.org/10.1017/S0305000908008787

Berman, Ruth A. (ed.). 2004. *Developing Discourse Stance across Adolescence*. Special issue of *Journal of Pragmatics* 37(2).

Berman, Ruth A., Hrafnhildur Ragnarsdóttir and Sven Strömqvist. 2002."Discourse stance: Written and spoken language." *Written Language and Literacy* 5(2): 255–289. https://doi.org/10.1075/wll.5.2.06ber

Besnier, Niko. 1989. "Literacy and feelings: The encoding of affect in Nukulaelae letters." *Text* 9(1): 69–92. https://doi.org/10.1515/text.1.1989.9.1.69

Besnier, Niko. 1990. "Language and affect." *Annual Review of Anthropology* 19: 419–451. https://doi.org/10.1146/annurev.an.19.100190.002223

Besnier, Niko. 1992. "Reported speech and affect on Nukulaelae Atoll." In *Responsibility and Evidence in Oral Discourse*, ed. by Jane H. Hill and Judith T. Irvine, 161–181. Cambridge: Cambridge University Press.

Biber, Douglas and Edward Finegan. 1988. "Adverbial stance types in English." *Discourse Processes* 11(1): 1–34. https://doi.org/10.1080/01638538809544689

Biber, Douglas and Edward Finegan. 1989. "Styles of stance in English: Lexical and grammatical marking of evidentiality and affect." *Text* 9(1): 93–124.

Bolinger, Dwight L. 1986. "Intonation and emotion." *Quaderni di Semantica* 7: 13–21.
Bruner, Jerome S. 1986. *Actual Minds, Possible Worlds. Cambridge*, MA: Harvard University Press.
Bucholtz, Mary. 2009. "From stance to style: Gender, interaction, and indexicality in Mexican immigrant youth slang." In *Stance: Sociolinguistic Perspectives*, ed. by Alexandra Jaffe, 146–170. New York: Oxford University Press. https://doi.org/10.1093/acprof:oso/9780195331646.003.0007
Bucholtz, Mary. 2010. *White Kids: Language, Race, and Styles of Youth Identity*. Cambridge: Cambridge University Press. https://doi.org/10.1017/CBO9780511975776
Bucholtz, Mary and Kira Hall. 2004. "Language and identity." In *A Companion to Linguistic Anthropology*, ed. by Alessandro Duranti, 369–394. Malden, MA: Blackwell.
Bucholtz, Mary and Kira Hall. 2005. "Identity and interaction: A sociocultural linguistic approach." *Discourse Studies* 7(4–5): 585–614. https://doi.org/10.1177/1461445605054407
Bühler, Karl. 1934. *Sprachtheorie: Die Darstellungsfunktion der Sprache*. Jena: Gustav Fischer Verlag.
Bybee, Joan. 2006. "From usage to grammar: The mind's response to repetition." *Language* 82(4): 711–733. https://doi.org/10.1353/lan.2006.0186
Bybee, Joan. 2007. *Frequency of Use and the Organization of Language*. New York: Oxford University Press. https://doi.org/10.1093/acprof:oso/9780195301571.001.0001
Bybee, Joan. 2010. *Language, Usage and Cognition*. Cambridge: Cambridge University Press. https://doi.org/10.1017/CBO9780511750526
Chafe, Wallace L. 1986. "Evidentiality in English conversation and academic writing." In *Evidentiality: The Linguistic Coding of Epistemology*, ed. by Wallace L. Chafe and Johanna Nichols, 261–272. Norwood, NJ: Ablex.
Chafe, Wallace L. 1994. *Discourse, Consciousness, and Time: The Flow and Displacement of Conscious Experience in Speaking and Writing*. Chicago: University of Chicago Press.
Channell, Joanna. 2000. "Corpus-based analysis of evaluative lexis." In *Evaluation in Text: Authorial Stance and the Construction of Discourse*, ed. by Susan Hunston and Geoff Thompson, 38–55. New York: Oxford University Press.
Clancy, Patricia M. 1999. "The socialization of affect in Japanese mother-child conversation." *Journal of Pragmatics* 31: 1397–1421. https://doi.org/10.1016/S0378-2166(98)00112-X
Clancy, Patricia M., Noriko Akatsuka and Susan Strauss. 1997. "Deontic modality and conditionality in discourse: A cross-linguistic study of adult speech to young children." In *Directions in Functional Linguistics*, ed. by Akio Kamio, 19–57. Amsterdam: John Benjamins. https://doi.org/10.1075/slcs.36.05cla
Clift, Rebecca. 2006. "Indexing stance: Reported speech as an interactional evidential." *Journal of Sociolinguistics* 10(5): 569–595. https://doi.org/10.1111/j.1467-9841.2006.00296.x
Conrad, Susan and Douglas Biber. 2000. "Adverbial marking of stance in speech and writing." In *Evaluation in Text: Authorial Stance and the Construction of Discourse*, ed. by Susan Hunston and Geoff Thompson, 56–73. New York: Oxford University Press.
Cornillie, Bert. 2008. "On the grammaticalization and (inter)subjectivity of evidential (semi-)auxiliaries in Spanish." In *Theoretical and Empirical Issues in Grammaticalization*, ed. by Elena Seoane and María J. López-Couso, 55–76. Amsterdam: John Benjamins.
Couper-Kuhlen, Elizabeth. 2012. "On affectivity and preference in responses to rejection." *Text & Talk* 32(4): 453–475. https://doi.org/10.1515/text-2012-0022
Damari, Rebecca R. 2010. "Intertextual stancetaking and the local negotiation of cultural identities by a binational couple." *Journal of Sociolinguistics* 14(5): 609–629. https://doi.org/10.1111/j.1467-9841.2010.00456.x
Damari, Rebecca R. 2012. Stancetaking as Identity Work: The Case of Mixed American Israeli Couples. Ph.D. dissertation. Linguistics Department, Georgetown University, Washington, D.C.

Dancygier, Barbara and Eve Sweetser (eds). 2012. *Viewpoint in Language: A Multimodal Perspective.* Cambridge: Cambridge University Press. https://doi.org/10.1017/CBO9781139084727

Davies, Bronwyn and Rom Harré. 1990. "Positioning: Conversation and the production of selves." *Journal of the Theory of Social Behavior* 20: 43–63. https://doi.org/10.1111/j.1468-5914.1990.tb00174.x

DeLancey, Scott. 1981. "An interpretation of split ergativity and related patterns." *Language* 57: 626–657. https://doi.org/10.2307/414343

Downing, Angela. 2002. "'Surely you knew!': Surely as a marker of evidentiality and stance." *Functions of Language* 8(2): 251–282. https://doi.org/10.1075/fol.8.2.05dow

Du Bois, John W. 1986. "Self-evidence and ritual speech." In *Evidentiality: The Linguistic Coding of Epistemology*, ed. by Wallace L. Chafe and Johanna Nichols, 313–336. Norwood, NJ: Ablex.

Du Bois, John W. 2002. "Stance and consequence." Paper presented at the Annual Meeting of the American Anthropological Association, New Orleans, LA, November 20–24.

Du Bois, John W. 2007. "The stance triangle." In *Stancetaking in Discourse: Subjectivity, Evaluation, Interaction*, ed. by Robert Englebretson, 139–182. Amsterdam: John Benjamins. https://doi.org/10.1075/pbns.164.07du

Du Bois, John W. 2014. "Towards a dialogic syntax." *Cognitive Linguistics* 25(3): 359–410.

Du Bois, John W. and Elise Kärkkäinen. 2012. "Taking a stance on emotion: Affect, sequence, and intersubjectivity in dialogic interaction." *Text & Talk* 32(4): 433–451. https://doi.org/10.1515/text-2012-0023

Du Bois, John W., R. Peter Hobson and Jessica A. Hobson. 2014. "Dialogic resonance and intersubjective engagement in autism." *Cognitive Linguistics* 25(3): 411–441.

Eckert, Penelope. 2008. "Variation and the indexical field." *Journal of Sociolinguistics* 12(4): 453–476. https://doi.org/10.1111/j.1467-9841.2008.00374.x

Eckert, Penelope and Sally McConnell-Ginet. 2011. "Communities of practice: Where language, gender, and power all live." In *Language and Gender: A Reader*, 2nd edition, ed. by Jennifer Coates and Pia Pichler, 573–582. Malden, MA: Blackwell.

Endo, Tomoko. 2013. "Epistemic stance in Mandarin conversation: The positions and functions of *wo juede* 'I think.'" In *Chinese Discourse and Interaction: Theory and Practice*, ed. by Yuling Pan and Daniel Kádár, 12–34. London: Equinox.

Enfield, Nicholas J. and Stephen C. Levinson. 2006. *Roots of Human Sociality: Culture, Cognition and Interaction*. Oxford: Berg.

Englebretson, Robert. 2007a. "Grammatical resources for social purposes: Some aspects of stancetaking in colloquial Indonesian conversation." In *Stancetaking in Discourse: Subjectivity, Evaluation, Interaction*, ed. by Robert Englebretson, 69–110. Amsterdam: John Benjamins. https://doi.org/10.1075/pbns.164.05eng

Englebretson, Robert. 2007b. "Stancetaking in discourse: An introduction." In *Stancetaking in Discourse: Subjectivity, Evaluation, Interaction*, ed. by Robert Englebretson, 1–25. Amsterdam: John Benjamins. https://doi.org/10.1075/pbns.164

Englebretson, Robert (ed.). 2007. *Stancetaking in Discourse: Subjectivity, Evaluation, Interaction.* Amsterdam: John Benjamins. https://doi.org/10.1075/pbns.164

Ensink, Titus and Christoph Sauer. 2003a. "Social-functional and cognitive approaches to discourse interpretation: The role of frame and perspective." In *Framing and Perspectivising in Discourse*, ed. by Titus Ensink and Christoph Sauer, 1–21. Amsterdam: John Benjamins. https://doi.org/10.1075/pbns.111.02ens

Ensink, Titus and Christoph Sauer (eds). 2003b. *Framing and Perspectivising in Discourse.* Amsterdam: John Benjamins. https://doi.org/10.1075/pbns.111

Fairclough, Norman. 2003. *Analysing Discourse: Textual Analysis for Social Research*. New York: Routledge.

Field, Margaret. 1997. "The role of factive predicates in the indexicalization of stance: A discourse perspective." *Journal of Pragmatics* 27(6): 799–814. https://doi.org/10.1016/S0378-2166(96)00047-1

Fillmore, Charles J. 1977. "The case for case reopened." In *Syntax and Semantics 8: Grammatical Relations*, ed. by Peter Cole and Jerrold M. Sadock, 59–81. New York: Academic Press.

Fitzmaurice, Susan M. 2004. "Subjectivity, intersubjectivity and the historical construction of interlocutor stance: From stance markers to discourse markers." *Discourse Studies* 6(4): 427–448.

Gardner, Rod. 2001. *When Listeners Talk: Response Tokens and Listener Stance*. Amsterdam. John Benjamins. https://doi.org/10.1075/pbns.92

Ginzburg, Jonathan. 2012. *The Interactive Stance: Meaning for Conversation*. New York: Oxford University Press. https://doi.org/10.1093/acprof:oso/9780199697922.001.0001

Goffman, Erving. 1974. *Frame Analysis: An Essay on the Organization of Experience*. New York: Harper & Row.

Goffman, Erving. 1979. "Footing." *Semiotica* 25(1–2): 1–29. https://doi.org/10.1515/semi.1979.25.1-2.1

Goffman, Erving. 1981. *Forms of Talk*. Philadelphia: University of Pennsylvania Press.

Goodwin, Charles. 1986. "Audience diversity, participation and interpretation." *Text* 6: 283–316.

Goodwin, Charles. 2006. "Retrospective and prospective orientation in the construction of argumentative moves." *Text & Talk* 26(4/5): 443–461. https://doi.org/10.1515/TEXT.2006.018

Goodwin, Charles. 2007a. "Interactive footing." In *Reporting Talk: Reported Speech in Interaction*, ed. by Elizabeth Holt and Rebecca Clift, 16–46. Cambridge: Cambridge University Press.

Goodwin, Charles. 2007b. "Participation, stance and affect in the organization of activities." *Discourse and Society* 18(1): 53–73. https://doi.org/10.1177/0957926507069457

Goodwin, Charles and Marjorie H. Goodwin. 1992. "Assessments and the construction of context." In *Rethinking Context: Language as an Interactive Phenomenon*, ed. by Alessandro Duranti and Charles Goodwin, 147–189. Cambridge: Cambridge University Press.

Goodwin, Marjorie H. 1998. "Games of stance: Conflict and footing in hopscotch." In *Kids Talk: Strategic Language Use in Later Childhood*, ed. by Carolyn T. Adger and Susan Hoyle, 23–46. New York: Oxford University Press.

Goodwin, Marjorie H. 2006. *The Hidden Life of Girls: Games of Stance, Status, and Exclusion*. Malden, MA: Blackwell. https://doi.org/10.1002/9780470773567

Goodwin, Marjorie H. and H. Samy Alim. 2010. "'Whatever (neck roll, eye roll, teeth suck)': The situated coproduction of social categories and identities through stancetaking and transmodal stylization." *Journal of Linguistic Anthropology* 20(1): 179–194. https://doi.org/10.1111/j.1548-1395.2010.01056.x

Goodwin, Marjorie H., Asta Cekaite and Charles Goodwin. 2012. "Emotion as stance." In *Emotion in Interaction*, ed. by Anssi Peräkylä and Marja-Leena Sorjonen, 16–41. New York: Oxford University Press. https://doi.org/10.1093/acprof:oso/9780199730735.003.0002

Goodwin, Marjorie H. and Charles Goodwin. 2000. "Emotion within situated activity." In *Communication: An Area of Development*, ed. by Nancy Budwig, Ina Č. Užgiris and James V. Wertsch, 33–54. Stanford, CT: Ablex.

Gumperz, John J. 1977. "Sociocultural knowledge in conversational inference." In *Georgetown University Round Table on Languages and Linguistics*, ed. by Muriel Saville-Troike, 191–212. Washington, DC: Georgetown University Press.

Gumperz, John J. 1982. *Discourse Strategies*. Cambridge: Cambridge University Press. https://doi.org/10.1017/CBO9780511611834

Gumperz, John J. 1992. "Contextualization and understanding." In *Rethinking Context: Language as an Interactive Phenomenon*, ed. by Alessandro Duranti and Charles Goodwin, 229–252. Cambridge: Cambridge University Press.

Günthner, Susanne. 1999. "Polyphony and the 'layering of voices' in reported dialogues: An analysis of the use of prosodic devices in everyday reported speech." *Journal of Pragmatics* 31(5): 685–708. https://doi.org/10.1016/S0378-2166(98)00093-9

Haddington, Pentti. 2007. "Positioning and alignment as activities of stancetaking in news interviews." In *Stancetaking in Discourse: Subjectivity, Evaluation, Interaction*, ed. by Robert Englebretson, 283–317. Amsterdam: John Benjamins. https://doi.org/10.1075/pbns.164.11had

Halliday, Michael A. K. 1981. "Text semantics and clause grammar: Some patterns of realization." In *The Seventh LACUS Forum*, ed. by James E. Copeland and Philip W. Davis, 31–59. Columbia, SC: Hornbeam Press.

Halliday, Michael A. K. 1994. *An Introduction to Functional Grammar*, 2nd edition. London: Edward Arnold.

Hanks, William F. 1990. *Referential Practice: Language and Lived Space among the Maya*. Chicago: University of Chicago Press.

Harrison, Annette R. 2011. "Representing the ideal self: Represented speech and performance roles in Fulfulde personal narratives." *Pragmatics* 21(2): 191–211. https://doi.org/10.1075/prag.21.2.02har

Haviland, John B. 1989. "'Sure, sure': Evidence and affect." *Text* 9(1): 27–68. https://doi.org/10.1515/text.1.1989.9.1.27

Hayano, Kaoru. 2011. "Claiming epistemic primacy: *Yo*-marked assessments in Japanese." In *The Morality of Knowledge in Conversation*, ed. by Tanya Stivers, Lorenza Mondada and Jakob Steensig, 58–81. Cambridge: Cambridge University Press. https://doi.org/10.1017/CBO9780511921674.004

Heritage, John. 2002. "'Oh'-prefaced responses to assessments: A method of modifying agreement/disagreement." In *The Language of Turn and Sequence*, ed. by Cecilia E. Ford, Barbara A. Fox and Sandra A. Thompson, 196–224. New York: Oxford University Press.

Heritage, John and Geoffrey Raymond. 2005. "The terms of agreement: Indexing epistemic authority and subordination in talk-in-interaction." *Social Psychology Quarterly* 68(1): 15–38. https://doi.org/10.1177/019027250506800103

Hodge, Robert and Gunther Kress. 1988. *Social Semiotics*. Cambridge: Polity.

Hopper, Paul J. and Elizabeth C. Traugott. 2003. *Grammaticalization*, 2nd edition. Cambridge: Cambridge University Press. https://doi.org/10.1017/CBO9781139165525

Hunston, Susan. 2007. "Using a corpus to investigate stance quantitatively and qualitatively." In *Stancetaking in Discourse: Subjectivity, Evaluation, Interaction*, ed. by Robert Englebretson, 27–48. Amsterdam: John Benjamins. https://doi.org/10.1075/pbns.164.03hun

Hunston, Susan and John Sinclair. 2000. "A local grammar of evaluation." In *Evaluation in Text: Authorial Stance and the Construction of Discourse*, ed. by Susan Hunston and Geoff Thompson, 74–101. New York: Oxford University Press.

Hunston, Susan and Geoff Thompson (eds). 2000. *Evaluation in Text: Authorial Stance and the Construction of Discourse*. New York: Oxford University Press.

Hyland, Ken. 2005. "Stance and engagement: A model of interaction in academic discourse." *Discourse Studies* 7(2): 173–192. https://doi.org/10.1177/1461445605050365

Hyland, Ken and Polly Tse. 2005. "Evaluative 'that' constructions: Signaling stance in research abstracts." *Functions of Language* 12(1): 39–63. https://doi.org/10.1075/fol.12.1.03hyl

Iwasaki, Shoichi and Foong Ha Yap (eds). 2015. *Stance-marking and Stance-taking in Asian Languages*. Special issue of *Journal of Pragmatics* 83.

Jaffe, Alexandra. 2009a. "Stance in a Corsican school: Institutional and ideological orders and the production of bilingual subjects." In *Stance: Sociolinguistic Perspectives*, ed. by Alexandra Jaffe, 119–145. New York: Oxford University Press. https://doi.org/10.1093/acprof:oso/9780195331646.001.0001

Jaffe, Alexandra. 2009b. "Introduction: The sociolinguistics of stance." In *Stance: Sociolinguistic Perspectives*, ed. by Alexandra Jaffe, 3–28. New York: Oxford University Press. https://doi.org/10.1093/acprof:oso/9780195331646.001.0001

Jaffe, Alexandra (ed.). 2009c. *Stance: Sociolinguistic Perspectives*. New York: Oxford University Press. https://doi.org/10.1093/acprof:oso/9780195331646.001.0001

Jakobson, Roman. 1960. "Closing statement: Linguistics and poetics." In *Style in Language*, ed. by Thomas A. Sebeok, 350–377. Cambridge, MA: MIT Press.

Jakobson, Roman. 1971. "Shifters, verbal categories, and the Russian verb." In *Roman Jakobson Selected Writings 2: Word and Language*, 130–147. The Hague: Mouton.

Jaworski, Adam and Crispin Thurlow. 2009. "Taking an elitist stance: Ideology and the discursive production of social distinction." In *Stance: Sociolinguistic Perspectives*, ed. by Alexandra Jaffe, 195–226. New York: Oxford University Press. https://doi.org/10.1093/acprof:oso/9780195331646.003.0009

Johnstone, Barbara. 2007. "Linking identity and dialect through stancetaking." In *Stancetaking in Discourse: Subjectivity, Evaluation, Interaction*, ed. by Robert Englebretson, 49–68. Amsterdam: John Benjamins. https://doi.org/10.1075/pbns.164.04joh

Johnstone, Barbara. 2009. "Stance, style, and the linguistic individual." In *Stance: Sociolinguistic Perspectives*, ed. by Alexandra Jaffe, 29–52. New York: Oxford University Press. https://doi.org/10.1093/acprof:oso/9780195331646.003.0002

Kärkkäinen, Elise. 2003. *Epistemic Stance in English Conversation: A Description of Its Interactional Functions, with a Focus on 'I Think'*. Amsterdam: John Benjamins. https://doi.org/10.1075/pbns.115

Kärkkäinen, Elise. 2006. "Stance taking in conversation: From subjectivity to intersubjectivity." *Text & Talk* 26: 699–731. https://doi.org/10.1515/TEXT.2006.029

Kärkkäinen, Elise. 2007. "The role of 'I guess' in conversational stancetaking." In *Stancetaking in Discourse: Subjectivity, Evaluation, Interaction*, ed. by Robert Englebretson, 183–219. Amsterdam: John Benjamins. https://doi.org/10.1075/pbns.164.08kar

Kärkkäinen, Elise. 2012a. "'I thought it was very interesting': Conversational formats for taking a stance." *Journal of Pragmatics* 44(15): 2194–2210. https://doi.org/10.1016/j.pragma.2012.09.005

Kärkkäinen, Elise. 2012b. "On digressing with a stance and not seeking a recipient response." *Text & Talk* 32(4): 477–502. https://doi.org/10.1515/text-2012-0023

Kärkkäinen, Elise and John W. Du Bois (eds). 2012. *Stance, Affect, and Intersubjectivity in Interaction: Sequential and Dialogic Perspectives*. Special issue of *Text & Talk* 32(4).

Keisanen, Tiina. 2007. "Stancetaking as an interactional activity: Challenging the prior speaker." In *Stancetaking in Discourse: Subjectivity, Evaluation, Interaction*, ed. by Robert Englebretson, 253–281. Amsterdam: John Benjamins. https://doi.org/10.1075/pbns.164.10kei

Kiesling, Scott F. 2001. "Stances of whiteness and hegemony in fraternity men's discourse." *Journal of Linguistic Anthropology* 11(1): 101–115. https://doi.org/10.1525/jlin.2001.11.1.101

Kiesling, Scott F. 2009. "Style as stance: Stance as the explanation for patterns." In *Stance: Sociolinguistic Perspectives*, ed. by Alexandra Jaffe, 171–194. New York: Oxford University Press. https://doi.org/10.1093/acprof:oso/9780195331646.003.0008

Kockelman, Paul. 2004. "Stance and subjectivity." *Journal of Linguistic Anthropology* 14(2): 127–150. https://doi.org/10.1525/jlin.2004.14.2.127
Kuno, Susumu. 1987. *Functional Syntax: Anaphora, Discourse, and Empathy*. Chicago: University of Chicago Press.
Labov, William and Joshua Waletzky. 1967. "Narrative analysis: Oral versions of personal experience." In *Essays on the Verbal and Visual Arts*, ed. by June Helm, 12–44. Seattle: University of Washington Press.
Langacker, Ronald W. 1985. "Observations and speculations on subjectivity." In *Iconicity in Syntax*, ed. by John Haiman, 109–150. Amsterdam: John Benjamins. https://doi.org/10.1075/tsl.6.07lan
Langacker, Ronald W. 1987. *Foundations of Cognitive Grammar 1: Theoretical Prerequisites*. Stanford: Stanford University Press.
Langacker, Ronald W. 1999. *Grammar and Conceptualization*. Berlin: Mouton de Gruyter. https://doi.org/10.1515/9783110800524
Laury, Ritva. 2012. "Taking a stance and getting on with it: The form and function of the Finnish finite clausal extraposition construction." *Text & Talk* 32(4): 503–524. https://doi.org/10.1515/text-2012-0024
Lemke, Jay L. 1998. "Resources for attitudinal meaning: Evaluative orientations in text semantics." *Functions of Language* 5(1): 33–56. https://doi.org/10.1075/fol.5.1.03lem
Lempert, Michael. 2008. "The poetics of stance: Text-metricality, epistemicity, interaction." *Language in Society* 37(4): 569–592. https://doi.org/10.1017/S0047404508080779
Lempert, Michael. 2009. "On 'flip-flopping': Branded stance-taking in U.S. electoral politics." *Journal of Sociolinguistics* 13(2): 223–248.
Lempert, Michael. 2012. *Discipline and Debate: The Language of Violence in a Tibetan Buddhist Monastery*. Berkeley: University of California Press. https://doi.org/10.1525/california/9780520269460.001.0001
Linde, Charlotte. 1997. "Evaluation as linguistic structure and social practice." In *The Construction of Professional Discourse*, ed. by Britt-Louise Gunnarsson, Per Linell and Bengt Nordberg, 151–172. New York: Routledge.
Lucy, John A. (ed.). 1993. *Reflexive Language: Reported Speech and Metapragmatics*. Cambridge: Cambridge University Press. https://doi.org/10.1017/CBO9780511621031
Lyons, John. 1981. *Language, Meaning and Context*. London: Fontana.
Lyons, John. 1994. "Subjecthood and subjectivity." In *Subjecthood and Subjectivity: The Status of the Subject in Linguistic Theory*, ed. by Marina Yaguello, 9–17. Paris: Ophrys.
Macken-Horarik, Mary and James R. Martin (eds). 2003. *Negotiating Heteroglossia: Social Perspectives on Evaluation*. Special issue of *Text* 23(2).
MacWhinney, Brian. 1977. "Starting points." *Language* 53: 152–168. https://doi.org/10.2307/413059
Martin, James R. 2000. "Beyond exchange: APPRAISAL systems in English." In *Evaluation in Text: Authorial Stance and the Construction of Discourse*, ed. by Susan Hunston and Geoff Thompson, 142–175. New York: Oxford University Press.
Martin, James R. 2003. "Introduction" (in the special issue, *Negotiating Heteroglossia: Social Perspectives on Evaluation*). *Text* 23(2): 171–181. https://doi.org/10.1515/text.2003.007
Martin, James R. and Peter R.R. White. 2005. *The Language of Evaluation: Appraisal in English*. New York: Palgrave Macmillan. https://doi.org/10.1057/9780230511910
Matoesian, Greg. 2005. "Struck by speech revisited: Embodied stance in jurisdictional discourse." *Journal of Sociolinguistics* 9(2): 167–193. https://doi.org/10.1111/j.1360-6441.2005.00289.x
Maynard, Senko K. 1993. *Discourse Modality: Subjectivity, Emotion, and Voice in the Japanese Language*. Amsterdam: John Benjamins. https://doi.org/10.1075/pbns.24

Mushin, Ilana. 2001. *Evidentiality and Epistemological Stance: Narrative Retelling*. Amsterdam: John Benjamins. https://doi.org/10.1075/pbns.87

Norrick, Neal R. 1993. *Conversational Joking: Humor in Everyday Talk*. Bloomington, IN: Indiana University Press.

Ochs, Elinor. 1986. "From feelings to grammar: A Samoan case study." In *Language Socialization across Cultures*, ed. by Bambi B. Schieffelin and Elinor Ochs, 251–272. Cambridge: Cambridge University Press.

Ochs, Elinor. 1988. *Culture and Language Development: Language Acquisition and Language Socialization in a Samoan Village*. Cambridge: Cambridge University Press.

Ochs, Elinor. 1992. "Indexing gender." In *Rethinking Context: Language as an Interactive Phenomenon*, ed. by Alessandro Duranti and Charles Goodwin, 335–358. Cambridge: Cambridge University Press.

Ochs, Elinor. 1993. "Constructing social identity: A language socialization perspective." *Research on Language and Social Interaction* 26(3): 287–306. https://doi.org/10.1207/s15327973rlsi2603_3

Ochs, Elinor. 1996. "Linguistic resources for socializing humanity." In *Rethinking Linguistic Relativity*, ed. by John J. Gumperz and Steven C. Levinson, 407–437. Cambridge: Cambridge University Press.

Ochs, Elinor (ed.). 1989. *The Pragmatics of Affect*. Special issue of *Text* 9(1).

Ochs, Elinor and Bambi Schieffelin. 1989. "Language has a heart." *Text* 9(1): 7–25.

Onodera, Noriko O. and Ryoko Suzuki (eds). 2007. *Historical Changes in Japanese: With Special Focus on Subjectivity and Intersubjectivity*. Special issue of *Journal of Historical Pragmatics* 8(2).

Oropeza-Escobar, Minerva. 2011. *Represented Discourse, Resonance and Stance in Joking Interaction in Mexican Spanish*. Amsterdam: John Benjamins. https://doi.org/10.1075/pbns.204

Page, Ruth E. 2003. "An analysis of APPRAISAL in childbirth narratives with special consideration of gender and storytelling style." *Text* 23(2): 211–237. https://doi.org/10.1515/text.2003.009

Painter, Clare. 2003. "Developing attitude: An ontogenetic perspective on APPRAISAL." *Text* 23(2): 183–209. https://doi.org/10.1515/text.2003.008

Park, Joseph S-Y. 2011. "Framing, stance, and affect in Korean metalinguistic discourse." *Pragmatics* 21(2): 265–282. https://doi.org/10.1075/prag.21.2.05par

Park, Joseph S-Y. 2013. "Stance, style, and vocal mimicry." *Journal of Pragmatics* 53: 84–95. https://doi.org/10.1016/j.pragma.2013.04.004

Park, Joseph S-Y. and Hiroko Takanashi. 2011. "Introduction: Reframing framing: Interaction and the constitution of culture and society." *Pragmatics* 21(2): 185–190. https://doi.org/10.1075/prag.21.2.04tak

Peirce, Charles S. 1933. "Three kinds of signs." In *Collected Papers of Charles Sanders Peirce 3: Exact Logic*, ed. by Charles Hartshorne and Paul Weiss, 210–214. Cambridge, MA: Harvard University Press.

Peräkylä, Anssi and Marja-Leena Sorjonen (eds). 2012. *Emotion in Interaction*. New York: Oxford University Press. https://doi.org/10.1093/acprof:oso/9780199730735.001.0001

Pomerantz, Anita. 1984. "Agreeing and disagreeing with assessments: Some features found in preferred/dispreferred turn shapes." In *Structures of Social Action: Studies in Conversation Analysis*, ed. by John M. Atkinson and John Heritage, 57–101. Cambridge: Cambridge University Press.

Precht, Kristen. 2003. "Stance moods in spoken English: Evidentiality and affect in British and American conversation." *Text* 23(2): 239–257. https://doi.org/10.1515/text.2003.010

Rauniomaa, Mirka. 2003. "Stance accretion." Paper presented at the Language, Interaction, and Social Organization Research Focus Group, University of California, Santa Barbara, February.

Rauniomaa, Mirka. 2007. "Stance markers in spoken Finnish: *Minun mielestä* and *minusta* in assessments." In *Stancetaking in Discourse: Subjectivity, Evaluation, Interaction*, ed. by Robert Englebretson, 221–252. Amsterdam: John Benjamins. https://doi.org/10.1075/pbns.164.09rau
Reber, Elisabeth. 2012. *Affectivity in Interaction: Sound Objects in English*. Amsterdam: John Benjamins. https://doi.org/10.1075/pbns.215
Rocci, Andrea. 2012. "Modality and argumentative discourse relations: A study of the Italian necessity modal 'dovere'." *Journal of Pragmatics* 44(15): 2129–2149. https://doi.org/10.1016/j.pragma.2012.09.007
Sarangi, Srikant. 2003. "Editorial: Evaluating evaluative language" (in the special issue, *Negotiating Heteroglossia: Social Perspectives on Evaluation. Text* 23(2): 165–170. https://doi.org/10.1515/text.2003.006
Scheibman, Joanne. 2000. "'I dunno…': A usage-based account of the phonological reduction of 'don't' in American English conversation." *Journal of Pragmatics* 32: 105–124. https://doi.org/10.1016/S0378-2166(99)00032-6
Scheibman, Joanne. 2002. *Point of View and Grammar: Structural Patterns of Subjectivity in American English Conversation*. Amsterdam: John Benjamins. https://doi.org/10.1075/sidag.11
Scheibman, Joanne. 2007. "Subjective and intersubjective uses of generalizations in English conversations." In *Stancetaking in Discourse: Subjectivity, Evaluation, Interaction*, ed. by Robert Englebretson, 111–138. Amsterdam: John Benjamins. https://doi.org/10.1075/pbns.164.06sch
Schutz, Alfred. 1962. *Collected Papers I: The Problem of Social Reality*. The Hague: Martinus Nijhoff.
Shoaps, Robin A. 2004. Morality in Grammar and Discourse: Stance-taking and the Negotiation of Moral Personhood in Sakapultek (Mayan) Wedding Counsels. Ph.D. dissertation. Linguistics Department, University of California, Santa Barbara.
Shoaps, Robin A. 2007. "'Moral irony': Modal particles, moral persons and indirect stance-taking in Sakapultek discourse." *Pragmatics* 17(2): 297–335. https://doi.org/10.1075/prag.17.2.05sho
Shoaps, Robin A. 2009. "Moral irony and moral personhood in Sakapultek discourse and culture." In *Stance: Sociolinguistic Perspectives*, ed. by Alexandra Jaffe, 92–118. New York: Oxford University Press. https://doi.org/10.1093/acprof:oso/9780195331646.003.0005
Silverstein, Michael. 1976. "Shifters, linguistic categories, and cultural description." In *Meaning in Anthropology*, ed. by Keith H. Basso and Henry A. Selby, 11–55. Albuquerque: University of New Mexico Press.
Silverstein, Michael.1985. "Language and the culture of gender: At the intersection of structure, usage and ideology." In *Semiotic Mediation: Sociocultural and Psychological Perspectives*, ed. by Elizabeth Mertz and Richard Parmentier, 219–259. New York: Academic Press.
Silverstein, Michael. 2003. "Indexical order and the dialectics of sociolinguistic life." *Language and Communication* 23: 193–229. https://doi.org/10.1016/S0271-5309(03)00013-2
Siromaa, Maarit. 2012. "Resonance in conversational second stories: A dialogic resource for stance taking." *Text & Talk* 32(4): 525–545. https://doi.org/10.1515/text-2012-0025
Stockburger, Inge Z. 2015. "Stancetaking and the joint construction of *zine* producer identities in a research interview." *Journal of Sociolinguistics* 19(2): 222–240. https://doi.org/10.1111/josl.12118
Stubbs, Michael. 1986. "A matter of prolonged fieldwork: Notes towards a modal grammar of English." *Applied Linguistics* 7: 1–25. https://doi.org/10.1093/applin/7.1.1
Szatrowski, Polly. 2007. "Subjectivity, perspective and footing in Japanese co-constructions." In *The Grammar-Pragmatics Interface*, ed. by Nancy Hedberg and Ron Zacharski, 313–339. Amsterdam: John Benjamins. https://doi.org/10.1075/pbns.155.18sza
Tainio, Liisa. 2012. "Prosodic imitation as a means of receiving and displaying a critical stance in classroom interaction." *Text & Talk* 32(4): 547–568. https://doi.org/10.1515/text-2012-0026

Takanashi, Hiroko. 2001. "Stance differential in parallelism: Dialogic syntax of argumentation in Japanese." *Pragmatics in 2000: Selected Papers from the 7th International Pragmatics Conference* 2: 570–582.

Takanashi, Hiroko. 2004. The Interactional Co-construction of Play in Japanese Conversation. Ph.D. dissertation. Linguistics Department, University of California, Santa Barbara.

Takanashi, Hiroko. 2011. "Complementary stylistic resonance in Japanese play framing." *Pragmatics* 21(2): 231–264. https://doi.org/10.1075/prag.21.2.04tak

Takanashi, Hiroko and Joseph S-Y. Park (eds). 2011. Reframing Framing: Interaction and the Constitution of Culture and Society. Special issue of *Pragmatics* 21(2).

Tannen, Deborah (ed.). 1993. *Framing in Discourse*. New York: Oxford University Press.

Tannen, Deborah and Cynthia Wallat. 1993. "Interactive frames and knowledge schemas in interaction: Examples from a medical examination/interview." In *Framing in Discourse*, ed. by Deborah Tannen, 57–76. New York: Oxford University Press.

Thompson, Geoff and Susan Hunston. 2000. "Evaluation: An introduction." In *Evaluation in Text: Authorial Stance and the Construction of Discourse*, ed. by Susan Hunston and Geoff Thompson, 1–27. New York: Oxford University Press.

Thompson, Sandra A. 2002. "'Object complements' and conversation: Towards a realistic account." *Studies in Language* 26(1): 125–163. https://doi.org/10.1075/sl.26.1.05tho

Thompson, Sandra A. and Anthony Mulac. 1991. "A quantitative perspective on the grammaticization of epistemic parentheticals in English." In *Approaches to Grammaticalization 2: Focus on Types of Grammatical Markers*, ed. by Elizabeth C. Traugott and Bernd Heine, 313–329. Amsterdam: John Benjamins. https://doi.org/10.1075/tsl.19.2.16tho

Tomasello, Michael. 1999. *The Cultural Origins of Human Cognition. Cambridge*, MA: Harvard University Press.

Traugott, Elizabeth C. 1989. "On the rise of epistemic meanings in English: An example of subjectification in semantic change." *Language* 65(1): 31–55. https://doi.org/10.2307/414841

Traugott, Elizabeth C. and Bernd Heine. 1991. *Approaches to Grammaticalization* (2 volumes). Amsterdam: John Benjamins.

Verhagen, Arie. 2005. *Constructions of Intersubjectivity: Discourse, Syntax, and Cognition*. New York: Oxford University Press.

Voloshinov, Valentin N. 1973. *Marxism and the Philosophy of Language*, trans. by Ladislav Matejka and Irwin R. Titunik. Cambridge, MA: Harvard University Press.

Vygotsky, Lev S. 1986. *Thought and Language. Cambridge*, MA: MIT Press.

White, P. R. R. 2003. "Beyond modality and hedging: A dialogic view of the language of intersubjective stance." *Text* 23(2): 259–284. https://doi.org/10.1515/text.2003.011

Wu, Ruey-Jiuan R. 2004. *Stance in Talk: A Conversation Analysis of Mandarin Final Particles*. Amsterdam: John Benjamins. https://doi.org/10.1075/pbns.117

# Style and styling

Janus Mortensen & Nikolas Coupland
University of Copenhagen / Cardiff University

## 1. Introduction

In the most general, everyday understanding of the term, a style is a way of doing something. The blues is a particular style of music and so is jazz; surrealism is a style of painting and the same goes for pointillism. Cross-country skiers tend to stride forward in classic style or move at greater speed in what is known as skate style. When the term style is used in this manner – as a noun referring to a conventionalized way of doing something – we are likely to think of styles as relatively fixed entities, even though the categories in question are likely to be approximative generalizations: people might reasonably argue that the blues takes different forms in different contexts, and so on. However, a more important theoretical point is that, since styles always have to be 'brought off' in order to materialize, the notion of style inevitably also involves a more dynamic aspect, an aspect of *doing*. Style is not only a noun but also a verb, and any attempt at theorizing style will have to take this duality into consideration – 'style' as cultural form in relation to 'styling' as cultural practice.

In relation to speech and language, the study of style already has a long history, particularly in the areas of literary and general stylistics (Sebeok 1960; Enkvist, Spencer & Gregory 1964), but also in sociolinguistics (Labov 1972; Eckert & Rickford 2001; Auer 2007; Coupland 2007) and in neighbouring disciplines, including pragmatics (Lakoff 1979; Hickey 1989). In these fields, the concept refers to what are recognized to be different ways of using language, whether spoken or written, linked to the analysis of how particular styles are enacted in particular instances. This is the broad sense in which style will be discussed in the following. It will be important, however, to argue that a style perspective allows for a holistic view of meaning-making in the pragmatics of human communication and that the study of style should therefore not be restricted to spoken and written language, narrowly conceived.

In Labovian variationist sociolinguistics, styles have traditionally been conceptualized as situationally determined modes of speech. Building on data generated in sociolinguistic interviews and similar researcher-controlled environments, a central style-related finding emerging from the variationist paradigm is that speakers, in statistical terms, tend to modify their ways of speaking depending on how much attention they pay to their speech, which in turn will depend on the situation in which speech is produced. In this approach to style, which has counterparts in the field of general stylistics (e.g. Joos 1967), stylistic variation is largely seen as a consequence –

https://doi.org/10.1075/hop.21.sty2

or reflex, even – of contextual factors. Formal situations with a high degree of attention to speech are found to correlate with the use of relatively 'formal' or 'standard' features, whereas informal situations with relatively little attention paid to speech will exhibit the use of more informal styles, of which the most famous one is what Labov calls 'the vernacular' (for a recent discussion of this concept see Coupland 2016).

Against this traditional variationist view of style, which tends to invoke a one-dimensional scale of formality to account for variation in (individual) speech style, we find approaches that take an interest in the performative and meaning-making nature of styles and styling. In this tradition, which draws on insights from the work of Gumperz (1982), Hymes (1974) and several others (as reviewed below), styles and styling are conceptualized as dynamic processes that constitute an integral part of communicative situations and which may take part in the creation of many types of meaning. Each time a style is brought off, it invariably generates meaning in a dialectic interplay with various aspects of the situational context, rendering the idea that a style could be seen as a situational correlate insufficient as a theoretical starting point. Where the traditional variationist approach to style might be said to treat style mainly as a noun (as in Labov's use of the concept of 'contextual styles'), operating with a limited inventory of distinct styles organized along a continuum of formality, the alternative approach emphasizes the creative potential of styling, in the more verbal sense.

The two positions on style briefly outlined here, and which are treated in more detail elsewhere (e.g. Thøgersen, Coupland & Mortensen 2016), are not incompatible. In fact, as we will show in the following, current approaches to style tend to encompass 'consolidated' as well as 'dynamic' aspects, highlighting that both perspectives must be taken into consideration if we want to provide a satisfactory account of style and styling, or 'style in action'. In discussing style, we need to take account of the historically entrenched social meaning of particular styles as culturally familiar constructs, while at the same time recognizing the active, and potentially transformative, meaning-making potential of styling in local instances of interaction.

The text is organized as follows. In Section 2, we present a condensed historical overview of some of the central approaches to style and context in the literature. In Section 3, we look at more contemporary approaches to style and indexicality and investigate the relationship between social meaning and style. Section 4 broadens the scope and looks at the culturally reflexive use of styles in processes of stylization, while Section 5, by way of conclusion, offers an extended discussion of an example which illustrates some of the key topics covered in the chapter.

## 2. Style and context

The relationship between style and context is a central concern within disciplines that take an interest in language-in-use, including pragmatics, sociolinguistics and social semiotics. In this section we briefly review a selection of works concerned with this relationship. Much of the foundational work in the area was published in the 1960s, 1970s and 1980s. This means that the following section, though not ordered in a strictly chronological fashion, is something of a retrospective overview. It is, however, important to stress that the ideas we review, though not contemporary in origin, are nevertheless still very much current, as they continue to play an important role in present-day theories of style and styling.

The notion of register, principally associated with the work of Halliday (1978; see also Halliday, McIntosh, & Strevens 1964: 77), represents an early and influential conceptualization of the relationship between style and context. In Halliday's definition, which owes much to Malinowski's (1923) 'context of situation' and further developments of this concept by Firth (1950, 1957), register concerns linguistic variation relative to the situation within which language is used ('variation according to use'). If we take English as an example, the way the language is deployed in university lectures and textbooks differs considerably from the way it is used in, say, international air traffic. This gives rise to the possibility of identifying distinct registers ('academic English' vs. 'aviation English'), which are linked to – and to some extent shaped by – their contexts of use. Halliday specifies register as being composed of 'field of discourse' (that which language is being used to say something about, and in what setting), 'tenor of discourse' (concerning the social relationship between participants in the communicative situation) and 'mode of discourse' (relating to the communicative channel adopted in a particular communicative situation). Field, tenor and mode are contextual dimensions that are likely to influence the way language is used in particular situations, just as the 'dialect' of a speaker might result in different aspects of stylistic variation – 'variation according to user' in Halliday's terms.

Halliday suggests that register is 'a form of prediction: given that we know the situation, the social context of language use, we can predict a great deal about the language that will occur, with reasonable probability of being right' (Halliday 1978: 32). In this sense, Halliday's approach can be said to resemble the early variationist approaches outlined above, in that styles of speaking are viewed as being constrained by situational factors (register) and/or the speaker's provenance and sociocultural background (dialect). Yet Halliday's underlying functional view of language – the position that language is essentially motivated by the communicative needs of language users, allowing speakers to generate meaning in variable contexts on the basis of choices within a semiotic system – counteracts any simplistic or reductionist reading of the notions of register and dialect: Style may to some extent be constrained by contextual variables, but there is considerable scope for individual agency in Halliday's model as well.

In the Hymesian tradition of the *ethnography of speaking* – or the *ethnography of communication* (cf. Saville-Troike 2003) – style and context are even further integrated. Hymes explicitly takes issue with the purely statistical description of 'speech styles' (1972: 57–58), arguing that the meaning of styles also depends on 'qualitative judgments of appropriateness' in particular contexts. Although he does not include style explicitly in his SPEAKING grid, a mnemonic developed for the description of speech events, the grid nevertheless places style (in the sense we are discussing it here) squarely within the frame of the speech event, as an integral part of the meaning of any linguistically mediated communicative event. The 'A' in the 'SPEAKING' mnemonic refers to 'act sequences' which Hymes uses as a common term for 'message form' and 'message content'. He is particularly keen to stress that message content cannot be studied without paying due attention to form, arguing that 'it is a truism, but one frequently ignored in research, that *how* something is said is part of *what* is said' (Hymes 1972: 59, emphasis in original). This position would be difficult to uphold if the linguistic form facet of style were to be conceptualized as a reflex of the situational context. So, rather than a mere situational reflex, style comes to be seen as a central part of what *constitutes* a situation, or a speech event, in Hymes' terms. The way language is used by speakers – including choice of variety, level of formality, and so on – is not simply determined by contextual factors but is in itself part of shaping context and generating meaning.

Similar insights emerged from the tradition of interactional sociolinguistics, associated mainly with the work of Gumperz. In Gumperz's thinking, the notion of *contextualization cues* plays an important role in theorizing the relationship between style and context. Defined as 'constellations of surface features of message form' by which 'speakers signal and listeners interpret what the activity is, how semantic content is to be understood and *how* each sentence relates to what precedes or follows' (1982: 131, emphasis in original), Gumperz's notion of contextualization cues sits very comfortably with Hymes' insistence on the interdependence of 'message form' and 'message content'. The things we say *and the way we say them* creates context and, thereby, meaning. The meaning of contextualization cues, which can be realized at any 'level' of language use, including pronunciation, prosody, rhythm, tempo and code-switching (Gumperz 2015 [2003]), is *implicit* in interaction. While the meaning of words can – in principle, at least – be discussed in abstraction from any particular context, the meaning of contextualization cues is always tied to particular instances of use: They acquire and generate meaning in context, even when they are to some extent conventionalized within a particular community of language users.

A key insight generated by Gumperz's work is that the meaning of contextualization cues is not universal. People do not always 'read' cues the same way, and even if they do, they may misread them in terms of cultural stereotypes. In other words, the potential meanings of contextualization cues, realized as part of particular ways of speaking, are tied to particular sociocultural contexts, and often very local ones. To use terms introduced by Malinowski and Firth (see above), we might say that it takes a particular 'context of situation' (and possibly a particular 'context of culture') to successfully bring off contextualization. This is illustrated in one of the examples included in Gumperz's book on *Discourse Strategies* (1982), here presented as Extract 1.

**Extract 1.** I don't know

| | |
|---|---|
| Teacher: | James, what does this word say? |
| James: | I don't know. |
| Teacher: | Well, if you don't want to try someone else will. Freddy? |
| Freddy: | Is that a *p* or a *b*? |
| Teacher: | (encouragingly) It's a *p*. |
| Freddy: | Pen. |

(Gumperz 1982: 147)

James has an African-American background, and Gumperz argues that understanding the meaning of his utterance in the second line crucially hinges on this fact. What the transcript does not show is that James produces his utterance with rising intonation. This intonation pattern, Gumperz argues, amounts to a contextualization cue which may be taken as 'meaning' or 'signalling' that James is not unwilling to read the word in front of him; he is simply unsure about *how* to read it and he therefore – implicitly – requests the teacher's assistance in 'cracking the code'. The teacher, however, has a different sociocultural background and is not attuned to this meaning of a rising intonation contour. It does not carry a particular meaning in her primary discourse community and is therefore not effective in creating the context and the meaning that James, according to Gumperz, intended. Freddy's utterance, on the other hand, is styled in a fashion that matches her expectations, and is consequently met with greater success – although the intended communicative action is in principle no different from that of James.

Extract 1 suggests that Halliday's belief in the predictive power of register is severely challenged by language use in situations where participants do not share the same communicative norms, and therefore do not necessarily understand the same things by particular styles of speaking. James and the teacher may well have understood the field and tenor of the situation in Extract 1 in the same way, but that does not in itself determine the way they use language and the pragmatic force of their utterances. In fact, in the end, their stylistic choices arguably seem to have a greater effect on the situation than vice versa. This point extends well beyond communicative encounters of the kind discussed by Gumperz. In principle, contextualization cues hold the potential to reconfigure all aspects of Halliday's register, particularly field and tenor, but also mode. So, the predictive power of 'register' really only holds to the extent that participants act in accordance with what might be considered the expected behaviour – the 'appropriateness' that Hymes talked about. There is, of course, plenty of evidence to support the idea that context has a bearing on the way language is used in particular situations, but there is also plenty of evidence to support the inverse: that the way language is used in a particular situation is part of creating the context of that very situation – and the meanings generated therein. This last point has also been made within the framework of ethnomethodological conversation analysis, where the power of talk to create context for subsequent talk and members' methods for creating meaning in interaction have been described in great detail (see e.g. Drew & Heritage 1992). But it is interesting to note how both causal directions – context determining style and style determining context – recognize that there is on-going interplay between style as social object and styling as social practice.

Another perspective that Hymes and Gumperz both allude to is what might be called the *relational* potential of style. Using a particular style, as opposed to other styles, invariably positions the speaker in a particular way vis-à-vis other (groups of) speakers. This idea was more fully developed by Le Page and Tabouret-Keller who suggested that 'linguistic behaviour' (styling, we might call it) can be seen as 'a series of *acts of identity* in which people reveal both their personal identity and their search for social roles' (1985: 14). One of their examples, drawn from joint work with Mark Sebba in London in the early 1980s, concerns children of West Indian immigrants and their linguistic repertoires. For these kids, the recurring choice between 'London Jamaican' (on the one hand) and 'London English' or 'Standard English' (on the other) amounts to a complex series of acts of identity, presenting them as contenders for particular social roles. Le Page and Tabouret-Keller recognize the existence of contextual constraints on linguistic behaviour, noting that '*all* utterances are affected by the audience, the topic and the setting' (emphasis in original), but they also stress the considerable power that speakers have in creating (relational) social meaning through styling, arguing that 'the individual creates for himself the patterns of his linguistic behaviour so as to resemble those of the group or groups with which from time to time he wishes to be identified, or so as to be unlike those from whom he wishes to be distinguished' (Le Page & Tabouret-Keller 1985: 181).

The relational potential of verbal styling is also at the heart of Bell's theory of language style as audience design (1984, 2001). Bell's theory, which among other sources draws inspiration from the work of Le Page (McEntegart & Le Page 1982) as well as work on accommodation in social psychology (Giles & Powesland 1975), constitutes a refined model of the ways in which speakers may modify their 'language style' in an attempt to align or dis-align with various types of 'audiences,' ranging from the immediately present audience to idealized recipients – the 'referees' with whom the speaker may aspire to be associated. Bell (1984) makes an explicit distinction between what he calls 'responsive' and 'initiative' audience design which again encapsulates the bi-directional relationship between style and context that we have discussed in this section. In responsive audience design, the style of speaking is conditioned by contextual factors, particularly the speaker's audience (which Bell originally held to be the most important influential aspect of context on shaping language use). In initiative audience design, on the other hand, the speaker makes 'creative' stylistic choices in order to align with particular groups of speakers who may or may not be present in the interaction. In this process, we are able to discern the meaning-making potential of styling – the potential of stylistic choices to create social meaning.

## 3. Style and social meaning

In this section we turn to more recent approaches to style. The potential of style and styling to create social meaning has already been introduced in the previous section, but as we shall show in this section, later works have added considerable refinement to our understanding of how acts of styling and styles come to carry meaning in particular contexts and for particular groups of language users. These advances have been related to a general renewed theoretical interest in the relation between language and social meaning which has taken shape around concepts such as indexicality and enregisterment. In the following, we discuss these concepts – social meaning, indexicality and enregisterment – with a particular focus on their relation to style. (For a more general overview of current thinking on social meaning and language, see contributions by Silverstein, Eckert, Jaffe and Gal in Coupland (ed.) (2016)). We also expand the perspective on style by discussing how styles are established through other semiotic resources than language.

Social meaning is an essential but slippery notion in the study of language use. Eckert (2016: 81) argues that social meaning 'has been an untheorized subtext of all work on [language] variation' but this arguably holds true for many – if not most – approaches to the study of language. Although it does not define the concept or delimit its remit to any great extent, it may be useful to think of social meaning as the process of achieving 'the social significance of language' (Coupland 2007: 18). As this broad gloss suggests, social meaning is best seen as an open-ended cover term for distinctions that relate to social values and norms, power and status, social identities and stereotypes, prejudices and much more. The study of social meaning and *language* – as opposed to non-linguistic approaches to social meaning – takes a particular interest in how these distinctions are reflected in and constituted through the use of language. In the combination of its verbal and nominal meanings (style as verb, style as noun) the concept of style offers a particularly useful vantage point for theorizing the interplay between language use and social meaning.

In recent decades indexicality has been established as a key concept in attempts to theorize the link between language use and social meaning, centrally inspired by the work of Silverstein (1976, 2003). In its most general sense, indexicality is used in reference to the links that exist between linguistic forms and the social meanings they 'point to'. In English, the use of word-final [ɪn] rather than [ɪŋ] in words like *runnin/running* and *singin/singing* has an indexical value, pointing to aspects of the speaker's identity, perhaps as 'uneducated' or, alternatively, 'laidback'. However, the relationship between a linguistic form and what it meaningfully 'stands for' is not straightforward. In fact, one of the central insights emanating from work on indexicality is that the social meanings of linguistic forms (whether they are individual phonemes, words, or full-fledged styles) are generally 'underspecified' and therefore variable according to context of use, even within the same socio-cultural setting (Coupland 2007: 23).

Eckert's notion of the indexical field (Eckert 2008) maps how variants of sociolinguistic variables, as one particular type of linguistic form, may have very different meanings depending on context of use (cf. Kiesling 1998). Using the (ING) variable as one of her examples (building mainly on the work of Campbell-Kibler 2007, 2008), Eckert is able to show that the meaning of the variable's two variants (one realized with an apical alveolar nasal and one with a velar nasal, again as in *runnin* vs. *running*) depends crucially on their embeddedness within particular styles of speaking. In an abstract and decontextualized sense, the apical variant (*runnin*) is stereotypically related to meanings such as 'uneducated', 'lazy' and 'inarticulate' but also 'easy-going', 'unpretentious' and 'relaxed'. The velar variant (*running*), on the other hand, activates meanings such as 'educated', 'articulate' and 'formal' but also 'effortful' and 'pretentious'. Taken together, these meanings realize the indexical field of (ING), and it is only in particular contexts of use, as part of particular styles, that the meaning of either variant is potentially narrowed down. Eckert illustrates the general principle elegantly, even for readers who may not be familiar with the particular example, by reference to a fictional character, Lord Peter Wimsey, whose social persona as the 'archetype for the British gentleman detective' (as Wikipedia has it) is, in part, created by the consistent use of apical forms in the representation of his speech:

> Presumably the almost categorical use of the apical form by Lord Peter Wimsey in the murder mysteries of Dorothy Sayers indexes the effortlessness that comes of entitlement. And it is the embedding of this apical form in a broader upper-class style that allows it to take on this meaning. (Eckert 2008: 467)

This meaning of 'upper-class English effortlessness' is of course radically different from the lower-class, uneducated meaning that apical (ING) has been said to carry in some other contexts.

In traditional variationist approaches to style, the goal was to establish correlational patterns between linguistic forms and abstract social categories such as social class, gender or ethnicity. Approaches to style and styling which take their cue from theories of indexicality move beyond such correlational views of social meaning. In the approach represented by Eckert, which she has described as 'third wave' variationism (Eckert 2012, see also Eckert 2000), linguistic features are not seen as having inherent social meaning, defined by their statistical correlation with the speech of individuals assigned to predefined social groups. On the contrary, Eckert's approach stresses what has elsewhere been referred to as 'indexicality in interaction' (cf. Bucholtz 2008), highlighting the dynamic meaning-making potential of linguistic features in particular contexts of use, and thereby avoiding an over-simplified account of the relationship between linguistic forms and social meaning. This line of thought is also pursued within what has been called sociocultural linguistics (Bucholtz & Hall 2005) and has been re-theorized more recently by Jaffe (2016), although its essence was already apparent in some of the earliest sociolinguistic discussions of style (e.g. Bell 1984; Coupland 1985).

Styling can be characterized as meaning-making in interaction through the deployment of culturally familiar semiotic resources. So far, the semiotic resources considered in this section have been limited to two variants of a single sociolinguistic variable (ING), but the semiotic resources available for meaning-making are obviously many more and much more varied. In the following we will first look at how styles, seen as reified metacultural notions (style as noun), may be said to constitute composite semiotic resources in themselves, and then, subsequently, look at how non-linguistic semiotic resources may be deployed as part of styles for the purposes of social meaning-making.

It is quite common for particular ways of speaking (whether imagined or real) to acquire a degree of cultural salience which makes them recognizable as distinct styles with a particular meaning potential. Using 'the Queen's English' as his main example, Agha (2003, 2007) has theorized this phenomenon as a process of *enregisterment* in which a style comes to be established as a culturally salient 'register'. The process of enregisterment is by now well-documented in a range of settings. Drawing on Agha's work, Johnstone (2014) and colleagues (Johnstone, Andrus, & Danielson 2006; Johnstone et al. 2015) have studied the enregisterment of 'Pittsburghese' as a distinct style (and what many would refer to as a regional dialect) in the US context. Based on data going back to the beginning of the 20th century, they are able to show how the enregisterment of the style – the cultural consolidation of what it means to speak like someone from Pittsburgh – has involved extensive metalinguistic commentary in many different contexts as well as a proliferation of representations of 'sayings' associated with the style through a range of media, including t-shirts, refrigerator magnets, and YouTube videos (see e.g. Kiesling 2018). In the context of Denmark, researchers have identified registers with the labels 'integrated language' vs. 'street language' used amongst young kids from ethnically diverse backgrounds (Madsen, Møller & Jørgensen 2010). For people in the know, these labels again refer to distinct styles, each with its own set of indexical values. The stereotypical indexical values of integrated language include 'higher class culture (wealth)', 'sophistication', 'authority' and 'academic skills', while 'street language' is associated with, amongst other things, 'toughness', 'masculinity', 'pan-ethnic minority "street" culture' and 'academic non-prestige' (Madsen 2013). In essence, integrated language denotes a societally mainstream style, possibly even an 'establishment' style, while street language, as a counterpoint to this style, is anything but mainstream and establishment.

Culturally familiar styles like 'the Queen's English', 'Pittsburghese' or 'integrated language' do not have single, unified meanings. Like other semiotic signs, styles acquire their meaning in context, in part by being different from other styles (Irvine 2001; cf. Hymes 1972: 58). However, once established as culturally salient frames of reference, styles may be referred to or deployed in interaction to create situated local meanings and pragmatic effects. Enregistered styles become 'construct resources' – 'ideological postulates about language variation and social meaning' (Fabricius & Mortensen 2013: 377) – which speakers draw on in making sense of the sociolinguistic landscape they are part of – and in creating meaning in particular communicative situations (for an example from Jamaica see Bohmann 2016). In highlighting the social significance of the 'work' speakers do around styles, the study of language ideologies (see contributions in Schieffelin, Kroskrity & Woolard 1992 for early examples) has much to offer the study of style. Just as 'ideologies of language are significant for social as well as linguistic analysis because they are not only about language' (Woolard & Schieffelin 1994: 55), the analysis of style has a critical potential in drawing attention to the social significance of styles as indexes of linguistic and social hierarchies.

As we argued earlier, the view of styles as relatively durable and culturally salient phenomena is not at odds with the dynamic view of styles outlined in the discussion of indexicality above. Rather than seeing them as competing approaches, it is necessary to recognise both static and dynamic elements functioning within an integrated account of style. Styles like 'Pittsburghese' which have undergone a process of enregisterment and may therefore be discussed as 'nouns' are, after all, dependent on acts of styling (style as verb) for their creation and continued existence. No matter how sedimented a style may be, it will always have to be 'activated' in some sense in order to acquire and create meaning. Similarly, as discussed above, particular linguistic features tend to acquire their indexical meanings by being performed as part of culturally salient styles. The generation of indexical meaning in relation to a particular linguistic sign will depend on an association between that sign and the style it is seen (or heard) to form part of on that occasion of use.

Madsen's (2013) study provides a useful example here. In listing what she calls the 'performable signs' of 'integrated language', she mentions, among other things, the use of distinct pronunciation, a certain 'academic' vocabulary and polite expressions. Street language, on the other hand, is brought into being, *inter alia*, by the use of slang expressions and swear words, as well as 'polylingual practices' in which speakers draw on linguistic features from multiple named languages (cf. Jørgensen et al. 2011). Clearly, there is no one-to-one relationship between particular linguistic features or particular linguistic practices (like polylanguaging) and the enregistered style in question. Distinct pronunciation and polite expressions are not uniquely tied to what Madsen's participants call 'integrated language', just as the use of swearwords, jargon or even polylingual practices is not particular to 'street language'. Still, in the local social ecology, these are the meanings that are liable to be generated.

As the final point in this section, we need to briefly consider the multimodal nature of styles. Spoken language is only one type of semiotic resource deployed stylistically for meaning-making purposes. In his analysis of youth subculture in post-war Britain, Hebdige (1979) analysed the relationship between (group) identity and style as expressed, for example, through clothing, musical preferences, make-up, and modes of transport, thereby drawing attention to the inherent multimodal nature of styling as a communicative practice. Cultures tend to 'load up' particular semiotic resources for indexical purposes, and not others. But once a semiotic resource has become salient within a particular sociocultural setting, any act of styling involving that resource will generate meaning, irrespective of the specific kind of semiotic resource involved. Although this admittedly makes it difficult to define the remit of style analysis, it is also clear that a style perspective helps us theorize how meaning-making in human interaction is achieved not just through language, but through multiple semiotic means, across multiple communicative modes (Mortensen, Coupland & Thøgersen 2017).

## 4. Performing styles: Stylization and cultural reflexivity

In this fourth section, we take the discussion of style a step further, looking at *stylization* or *stylized performance* (Coupland 2001, 2007) as a particularly reflexive way in which styling can be used as a meaning-making resource. The concept of stylization draws inspiration from Bakhtin's (1981, 1986) ideas about the multi-voicedness of discourse, as it has been applied and extended in Rampton's work on 'crossing' (Rampton 1995, 2005, 2006). Coupland has defined stylization as 'a knowing and self-aware performance of a style or genre drawn from a pre-established repertoire' (Coupland 2001: 422). It is 'a mode of performance whereby a stylizer knowingly holds back from signalling full ownership of a voiced utterance' (Coupland & Mortensen 2017: 260), indicating that the deployed voice (or style) should not be taken at face value. By using stylistic resources in this way, speakers can generate social meaning 'on the basis of provisionality' (Coupland & Mortensen 2017: 260), by leaving their exact stance or communicative intention hanging in the air. When engaging in stylization speakers generate ambiguity, leaving it to their recipients to create meaning – without ever being entirely sure that what they come to understand is what was meant.

Stylization is closely bound up with discursive and cultural reflexivity. By activating someone else's voice through stylization – by means of what has been called "as if" voicing (Coupland 2011: 155) – the social meanings of that particular voice are activated and held up for (critical) scrutiny. This can be utilized for humorous purposes, as when stylization is employed as a means of making fun of or 'pointing fingers' at speakers who are stereotypically associated with particular ways of speaking (see e.g. Bell 2016). However, in another function, stylization can generate a more profound form of cultural reflexivity, which may even destabilize culturally established norms. This has been illustrated by Lorenzo-Dus (2017) in her analysis of the Spanish TV news program *Salvados* and the stylistic and stylizing practice of its anchor, Jordie Évole. In the program, Évole adopts a soft-spoken, apparently naïve style of interviewing that allows him to question perceived injustices in a seemingly innocent manner, thereby catching his interview victims unawares (not entirely unlike the actor Peter Falk in the role of Inspector Columbo). Lorenzo-Dus is able to show, through analyses of audience uptake on Twitter, that Évole is perceived by many as an important 'incisive' critical voice, exposing the wrongdoings of people in power, and thereby expanding the critical remit of political journalism in Spain.

In another recent study, Spilioti (2017) similarly addresses new modes of styling and stylization in broadcast media, and discusses their interaction with processes of social change. Her data are taken from a Greek political satire radio show called Ελληνοφρένεια ('Greekophrenia'), in which the host *Apostolis* deploys stylized performances of Greek and English in conversation with callers who are unaware that they have been framed as the 'dupes' (Bauman 1986) of on-air telephone pranks. In what initially seems to be a haphazard use of English, intertwined with distinctly different styles of Greek, *Apostolis* is activating a complex and ambiguous network of social meanings where callers and radio listeners alike are left to their own devices in figuring out exactly what is discursively going on. Spilioti argues that these acts of broadcast talk 'refract' (cf. Woolard with Bencomo & Carbonell 2013) speech practices of the wider community and point to on-going change in the ideological alignment between Greek and English in Greece. By means of an ambiguous use of various 'voices', *Apostolis* thus manages to hold current issues in Greece at the interface between language and social change up for critical scrutiny.[1]

Evolé and *Apostolis* can be seen as what Urban, in his (2001) theory of 'how culture moves through the world', refers to as *entrepreneurs*. The *entrepreneur* is someone who 'takes something old into a new world, or tries something new out on an old world' (Urban 2001: 2), thereby generating opportunities for cultural reflexivity (though this is not Urban's term). In doing so, the entrepreneur offers a new perspective on existing practices, and opens a potential for new ways of thinking and new ways of doing. Stylization is one way of achieving this goal, because the multi-voicedness that characterizes stylization holds a distinct critical potential (cf. Bakhtin's work

1. The summaries of Lorenzo-Dus (2017) and Spilioti (2017) offered here are partly reproduced from the discussion in Mortensen, Coupland and Thøgersen (2017).

on heteroglossia and his notion of the carnivalesque). In a similar fashion, Hebdige (1979) argues that the youth subcultures he studied – mods, punks, rockers, and so on – managed to create subversive meanings through the stylistic practice of *bricolage*. Following Levi-Strauss (1966), Hebdige describes the *bricoleur* as someone who deploys seemingly familiar signs in unexpected settings, thereby generating new and often unsettling meaning. Through bricolage, Hebdige argues, 'the conventional insignia of the business world – the suit, collar and tie, short hair, etc. – were stripped of their original connotations – efficiency, ambition, compliance with authority – and transformed into "empty" fetishes ...' as part of what Eco has called 'semiotic guerrilla warfare' (Hebdige 1979: 105, referring to Eco 1972).

## 5. An example

In closing the chapter, we would like to offer an analysis of a single case in order to show the analytical potential of the style concept in a little more detail. Considering a written and visual instance also offsets the bias towards spoken data in the discussion this far. Figure 1 is an Internet meme which circulated in various online forums in the days following the inauguration of Donald Trump as the President of the United States in January of 2017.

The meme is a juxtaposition of two pictures, presumably video stills. We will ignore the left-most segment of the image for the moment and start with the segment on the right. Here we see Sean Spicer who served as White House Press Secretary up until July of 2017. He is standing behind a lectern with the inscription 'The White House – Washington' (in seriffed capital letters), with an upright American flag nearby, against the backdrop of a framed image of the northern façade of the White House. Underneath the visual depiction of the White House the inscription 'The White House – Washington' appears again, though we only see part of the text. To Spicer's left, at

**Figure 1.** 'The inauguration crowds where yuge' meme (https://imgflip.com/i/1i6g7i)

the very right of the meme, a photo (or perhaps a video still) from the day of Trump's inauguration is displayed on a monitor. The photo shows Trump (the small solitary figure in the centre of the right-most image) walking away from camera in a carefully orchestrated procession from the White House towards a podium facing the National Mall, filled with people who have come to witness the inauguration.

Any viewer familiar with US politics is likely to recognize the photo of Spicer as a scene from a White House press conference. The visual context is instantly recognizable, but in detailing the components which make up the totality of the visual imagery, as we have done above, it is obvious that this visualization is really the result of careful styling – styling of everything from the choice of colours and typography to furniture and various objects with referential as well as symbolic meaning (e.g. the flag and the representation of the White House) as well as spatial layout and, perhaps less obviously, the choice of camera angle and other technical aspects of the mediation of the event. In sum, the image may be said to depict a situation which in every respect has been styled to lend the speaker a distinct air of authority and power and to instil in the viewer a sense of reverence or at least conventionalized respect. As such, the photo illustrates an output from a process of styling, which includes relational styling (manipulation of how a represented politician is conventionally to be seen and heard).

The day before the press conference, Reuters had released side-by-side aerial photos of the National Mall showing the crowds attending the inauguration ceremonies of Barack Obama in 2009 and Trump in 2017 (Trotta 2017). The side-by-side images soon went viral on Twitter and other social media, and the general consensus was that Trump's crowd had been much smaller than Obama's. At the press conference, Spicer took issue with this view, claiming that established news media had engaged in 'deliberately false reporting' (The White House 2017) – i.e. essentially claiming that the media were lying about the size of Trump's crowd. This claim was considered highly controversial and made the press conference the topic of intense debate in various media. Spicer's briefing also became the topic of debate due to the particular rhetorical, visual and sartorial style he adopted. Comments were made regarding his suit, which was believed to be oversized and ill-fitting, resulting in Spicer being likened 'to a graduate of clown college and a used-car salesman' (Trebay 2017); others noticed his speaking tone, which was described as 'irate'; some focused on his decision not to take questions after his statement, which was described as 'a highly unusual move' (Wagner 2017). The main issue, of course, was his way of handling facts. In claiming that 'this was the largest audience to ever witness an inauguration—period—both in person and around the globe' Spicer was in blatant denial of the facts, lying in plain daylight. These comments on Spicer's behaviour – and many others like them – arguably helped to draw attention to a perceived mismatch between the setting of a White House press briefing and Spicer's personal style (or self-styling). By performing stylistic acts in multiple semiotic modes which were all seen to index anything but 'high-class', 'authority' and 'honesty', Spicer's way of 'doing a press conference' was at odds with sociocultural expectations, making him the object of ridicule.

In Figure 1 the theme of ridicule is activated most directly in the interplay between the left and right segments of the composite meme. Based on the presence of two large microphones in front of the speaker on the left, we can recognize another representation of a press conference. Though literally not 'staged' to the same extent as the White House event, this press conference is no less styled. The speaker's attire – beret and an army green shirt, both with various insignia – index him as a military figure. Because the speaker appears in front of palm trees, we get the impression that the press conference takes place outdoors, perhaps 'in the field', in some warm and seemingly dusty environment. Overall, we are presented with a military man of action, seemingly making an insistent point (raised palms) to a mediated audience.

For viewers with the relevant sociocultural frame of reference, the speaker will in fact be recognizable as Mohammed Saeed al-Sahhaf who was Iraqi Information Minister and spokesperson for President Saddam Hussein during the US-led invasion of Iraq in 2003. In international news media he earned the derogatory nickname 'Comical Ali' – a phonological play on the phrase 'Chemical Ali', which was the even more derogatory nickname of a former Iraqi defence minister. Comical Ali was so-called because he tirelessly engaged in daily press briefings where he denied any suggestion that the Iraqi regime was threatened by the invasion, although the Iraqi forces were quite obviously, according to Western news media at least, on the verge of collapse. In Western media, the press briefings by Mohammed Saeed al-Sahhaf were generally considered laughable because of the perceived outrageous nature of the claims he made, and the humorous style he adopted. By deploying this image of Comical Ali, and indexing the visual and discursive style that he epitomizes as a mediated prototype, the meme producer activates a highly particular meaning potential. By associating Spicer with this meaning potential, through the juxtaposition of photos showing the two men in similar situations and with similar facial expressions, thereby activating a much more powerful intertextual connection, the meme invites viewers (at least, viewers with the necessary metacultural awareness) to see Spicer as acting disingenuously.

The meme caption ('The inauguration crowds where yuge') brings us back to verbal style and styling, adding insult to the injury already achieved in other semiotic modes. The misspelling of 'were' as <where>, but also perhaps the h-dropping suggested by the spelling <yuge> (for 'huge'), conjure up a particular social persona for the individual making the claim. The indexical fields of these features are wide, but it is reasonable to assume that the features are included in order to invite us to think of a speaker that is 'uneducated', 'lazy' and 'inarticulate' (cf. the meanings of the apical meanings of ING discussed above). Interestingly, the viewer cannot be sure who 'owns' the salient voice or voices: Is the caption implied to be what Spicer is saying – he did not in fact utter these words at the press briefing – or perhaps what Mohammed Saeed al-Sahhaf is saying or once said – he would very probably not have an opinion on the matter at all? Or is this something actually or potentially said by Donald Trump? Looking at the folk wisdom available at the website 'know your meme', we see that its account of 'yuge' indicates that there was, at the time, a view in circulation which suggests that Trump may well have been the intended referent:

**Extract 2.** Yuge

**Yuge** (sometimes spelled yooge) is the pronunciation of the English adjective "huge" in a dialect called "New York City English", which causes the /h/ to be reduced to a /y/ sound because of the presence of /u/ and /j/. The pronunciation became popular during the 2016 Presidential Election because of its frequent use by both Bernie Sanders and Donald Trump, both of whom are New York City natives that speak New York City English.
(http://knowyourmeme.com/memes/yuge)

In this context, then, 'yuge' seems to be constructed as a styling shibboleth that indexes 'New York City English' – an enregistered style of American English which is traditionally seen as less than prestigious. Sean Spicer is also a native of New York, so the joke could still be on him. But arguably, as its main impacting quality, the meme generates a deliberate ambiguity over who is voicing the caption, and who therefore is making the spurious claim about the size of the inauguration crowd, and with what consequences. In sum, through the deployment of various forms of culturally salient styles in multiple semiotic modes, and through complex and multi-dimensional laminations of style, which certainly include verbal stylization, the meme manages to deliver a metacomment on the political situation in the US around the time of Donald Trump's election and his inauguration. This act of styling/stylization, moreover, invites viewers to engage their critical faculty of metacultural reflexivity. This is not style as a simple reflex of social arrangements; it is styling as a critical resource for exposing social congruities and incongruities, and therefore also for construing cultural alternatives.

## References

Agha, Asif. 2003. "The social life of cultural value." *Language & Communication* 23(3–4): 231–273. https://doi.org/10.1016/S0271-5309(03)00012-0

Agha, Asif. 2007. *Language and Social Relations*. Cambridge: Cambridge University Press.

Auer, Peter (ed.). 2007. *Style and Social Identities: Alternative Approaches to Linguistic Heterogeneity*. Berlin: Mouton de Gruyter.

Bakhtin, Mikhail. 1981. *The Dialogic Imagination: Four Essays*. Translated by Michael Holquist. Austin: University of Texas Press.

Bakhtin, Mikhail. 1986. *Speech Genres and Other Late Essays*. Translated by Caryl Emerson and Michael Holquist. Austin: University of Texas Press.

Bauman, Richard. 1986. *Story, Performance, and Event: Contextual Stories of Oral Narrative*. Cambridge: Cambridge University Press. https://doi.org/10.1017/CBO9780511620935
Bell, Allan. 1984. "Language style as audience design." *Language in Society* 13(2): 145–204. https://doi.org/10.1017/S004740450001037X
Bell, Allan. 2001. "Back in style: Reworking audience design." In *Style and Sociolinguistic Variation*, ed. by Penelope Eckert and John R. Rickford, 139–169. Cambridge: Cambridge University Press.
Bell, Allan. 2016. "An evil version of our accent." In *Style, Media and Language Ideologies*, ed. by Jacob Thøgersen, Nikolas Coupland and Janus Mortensen, 235–258. Oslo: Novus.
Bohmann, Axel. 2016. "'Nobody canna cross it': Language-ideological dimensions of hypercorrect speech in Jamaica." *English Language and Linguistics* 20(1): 129–152. https://doi.org/10.1017/S1360674315000374
Bucholtz, Mary. 2008. *Indexicality in Interaction*. Themed panel at Sociolinguistics Symposium 17, 3–5 April, Amsterdam. http://www.meertens.knaw.nl/ss17/contributions/abstract.php?paperID=158
Bucholtz, Mary, and Kira Hall. 2005. "Identity and interaction: A sociocultural linguistic approach." *Discourse Studies* 7(4–5): 585–614.
Campbell-Kibler, Kathryn. 2007. "Accent, (ING), and the social logic of listener perceptions." *American Speech* 82(1): 32–64. https://doi.org/10.1215/00031283-2007-002
Campbell-Kibler, Kathryn. 2008. "I'll be the judge of that: Diversity in social perceptions of (ING)." *Language in Society* 37(5): 637–659. https://doi.org/10.1017/S0047404508080974
Coupland, Nikolas. 1985. "Hark, hark the lark!": Social motivations for phonological style-shifting. *Language and Communication* 5: 153–172. https://doi.org/10.1016/0271-5309(85)90007-2
Coupland, Nikolas. 2001. "Stylization, authenticity and TV news review." *Discourse Studies* 3(4): 413–442. https://doi.org/10.1177/1461445601003004006
Coupland, Nikolas. 2007. *Style: Language Variation and Identity*. Cambridge: Cambridge University Press. https://doi.org/10.1017/CBO9780511755064
Coupland, Nikolas. 2011. "The Sociolinguistics of style." In *The Cambridge Handbook of Sociolinguistics*, ed. by Rajend Mesthrie, 138–156. Cambridge: Cambridge University Press. https://doi.org/10.1017/CBO9780511997068.013
Coupland, Nikolas. 2016. "Labov, vernacularity and sociolinguistic change." *Journal of Sociolinguistics* 20(4): 409–430. https://doi.org/10.1111/josl.12191
Coupland, Nikolas (ed.). 2016. *Sociolinguistics: Theoretical Debates*. Cambridge: Cambridge University Press. https://doi.org/10.1017/CBO9781107449787
Coupland, Nikolas and Janus Mortensen. 2017. "Style as a unifying perspective for the sociolinguistics of talking media." In *Style, Mediation, and Change: Sociolinguistic Perspectives on Talking Media*, ed. by Janus MortensenJanus Mortensen, Nikolas Coupland and Jacob Thøgersen, 251–261. New York: Oxford University Press. https://doi.org/10.1093/acprof:oso/9780190629489.003.0012
Drew, Paul and John Heritage. 1992. *Talk at Work: Interaction in Institutional Settings*. Cambridge: Cambridge University Press.
Eckert, Penelope. 2000. *Linguistic Variation as Social Practice: The Linguistic Construction of Identity in Belten High*. Malden: Blackwell.
Eckert, Penelope. 2008. "Variation and the indexical field." *Journal of Sociolinguistics* 12(4): 453–76. https://doi.org/10.1111/j.1467-9841.2008.00374.x
Eckert, Penelope. 2012. "Three waves of variation study: The emergence of meaning in the study of sociolinguistic variation." *Annual Review of Anthropology* 41(1): 87–100. https://doi.org/10.1146/annurev-anthro-092611-145828

Eckert, Penelope. 2016. "Variation, meaning and social change." In *Sociolinguistics: Theoretical Debates*, ed. by Nikolas Coupland, 68–85. Cambridge: Cambridge University Press. https://doi.org/10.1017/CBO9781107449787.004

Eckert, Penelope and John R. Rickford (eds). 2001. *Style and Sociolinguistic Variation*. Cambridge: Cambridge University Press.

Eco, Umberto. 1972. "Towards a semiotic enquiry into the television message". In *W.P.C.S.* 3, University of Birmingham.

Enkvist, Nils Erik, John Spencer and Michael J. Gregory. 1964. *Linguistics and Style*. London: Oxford University Press.

Fabricius, Anne and Janus Mortensen. 2013. "Language ideology and the notion of construct resources: A case study of modern RP." In *Language (De)Standardisation in Late Modern Europe: Experimental Studies*, ed. by Tore Kristiansen and Stefan Grondelaers, 375–401. Oslo: Novus.

Firth, John R. 1950. "Personality and language in society." *The Sociological Review* 42 (1): 37–52. https://doi.org/10.1111/j.1467-954X.1950.tb02460.x

Firth, John R. 1957. *Papers in Linguistics, 1934–1951*. London: Oxford University Press.

Giles, Howard and Peter F. Powesland. 1975. *Speech Style and Social Evaluation*. London: Academic Press.

Gumperz, John J. 1982. *Discourse Strategies*. Cambridge: Cambridge University Press. https://doi.org/10.1017/CBO9780511611834

Gumperz, John J. 2015. "Interactional sociolinguistics: A personal perspective." In *The Handbook of Discourse Analysis*, 2nd edition, ed. by Deborah Tannen, Heidi E. Hamilton and Deborah Schiffrin, 309–323. Malden: Blackwell. [Originally published in 2003].

Halliday, Michael A. K. 1978. *Language as Social Semiotic: The Social Interpretation of Language and Meaning*. London: Edward Arnold.

Halliday, Michael A. K., Angus McIntosh and Peter Strevens. 1964. *The Linguistic Sciences and Language Teaching*. London: Longmans.

Hebdige, Dick. 1979. *Subculture: The Meaning of Style*. London: Routledge.

Hickey, Leo (ed.). 1989. *The Pragmatics of Style*. London: Routledge.

Hymes, Dell. 1972. "Models of the interaction of language and social life." In *Directions in Sociolinguistics*, ed. by John J. Gumperz and Dell Hymes, 35–71. New York: Holt, Rinehart and Winston.

Hymes, Dell. 1974. *Foundations in Sociolinguistics: An Ethnographic Approach*. Philadelphia: University of Pennsylvania Press.

Irvine, Judith. 2001. "'Style' as distinctiveness: The culture and ideology of linguistic differentiation." In *Style and Sociolinguistic Variation*, ed. by Penelope Eckert and John R. Rickford, 21–43. Cambridge: Cambridge University Press.

Jaffe, Alexandra. 2016. "Indexicality, stance and fields in sociolinguistics." In *Sociolinguistics: Theoretical Debates*, ed. by Nikolas Coupland, 86–112. Cambridge: Cambridge University Press. https://doi.org/10.1017/CBO9781107449787.005

Johnstone, Barbara. 2014. *Speaking Pittsburghese: The Story of a Dialect*. New York: Oxford University Press.

Johnstone, Barbara, Jennifer Andrus and Andrew E. Danielson. 2006. "Mobility, indexicality, and the enregisterment of 'Pittsburghese.'" *Journal of English Linguistics* 34(2): 77–104. https://doi.org/10.1177/0075424206290692

Johnstone, Barbara, Daniel Baumgardt, Maeve Eberhardt and Scott Kiesling. 2015. *Pittsburgh Speech and Pittsburghese*. Berlin: De Gruyter Mouton. https://doi.org/10.1515/9781614511786

Joos, Martin. 1967. *The Five Clocks: A Linguistic Excursion into the Five Styles of English Usage*. New York: HBJ.
Jørgensen, Jens Normann, Martha Sif Karrebæk, Lian Malai Madsen and Janus Spindler Møller. 2011. "Polylanguaging in superdiversity." *Diversities* 13(2): 23–37.
Kiesling, Scott Fabius. 1998. "Men's identities and sociolinguistic variation: The case of fraternity men." *Journal of Sociolinguistics* 2(1): 69–99. https://doi.org/10.1111/1467-9481.00031
Kiesling, Scott Fabius. 2018. "YouTube Yinzers: Stancetaking and the performance of Pittsburghese." In *Identity and Dialect Performance: A Study of Communities and Dialects*, Chapter 14 [Routledge Studies in Language and Identity], ed. by Reem Bassiouney. Abingdon: Routledge.
Labov, William. 1972. *Sociolinguistic Patterns*. Philadelphia: University of Pennsylvania Press.
Lakoff, Robin Tolmach. 1979. "Stylistic Strategies Within a Grammar of Style." *Annals of the New York Academy of Sciences* 327(1): 53–78. https://doi.org/10.1111/j.1749-6632.1979.tb17753.x.
Le Page, Robert Brock and Andrée Tabouret-Keller. 1985. *Acts of Identity: Creole-Based Approaches to Language and Ethnicity*. Cambridge: Cambridge University Press.
Levi-Strauss, Claude. 1966. *The Savage Mind: La Pensee Sauvage*. London: Weidenfeld and Nicolson.
Lorenzo-Dus, Nuria. 2017. "Style, sociolinguistic change, and political broadcasting: The case of the Spanish news show *Salvados*." In *Style, Mediation, and Change: Sociolinguistic Perspectives on Talking Media*, ed. by Janus Mortensen, Nikolas Coupland and Jacob Thøgersen, 27–50. New York: Oxford University Press. https://doi.org/10.1093/acprof:oso/9780190629489.003.0002
Madsen, Lian Malai. 2013. "'High' and 'Low' in urban Danish speech styles." *Language in Society* 42(2): 115–138. https://doi.org/10.1017/S0047404513000018
Madsen, Lian Malai, Janus Spindler Møller and Jens Normann Jørgensen. 2010. "'Street Language' and 'Integrated': Language use and enregisterment among late modern urban girls." In *Ideological Constructions and Enregisterment of Linguistic Youth Styles* [Copenhagen Studies in Bilingualism 55], ed. by Lian Malai Madsen, Janus Spindler Møller and Jens Normann Jørgensen, 81–113. Copenhagen: University of Copenhagen.
Malinowski, Bronislaw. 1923. "The problem of meaning in primitive languages." In *The Meaning of Meaning: A Study of the Influence of Language upon Thought and of the Science of Symbolism*, ed. by Charles Kay Ogden and Ivor Armstrong Richards, Supplement 1, 296–336.
McEntegart, Damian and Robert B. Le Page. 1982. "An appraisal of the statistical techniques used in the Sociolinguistic Survey of Multilingual Communities." In *Sociolinguistic Variation in Speech Communities*, ed. by Suzanne Romaine, 105–124. London: Hodder Arnold.
Mortensen, Janus, Nikolas Coupland and Jacob Thøgersen. 2017. "Introduction: Conceptualizing style, mediation, and change." In *Style, Mediation, and Change: Sociolinguistic Perspectives on Talking Media*, ed. by Janus Mortensen, Nikolas Coupland and Jacob Thøgersen, 1–24. New York: Oxford University Press. https://doi.org/10.1093/acprof:oso/9780190629489.001.0001
Rampton, Ben. 1995. *Crossing*. London: Longman.
Rampton, Ben. 2005. *Crossing, Language and Ethnicity among Adolescents*, 2nd edition. Manchester: St. Jerome Publishing.
Rampton, Ben. 2006. *Language in Late Modernity: Interaction in an Urban School*. Cambridge: Cambridge University Press. https://doi.org/10.1017/CBO9780511486722
Saville-Troike, Muriel. 2003. *The Ethnography of Communication: An Introduction*. Malden: Blackwell. https://doi.org/10.1002/9780470758373
Schieffelin, Bambi B., Paul V. Kroskrity and Kathryn A. Woolard (eds). 1992. *Language Ideologies. Special Issue. Pragmatics* 2(3).
Sebeok, Thomas A. 1960. *Style in Language. Cambridge*, Mass: MIT Press.

Silverstein, Michael. 1976. "Shifters, linguistic categories, and cultural description." In *Meaning in Anthropology*, ed. by Keith H. Basso and Henry A. Selby, 11–55. Albuquerque: University of New Mexico Press.

Silverstein, Michael. 2003. "Indexical order and the dialectics of sociolinguistic life." *Language and Communication* 23(3–4): 193–229. https://doi.org/10.1016/S0271-5309(03)00013-2

Spilioti, Tereza. 2017. "Radio talk, pranks, and multilingualism: Styling Greek identities at a time of crisis." In *Style, Mediation, and Change: Sociolinguistic Perspectives on Talking Media*, ed. by Janus Mortensen, Nikolas Coupland and Jacob Thøgersen, 51–76. New York: Oxford University Press. https://doi.org/10.1093/acprof:oso/9780190629489.003.0003

The White House. 2017. *The White House Press Secretary Makes A Statement*. Recorded YouTube live stream. https://www.youtube.com/watch?v=9AjjVMAdWm4&feature=youtu.be&t=1h33m25s.

Thøgersen, Jacob, Nikolas Coupland and Janus Mortensen. 2016. "Introduction: Style, Media and Language Ideologies." *In Style, Media and Language Ideologies*, ed. by Jacob Thøgersen, Nikolas Coupland and Janus Mortensen, 11–49. Oslo: Novus.

Trebay, Guy. 2017. "Sean Spicer fixed his suits. What about the ties?" *The New York Times*, March 4, 2017, sec. Fashion & Style. https://www.nytimes.com/2017/03/04/fashion/sean-spicer-white-house-press-secretary-trump-style-suits-ties.html.

Trotta, Daniel. 2017. "Crowd controversy: The making of an inauguration day photo." *Reuters*, January 24, 2017. https://www.reuters.com/article/us-usa-trump-inauguration-image/crowd-controversy-the-making-of-an-inauguration-day-photo-idUSKBN1572VU.

Urban, Greg. 2001. *Metaculture: How Culture Moves through the World*. Minneapolis: University of Minnesota Press.

Wagner, John. 2017. "Trump's press secretary lashes out at press, calling crowd coverage 'shameful and wrong.'" *Washington Post*, January 21, 2017, sec. Post Politics. https://www.washingtonpost.com/news/post-politics/wp/2017/01/21/trumps-press-secretary-lashes-out-at-press-calling-crowd-coverage-shameful-and-wrong/.

Woolard, Kathryn A., Aida Ribot Bencomo and Josep Soler Carbonell. 2013. "What's so funny now? The strength of weak pronouns in Catalonia." *Journal of Linguistic Anthropology* 23(3): 127–141. https://doi.org/10.1111/jola.12024

Woolard, Kathryn A. and Bambi B. Schieffelin. 1994. "Language ideology." *Annual Review of Anthropology* 23(1): 55–82. https://doi.org/10.1146/annurev.an.23.100194.000415

# Superdiversity

Zane Goebel
University of Queensland, Brisbane

## 1. Introduction

Discourses about superdiversity can be traced back to Vertovec's (2007b) paper "Super-diversity and its implications". In this paper, superdiversity referred to the diversification of diversity in Western European contexts, especially the UK, where this diversification was experienced, commented upon, and bureaucratized (in policy) as a new and potentially troublesome phenomenon. Vertovec offers the following definition of superdiversity:

> ... [A] notion intended to underline a level and kind of complexity surpassing anything the country has previously experienced. Such a condition is distinguished by a dynamic interplay of variables among an increased number of new, small and scattered, multiple-origin, transnationally connected, socio-economically differentiated and legally stratified immigrants who have arrived over the last decade. ... Such additional variables include differential immigration statuses and their concomitant entitlements and restrictions of rights, divergent labour market experiences, discrete gender and age profiles, patterns of spatial distribution, and mixed local area responses by service providers and residents. Rarely are these factors described side by side. The interplay of these factors is what is meant here, in summary fashion, by the notion of 'super-diversity'. (Vertovec 2007b: 1024–1025)

The above definition is a descriptor for a particular situation, which contrasts with what was seen as a common and problematic way of describing multiculturalism and transnationalism (Tsuda 2003; Brettell 2003; Vertovec 2007a). One cluster of issues related to the conceptualization of identity as constant, rather than context dependent. For example, the ideas of multiculturalism and transnationalism often constructed borders between migrants and their hosts by discursively positioning them as members of a homogenous national group moving to another nation populated by another homogenous group. This essentialization process erased the heterogeneous nature of both populations. Just as importantly, Vertovec (2007a, b) pointed out that the complexity covered by the term superdiversity invited social scientists to seek interdisciplinary engagement. Such engagement would assist in understanding how people practiced everyday mundane multiculturalism in settings characterized by superdiversity (Vertovec 2007b: 1045).

Sociolinguistics was in a position to take up this invitation. This was so because of its long history of pursuing issues around identity, contact, and social cohesion

https://doi.org/10.1075/hop.21.sup1

together with a methodological toolkit for examining how people practiced everyday multiculturalism (Milroy & Muysken 1995; Eastman 1992; Auer 1998; Le Page & Tabouret-Keller 1985; Antaki & Widdicombe 1998; Gumperz 1982; Tannen 1984; Blommaert 2001; Rampton 1995; Scollon & Scollon 1981). A group of scholars took up this invitation and formed a research community in 2010: the International Consortium on Language and Super-diversity (InCoLaS). The formation of InCoLaS co-occurred with the publication of a book by Blommaert (2010) that invited us to link the idea of superdiversity to concerns over globalization and inequality more generally. This was shortly followed by a special issue, which used a sociolinguistic lens to discuss questions of identity, contact, social cohesion, and methodology, especially the strengths of linguistic anthropology/ethnography for understanding these issues (Blommaert & Rampton 2011). At the same time, these two volumes invited us to evaluate concepts we work with in sociolinguistics. This included our conceptions of language; the connections between language and social relations; the processes, infrastructures, and conditions that enabled the circulation and association of language with social relations, identities, and interactional practices.

Since then, the idea of superdiversity has received rapid uptake within sociolinguistics. This is evidenced by a cursory glance at special issues, edited books, and monographs that have been published since 2013 (Arnaut et al. eds. 2016; Faudree & Schulthies 2015; Arnaut 2012; Kusters et al. 2017; Blackledge & Creese eds. 2014; De Fina, Ikiszoglu & Wegner 2017; Pennycook & Otsuji 2015; Garcia & Li 2014; Flores 2016; Goebel 2015; Duarte & Gogolin 2013; Blommaert & Varis eds. 2015; Arnaut et al. eds. 2015; Blommaert 2013). Within this literature, superdiversity is used in multiple ways. Sometimes it is used as a descriptor of contemporary city and urban sociolinguistic life, as in "contact in conditions of superdiversity". More commonly, however, the term superdiversity continues to index an invitation to evaluate and engage in intellectual exchange about sociolinguistic concepts and methods (Arnaut et al. 2016; Blommaert 2015).

Like all concepts and processes of knowledge circulation, the meanings associated with the term superdiversity are also constantly emerging and contested, in Vološinov's (1973 [1929]) sense. Superdiversity has been critiqued as an exemplar of the dark side of academic branding (Pavlenko 2017), for its Eurocentrism, scale-lessness, and proclivity to view superdiversity as only an outcome of migration (Reyes 2014; Goebel 2015; Silverstein 2015; Albury 2017; Goebel 2016). For example, what role do institutions play in diversification and diversity management, and for how long has this been happening, and how does all this relate to the discursive construction of social relations (Silverstein 2015; Moore 2015; Goebel 2015, 2016).

Many of the major contours of these critiques have been nicely summarized elsewhere (Varis 2016). Accordingly, in the rest of the entry I align with Blommaert and Rampton (2011) and Blommaert (2015) to argue that more than anything else the idea of superdiversity has created an important point of reference and synthesis for thinking about many sociolinguistic concepts. In particular, concepts relating to the mobility and connection of people, material things, and ideas, and the relationship of all of this to this thing called language and to diversity management. In Section 2 I point out that these concepts are underpinned by an acknowledgement that most settings can be characterized as contact settings, and that the communicative uncertainty in such settings is policed or managed in a multitude of complex and inter-related ways. The concept of language has received sustained attention too and I discuss these ideas in Section 3, before then moving to the relationship of language to notions of identity in Section 4. In Section 5, I relate reconceptualizations about language and identity to conceptual work around the idea of community, before examining how all of these ideas relate to discussions about theory and method more generally in Section 6.

## 2. Ideas about contact

One of the starting assumptions of superdiversity scholarship is that many interactions in neighborhoods and institutions involve contact between those who share few semiotic resources. This assumption is underpinned by forty years of sociolinguistic research in contact settings that tell us that all understanding in interaction is jointly negotiated and constructed no matter how much background is shared between participants (Gumperz 1982; Rampton 1995; Hanks 2006; Enfield 2006; Philips 1983; Scollon & Scollon 1981; Tannen 1984). The above-mentioned work, as well as other related work, also tells us that these contact situations influence the life trajectories of participants in all sorts of ways. For example, the inability to interact using an expected way of speaking can lead to incarceration in police-suspect interviews (Eades 1995), deportation in bureaucrat-asylum seeker interviews (Maryns 2006; Jacquemet 2015), inability to obtain a post in a job interview (Scheuer 2003; Gumperz 1982), being labelled as deviant in classroom settings (Philips 1983; Scollon & Scollon 1981), being labelled as deviant in urban neighbourhoods (Goebel 2010), and so on.

One way of viewing the discourses that occur in these contact settings, is to seek to understand the relationship of discourses about contact to social value (e.g. the papers in Faudree & Schulthies 2015). These reflexive discourses about social value also police interactional practice. In doing so, they construct and project normativities around such practice. These normativities emerge within different participation frameworks. For example, conversational narratives about the unexpected events that happen in contact (de)value the practices and participants in the story world, while policing social practice and (re)creating normativities for small participant constellations (Faudree 2015; Goebel 2010). At another scale, institutionally sponsored chains of "diversity talk" (Faudree & Schulthies 2015) – that is discourses about diversity – help to construct, model, and project particular ways of speaking as standard, normative, and part of national citizenship or pan-ethnic belonging (Moore 2015; Silverstein 2015; Schulthies 2015). In other cases, these familiar ideologies that link a standard language with a community and state are recontextualized and used as yardsticks to manage diversity in contact situations, such as asylum interviews (Jacquemet 2015), television program production (Schulthies 2015; Goebel 2015), and school classrooms (Karrebæk 2016). Commentaries about diversity are often conducted in multiple languages, which has also been a major conceptual focus for those working on superdiversity.

## 3. Ideas about language, continuity, and change

Sociolinguistic scholarship on superdiversity has also invited us to reconceptualize this thing called language, while considering the reflexive nature of all language use, how resources used in one setting relate to resources in another, and how all of this relates to change more generally (Blommaert and Rampton 2015; Blommaert 2010, 2013; Arnaut, Karrebæk & Spotti 2016). This invitation builds on sociolinguistic work on language ideologies and work on codeswitching.

Work on language ideologies questioned the usefulness of a purely linguistically inspired idea of language given that meaning-making is not just context specific in terms of who says what to whom, where, when, and about what, but that it is also multimodal and highly reflexive in two main ways. First, it has the capacity to be used to comment upon usage and users as interaction unfolds (Agha 2007a; Lucy 1993; Jaworski, Coupland & Galasiński 2004; Bauman & Briggs 2003; Schieffelin, Woolard & Kroskrity 1998; Kroskrity 2000; Agha 2007b). Second, connection is always seen as a part of any instance of situated usage because typically it involves the imitation of semiotic resources from another time and space (e.g. Agha 2007a; Lempert 2014; Bauman & Briggs 1990; Silverstein & Urban 1996). In its discursive form, imitation is a form of semiosis that involves replication of a semiotic fragment from one scale as well as a response to or (e)valuation of this fragment at the situated ongoing interactional scale. The old fragment helps to make a piece of discourse recognizable, while the new commentary increases the possibility of the whole configuration receiving uptake.

Invitations to think about connection also extend to thinking about continuity and change more generally (Blommaert 2010, 2013). Commenting on studies of language endangerment for example, Blommaert (2010: 134) invites us to look at where continuities may lie rather than focusing just on change. The invitation to historicize our accounts of contact, especially through examining imitation, also opens up other possibilities for looking at continuity and change. Indeed, we could even say that in contact settings we are seeing both continuity and change in one utterance: the copied fragments represent continuity and the addition of a response represents change. Where part of a new configuration receives further uptake in a subsequent speech event we are starting to see continuity across events; that is cultural reproduction in action. A focus on change as imitation can thus provide some insights into change that may not be obvious from studies that conceptualize change as change between two time-separated points (e.g. discursive patterns of thirty year olds and seventy year olds).

Work on codeswitching in contact settings has problematized the brought-along essentialist notions of language as pure, unbounded, nameable, and unproblematically linked to territorially bound groups of native speakers (e.g. Rampton 1995; Meeuwis & Blommaert 1994; Blommaert, Collins & Slembrouck 2005; Auer 1995; Alvarez-Cáccamo 1998; Gafaranga & Torras 2002; Swigart 1992). In contrast to this earlier work on codeswitching in contact settings, superdiversity scholarship has also embraced an approach that combines fine-grained examination of the talk that occurs in contact settings with the use of ethnography to help interpret this talk (I will discuss this further in Section 6). Concerns about the nature of language and/or unwittingly seeing codes as similar to bounded languages and thus codeswitching as the use of two bounded codes generated a whole host of competing terminological alternatives within superdiversity discourses. These include polylanguaging (Jørgensen et al. 2011), translanguaging (Garcia & Li 2014), enoughness (Blommaert & Varis 2013), heteroglossia (Blackledge & Creese 2014; Rampton 2011), metrolingualism (Pennycook & Otsuji 2015), signswitching and knowledging (Goebel 2010, 2015), semiotic repertoires (Kusters et al. 2017). Some of these terms and their underlying concepts have been critiqued because they sometimes don't pay enough attention to the importance of connections between the embodied use of resources in one setting to resources from another setting (Albury 2017; Jørgensen et al. 2011; Pennycook 2017). Even so, those that incorporate insights from the language ideological scholarship on reflexivity and connection are increasing in number too (e.g. Blommaert & Varis 2013; Karrebæk 2016; Goebel 2010, 2015, and the papers in Faudree & Schulthies 2015).

Excerpt 1 provides an example that takes into account concerns about the multiple use of semiotic resources in situated interaction and their connection to language ideologies from elsewhere. This snippet of talk is from a conversation involving mobile Indonesians who have temporarily settled in an urban ward in Indonesia. A ward consists of roughly 18–24 families who typically live in the same street. This ward was located in an ethnic homeland of Javanese speakers. Javanese as well as other ethnolinguistic identities had become natural social categories over the previous two centuries, becoming especially focused through the intense nation-building efforts that occurred between 1966 to the mid-1990s (Goebel 2010, 2015). Among the relevant named languages are Indonesian, which has been constructed as the language for communication among strangers and with ethnic others, as well as the language of public address, while Javanese and other ethnic languages have been constructed as the language of co-ethnic and intimate communication. Within this ward there were neighbours who came from both central and peripheral Javanese speaking areas, as well as total ethnolinguistic outsiders (I have put an asterisk after the names of neighbours who self-identified as non-Javanese).

Excerpt 1 is drawn from a two-hour-long recording of a ward meeting where there were thirteen attendees, five of whom self-identified as non-Javanese. I recorded this meeting during thirty months of fieldwork in this ward where these meetings were a monthly event (Goebel 2010: 89–90). These meetings functioned as a forum to disseminate government development policies, gather and disseminate co-operative finance, gather and distribute funds for the upkeep of ward infrastructure and health initiatives, and for socializing. In the conversation before the talk in Excerpt 1, we hear commentaries about the non-present Mrs. Tobing's* inabilities to embody ward normativities, including attending monthly meetings, paying contributions toward the upkeep of the ward, socializing with neighbors, smiling at them when interacting with them, and asking after neighbors as they pass by other ward members' houses. In much of this talk, four participants, Mrs. Naryono, Mrs. Nurholis, Mrs. Joko and Mrs. Sumaryono*, use linguistic resources associated with Javanese and Indonesian. For readability, I have deleted conversation analytic conventions for representing interaction, but I have differentiated between linguistic resources stereotypically associated with Indonesian (plain font) and those stereotypically associated with Javanese (bold font).

**Excerpt 1.** Interpreting interaction in contact settings[1]

| | |
|---|---|
| **Mrs Naryono** | |
| 1 (eh ???) anu **karepé iki**, pokoknya saya<br>2 tuh di sini tuh, cuma sebentar, **ngono loh** | Eh, ah **her wish is like this**, "As it stands. I'm here just for a while", [she] **said it like that.** |
| **Mrs. Sumaryono*** | |
| 3 **ngomongé ngono** | **She said that?** |
| **Mrs. Naryono** | |
| 4 heeh, saya tuh di sini, cuma sebentar<br>5 nanti sewaktu waktu saya tuh bisa pindah,<br>6 tapi kan, selama bertempat tinggal di sini<br>7 seharusnya, ya | That is right. "I'm only here for a while, latter on at any time I will move." But don't [you] agree, as long as [she] lives here [she] has to, you agree? |

1. Extracts 1 and 2 were originally published in 2010 in my book *Language, Migration, and Identity: Neighborhood Talk in Indonesia* (pp. 101 and 89), and have been reprinted with permission of Cambridge University Press.

**Mrs. Sumaryono***

| | |
|---|---|
| 8 ya semua orang (???) itu bu muslim dulu | Yes all people (???), a while back Mrs. |
| 9 apa, nggak tuh | Muslim or [I] don't know |

There are a number of points we can make about the talk in Excerpt 1. First, we see that both Mrs. Naryono and Mrs. Sumaryono* move between using linguistic resources stereotypically associated with Javanese (bold font) and Indonesia (plain font). With reference to ethnographically recoverable information, we find out that Mrs. Naryono has been identified and self-identifies as a Javanese, while Mrs. Sumaryono* has been identified and self identifies as a non-Javanese migrant. Their use of linguistic resources provides an example where these resources do not align in a straightforward way with identity-language relationships, such as one where Javanese might be seen as a language of co-ethnic interaction because Mrs. Sumaryono* is not Javanese, but uses Javanese. It is also the case, that my data from other speech events involving these two participants demonstrates that both could have conducted this conversation in either Indonesian or Javanese had they wished, and thus this usage is not simply a matter of lack of competence in one language or another. This puts us in a position to ask why this now?

We can start to answer this question by paying further attention to this talk, as well as bringing in data from outside this conversation, including further ethnographically recoverable information, and information about the construction of language ideologies by the Indonesian state. In looking further at this talk, we see that as Mrs. Naryono engages in a change in activity type; from talking about a deviant ward member to quoting this members thoughts or wishes (lines 1–2). This language choice is made more significant through how Mrs. Sumaryono* aligns with Mrs. Naryono's representation of Mrs. Tobing's* Indonesian talk. In this case, we have Sumaryono* using Javanese (line 3) with her Javanese interlocutor (Mrs. Naryono), which demonstrates that she is different to the Indonesian speaking Mrs. Tobing* because Mrs. Sumaryono* uses Javanese with neighbors. While here we only have evidence of two turns, examination of Mrs. Sumaryono's* talk in other parts of the meeting, as well as ethnographic observations of her usage elsewhere shows that she habitually pursues social sameness with her neighbors through the use of Javanese resources.

With reference to language ideologies emanating from the state, we can also see connections between these ideologies and this situated talk. In this case, and contrary to the national ideology where Indonesian is the language of unity in diversity, Indonesian speakerhood is projected as inappropriate for interaction amongst this group of ethnically diverse women, and thus helps exclude Mrs. Tobing* from the group of people who are considered good neighbors. This bit of talk exemplifies the everyday multiculturalism that Vertovec (2007b) invited us to investigate. From this brief look we can say that while everyday multiculturalism is ideologized in Indonesia as requiring Indonesian, its continued use in settings where social cohesion is built via another language turns this interactional asset into a an interactional liability.

## 4. Ideas about identity

As noted in the last section, some of the sociolinguistic work on superdiversity relates to rethinking ideas around identity in contact settings, and its relationship with named languages (Arnaut et al. 2015; Goebel 2010, 2015; Blommaert 2013; Blommaert & Rampton 2015; Arnaut et al. 2016). In taking up Vertovec's (2007b) invitation to understand identity and forms of social identification in settings characterized by superdiversity, this scholarship builds upon more general sociolinguistic work on identity. It has drawn on research on talk-in-interaction that has demonstrated the identities are multiple, situated, emergent, and connected to identities at other scales (Bucholtz & Hall 2004; Agha 2007a; Antaki & Widdicombe 1998; Le Page & Tabouret-Keller 1985; Wortham 2006; Hester & Eglin 1997). For example, it has shown how small participant constellations recognize and align with signs associated with identities from other scales, while pursuing social sameness or difference (Bucholtz & Hall 2004; Antaki & Widdicombe 1998; Wortham 2006).

More recently, sociolinguistic work on superdiversity and semiotics has also helped to reconceptualize notions of identity by building on the above-mentioned work, work on scale (Blommaert 2010; Blommaert, Westinen & Leppänen 2015), imitation (Lempert 2014; Bauman & Briggs 1990; Silverstein & Urban 1996), and chronotope (Lempert & Perrino 2007). This work has started to develop the concept of chronotopic identity (Blommaert & De Fina 2017; Blommaert 2016; Goebel 2017). In short, a chronotopic identity is a semiotic configuration that is constructed – often through institutionally authorized one-to-many participation frameworks – at a particular scale. This configuration (e.g. linguistic signs, place, social practice, time, demeanors) or fragments of it are then available for imitation at another scale. For example, multiple Hollywood and television representations in the past of men wearing thick black plastic rimmed eyewear can become interpretive resources for socially identifying someone who wears them now as "old fashioned".

## 5. Ideas about community

Work on superdiversity has invited us to re-examine ideas about community, often via the work on identity noted in the previous section. This work also builds upon sociolinguistic work that uses a micro-analytical perspective to examine how those in contact settings pursue social sameness and/or positive social relations. This includes the examination of the role of conversational narrative (Ochs & Capps 2001; Georgakopoulou 2007), gossip (Besnier 2009), repetition (Tannen 1989), prosody and other embodied signs (Tannen 1984; Bjork-Willen 2007), and small talk (Coupland 2000), in the pursuit of common ground (Enfield 2006), and in the building and maintenance of social relations. More specifically, within superdiversity discourse, community is seen as being interactionally achieved. This is achieved through the recontextualization of chronotopic identities, through the interactional use of small talk to construct common ground, and often through a combination of these (Arnaut et al. 2015; Williams & Stroud 2013; Blommaert & Varis 2015; Goebel 2010, 2015; Blommaert 2013; Blommaert & Rampton 2015; Arnaut et al. 2016).

The conceptualization of community within superdiversity scholarship builds on a diverse set of ideas that challenge older notions of community, and the types of competences one needs to display and enact community. These include emergent communities that are the outcome of situated face-to-face interaction (Bucholtz & Hall 2004). A series of interactions across time in a locale produces another type of community, which are often referred to as "communities of practice" (Wenger 1998). The existence of multiple communities of practice (COP) also enables distinctions between COP (Bourdieu 1984). The practice of making such distinctions helps to sharpen the boundaries between each of these COP (Irvine 2001). Publics or audiences represent another type of community. Publics and audiences not only live in the imaginations of media professionals, writers, and bureaucrats (Anderson 2006 [1991, 1983]; Ang 1996; Livingstone 2005), but they are also constituted through acts of media consumption in living rooms and elsewhere, as well as lesson consumption in classrooms, lecture theatres, and other teaching venues.

In superdiversity discourse, each of these types of communities and the semiotic resources associated with them (e.g. chronotopic identities) become resources for interactional work, or for representations of community in contact settings in the case of mass mediated models of contact (Goebel 2015). At this stage, another example is useful. Excerpt 2 represents a conversation that occurred in the same ward meeting as Excerpt 1, but occurs a few minutes earlier. This talk occurs after discussion about who has and has not paid contributions towards the upcoming Independence Day celebrations in this ward. For readability, I have deleted most conversation analytic conventions for representing interaction, but I have kept some that I will explain as I move through the analysis.

**Excerpt 2.** Community building

| | |
|---|---|
| **Mrs. Abdurrahman*** | |
| 1 bu tobing tuh yang mana | Which one is Mrs. Tobing? |
| **Mrs. Nurholis** | |
| 2 itu loh sebelah bu matius itu loh | You know the one beside Mrs. Matius. |
| **Mrs. Sumaryono*** | |
| 3 sebelah bu roni itu bu tobing toh | The one beside Mrs. Roni is Mrs Tobing, you with me. |
| **Mrs. Naryono** | |
| 4 bu tobing, tobing, tobing | Mrs. Tobing, Tobing, Tobing. |

| | |
|---|---|
| **Mrs. Nurholis** | |
| 5 nggak pernah datang kok | [She] has never attended, disappointingly. |
| **Mrs. Naryono** | |
| 6 lah iya, arisan >nggak pernah | That is right, [she] has never attended a meeting. |
| 7 datang> | |
| **Mrs. Nurholis** | |
| 8 >patungan sepuluh ribu> #nggak | [she] has never contributed her share of 10000 |
| 9 pernah datang'# | [rupiah toward celebrations] [at an arisan]. |
| **Mrs. Sumaryono*** | |
| 10 padahal rt penting butuh kenal ya, | But the ward is important [we] need acquaintances, yes? |

The import of this excerpt is that from line 5 onwards we see that Mrs. Nurholis, Mrs. Naryono, and Mrs. Sumaryono* jointly construct what is seen as normative practice in this ward. In this case, it is attendance at monthly meetings and paying contributions toward upcoming celebrations. Non-attendance is the unexpected event. The social value of attendance is framed in terms of how attendance relates to having acquaintances. If we examine all of the talk in this meeting, then we see the beginning of a neighborhood voice about an emergent ward normativity. This includes how one should interact with neighbours, including the facial expressions one should use upon contact, the language one should use (e.g. Javanese or Indonesian), how regularly one should attend meetings, and so on. In short, the attention to discursive practices in this example not only provide us with an example of how everyday mundane multiculturalism is practiced (Vertovec 2007b), but it also provides us with an insight into how notions of community develop interactionally. In this contact setting, shared understandings about what constitutes a community are constructed in situ. In this case, it is done through both the pursuit of sameness (we speak the same language, we think about this person in the same way, etc.), and difference (we are different to this deviant person by way of actually attending meetings and making financial contributions).

The social pursuit of sameness and the pursuit of positive social relations is also achieved through the minutiae of interactional performance. Here it is achieved via a chain of repetitions that occur after Mrs. Abdurrahman's* query about where one of several meeting absentees lives. These repetitions have a copy of others' talk *nggak pernah datang* "never attends" (lines 5–9), together with a response with some new information from lines 6-8. We also see that copies are not just copies of words, but also of the talk's tempo. For example, we see that on line 8 Nurholis copies the tempo of Naryono's talk on line 7. In this case, Nurholis speeds up her talk (indicated by > surrounding pieces of talk), as done by Naryono before copying the actual words *nggak pernah datang*. In addition to constructing common ground around a topic, the regular occurrence of imitation here and elsewhere also constructs common ground in opinions about normative behavior (Goebel 2010). Put in terms of one of Vertovec's (2007b) concerns about how people do everyday mundane multiculturalism, we can say that through a micro-analytical examination of talk, coupled with ethnographic and language ideological information, we can see that people pursue social sameness in multiple ways: sameness in utterance forms, sameness in opinion, sameness in language choice.

## 6. Ideas about approaches

In the discussion so far, we can identify a number of sometimes overlapping approaches, including conversation analysis, membership category analysis, Goffmanian (1969 [1959]) dramaturgy, ethnography, history, and cultural and media studies. In line with broader appeals to be more multidisciplinarity (e.g. Wallerstein 2004; Clifford 1986; Hymes 1974), superdiversity scholarship has modelled the use of multiple methodologies and theoretical perspectives to understand the complexities surrounding contact. What is common to many of these approaches, is that they share similar epistemological stances about the need to examine communicative practice from the participants' perspective, while also acknowledging anthropological discourses that problematize ethnographic representations, anthropological authority, and authenticity (Clifford & Marcus 1986).

Sometimes, examining communicative practice from the participants' perspective means focusing on small participant constellations via linguistic ethnography or linguistic anthropology (for a discussion of both approaches see Duranti 2009; Rampton et al. 2004). Both approaches use methods that involve a mixture of paying close attention to recordings and/or transcripts of recordings of talk in these situations of contact, and ethnographic methods (interviewing, participation, and observation). Indeed, this approach has become a staple in the epistemological and methodological toolkit of scholars interested in superdiversity (Blommaert 2013; Blommaert and Rampton 2015; Blommaert et al. 2015; Goebel 2010; Pennycook & Otsuji 2015; Arnaut, Karrebæk, & Spotti 2016).

Sometimes, linguistic ethnographic approaches are combined with insights from language ideology scholarship and work on nation building, as in the example provided in the last section. The use of extra theoretical and methodological machinery used in my analysis of Excerpts 1 and 2 helped to interpret this talk, including whether, to what extent and how my interpretations related to the participants' interpretations of their life worlds. At the same time, this extra contextual data about nation-building and the conditions of the ward where I was working helped me to interpret how this talk was connected to social practices from elsewhere.

## 7. Conclusion

This entry started with Vertovec's (2007a, b) original definition of superdiversity and the context within which it was proposed. We then examined the uptake of this term within sociolinguistics in terms of:

1. uptake by a research community,
2. uptake as a descriptor for settings that are more complex than settings described as multicultural, and
3. uptake as an invitation to rethink some of the theories, methods, and related concepts used in social science in general and sociolinguistics in particular.

The bulk of the discussion revolved around ideas about contact, language, identity, community, and approaches to contact settings. I argued that more than anything else, the idea of superdiversity has provided inspiration for a rethinking of a host of sociolinguistic concepts that focus on the connections between contact, language, identity, and community, and approaches to understanding all of this.

The now regular use of ethnography and discourse analysis, informed by work in semiotics and social theory, have provided new concepts, such as scale and chronotopic identity. These new concepts present special promise for understanding the relationships between contact, continuity, and change. At the same time, related work on how social value and normativity is reflexively created, circulated, policed, and tied to identity has provided new ways of understanding how diversity is managed through diversity talk that occurs at several scales: from face-to-face talk about contact to commentaries about contact. Together, this work has highlighted a need to strive to understand the complexities surrounding contact.

## References

Agha, Asif. 2007a. *Language and Social Relations*. Cambridge: Cambridge University Press.

Agha, Asif. 2007b. "The Object Called 'Language' and the Subject of Linguistics." *Journal of English Linguistics* 35(3): 217–235. https://doi.org/10.1177/0075424207304240

Albury, Nathan. 2017. "Mother tongues and languaging in Malaysia: Critical linguistics under critical examination." *Language in Society* 46(4): 567–589. https://doi.org/10.1017/S0047404517000239

Alvarez-Cáccamo, Celso. 1998. "From 'switching code' to code-switching." In *Code-switching in Conversation: Language, Interaction and Identity*, ed. by Peter Auer, 29–48. New York: Routledge.

Anderson, Benedict. 2006 [1991, 1983]. *Imagined Communities: Reflections on the Origin and Spread of Nationalism*, Revised edition. London: Verso.

Ang, Ien. 1996. *Living Room Wars: Rethinking Media Audiences for a Postmodern World*. London: Routledge. https://doi.org/10.4324/9780203289549

Antaki, Charles and Sue Widdicombe (eds). 1998. *Identities in Talk*. London: Sage Publications.

Arnaut, Karel. 2012. "Super-diversity: Elements of an emerging perspective." *Diversities* 14(2): 1–16.

Arnaut, Karel, Jan Blommaert, Ben Rampton and Massimiliano Spotti. 2015. "Introduction: Superdiversity and sociolinguistics." In *Language and Superdiversity*, ed. by Karel Arnaut, Jan Blommaert, Ben Rampton and Massimiliano Spotti, 11–27. New York: Routledge.

Arnaut, Karel, Jan Blommaert, Ben Rampton and Massimiliano Spotti (eds). 2015. *Language and Superdiversity*. New York: Routledge.

Arnaut, Karel, Martha Karrebæk, Massamiliano Spotti and Jan Blommaert (eds). 2016. *Engaging Superdiversity: Recombining Spaces, Times and Language Practices*. Bristol: Multilingual Matters. https://doi.org/10.21832/9781783096800

Arnaut, Karel, Martha Karrebæk and Massimiliano Spotti. 2016. "Engaging superdiversity: The poiesis-infrastructure nexus and language practices in combinatorial spaces." In *Engaging Superdiversity: Recombining Spaces, Times and Language Practices,*, ed. by Karel Arnaut, Martha Sif Karrebæk, Massimilo Spotti and Jan Blommaert, 3–24. Bristol: Multilingual Matters. https://doi.org/10.21832/9781783096800-003

Auer, Peter. 1995. "The pragmatics of code-switching: A sequential approach." In *One Speaker, Two Languages: Cross-disciplinary Perspectives on Code-switching*, ed. by Lesley Milroy and Pieter Muysken, 115–135. Cambridge: Cambridge University Press. https://doi.org/10.1017/CBO9780511620867.006

Auer, Peter (ed.) 1998. *Code-Switching in Conversation: Language, Interaction and Identity*. New York: Routledge.

Bauman, Richard and Charles Briggs. 1990. "Poetics and performance as critical perspectives on language and social life." *Annual Review of Anthropology* 19: 59–88. https://doi.org/10.1146/annurev.an.19.100190.000423

Bauman, Richard and Charles Briggs. 2003. *Voices of Modernity: Language Ideologies and the Politics of Inequality*. Cambridge: Cambridge University Press. https://doi.org/10.1017/CBO9780511486647

Besnier, Niko. 2009. *Gossip and the Everyday Production of Politics*. Honolulu: University of Hawai'i Press. https://doi.org/10.21313/hawaii/9780824833381.001.0001

Bjork-Willen, Polly. 2007. "Participation in multilingual preschool play: Shadowing and crossing as interactional resources." *Journal of Pragmatics* 39(12): 2133–2158. https://doi.org/10.1016/j.pragma.2007.05.010

Blackledge, Adrian and Angela Creese. 2014. "Heteroglossia as practice and pedagogy. In *Heteroglossia as Practice and Pedagogy*, ed. by Adrian Blackledge and Angela Creese, 1–20. New York: Springer. https://doi.org/10.1007/978-94-007-7856-6

Blackledge, Adrian and Angela Creese (eds). 2014. *Heteroglossia as Practice and Pedagogy*. New York: Springer. https://doi.org/10.1007/978-94-007-7856-6

Blommaert, Jan. 2001. "Investigating narrative inequality: African asylum seekers' stories in Belgium." *Discourse & Society* 12: 413–449. https://doi.org/10.1177/0957926501012004002

Blommaert, Jan. 2010. *The Sociolinguistics of Globalization*. Cambridge: Cambridge University Press. https://doi.org/10.1017/CBO9780511845307

Blommaert, Jan. 2013. *Ethnography, Superdiversity and Linguistic Landscapes: Chronicles of Complexity*. Bristol: Multilingual Matters. https://doi.org/10.21832/9781783090419

Blommaert, Jan. 2015. "Commentary: Superdiversity old and new." *Language & Communication* 44: 82–88. https://doi.org/10.1016/j.langcom.2015.01.003

Blommaert, Jan. 2016. "Chronotopes, scales and complexity in the study of language in society." In *Engaging Superdiversity: Recombining Spaces, Times and Language Practices*, ed. by Karel Arnaut, Martha Karrebæk, Massimiliano Spotti and Jan Blommaert, 47–62. Bristol: Multilingual Matters. https://doi.org/10.21832/9781783096800-005

Blommaert, Jan, James Collins and Stef Slembrouck. 2005. "Spaces of multilingualism." *Language and Communication* 25(3): 197–216. https://doi.org/10.1016/j.langcom.2005.05.002
Blommaert, Jan and Anna De Fina. 2017. "Chronotopic identities: On the timespace organization of who we are." In *Diversity and Superdiversity: Sociocultural Linguistic Perspectives*, ed. by Anna De Fina, Didem Ikiszoglu and Jeremy Wegner, 1–15. Washington: Georgetown University Press.
Blommaert, Jan and Ben Rampton. 2011. "Language and superdiversity." *Diversities* 13(2): 1–21.
Blommaert, Jan and Ben Rampton. 2015. "Language and superdiversity." In *Language and Superdiversity*, ed. by K. Arnaut, Jan Blommaert, Ben Rampton and M. Spotti, 29–59. New York: Routledge.
Blommaert, Jan and Piia Varis. 2013. "Enough is enough: The heuristics of authenticity in superdiversity." In *Linguistic superdiversity in urban areas*, ed. by Joana Duarte and Ingrid Gogolin, 143–159. Amsterdam: John Benjamins Publishing Company. https://doi.org/10.1075/hsld.2.10blo
Blommaert, Jan and Piia Varis. 2015. "The importance of unimportant language." *Multilingual Margins* 2(1): 4–9.
Blommaert, Jan and Piia Varis (eds) 2015. *The Importance of Unimportant Language*. Special issue of *Multilingual Margins* 2(1).
Blommaert, Jan, Elina Westinen and Sirpa Leppänen. 2015. "Further notes on sociolinguistic scales." *Intercultural Pragmatics* 12(1): 119–127.
Bourdieu, Pierre. 1984. *Distinction: A Social Critique of the Judgement of Taste*. Cambridge, Mass.: Harvard University Press.
Brettell, Caroline. 2003. *Anthropology and Migration: Essays on Transnationalism, Ethnicity, and Identity*. Walnut Creek, Calif.: Altamira Press.
Bucholtz, Mary and Kira Hall. 2004. "Theorizing identity in language and sexuality research." *Language in Society* 33(4): 469–515.
Clifford, James and George Marcus (eds). 1986. *Writing Culture: The Poetics and Politics of Ethnography*. Berkeley: University of California Press.
Coupland, Justine (ed.). 2000. *Small Talk*. London: Longman.
De Fina, Anna, Didem Ikiszoglu and Jeremy Wegner (eds). 2017. *Diversity and Super-diversity: Sociocultural Linguistic Perspectives*. Washington: Georgetown University Press.
Duarte, Joana and Ingrid Gogolin (eds). 2013. *Linguistic Superdiversity in Urban Areas : Research Approaches*. Amsterdam: John Benjamins Publishing Company. https://doi.org/10.1075/hsld.2
Duranti, Alessandro. 2009. "Linguistic anthropology: History, ideas and issues." In *Linguistic Anthropology: A Reader*, ed. by Alessandro Duranti, 1–60. London: Blackwell.
Eades, Diana. 1995. "Aboriginal English on trial: The case for Stuart and Condren." In *Language in Evidence: Issues Confronting Aboriginal and Multicultural Australia*, ed. by Diana Eades, 147–174. Sydney: University of New South Wales Press.
Eastman, Carol (ed.) 1992. *Codeswitching*. Clevedon, Avon, UK: Multilingual Matters.
Enfield, Nicholas. 2006. "Social consequences of common ground." In *Roots of Human Sociality: Culture, Cognition and Interaction*, ed. by Nicholas Enfield and Stephen Levinson, 399–430. Oxford: Berg.
Faudree, Paja. 2015. "Singing for the dead, on and off line: Diversity, migration, and scale in Mexican Muertos music." *Language & Communication* 44: 31–43. https://doi.org/10.1016/j.langcom.2014.11.004
Faudree, Paja and Becky Schulthies. 2015. "Introduction: 'diversity talk' and its others." *Language & Communication* 44: 1–6. https://doi.org/10.1016/j.langcom.2014.10.010
Flores, Nelson. 2016. "Introduction: US perspectives on super-diversity and schooling." *International Journal of the Sociology of Language* 241: 11–7.

Gafaranga, Joseph and Maria-Carma Torras. 2002. "Interactional otherness: Towards a redefinition of codeswitching." *The International Journal of Bilingualism* 6(1): 1–22. https://doi.org/10.1177/13670069020060010101
Garcia, Ofelia and Li Wei. 2014. *Translanguaging: Language, Bilingualism and Education*. London: Palgrave Macmillan.
Georgakopoulou, Alexandra. 2007. *Small Stories, Interaction and Identities*. Amsterdam: John Benjamins Publishing Company. https://doi.org/10.1075/sin.8
Goebel, Zane. 2010. *Language, Migration and Identity: Neighborhood Talk in Indonesia*. Cambridge: Cambridge University Press. https://doi.org/10.1017/CBO9780511778247
Goebel, Zane. 2015. *Language and Superdiversity: Indonesians Knowledging at Home and Abroad*. New York: Oxford University Press. https://doi.org/10.1093/acprof:oso/9780199795413.001.0001
Goebel, Zane. 2016. "Superdiversity from within: The case of ethnicity in Indonesia." In *Engaging Superdiversity: Recombining Spaces, Times and Language Practices*, ed. by Karel Arnaut, Martha Karrebæk, Max Spotti and Jan Blommaert, 251–276. Bristol: Multilingual Matters. https://doi.org/10.21832/9781783096800-013
Goebel, Zane. 2017. "Imitation, interdiscursive hubs, and chronotopic configuration." *Language & Communication* 53: 1–10. https://doi.org/10.1016/j.langcom.2017.01.003
Goffman, Erving. 1969 [1959]. *The Presentation of Self in Everyday Life*. London: Allen Lane The Penguin Press.
Gumperz, John. 1982. *Discourse strategies*. Cambridge: Cambridge University Press. https://doi.org/10.1017/CBO9780511611834
Hanks, William. 2006. "Joint commitment and common ground in a ritual event." In *Roots of Human Sociality: Culture, Cognition and Interaction*, ed. by Nicholas Enfield and Stephen Levinson, 299–328. Oxford: Berg.
Hester, Stephen and Peter Eglin (eds). 1997. *Culture in Action: Studies in Membership Categorization Analysis*. Maryland: International Institute for Ethnomethodology and Conversation Analysis, and University Press of America, Inc.
Hymes, Dell. 1974. *Foundations in Sociolinguistics: An Ethnographic Approach*. Philadelphia: University of Pennsylvania Press.
Irvine, Judith. 2001. "'Style' as distinctiveness: The culture and ideology of linguistic differentiation." In *Style and Sociolinguistic Variation*, ed. by Penelope Eckert and John Rickford, 21–43. Cambridge: Cambridge University Press.
Jacquemet, Marco. 2015. "Asylum and superdiversity: The search for denotational accuracy during asylum hearings." *Language & Communication* 44: 72–81. https://doi.org/10.1016/j.langcom.2014.10.016
Jaworski, Adam, Nikolas Coupland and Dariusz Galasiński (eds). 2004. *Metalanguage: Social and Ideological Perspectives*. Berlin: Mouton de Gruyter. https://doi.org/10.1515/9783110907377
Jørgensen, J. Normann, Martha S. Karrebæk, Lian Malai Madsen and Janus Spindle Møller. 2011. "Polylanguaging in superdiversity." *Diversities* 13(2): 22–37.
Karrebæk, Martha. 2016. "Rye bread for lunch, lasagne for breakfast: Enregisterment, classrooms and national food norms in superdiversity." In *Engaging Superdiversity: Recombining Spaces, Times and Language Practices*, ed. by Karel Arnaut, Martha Karrebæk, Massamiliano Spotti and Jan Blommaert, 89–122. Bristol: Multilingual Matters. https://doi.org/10.21832/9781783096800
Kroskrity, Paul V. (ed.). 2000. *Regimes of Language: Ideologies, Polities, and Identities*. Santa Fe: School of American Research.
Kusters, Annelies, Massimiliano Spotti, Ruth Swanwick and Elina Tapio. 2017. "Beyond languages, beyond modalities: Transforming the study of semiotic repertoires." *International Journal of Multilingualism* 14(3): 219–232. https://doi.org/10.1080/14790718.2017.1321651

Le Page, Robert B. and Andrée Tabouret-Keller. 1985. *Acts of Identity: Creole-based Approaches to Language and Ethnicity*. Cambridge: Cambridge University.

Lempert, Michael. 2014. "Imitation." *Annual Review of Anthropology* 43(1): 379–395. https://doi.org/10.1146/annurev-anthro-102313-030008

Lempert, Michael and Sabina Perrino. 2007. "Entextualization and the ends of temporality." *Language & Communication* 27(3): 205–211. https://doi.org/10.1016/j.langcom.2007.01.007

Livingstone, Sonia. 2005. "On the relation between audiences and publics." In *Audiences and Publics: When Cultural Engagement Matters for the Public Sphere*, ed. by Sonia Livingstone, 17–41. Bristol: Intellect.

Lucy, John A. (ed.). 1993. *Reflexive Language: Reported Speech and Metapragmatics*. Cambridge: Cambridge University Press. https://doi.org/10.1017/CBO9780511621031

Maryns, Katrijn. 2006. *The Asylum Speaker: Language in the Belgian Asylum Procedure*. Manchester: St Jerome.

Meeuwis, Michael and Jan Blommaert. 1994. "The 'markedness model' and the absence of society: Remarks on codeswitching." *Multilingua* 13(4): 387–423. https://doi.org/10.1515/mult.1994.13.4.387

Milroy, Lesley and Pieter Muysken (eds). 1995. *One Speaker, Two Languages: Cross-Disciplinary Perspectives on Code-Switching*. Cambridge: Cambridge University Press. https://doi.org/10.1017/CBO9780511620867

Moore, Robert. 2015. "From revolutionary monolingualism to reactionary multilingualism: Top-down discourses of linguistic diversity in Europe, 1794-present." *Language & Communication* 44: 19–30. https://doi.org/10.1016/j.langcom.2014.10.014

Ochs, Elinor and Lisa Capps. 2001. *Living Narrative*. Cambridge, Mass.: Harvard University Press.

Pavlenko, Aneta. 2017. "Superdiversity and why it isn't: Reflections on terminological innovation and academic branding." In *Sloganizations in Language Education Discourse*, ed. by Stephan Breidbach, Lutz Küster and Barbara Schmenk. Bristol, UK: Multilingual Matters.

Pennycook, Alastair. 2017. "Translanguaging and semiotic assemblages." *International Journal of Multilingualism* 14(3): 269–282. https://doi.org/10.1080/14790718.2017.1315810

Pennycook, Alastair and Emi Otsuji. 2015. *Metrolingualism: Language in the City*. New York: Routledge.

Philips, Susan U. 1983. *The Invisible Culture: Communication in Classroom and Community on the Warm Springs Indian Reservation*. New York: Longman.

Rampton, Ben. 1995. *Crossing: Language and Ethnicity among Adolescents*. London: Longman.

Rampton, Ben. 2011. "From 'Multi-ethnic adolescent heteroglossia' to 'Contemporary urban vernaculars.'" *Language & Communication* 31(4): 276–294. https://doi.org/10.1016/j.langcom.2011.01.001

Rampton, Ben, Karin Tusting, Janet Maybin, Richard Barwell, Angela Creese and Vally Lytr. 2004. *UK Linguistic Ethnography: A Discussion Paper.* London: Coordinating committee of the UK Linguistic Ethnography Forum.

Reyes, Angela. 2014. "Linguistic anthropology in 2013: Super-new-big." *American Anthropologist* 116(2): 366–378. https://doi.org/10.1111/aman.12109

Scheuer, Jann. 2003. "Habitus as the principle for social practice: A proposal for critical discourse analysis." *Language in Society* 32(2): 143–175. https://doi.org/10.1017/S0047404503322018

Schieffelin, Bambi, Kathryn Woolard and Paul Kroskrity (eds). 1998. *Language Ideologies: Practice and Theory*. New York: Oxford University Press.

Schulthies, Becky. 2015. "Do you speak Arabic? Managing axes of adequation and difference in pan-Arab talent programs." *Language & Communication* 44: 59–71. https://doi.org/10.1016/j.langcom.2014.10.010

Scollon, Ron and Suzanne Wong Scollon. 1981. *Narrative, Literacy, and Face in Interethnic Communication*. Norwood, N.J.: Ablex Pub. Corp.
Silverstein, Michael. 2015. "How language communities intersect: Is 'superdiversity' an incremental or transformative condition?" *Language & Communication* 44(Supplement C): 7–18. https://doi.org/10.1016/j.langcom.2014.10.015
Silverstein, Michael and Greg Urban (eds). 1996. *Natural Histories of Discourse*. Chicago: University of Chicago Press.
Swigart, Leigh. 1992. "Two codes or one? The insiders' view and the description of codeswitching in Dakar." In *Codeswitching*, ed. by Carol Eastman, 83–102. Clevedon, Avon, UK: Multilingual Matters.
Tannen, Deborah. 1984. *Conversational Style: Analyzing Talk among Friends. Norwood*, New Jersey: Ablex.
Tannen, Deborah. 1989. *Talking Voices: Repetition, Dialogue, and Imagery in Conversational Discourse*. Cambridge: Cambridge University Press.
Tsuda, Takeyuki. 2003. *Strangers in the Ethnic Homeland: Japanese Brazilian Return Migration in Transnational Perspective*. New York: Columbia University Press. https://doi.org/10.7312/tsud12838
Varis, Piia. 2016. "Superdiverse times and places: Media, mobility, conjunctures, and structures of feelings." In *Engaging Superdiversity: Recombining Spaces, Times and Language Practices*, ed. by Karel Arnaut, Martha Karrebæk, Massimiliano Spotti and Jan Blommaert, 25–46. Bristol: Multilingual Matters. https://doi.org/10.21832/9781783096800-004
Vertovec, Steven. 2007a. "Introduction: New directions in the anthropology of migration and multiculturalism." *Ethnic and Racial Studies* 30(6): 961–978. https://doi.org/10.1080/01419870701599416
Vertovec, Steven. 2007b. "Super-diversity and its implications." *Ethnic and Racial Studies* 30(6): 1024–1053. https://doi.org/10.1080/01419870701599465
Vološinov, Valentin. 1973 [1929]. *Marxism and the Philosophy of Language*. Translated by Ladislav Matejka and I. R. Titunik. New York: Seminar Press.
Wallerstein, Immanuel. 2004. *World-System Analysis: An Introduction*. Durham: Duke University Press.
Wenger, Etienne. 1998. *Communities of Practice*. Cambridge: Cambridge University Press. https://doi.org/10.1017/CBO9780511803932
Williams, Quentin and Christopher Stroud. 2013. "Multilingualism in transformative spaces: Contact and Conviviality. *Language Policy* 12(4): 289–311. https://doi.org/10.1007/s10993-012-9265-4
Wortham, Stanton. 2006. *Learning Identity: The Joint Emergence of Social Identification and Academic Learning*. Cambridge: Cambridge University Press.

# Tactile sign languages

Louisa Willoughby, Shimako Iwasaki, Meredith Bartlett & Howard Manns
Monash University, Melbourne

## 1. Introduction

Within the field of sign language linguistics, an emerging area of interest is the sign language forms used by people who are both deaf and blind. In very simple terms, a deafblind signer will follow a conversation by placing one or both hands on top of the hands of someone who is signing. However, as this chapter will explore, the move from a visual to tactile mode of perception necessitates a number of adaptations in the way a message is communicated. Whether these changes lead to minor modifications of the existing visual sign language, the emergence of a new language specifically designed for tactile production and reception or something in between arguably differs depending on both the individual deafblind signer and the communities in which they are imbedded. In this entry we set out to give an overview of what is known about distinctive pragmatic strategies employed by deafblind signers around the world, be they linguistic or non-linguistic; highly codified or somewhat idiosyncratic adaptions. Our goal in taking a broad-sweeping view in this chapter is to give an overview of the different ways in which deafblind people respond to the challenge of communication with limited or no access to the visual or auditory channel, and to consider what (if any) insights this might give about pragmatics in human communication more generally. We note that the choice of terms to describe these ways of signing is potentially problematic, as calling something a "tactile sign language" might seem to be making claims that the variety has diverged markedly from the parent sign language (i.e. is a 'new' language) and/or has been specifically optimised for tactile delivery. However, within this relatively new field of research and interpreting practice "tactile sign language" or "tactile [sign language name]"[1] has become the default way of referring to the form of signing used by deafblind people, and is thus our umbrella term of choice in this entry.

In talking about the ways in which deafblind people use and adapt sign languages it is important to be clear about several points from the outset. Because deafblindness

1. E.g. tactile Auslan in Australia, tactile SSL (Swedish Sign Language) in Sweden, tactile JSL (Japanese Sign Language) in Japan. For examples of this usage, see e.g. Bono et al. (2018), Mesch (2001), Napier, McKee & Goswell (2010).

https://doi.org/10.1075/hop.21.tac1

is a low incidence condition – and one that can severely impact a person's ability to travel independently – many deafblind people experience social isolation (Hepp 1998) and may have limited experience using tactile sign languages with other deafblind people. Edwards' work in the Seattle deafblind community (e.g. Edwards 2012, 2014a, 2014b, 2018) documents how the process of deafblind people coming together more and sharing their views and experience was inseparable from the process of language change that led to the emergence of a distinctive Tactile American Sign Language. In contexts where deafblind people are more isolated, the adaptations an individual uses may be more idiosyncratic and also less effective for conveying information or avoiding ambiguity. A related point is the level of experience or fluency someone has as a tactile sign language user. Deafblind signers are typically adults who were born deaf (and learnt a visual sign language as children) before losing their sight later in life due to degenerative conditions such as retinitis pigmentosa (RP) or glaucoma. For some tactile sign language users, vision loss is total and happens relatively early in life, but there remains a cohort who make the transition to tactile reception only in their 50s or later, and/or who have some residual vision that they make use of in interpreting aspects of an interaction (such as perceiving nodding). Added to this diversity are small numbers of tactile signers with other physical or intellectual disabilities, and people who first learnt to sign after losing their sight. It is thus often remarked upon that deafblind signers are a very heterogeneous bunch (e.g. Collins & Petronio 1998; Mesch 2001; Willoughby, Manns, Iwasaki & Bartlett 2014). If and how sociolinguistic factors (such as gender) or fluency factors (such as age of acquisition of a sign language or age at transition to tactile reception) affect the ways in which a deafblind person signs remains poorly understood – though Petronio and Dively (2006) provide some early data on these factors that will be discussed in Section 5.

In visual sign languages a great deal of syntactic and pragmatic information is conveyed via non-manual channels. Janzen, Shaffer & Wilcox (1999) on *signed language pragmatics* includes numerous examples of how features such as head nods and tilts, eyebrow movement and pursed lips are used to modify the meaning of the manually signed utterance – for example, to express degree of certainty or to turn statements into polar questions. These non-manual features are also frequently used to provide backchannelling responses (Petronio & Dively 2006), while eye-gaze plays an important role in regulating turn-taking in visual signing (see Janzen et al. 1999), as it does in spoken language interactions. While some tactile sign language users may have enough residual sight to perceive occasional non-manual features visually, the majority will not. A question thus becomes if and how tactile sign language users adapt the parent visual sign language or draw on different interactional cues to recover information that the parent visual sign language encodes through non-manuals. A further challenge in describing tactile sign languages is that a fulsome pragmatic discussion needs to account not only for the ways in which the language encodes linguistic information, but also for the ways in which deafblind signers might reinscribe or otherwise access relevant interactional information that participants normally perceive through the visual or aural channels (such as who is in the room, whether their conversation partner is listening attentively, who is making a bid for the floor). One option, of course, is to use linguistic means to make such points explicitly (such as using the lexical sign YES for back-channelling), but in Sections 4–6 we explore a number of evolving conventions that draw on what in an oral language environment might be termed "non-verbal communication". Academic research around tactile signing remains relatively scant and a number of questions remain about the degree to which deafblind communities around the globe are responding in similar ways to the challenges of tactile communication. To date, tactile American Sign Language (ASL) has attracted the most academic attention (Collins & Petronio 1998; Edwards 2012, 2014b, 2014a, 2018; Haas, Fleetwood & Ernest 1995; Quinto-Pozos 2002; Reed, Delhorne, Durlach & Fischer 1995), but studies have also explored tactile Swedish Sign Language (SSL) (e.g. Mesch 2001, 2013), tactile French Sign Language (Schwarz 2004, 2009), tactile Norwegian Sign Language (e.g. Berge & Raanes 2013; Mesch, Raanes & Ferrara 2015; Raanes 2011; Raanes & Berge 2017), tactile Japanese Sign Language (Bono et al. 2018) and tactile Australian Sign Language (Auslan) (Iwasaki, Bartlett, Manns & Willoughby in press; Willoughby et al. 2014).

## 2. Body position and contact in tactile signing

Tactile communication requires the creation of norms surrounding what is or is not appropriate touching that are often radically different to those of the wider community. Deafblind people get their information about the world primarily through touch, and a logical extension of this (when people are comfortable doing so) is to touch each others' bodies to convey information such as what a new hairstyle or blouse is like (Edwards 2014b). Similarly, a deafblind person might lightly feel the hands of a friend to see what they are doing or whom they are talking to. Such touch behaviours are at the core of what in the US is referred to as the "pro-tactile" movement, a deafblind-led movement that has sought to develop and promote interactional conventions that allow deafblind people to more fully participate in society (for more information, see www.protactile.org/).

The creation of new norms around intimacy and personal space is not without problems. Raanes (2011) recounts that at a focus group with four users of tactile NTS (Norwegian Sign Language) participants complained that they do not like it when interpreters sit too close and invade their personal space. Yet, in data that Raanes collected from these same individuals she noted that they generally sat very close together and frequently coarticulated signs on the recipient's face, head and body (e.g. a sign that would normally be made on the signer's own face can be made on the recipient's face so that it is clearer for the deafblind person where the sign contacts the body). This was not seen as an invasion of personal space, and indeed, has been attested in at least two other tactile sign languages (tactile ASL and tactile SSL. See Edwards 2014b; Mesch et al. 2015). But Raanes notes that it leaves unresolved the issue of what it is exactly that interpreters are doing that her participants viewed as an invasion of personal space. How people become socialised into these norms of bodily contact – and what happens when people who are comfortable with these norms interact with those who are not – is also a complex issue requiring frequent compromise and habituation as people learn to leave their comfort zones (Edwards 2014b).

Tactile signers may make use of a wide variety of hand and body positions for tracking the signing of their interlocutor. As noted in the introduction, the primary way that deafblind interlocutors track the signing of their conversation is by placing one or both hands over those of their interlocutor. But valuable haptic feedback can also be gained from contact with other parts of interlocutor's body and for this reason many tactile signers prefer to converse in postures that allow legs or other body parts to touch in addition to hands – for example, by sitting opposite each other with legs or knees touching (for an example of this, see images in Edwards 2018). Deafblind people report that postures like this will alert them to a range of subtle movements made by the interlocutor that are relevant to the interaction – such as allowing them to perceive a nodding head, a head turn or body twist that may indicate something else has caught their interlocutor's attention.

Tactile sign languages around the globe seem to differ in the preferred hand positions used for sign reception. For example, in tactile ASL there is a preference for one handed reception, where the recipient follows only the dominant hand of the signer (Collins & Petronio 1998; Edwards 2014b). This position is also used to follow interpreted monologues in tactile SSL in Sweden (Mesch 2001). When both signers share the same dominant hand, this position can form what Mesch calls "dialogue position" – i.e. each signer places their non-dominant hand on top of the dominant hand of their interlocutor, allowing transition between speaking turns without having to change hand position. Dialogue position is frequently used in recordings of tactile signers in Sweden (Mesch 2001) and it is also noted in France (Schwarz 2004), but is not used in Norway (Raanes 2011) or Australia (Willoughby et al. 2014). In the latter countries – and anecdotally also in the UK, New Zealand and Japan – the only hand configuration commonly seen is for the receiver to place both hands on top of the signer – necessitating a change of hand position each time the turn changes in conversation. Figure 1 illustrates this position. It is not yet clear whether these different preferences for hand position are connected to structural differences in the parent visual sign language (e.g. proportion of one-handed vs. two-handed signs, or of signs involving two hands moving asymmetrically), or the degree of conventionalisation/development tactile signing has undergone in these countries, or indeed any other factors.

The hand positions described so far imply that a deafblind signer can only participate in dyadic conversation. When deafblind people come together in groups

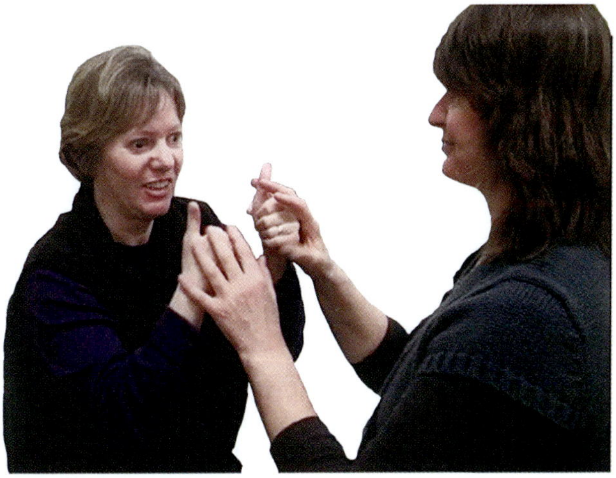

Figure 1. Hand positions of two deafblind signers (Left = speaker; Right = recipient)

– such as committee meetings or recreational activities – the traditional approach has been to provide each deafblind signer with an interpreter,[2] who relays communication between the individual and the group (Berge & Raanes 2013). The downside of this approach is that it makes gatherings of deafblind people both logistically complex and very expensive to organise, especially in areas experiencing interpreter shortages. For these reasons, the pro-tactile movement in Seattle has developed a number of complex adaptations of ASL that allow for direct communication between three or more deafblind people. This is primarily achieved by turning two-handed signs into one-handed forms that can then be made with both hands simultaneously and followed by two people at once (Edwards 2014b). However, it should be noted that this adaptation occurs in a context where the community is developing a language that diverges at the sub-lexical level from many of the articulatory constraints of the parent visual sign language, so it is not simply a case of signing visual ASL with weak hand drop (see Edwards 2014b, 2018 for further details).

## 3. Question formation

Cross-linguistically, sign languages use non-manual features (such as head tilt and changes in eyebrow position) to syntactically mark questions (see Janzen et al. 1999

2. In practice, the risk of occupational overuse injuries for all sign language interpreters mean that interpreters normally work in tandem to allow appropriate rest breaks (Australian Sign Language Interpreters' Association 2014). Overuse injuries are a particular concern for tactile interactions because of the pressure of having one's signing even lightly tracked by a tactile sign language user.

for further details). These can be thought of as loosely equivalent to questioning intonation in English and are inaccessible to deafblind signers. However, just as spoken languages will have myriad possible structures for forming questions, so visual sign languages develop a host of phrasing conventions that can cue the recipient to interpret the utterance as a question. The question thus becomes whether tactile signers vary categorically or statistically in the ways in which they mark questions in their utterances, compared to visual signers, and whether they experience difficulty in correctly identifying questions in interactional discourse.

One of the earliest published studies to explore features of a tactile sign language is Haas et al.'s (1995) analysis of a conversation between two users of tactile ASL. Haas et al. note that their two interlocutors (referred to as A and W) use a wide variety of structures for marking polar questions, and that they employ these structures at different rates. Participant A ends the majority of his polar questions with either a tag RIGHT, or a final YOU to make clear that the other party is being addressed, as in:

(1) YOU COMFORTABLE HERE YOU
Are you comfortable here?

(2) YOU YUCK MATH RIGHT
You don't like maths, do you? (Haas et al. 1995: 109)

Participant W does not show a clear preference in structures and uses an eclectic mix of markers including manually signing a question mark at the end of a phrase. This sign (glossed as QUESTION) does exist in visual ASL, but is used optionally to convey emphasis/incredulity (etc.) in a question (Collins & Petronio 1998: 31), whereas in deafblind contexts it does not appear to have these associations. Additionally, W used explicit question phrases, as in (3) and left questions unmarked when their intention is clear from the context, as in (4)

(3) DO YOU BELIEVE PARENT HAVE-TO INFORM CHILDREN
Do you believe that parents have to inform their children?

(4) I VERY COMFORTABLE, YOU
I'm very comfortable, are you? (Haas et al. 1995: 109)

Collins and Petronio (1998) provide the first broad account of tactile ASL features, based on a corpus from 14 deafblind signers – 11 signing naturally at a social event in Seattle and three signing stories to each other as part of a more structured data elicitation task. They noted that signers in their study also formed polar questions with the question mark sign, as in (5)

(5) NOW QUESTION
Right now? (Collins & Petronio 1998: 31)

However, in later deafblind interview data less than 11% of polar questions used this sign (Dively & Petronio 2006; cited in Petronio 2010: 255), suggesting that it may have been a short-lived convention of tactile ASL.

Collins and Petronio (1998) state that wh-questions in their data always included an overt WH-sign. Mesch's study of tactile Swedish Sign Language also found a strong preference for wh-questions to use an overt WH-sign. However, in her data their use is not obligatory – around 13% of wh-questions in her data were unmarked (Mesch 2001: 164), while in Dively and Petronio's interview data that figure rises to 22% (Dively & Petronio 2006; cited in Petronio 2010: 255). As sign languages follow a topic-comment word order (see Janzen et al. 1999), WH-signs may appear in a range of positions within the utterance in both visual and tactile sign languages – including initially, finally and both initially and finally, as in (6) (Collins & Petronio 1998; Haas et al. 1995; Mesch 2001).

(6) WHAT PLANE LOOK-LIKE WHAT
What did the plane look like (Collins & Petronio 1998: 30)

Mesch (2001: 163) quantified the position of wh-words in her corpus and found that initial position was strongly preferred (used in 73% of cases), suggesting that the word order is being used as an important cue that a question is incoming. Collins and Petronio (1998) additionally note that wh-questions often began with YOU as an attention-getter, as in (7)

(7) YOU HOW YOU
How are you? (Collins & Petronio 1998: 30)

These forms are possible, but not obligatory in ASL grammar. However, deafblind signers also made regular use of YOU as an attention getter at the start of questions about third parties, as in (8). This use was initially thought to be unique to tactile ASL, but has now also been attested in visual ASL, albeit as a rarely used form (Petronio 2010: 259).

(8) YOU WHY VISIT 7 FLOOR GIRL WANT VISIT 7 FLOOR FOR++
Why did the girl want to visit the 7th floor?
(Collins & Petronio 1998: 30; see also Petronio 2010)

Mesch (2001) considered pointing behaviour in polar questions and found that YOU was present in around 70% of cases. But, unlike Collins and Petronio (1998), she found that around half of all YOU attention getters were at the end of the question and only a quarter occurred at the start of the utterance. In tactile Norwegian Sign Language, Raanes (2011) also reports that emphatic questioning is performed by the signer moving their hands away from their own body and into what would normally be the signing space of the recipient (i.e. close to the recipient's body). This may be accompanied by YOU pronouns that make contact with the interlocutor's chest.[3] Mesch (2001: 149–151) notes that this type of questioning is also used in tactile Swedish Sign Language, and specifically that YOU signs that make contact occur utterance-finally. They thus act as a cue that the turn is about to change. This raises the important issue of the ways that the signing space more generally might be manipulated to give clues to turn-taking mechanics, which are explored in the following section. The findings presented in this section also strongly suggest that tactile sign languages do not have clear-cut grammatical forms for marking questions in the same way that visual sign languages do. Rather, they are recruiting or developing a range of manual and discourse features to signal that the utterance is to be read as a question.

## 4. Turn-taking

Language and interaction is a broad topic and can cover various aspects of pragmatics. Human interaction involves rapid exchanges of turns at talk. There are two major approaches to turn-taking. The first approach is a sociological approach proposed by Sacks, Schegloff and Jefferson (1974), which reveals a fundamental orderliness in the organization of turn-taking and initiated the modern literature on conversational turn-taking by outlining how turn-taking practices constitute a system of social interaction. Conversation Analysis (CA) has contributed to our understanding of this system. A psychological alternative is the signalling approach suggested by Duncan (1972). Contemporaneous with the approach by Sacks et al. (1974), Duncan (1972) proposed a set of turn-taking signals. The main set is turn-handing-over signals and consists of prosodic, gestural, lexical and syntactic cues. In this model, the turn-taking system is under the control of the current speaker. There have been relatively few studies on turn-taking in sign languages, but earlier studies in sign language interaction followed the signal-based approach (e.g. Baker 1977). Recently, sign language researchers have carried out studies within the framework of CA (e.g. Groeber & Pochon-Berger 2014; Kikuchi 2011; McCleary & Leite 2013). As we discuss below, for tactile signed conversations, most work follows the signal-based approach and fewer studies on tactile signed interaction employ the CA framework.

In spoken conversations, speakers intricately coordinate their turns, minimizing gap and overlap by managing a flow of multimodal information. It has been suggested that turn-taking is universal cross-linguistically (e.g. Stivers et al. 2009). In

3. In pro-tactile ASL the default form of YOU seems to be to make contact with the interlocutor's body (Edwards 2014a), whereas in other tactile sign languages described to date body contact with YOU appears to retain an emphatic effect.

conversations in sign languages, which are described as visual-gestural languages, turns are produced with the hands, body, and face, and perceived visually (see Janzen et al. 1999 for further details). In contrast, deafblind signers who have no access to auditory and visual resources require modified resources through tactile and kinetic inputs to initiate, sustain, and terminate their social encounters.

Studies on tactile signed interaction find the importance of contact and hand position in accomplishing turn-taking. For example, following the work of Baker (1977), who employed the signalling approach, Haas et al. (1995: 128–129) found that the major turn-yielding signal their participants used was returning their hands to rest position, but that turn-yielding was also accomplished by a more general decrease in signing speed and the indexing of addressee at the end of a turn, with a held question. Turn-claiming was accomplished by an increase in size and quantity of head-nodding, switching to palm, moving out of rest position, shifting posture, and interrupting and repeating the first few signs. The latter strategy was found to be a particularly effective way of initiating turn change in their data.

Employing the signal-based approach, Mesch (2001) explores turn-taking in tactile Swedish Sign Language. The preference for signing in 'dialogue position' (see Section 2, above) creates a unique turn-taking environment in this language, since (unlike other documented positions) it allows for either party to talk without the need to change hand positions. Mesch posits that changes in hand height (levels) and position in signing space (zones) are used to regulate turn-taking in tactile Swedish Sign Language interactions. At 'rest' level the hands are in the lap or otherwise disengaged from signing – what is commonly referred to as the home position in other sign language studies (see e.g. Cibulka 2015). The default height for hands engaged in conversation is called the turn level, with Mesch (2001) stating that hands are raised somewhat from this position in order to indicate hesitation and lowered somewhat (but not returned to rest) to signal turn change. She further suggests that hands move on the horizontal plane to indicate turns at talk – with whoever has the floor bringing their hands into signing space directly in front of their body and indicating that they are giving up the floor by moving back into a shared signing space between the two interlocutors. Raanes (2011) also notes that hesitation in tactile Norwegian Sign Language can be indicated by raising the height at which signs are produced, but other features of turn zones and levels have not been attested in tactile sign languages that make use of other hand configurations for reception.

In recent years researchers working with visual sign languages have become increasingly interested in the role of micro-pauses and sign lengthening as resources for managing turn-taking (Cibulka 2015, 2016; Groeber & Pochon-Berger 2014). This is likely an important resource for turn-taking in tactile sign languages, though it is yet to be the subject of sustained research. We do, however, see a hint of this in Mesch's observation (2001: 140) that over 50% of the polar questions in her data saw the final sign held for 300 ms or longer. Both Raanes (2011) and Iwasaki et al. (in press) also discuss the importance of subtle changes in pressure/ body contact between participants as a way of signalling impending turn change – for example, Iwasaki et al.'s frame-by-frame analysis, reproduced in Figure 2 below, captures a signer's non-dominant hand breaking contact with the recipient and moving towards the recipient position while his dominant hand is still engaged in producing the final sign of the utterance. Iwasaki et al.'s work is strongly informed by CA and suggests not only the utility of a CA approach to understanding signed interaction (a point being increasingly taken up by sign language linguists, cf. Girard-Groeber 2015; Groeber & Pochon-Berger 2014; Kikuchi 2011; McCleary & Leite 2013), but that careful analysis of tactile signed interactions may help shed light on conversational processes and structures that are present in all language and modalities, but may become more obvious to the analyst in the tactile mode.

| | | |
|---|---|---|
| 14 | AL: | WANT ASK ASK YOU UMM WANT ASK WANT ASK<br>*I want to ask you a question* |
| 15 | | YOU HEAE HAVE GOOD N-E-W-S WHAT<br>*Have you heard the good news?* |
| 16 → | | (0.4) ((Frame 1)) |
| 17 → | DH: | WHAT AGAIN<br>*Again?* |

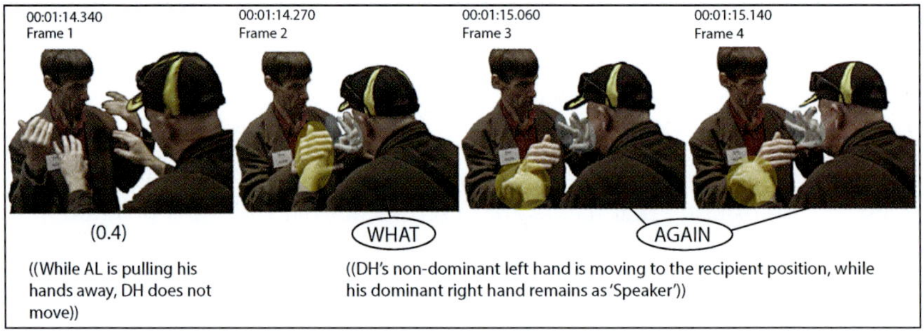


**Figure 2.** Frame-by-frame analysis of hand position (taken from Iwasaki et al. in press)

## 5. Feedback

Arguably, the most distinctive feature of tactile signing is the way in which addressee feedback is given. Since deafblind signers cannot reliably access their addressee's facial expressions, nodding and laughter (as well as less common cues, such as crying), alternate conventions for displaying addressee involvement in conversation are required. The precise conventions used vary somewhat across the different tactile signed languages, but all use a variety of conventionalised taps and squeezes, which are unique to tactile signing. They also make use of manual signs such as YES or RIGHT and repeating the last sign of the signer's utterance, which are also commonly used back-channel devises in visual sign languages (Coates & Sutton-Spence 2001; Mesch 2016). Repetition of the prior signed utterances serves both a turn-taking function, binding the turns together and allows the recipient to signal acceptance of the contribution of the prior speaker.

For tactile Swedish Sign Language, Mesch (2001) reports two distinct tapping conventions. As the name suggests, an addressee performs a 'thumb tap' by using their thumb to give one or more taps on the signer's hand. In 'YES-tapping' by contrast, the addressee uses all four fingers to tap on the signer's hand. The thumb tap is used frequently as feedback to show that the addressee is still paying attention. As Mesch notes (2001: 112), its function is to show understanding, but it may also be used in contexts where the addressee has not in fact understood, but does not wish to initiate repair. YES-tapping, by contrast, seems to serve a more emphatic or affiliative function than the thumb tap, but Mesch reports that for true emphasis tactile Swedish Sign Language users produce full lexical signs such as OH-YES, AGREE, OY! (an exclamative) or repeat part of the prior utterance.

Collins and Petronio (1998) also found two distinct feedback taps in tactile ASL. As in tactile Swedish Sign Language, an one-fingered tap on the signers hand signals attentiveness to the message and a four-fingered tap carries senses such as "OK", "Oh I see" and "I agree" (1998: 32). Both Mesch and Collins and Petronio note that the speed and number of repetition given to taps subtly changes the meaning – as is common in sign language grammars more generally, repetition is perceived as adding intensity or emphasis to the base sign, which depending on its placement in the discourse may signal meaning such as "Yes, I know that already", "Yes, I agree with you", "So true", etc. Collins and Petronio discuss three other back-channel forms used in their data. The first they name the 'tactile nod'. It is formed by the recipient lightly nodding the signer's hand back and forth – reminiscent of the nodding motion of the ASL sign YES (and indeed a nodding head). A gentle repeated squeeze to the signer's hand served a similar discourse function as the tactile nod, while a single firm squeeze functioned as a repair initiator, indicating that the addressee had failed to catch what had just been signed (Collins & Petronio 1998: 33).

Collins and Petronio only discuss feedback forms being given on the hands, but both Mesch and Raanes (who records similar tapping behaviour in tactile Norwegian Sign Language) note that taps can also be applied to other body parts, such as the upper arms, knees or thighs. In pro-tactile ASL, the convention has now moved so that back-channelling is now done solely on other body parts (usually the knees or thighs when seated or the forearm when standing), never the signer's hands. As aj granda and Jelica Nuccio explain in their vlog (www.protactile.org/2016/03/english-transcription-of-aj-

and-jelicas.html), this allows for more frequent, less intrusive feedback to be given and can allow the simultaneous reception of single-word lexical signs (such as RIGHT or AGREE made onto the leg) without the switch in hand-position that such simultaneous talk would normally entail.

While back-channelling in visual sign languages is commonly given through non-manual features, linguistic signs can also fulfil this role. In a study of the Swedish Sign Language corpus, Mesch (2016) found that around 20% of all back-channels given in Swedish Sign Language are manual. The most frequently used manual back-channels are a reduced form of the sign for YES (cf. the discussion of YES-tapping above) and the palm-up gesture, which is also attested in tactile SSL.

Petronio and Dively (2006) were interested in if and how tactile and visual users of ASL varied in their use of the manual signs YES and #NO. The data for their study came from 14 interviews in which both the interviewer and interviewees were deafblind users of tactile ASL, matched for age and gender with 14 interviews conducted in visual ASL. The visual ASL interviews included eight two-party interactions and six multi-party interactions. As might be expected, they found that tactile signers made higher use of YES and #NO signs than signers in either visual condition. However, they also found a significant difference in the use of manual feedback depending on whether the interaction was a two-party or multi-party conversation. On average every 15 minutes, tactile signers used manual YES or #NO 34.4 times, as against 23.5 times in the multi-party interactions and only 9.8 times in the two-party visual ASL interactions (Petronio & Dively 2006: 69). This meant that there was a significant difference between the two-party visual ASL interview and both other conditions, but not between the tactile ASL and multi-party visual interaction. The authors hypothesise that this is linked to visibility conditions within an interaction. In a two-party interaction, both interlocutors can attend to the face of their conversation partner, and thus non-manual feedback is highly accessible. However, in multi-party interactions the risk that the interlocutor's gaze is elsewhere is higher, and thus non-manuals may not be perceived (cf. Bono, Kikuchi, Cibulka & Osugi 2014). The greater movement involved in producing a manual sign, by contrast, is likely to register in a signer's peripheral vision.

Petronio and Dively (2006) also provide some of the only analysis to date of sociolinguistic variation in tactile signing. They note that in their corpus deafblind women produce 965 tokens of YES and #NO compared to 586 from deafblind men; and tentatively link this to claims of gender differences in conversation styles between men and women in spoken languages (cf. Coates & Givon 1997; Tannen 1990). There is also clear variation in the feedback interviewees provided depending on the age at which they first started using tactile ASL. Three late users (who transitioned to tactile aged 55 or above) provided minimal feedback compared to other participants, who all began using tactile ASL before age 40. One of the heaviest users of feedback in the study also grew up with deafblind parents (and thus had used expressive tactile ASL from a young age) further suggesting that early exposure and/ or level of familiarity with tactile ASL influences feedback behaviour.

Petronio and Dively (2006) classified 12 different discourse functions that YES and #NO served in their data, all of which can also occur in visual ASL. However, there was one environment where YES frequently occurred in tactile ASL but not in visual ASL: as an acknowledgement token following a wh-question as in (9):

(9) Interviewer: "How old were you when you started having vision problems?"
Interviewee: YES+++ PRO.1 START OLD-38 YEAR OLD.
"[Yes,] I started when I was 38 years old."
(Petronio & Dively 2006: 74)

YES responses in such cases were articulated as relatively small signs and were often accompanied by pauses as the addressee constructed their response. Pragmatically the YES in this context is arguably functioning like a hesitation marker such as HMM (which has its own ASL sign). But it remains a question for further research why YES has been recruited by tactile ASL signers to fulfil this function, and whether similar usages are found in other tactile signed languages.

Finally, tactile signers might give feedback about whether an utterance has been understood through grip cues. Raanes (2011: 69) discusses a case where an addressee fails to follow an instance of fingerspelling and initiates repair by gripping the interlocutor's hands tightly, so that it would be difficult to continue signing. The signer stops immediately and waits for the recipient's grip to relax before respelling the name slower and more deliberately. Certain signs, or types of signs, may also become conventionalised as needing different hand configurations to be correctly discerned, leading signers to pre-emptively hold the articulation of such signs to allow the addressee time to fully comprehend the sign. Numbers are one such category of signs, since in fast-paced signing it might be difficult for a tactile recipient to accurately perceive how many fingers were extended or the difference between certain similar movement paths. Numbers are also often less predictable than the surrounding discourse, so are harder to recover from context. For these reasons, tactile ASL and tactile Auslan signers routinely hold number signs (Collins & Petronio 1998: 22; Willoughby et al. 2014). Figure 3 illustrates the quite dramatic change in hand position (including recruiting the second hand for probing) that an unexpected number might prompt. Note that the cue for the signer that the number has been comprehended is the return of the addressee's hands to the default reception position.

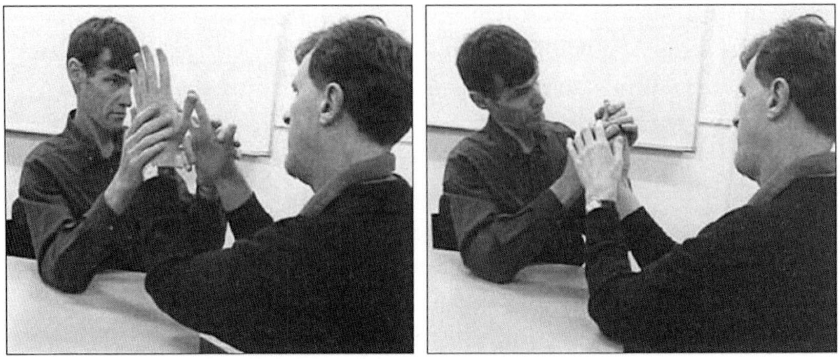

**Figure 3.** Initial and subsequent hand position when checking a troublesome number (reproduced with permission from Willoughby et al. 2014: 435)

## 6. Environmental information

Since deafblind signers do not have visual access to their surrounding environment, there is a potential need to develop new conventions to convey this information quickly and succinctly. Social-haptic communication (often shorted to 'haptics') is the name given to a range of communicative symbols and practices used to convey environmental information to deafblind people in a way outside of standard tactile signing – for example, by drawing the outline of a room on the back of a deafblind person in order to convey the location of doors, tables, etc. or where different people are sitting. Social-haptics as a distinct methodology has its origins in a collaboration between an interpreter and deafblind man (Palmer & Lahtinen 2015), growing from a range of hand taps and squeezes used to convey feedback into a wide range of conventionalised signs that can be articulated on the addressee's arms, back, etc. to indicate things such as the emotional states of others (laughter, applause, crying), directions (door, forwards) and even brief options that one might find at a buffet (coffee, chocolate). Haptics is commonly used to augment tactile signing in Scandinavia, and has been somewhat codified through the publication of a dictionary of 103 haptic signs by the Danish Association of the Deafblind (Neilsen 2012). Haptics has spread beyond Scandinavia through the Danish dictionary, translations of the Scandinavian materials and workshops held throughout Europe and the world. Part of the perceived usefulness of social-haptic symbols is that they can be delivered simultaneously with more formal signed information. For example, Berge and Raanes (2013) show how a deafblind woman chairing a meeting could receive haptic information about who was making bids for the floor once her turn concluded while she herself was signing. Likewise, information such as whom the chair was allocating the turn to next could be conveyed back to the participants via haptics without needing to break into the stream of dialogue. Social-haptic signs can also be used in crowded situations or other contexts where there is not the space or time to assume a normal tactile signing posture – for example, to quickly inform a deafblind person about what food or drink options are on offer at a function.

Social-haptic communication raises a few thorny issues, both in terms of the linguistic and the social. A full treatment of these issues is beyond the scope of this piece, but these issues require brief introduction for the linguists, interpreters, and other readers, who might consult this handbook entry. First, in terms of the linguistic, and as we noted above, a challenge in analysing deafblind communication is whether/where it is useful and appropriate to draw a distinction between 'linguistic' and 'non-verbal' communication. This is particularly clear in the realm of social-haptics. Haptics as a general topic of human communication is often included in accounts of 'non-verbal' communication (e.g. Matsumoto, Hwang & Frank 2016). However, as should be clear from the above (and Janzen et al. 1999), the conceptualisation and use of 'touch' haptics is very different in deaf communication (see also Napoli 2014), and deafblind communication again (e.g. Edwards 2012; Palmer & Lahtinen 2015). The term haptics in deafblind communication is most commonly understood to mean the social-haptic symbols invented by Palmer and Lahtinen (see 2015), and codified in Nielsen (2012). These symbols enable descriptions of the environment to be conveyed to deafblind signers through messages (which Lahtinen (2008) labels 'haptices') through the combination of individual symbols (labelled 'haptemes'). For instance, the hapteme YES (indexed by the tapping of an index finger) might be combined with the hapteme 'FAST.SPEED' (indexed by fast tapping) to index an 'emphatic yes'. Lahtinen, Palmer and Ojala (2012) propose the combination of haptemes to form haptices necessitates obeying "the grammar of touch", but it is unclear from this article how or whether this should be considered grammar in any traditional linguistic sense (though it should also be clarified that Lahtinen does not seem to suggest it should be).

This leads to the second thorny issue in a discussion of haptics: the social. The US pro-tactile movement has been vocal in criticising haptics on a number of fronts. Central to this critique is that haptics is a hearing- and sight-led phenomenon, which by consequence privileges sighted conventions and sighted orientations to the environment. In other words, haptics is perceived to fit deafblind people into a sighted world, without considering how the deafblind themselves orient to, and describe, their own experiences and environment.[4] It is also generally non-reciprocal: a sighted person might use social-haptic symbols with a deafblind person, but we are not aware of deafblind people routinely using these symbols in conversation with each other. Edwards' work (e.g. 2012, 2014a, 2014b), focusing on the pro-tactile movement, stands as an

4. We owe this critical point to one of the anonymous reviewers of this piece.

implicit critique of the sight-led orientation to, and/or the need for, haptics to convey information about the environment. For instance, Edwards (2012) outlines how an interpreter might work with a deafblind signer, using conventional ASL signs, to negotiate the relationship between the visual and deafblind understanding of spatio-temporal orientation. Implicit in this observation is a critique that not only do interpreters not need haptics, but in fact the use of haptics (codified and with a visual orientation) may leave deafblind signers unable to express or elaborate upon their own view of the world in interaction.

At the time of writing, social-haptic symbols have attracted wide interest and some traction of used from deafblind signers and interpreters in many parts of the world. However, there is a lack of concrete research data on if/how the use of social-haptics is being used in different countries or interactional settings and the ways or degree to which either interpreters or deafblind people find it a helpful communicative resource. Edwards' work also provides an alternative example of how visual signs may evolve, and be used in interaction, to convey a deafblind rather than a sighted orientation to the immediate environment. It will be interesting to see if and how conventions for conveying this non-linguistic communication develop in tactile signing in coming years.

## 7. A note on data collection

Perhaps the greatest challenge in conducting research on tactile sign languages is that the current state of the art is to rely on a visual facsimile (i.e. a video-recording) as a record of what transpired in an interaction that was perceived (by at least one party) primarily through touch. The complex sensory relationship between touching an object or person and watching someone/thing perform that same touch has been theorised somewhat in the context of surgery (Bell 2017; Bezemer & Kress 2014),[5] but is yet to be seriously explored by researchers documenting tactile sign languages, though Iwasaki et al. (in press) make a number of important strides in this direction. A number of researchers are, however, cognisant of the many practical issues that confront one in filming tactile sign data. Corpus-based studies of visual sign languages generally use studio set-up for recording conversations, carefully controlling lighting conditions, backgrounds, seating set-ups, camera angles and participant clothing to

5. These studies theorize touch in the context of robot-assisted prostate surgery, where surgeons guide the robot via a camera for an operation that was formerly performed entirely through touch (Bell 2017) and how experienced surgeons evaluate the touching behaviour of registrars (Bezemer & Kress 2014).

maximise the quality and visibility conditions of the recordings (Perniss 2015; Schembri, Fenlon, Rentelis, Reynolds & Cormier 2013). A standard set up under these conditions will include three HD video cameras: one focussed on each interlocutor and a third with a wider view of both interlocutors (Schembri et al. 2013). However, a uniform studio set-up may not suit the unique signing postures preferred by many tactile sign language users, and studio lighting is not practical in many cases because photosensitivity is common in people with Usher Syndrome (a leading cause of deafblindness). Occlusion, while always a potential issue in sign language research, is particularly problematic for tactile sign language research as the hands of the recipient may obscure the sign that is being received. For all of these reasons, studies of tactile signing to date have largely eschewed formal studio setups (an exception is Petronio & Dively 2006; both Mesch's and Collins and Petronio's corpus also include some studio recordings). It should also be noted, too that while studio setup has become the norm for visual sign language work, van Herreweghe and Vermeerbergen (2012) note that it is perfectly possible to still gather high quality sign language data through careful filming of naturally occurring conversations.

Deafblind signing data to date also differs from much of the visual sign language corpus data that has been collected to date because of a preponderance of data from naturally occurring talk, as opposed to pre-arranged conversations. Whether due to deliberate methodological design or simply convenience, a number of major studies of deafblind signing to date have dealt with data collected from deafblind people as they engage in other activities – whether that be social events (Collins & Petronio 1998; Iwasaki et al. in press; Willoughby et al. 2014), meetings (Berge & Raanes 2013) or training sessions and camps (Edwards 2014b; Raanes 2011). This naturalistic data gives insight into how deafblind interlocutors manage quite complex joint attention tasks – such as learning how to use woodworking equipment (Edwards 2014b) or conversing while eating a meal (Raanes 2011) – but there is little comparative data to date about how visual sign language users manage comparable interactions.

## 8. Conclusion

Deafblind signing is a relatively new area of interest for sign language linguists, but one that is gaining traction internationally. As Hepp (1998) notes, up until the 1990s Deaf people who lost their sight were commonly told that they would need to give up signing and switch to another communication mode such as Print-on-Palm (essentially tracing the letter of each word onto a person's hand). Such methods are often cumbersome and burdensome to use and made it difficult for many deafblind people to remain active members of their local Deaf community. The growing uptake and acceptance of tactile signing provides an important avenue of expression for deafblind people, as well as increasing demand for specialist tactile sign language interpreters. In many places around the world, tactile sign languages are still developing stable conventions, and interactions between two deafblind signers (as opposed to a deafblind person and a sighted signer, such as an interpreter) remain somewhat limited. It will be interesting to see in coming years if and how conventions for tactile signing develop in different places and whether the overarching trend is one of convergence or divergence between the different tactile sign languages globally.

## References


Australian Sign Language Interpreters' Association. 2014. *ASLIA Workplace Health and Safety Policy.* https://aslia.com.au/wp-content/uploads/ASLIA-OHS-Policy.pdf

Baker, C. 1977. "Regulators and turn-taking in American Sign Language discourse." In *On the Other Hand*, ed. by L. Friedman, 215–236. New York: Academic Press.

Bell, L. 2017. "'You feel with your eyes': The creation of 'New' prostates and surgeons in and through Robotic-assisted radical prostatectomy." Presented at the The anatomy of the Image, Melbourne, Monash University.

Berge, S. S. and E. Raanes. 2013. "Coordinating the chain of utterances: An analysis of communicative flow and turn taking in an interpreted group dialogue for deaf-blind persons." *Sign Language Studies* 13(3): 350–371. https://doi.org/10.1353/sls.2013.0007

Bezemer, J. and G. Kress. 2014. "Touch: A resource for making meaning." *Australian Journal of Language and Literacy* 37(2): 77.

Bono, M., K. Kikuchi, P. Cibulk and Y. Osugi. 2014. "A colloquial corpus of Japanese Sign Language: Linguistic resources for observing sign language conversations." Presented at the *LREC*.

Bono, M., R. Sakaida, R. Makino, T. Okada, K. Kikuchi, M. Cibulka, L. Willoughby, S. Iwasaki, and S. Fukushima. 2018. "Tactile Japanese Sign Language and Finger Braille: An example of data collection for minority languages in Japan." Presented at the *8th Workshop on the Representation & Processing of Sign Languages: Involving the Language Community*, Miyazaki. http://lrec-conf.org/workshops/lrec2018/W1/pdf/18027_W1.pdf

Cibulka, P. 2015. "When the hands do not go home: A micro-study of the role of gesture phases in sequence suspension and closure." *Discourse Studies* 17(1): 3–24. https://doi.org/10.1177/1461445614557756

Cibulka, P. 2016. "On how to do things with holds: Manual movement phases as part of interactional practices in signed conversation." *Sign Language Studies* 16(4): 447–472. https://doi.org/10.1353/sls.2016.0015

Coates, J. and T. Givon. 1997. "The construction of a collaborative floor in women's friendly talk." *Typological Studies in Language* 34: 55–90. https://doi.org/10.1075/tsl.34.04coa

Coates, J. and R. Sutton-Spence. 2001. "Turn-taking patterns in deaf conversation." *Journal of Sociolinguistics* 5(4): 507–529. https://doi.org/10.1111/1467-9481.00162

Collins, S. and K. Petronio. 1998. "What happens in tactile ASL." In *Pinky Extension and Eye Gaze: Language Use in Deaf Communities*, ed. by C. Lucas, 18–37. Washington D.C.: Gallaudet University Press.

Duncan, S. 1972. "Some signals and rules for taking speaking turns in conversations." *Journal of Personality and Social Psychology* 23(2): 283. https://doi.org/10.1037/h0033031

Edwards, T. 2012. "Sensing the rhythms of everyday life: Temporal integration and tactile translation in the Seattle Deaf-Blind community." *Language in Society* 41(1): 29–71. https://doi.org/10.1017/S004740451100090X

Edwards, T. 2014a. "From compensation to integration: Effects of the pro-tactile movement on the sublexical structure of Tactile American Sign Language." *Journal of Pragmatics* 69: 22–41. https://doi.org/10.1016/j.pragma.2014.05.005

Edwards, T. 2014b. *Language Emergence in the Seattle DeafBlind Community*. Berkeley: University of California. http://search.proquest.com/openview/63cb352317bb90097011b9a64d105b52/1?pq-origsite=gscholar

Edwards, T. 2018. "Sign-creation in the Seattle DeafBlind community." *Gesture* 16(2): 305–328. https://doi.org/10.1075/gest.16.2.06edw

Girard-Groeber, S. 2015. "The management of turn transition in signed interaction through the lens of overlaps." *Frontiers in Psychology* 6: 741.

Groeber, S. and E. Pochon-Berger. 2014. "Turns and turn-taking in sign language interaction: A study of turn-final holds." *Journal of Pragmatics* 65: 121–136. https://doi.org/10.1016/j.pragma.2013.08.012

Haas, C., E. Fleetwood and M. Ernest. 1995. "An analysis of ASL Variation within DeafBlind-Deaf-Blind interaction: Question forms, backchanneling, and turn taking." *School of Communication Student Forum* 103–40.

Hepp, P. 1998. "Taubblindheit - Doppplte Kommunikationsbehinderung: Die Bedeutung der 'taktilen Gebärdensprache' in Deutschland [Deafblindness – double communication handicap. The meaning of tactile sign language in Germany]." *Das Zeichen* 12(45): 384–391.

Iwasaki, S., M. Bartlett, H. Manns and L. Willoughby. (in press). "The Challenges of multimodality and multi-sensoriality: Methodological issues in analyzing tactile signed interaction." *Journal of Pragmatics*. https://doi.org/10.1016/j.pragma.2018.05.003

Janzen, Terry, Barbara Shaffer, and Sherman Wilcox. 1999. "Signed language pragmatics." *In Handbook of Pragmatics*, ed. by Jan-Ola Östman & Jef Verschueren. Amsterdam: John Benjamins.

Kikuchi, K. 2011. "Nishakan no shuwa kaiwa deno junban koutai ni okeru shisen idou no bunseki [An analysis of gaze shifts in turn-taking in sign language conversations]." *The Japanese Journal of Language in Society* 14(1): 154–168.

Lahtinen, R. 2008. Haptices and Haptemes: A Case Study of Developmental Process in Touch-Based Communication of Acquired Deafblind People. PhD Dissertstion, Helsinki University.

Lahtinen, R., R. Palmer and S. Ojala. 2012. "Visual art experiences through touch using haptices." *Procedia-Social and Behavioral Sciences* 45: 268–276. https://doi.org/10.1016/j.sbspro.2012.06.563

Matsumoto, D., H. Hwang and M. Frank. 2016. "The body: Postures, gait, proxemics, and haptics." In *APA Handbook of Nonverbal Communication*, 387–400. Washington, DC: American Psychological Association. https://doi.org/10.1037/14669-015

McCleary, L. and T. de A. Leite. 2013. "Turn-taking in Brazilian sign language: Evidence from overlap." *Journal of Interactional Research in Communication Disorders* 4(1): 123–154.

Mesch, J. 2001. *Tactile Sign Language: Turn Taking and Question in Signed Conversations of Deaf-Blind People*. Hamburg: Signum.

Mesch, J. 2013. "Tactile signing with one-handed perception." *Sign Language Studies* 13(2): 238–263. https://doi.org/10.1353/sls.2013.0005

Mesch, J. 2016. "Manual backchannel responses in signers' conversations in Swedish Sign Language." *Language & Communication* 50: 22–41. https://doi.org/10.1016/j.langcom.2016.08.011

Mesch, J., E. Raanes and L. Ferrara. 2015. "Co-forming real space blends in tactile signed language dialogues." *Cognitive Linguistics* 26(2): 261–287. https://doi.org/10.1515/cog-2014-0066

Napier, J., R. McKee and D. Goswell. 2010. *Sign Language Interpreting: Theory and Practice in Australia and New Zealand*, 2nd edition. Annandale, N.S.W: Federation Press.

Napoli, D. J. 2014. "A magic touch: Deaf gain and the benefits of tactile sensation." In *Deaf Gain: Raising the Stakes for Human Diversity*, ed. by H. Dirksen. L. Bauman and J. J. Murray, 211–232. Minneapolis: University of Minnesota Press.

Nielsen, G. (ed.). 2012. *103 Haptic Signs - A Reference Book*. The Danish Association of the Deafblind.

Palmer, R. and R. Lahtinen. 2015. "History of social-haptic communication." http://www.deafblindinformation.org.au/wp-content/uploads/2016/01/history-of-social-haptic-communication.pdf.

Perniss, P. 2015. "Collecting and anlysing sign language data: Video requirements and use of annotation software." In *Research Methods in Sign Language Studies: A Practical Guide*, ed. by E. Orfanidou, B. Woll and G. Morgan, 55–73. Oxford: Wiley-Blackwell.

Petronio, K. 2010. "Deaf-Blind interpreting: Building on what you already know." *Cadernos de Tradução* 2(26): 237–273. https://doi.org/10.5007/2175-7968.2010v2n26p237

Petronio, K. and V. Dively. 2006. "Yes, no, visibility, and variation in ASL and Tactile ASL." *Sign Language Studies* 7(1): 57–98. https://doi.org/10.1353/sls.2006.0032

Quinto-Pozos, D. 2002. "Deixis in the visual/gestural and tactile/gestural modalities." In *Modality and Structure in Signed and Spoken Languages*, ed. by R. P. Meier, K. Cormier and D. Quinto-Pozos, 442–467. Cambridge: Cambridge University Press. https://doi.org/10.1017/CBO9780511486777.021

Raanes, E. 2011. "Tegnrom og taktilt tegnspråk." *Norsk Lingvistisk Tidsskrift* 29: 54–86.

Raanes, E. and S. S. Berge. 2017. "Sign language interpreters' use of haptic signs in interpreted meetings with deafblind persons." *Journal of Pragmatics* 107: 91–104. https://doi.org/10.1016/j.pragma.2016.09.013

Reed, C. M., L. A. Delhorne, N. I. Durlach and S. D. Fischer. 1995. "A study of the tactual reception of sign language." *Journal of Speech and Hearing Research* 38(2): 477–489. https://doi.org/10.1044/jshr.3802.477

Sacks, H., E. A. Schegloff and G. Jefferson. 1974. "A simplest systematics for the organization of turn-taking for conversation." *Language* 50: 696–735. https://doi.org/10.1353/lan.1974.0010

Schembri, A., J. Fenlon, R. Rentelis, S. Reynolds and K. Cormier. 2013. "Building the British Sign Language Corpus." *Language Documentation and Conservation* 7: 136–154.

Schwarz, S. 2004. *Eléments pour une analyse de la langue des signes tactile pratiquée par les personnes sourdes-aveugles*. Université Paris VIII - St Denis, Département de Sciences du Langage.

Schwarz, S. 2009. *Stratégies de synchronisation interactionnelle: alternance conversationnelle et rétro-action en cours de discours chez des locuteurs sourdaveugles pratiquant la Langue des Signes Française tactile* [*Interactional synchronization strategies: Alternating and conversational communication and feedback signals in French tactile sign language*]. Université Paris VIII - St Denis, Département de Sciences du Langage.

Stivers, T., N.J. Enfield, P. Brown, C. Englert, M. Hayashi, T. Heinemann et al. 2009. "Universals and cultural variation in turn-taking in conversation." *Proceedings of the National Academy of Sciences USA* 106: 10587–10592. doi: 10.1073/pnas.0903616106

Tannen, D. 1990. *You Just Don't Understand: Women and Men in Conversation*. New York: Ballantine Books.

van Herreweghe, M. and M. Vermeerbergen. 2012. "Data collection." In *Sign Language: An International Handbook*, ed. by B. Woll, M. Steinbach and R. Pfau, 401–420. Berlin: Mouton de Gruyter.

Willoughby, L., H. Manns, S. Iwasaki and M. Bartlett. 2014. "Misunderstanding and repair in Tactile Auslan." *Sign Language Studies* 14(4): 419–443. https://doi.org/10.1353/sls.2014.0014

# Cumulative index

This index refers to the whole of the *Handbook of Pragmatics*, its **Manual** as well as the 21 installments (the present one included), and it lists:

i. all labels used as entry headings in some part of the Handbook, with an indication of the part in which the entry is to be found, and with cross-references to other relevant entries;
ii. labels for traditions, methods, and topics for which separate entries have not (yet) been provided, indicating the entry-labels under which information can be found and the part of the Handbook where this is to be found.

The following abbreviations are used:

(MT) the Traditions section of the Manual
(MM) the Methods section of the Manual
(MN) the Notational Systems section of the Manual
(H) the thematic main body of the loose-leaf Handbook or (from the 21st installment onwards) of the specific annual installment (marked as H21, H22, etc.)
(T) the Traditions update/addenda of the printed Handbook (further specified for the bound volumes as T21, T22, etc.)
(M) the Methods update/addenda of the printed Handbook (further specified for the bound volumes as M21, M22, etc.)
(N) the Notational Systems update/addenda of the printed Handbook (further specified for the bound volumes as N21, N22, etc.)

References in the index may take the following forms:

"**Label (section reference**) (abbreviated as above)" — for labels which occur only as headings of an autonomous article
"**Label (section reference**); label(s)" — for labels which occur as article headings and for which it is relevant to refer to other articles as well
"**Label** label(s)" — for labels which do not (yet) occur as article headings, but which stand for topics dealt with under the label(s) indicated
"**Label** → label(s)" — for labels that are considered, for the time being and for the purposes of the Handbook, as (near)equivalents of the label(s) following the arrow; a further search must start from the label(s) following the arrow

**Abduction** Grounded theory (M); Language change (H)
**Academic concept** Vygotsky (H)
**Academic language** Applied linguistics (MT)
**Acceptability** Generative semantics (MT)
**Accessibility** Anaphora (H)
**Accommodation** Contact (H); Presupposition (H)
**Accommodation theory (MT)**; Adaptability (H); Age and language use (H); Bilingualism and multilingualism (H); Context and contextualization (H); Social psychology (MT)
**Accounting** Collaboration in dialogues (H); Social psychology (MT)
**Acoustics** Sound symbolism (H)
**Action** Action theory (MT); Agency and language (H); Austin (H); Bühler (H); Cognitive psychology (MT); Ethnomethodology (MT); Intentionality (H); Nexus analysis (T); Perception and language (H); Philosophy of action (MT); Speech act theory (MT)
**Action theory (MT)**; Agency and language (H); Grounded theory (M); Philosophy of action (MT)
**Activation** Relational ritual (H)
**Activity** Action theory (MT)
**Adaptability (H)**; Evolutionary pragmatics (T); (The) pragmatic perspective (M)
**Adjacency pair** Prosody (H); Sequence (H)
**Adjective** Experimental pragmatics (M)
**Adjunct control** Control phenomena (H)
**Adorno, T.** Critical theory (MT)
**Affect** Appraisal (H); Computational pragmatics (T); Discourse analysis (MT); Emotions (H21); Emotion display (H); Emphasis (H); Interpreter-mediated interaction (H); Laughter (H); Overlap (H); Stance (H21); Text and discourse linguistics (T); Think-aloud protocols (M)
**Affiliation/disaffiliation** → Affect
**Affirmation** Negation (H)
**Age and language use (H)**; 'Other' representation (H)
**Ageism** Age and language use (H)
**Agency and language (H)**; Action theory (MT); Case and semantic roles (H); Computational pragmatics (T); Intentionality (H); Metapragmatics (MT); Motivation and language (H)
**Agreement** Therapeutic conversation (H)
***Aisatsu* (H)**
**Aktionsart** Tense and aspect (H)
**Alignment** Stance (H21)
**Allegory** Conceptual integration (H)
**Ambiguity** Indeterminacy and negotiation (H); Mental spaces (H); Polysemy (H); Truthfulness (H); Sound symbolism (H)
**Amerindian languages** Anthropological linguistics (MT); Boas (H)
**Analysis** Analytical philosophy (MT)
**Analytical philosophy (MT)**; Austin (H); Conversational implicature (H); Hermeneutics (M); Philosophy of language (MT); Speech act theory (MT); Truth-conditional semantics (MT); Wittgenstein (H)
**Anaphora (H)**; Indexicals and demonstratives (H); Grounding (H); Tense and aspect (H)
**Anderson, B.** (H21)
**Animal communication** Adaptability (H); Communication (H); Primate communication (H)
**Annotation** Corpus analysis (MM); Corpus pragmatics (M)
**Antecedent** Anaphora (H)
**Anthropological linguistics (MT)**; Anderson (H21); Bilingualism and multilingualism (H); Cognitive anthropology (MT); Componential analysis (MT); Context and contextualization (H); Ethnography of speaking (MT); Fieldwork (MM); Gumperz (H); Hermeneutics (M); Intercultural communication (H); Language ideologies (H); Malinowski (H); Metalinguistic awareness (H); Metapragmatics (MT); Nexus analysis (T); Phatic communion (H); Sapir (H); Sociolinguistics (MT); Taxonomy (MM); (The) pragmatic perspective (M); Truthfulness (H); Whorf (H)
**Anti-language** Jargon (H)
**Apel, K. O.** Universal and transcendental pragmatics (MT)
**Aphasia** Adaptability (H); Cerebral representation of language; Clinical pragmatics (T); Jakobson (H21); Neurolinguistics (MT)
**Apology** Corpus pragmatics (M); Mediated performatives (H)
**Appeal** → Functions of language
**Applied linguistics** (MT); Forensic linguistics (T); Intercultural communication (H); Language policy, language planning and standardization (H); Sociolinguistics (MT)
**Appraisal (H)**; Emphasis (H)
**Appreciation** Appraisal (H); Ọmọlúàbí (H)
**Appropriateness** Creativity in language use (H)
**Arbitrariness** Adaptability (H); Iconicity (H); Structuralism (MT); Sound symbolism (H)
**Areal linguistics** Contact linguistics (MT); Language change (H)
**Argument structure** → Dependency
**Argumentation** Argumentation theory (MT); Rhetoric (MT); Argumentation in discourse and grammar (H)

**Argumentation in discourse and grammar (H)**; Argumentation theory (MT)
**Argumentation theory (MT)**; Rhetoric (MT); Argumentation in discourse and grammar (H)
**Articulation** Humboldt (H); Sound symbolism (H)
**Artificial intelligence (MT)**; Communication (H); Computational linguistics (MT); Cognitive psychology (MT); Cognitive science (MT); Connectionism (MT); Context and contextualization (H); Frame analysis (M); Frame semantics (T); Speech act theory (MT)
**Artificial life** Language acquisition (H)
**Ascription** Functional discourse grammar (T)
**Aspect** Markedness (H); Tense and aspect (H)
**Assertion** Austin (H); Speech act theory (MT)
**Assimilation** Language rights (H)
**Asymmetric interaction** Applied linguistics (MT); Communicative success vs. failure (H); Computer-mediated communication (H); Conversation types (H); Frame analysis (M); Mass media (H)
**Attention and language (H)**
**Attitude** Appraisal (H); Dialectology (MT); Social psychology (MT); Stance (H21)
**Attribution theory** Social psychology (MT)
**Audience** → Hearer
**Audience design** → Recipient design
**Audience effect** Primate communication (H)
**Augmentative** Morphopragmatics (T)
**Austin, J. L. (H)**; Analytical philosophy (MT); Communicative success vs. failure (H); Contextualism (T); Grice (H); Speech act theory (MT)
**Authenticity (H)**; Reported speech (H)
**Authier-Revuz, J.** Énonciation (H)
**Authority (H)**; Honorifics (H)
**Authorship** Experimental pragmatics (M); Forensic linguistics (T)
**Autism** Clinical pragmatics (T); Conceptual integration (H)
**Automata theory** Computational linguistics (MT)
**Automaticity** Think-aloud protocols (M)
**Autonomous vs. non-autonomous syntax** (MT); Chomskyan linguistics (MT); Functionalism vs. formalism (MT); Structuralism (MT)
**Awareness** Metalinguistic awareness (H)
**Axiology** Morris (H)

**Baby talk** → Motherese
**Back channel cue** Listener response (H)
**Background information** Collaboration in dialogues (H); Communication (H); Common ground (H); Context and contextualization (H); Cognitive science (MT); Discourse analysis (MT); Text and discourse linguistics (T)
**Backgrounding** Grounding (H)
**Bakhtin, M. M. (H)**; Collaboration in dialogues (H); Dialogical analysis (MM); Genre (H); Ideology (H); Intertextuality (H); Polyphony (H); Reported speech (H)
**Bally, C.** Énonciation (H)
**Basilect** Creole linguistics (MT)
**Bateson, G. (H)**; Communication (H)
**Behaviorism (MT)**; Cognitive psychology (MT); Grice (H); Morris (H); Objectivism vs. subjectivism (MT)
**Benveniste, E. (H)**; Énonciation (H)
**Bernstein, B.** Applied linguistics (MT); Communicative success vs. failure (H)
**Bilingual interactive activation (BIA)** The multilingual lexicon (H)
**Bilingualism and multilingualism (H)**; Accommodation theory (MT); Anderson (H21); Anthropological linguistics (MT); Borrowing (H); Code-switching (H); Contact (H); Contact linguistics (MT); Developmental psychology (MT); Intercultural communication (H); Language contact (H); Language dominance and minorization (H); Language maintenance and shift (H21); Language policy, language planning and standardization (H); The multilingual lexicon (H); Social psychology (MT); Sociolinguistics (MT)
**Binding** Anaphora (H)
**Biodiversity** Language ecology (H)
**Biology** Morris (H)
**Biosemiotics** Communication (H)
**Boas, F. (H)**; Anthropological linguistics (MT); Culture (H); Fieldwork (MM); Sapir (H); Typology (MT); Whorf (H)
**Body** Tactile sign languages (H21)
**Bootstrapping** Language acquisition (H)
**Borrowing (H)**; Contact (H); Interjections (H); Language contact (H)
**Bourdieu, P. (H)**; Anderson (H21); Ideology (H); Social institutions (H)
**Brain** Clinical pragmatics (T); Developmental dyslexia (H); Emotions (H21); Neurolinguistics (MT); Neuropragmatics (T)
**Brain imaging** → Cerebral representation of language; Cognitive science (MT); Language acquisition (H); Neurolinguistics (MT); Neuropragmatics (T); Perception and language (H); Psycholinguistics (MT)
**Bureaucratic language** Applied linguistics (MT)
**Business communication** Communication (H)

**Bühler, K.** (H); Language psychology (T21); Phatic communion (H)
**Caretaker discourse** Age and language use (H)
**Carnap, R.** Analytical philosophy (MT); Intensional logic (MT)
**Carnival(esque)** Bakhtin (H); Intertextuality (H)
**Cartesian philosophy** Chomskyan linguistics (MT)
**Case and semantic roles** (H); Agency and language (H); Case grammar (MT); Cognitive grammar (MT); Cognitive linguistics (MT); Dependency and valency grammar (MT); Functional grammar (MT); Role and reference grammar (MT)
**Case grammar** (MT); Case and semantic roles (H); Construction grammar (MT); Dependency and valency grammar (MT); Frame semantics (T); Functional grammar (MT); Role and reference grammar (MT)
**Catastrophe theory** (MT)
**Categorial imperative** Truthfulness (H)
**Categorization** (H); Adaptability (H); Cognitive grammar (MT); Cognitive linguistics (MT); Language dominance and minorization (H); Polysemy (H)
**Causality** (H)
**Centering theory** Tense and aspect (H)
**Cerebral division of labour in verbal communication** (H)
**Cerebral representation of language** Cerebral division of labour in verbal communication (H); Neurolinguistics (MT)
**Channel** (H); Computer-mediated communication (H); Conversation types (H); Discourse analysis (MT); Literacy (H); Mass media (H); Nonverbal communication (H); Politeness (H)
**Chaos theory** Catastrophe theory (MT)
**Chat** Computer-mediated communication (H)
**Child language** Ellipsis (H); Language acquisition (H)
**'CHILDES'** Language acquisition (H)
**Choice-making** Adaptability (H)
**Chomskyan linguistics** (MT); Autonomous vs. non-autonomous syntax (MT); Interpretive semantics (MT); Language acquisition (H); Mentalism (MT)
**Chronometric studies** Psycholinguistics (MT)
**Chronotope** Bakhtin (H)
**Chunking** Linear Unit Grammar (T21)
**Cicourel, A. V.** Cognitive sociology (MT)
**Class** Social class and language (H)
**Classification1** Typology (MT)
**Classification2** Taxonomy (MM)
**Classroom interaction** Applied linguistics (MT); Communicative success vs. failure (H); Language learning in immersion and CLIL classrooms (H)
**Clause structure** Attention and language (H); Control phenomena (H); Role and reference grammar (MT)
**Clinical pragmatics** (T); Cerebral representation of language; Perception and language (H)
**Co-ordination** Cognitive psychology (MT); Ellipsis (H)
**Code** Metalinguistic awareness (H); Register (H); Semiotics (MT)
**Code-switching** (H); Bilingualism and multilingualism (H); Borrowing (H); Contact linguistics (MT); Language contact (H); Language learning in immersion and CLIL classrooms (H); Language maintenance and shift (H21)
**Codemixing** Code-switching (H)
**Coding** Bateson (H)
**Cognate** The multilingual lexicon (H)
**Cognition** Language acquisition (H); Adaptability (H)
**Cognitive anthropology** (MT); Anthropological linguistics (MT)
**Cognitive grammar** (MT); Case and semantic roles (H); Cognitive linguistics (MT); Metaphor (H)
**Cognitive linguistics** (MT); Attention and language (H); Case and semantic roles (H); Cognitive grammar (MT); Cognitive science (MT); Embodiment (H); Emotions (H21); Hermeneutics (M); Language psychology (T21); Mental spaces (H); (The) pragmatic perspective (M)
**Cognitive pragmatics** Clinical pragmatics (T); Philosophy of mind (MT)
**Cognitive psychology** (MT); Artificial intelligence (MT); Behaviorism (MT); Clinical pragmatics (T); Cognitive science (MT); Comprehension vs. production (H); Connectionism (MT); Developmental psychology (MT); Experimentation (MM); Frame semantics (T); Intentionality (H); Perception and language (H); Psycholinguistics (MT)
**Cognitive science** (MT); Artificial intelligence (MT); Cognitive linguistics (MT); Cognitive psychology (MT); Connectionism (MT); Context and contextualization (H); Experimentation (MM); Grice (H); Perception and language (H); Mentalism (MT); Philosophy of mind (MT)
**Cognitive semantics** Cognitive science (MT); Componential analysis (MT); Conceptual semantics (T); Frame semantics (T); Lexical semantics (T)

**Cognitive sociology** (MT); Discourse analysis (MT); Emphasis (H); Ethnomethodology (MT); Sociolinguistics (MT); Symbolic interactionism (MT)
**Cohesion and coherence** (H); Communicative success vs. failure (H); Computational pragmatics (T); Discourse analysis (MT); Ellipsis (H); Frame analysis (M); Systemic functional grammar (MT); Tense and aspect (H); Text and discourse linguistics (T)
**Collaboration in dialogues** (H); Common ground (H); Conversational implicature (H); Conversational logic (MT); Listener response (H)
**Colligation** Metaphor (H); Collocation and colligation (H)
**Collocation and colligation** (H)
**Colonization** Language dominance and minorization (H)
**Color terms** Anthropological linguistics (MT); Lexical semantics (T); Perception and language (H)
**Commodification** Ideology (H)
**Common ground** (H); Collaboration in dialogues (H); Communication (H); Context and contextualization (H); Cognitive science (MT); Discourse analysis (MT); Text and discourse linguistics (T)
**Common sense** Ethnomethodology (MT)
**Communication** (H); Common ground (H)
**Communication disorders** → Language disorders
**Communication failure** Applied linguistics (MT)
**Communicational dialectology** Dialectology (MT)
**Communicative competence** Ethnography of speaking (MT); Gumperz (H); Linguistic explanation (MM); Motivation (H)
**Communicative dynamism** (H); Functional sentence perspective (H); Word order (H); Ọmọlúàbí (H)
**Communicative effect** Interlanguage pragmatics (T)
**Communicative style** (H); Cultural scripts (H); Non-verbal communication (H); Register (H)
**Communicative success vs. failure** (H)
**Community of practice** Social class and language (H)
**Comparative method** Contrastive analysis (MM)
**Competence vs. performance** → Cerebral representation of language; Chomskyan linguistics (MT)
**Complement control** Control phenomena (H)
**Compliment** Corpus pragmatics (M)
**Componential analysis** (MT); Anthropological linguistics (MT); Cultural scripts (H); Generative semantics (MT); Lexical field analysis (MT); Lexical semantics (T); Structuralism (MT)
**Comprehension vs. production** (H); Cohesion and coherence (H); Communication (H); Irony (H); Mediated performatives (H); Psycholinguistics (MT); Speech act theory (MT); Text comprehension (H)
**Compression** Conceptual integration (H)
**Computational linguistics** (MT); Artificial intelligence (MT); Discourse analysis (MT); Lexical functional grammar (MT)
**Computational pragmatics** (T)
**Computer communication** Artificial intelligence (MT); Computational pragmatics (T)
**Computer corpora** Notation Systems in Spoken Language Corpora (N)
**Computer modeling** Cognitive science (MT)
**Computer programming** Artificial intelligence (MT)
**Computer-mediated communication** (H); Literacy (H); Computational pragmatics (T)
**Conceptual blending** Conceptual integration (H); Metaphor (H)
**Conceptual dependency theory** Artificial intelligence (MT)
**Conceptual integration** (H)
**Conceptual metaphor theory** Metaphor (H)
**Conceptual semantics** (T); Interpretive semantics (MT)
**Conceptual vs. linguistic representation** Cognitive anthropology (MT); Cognitive psychology (MT)
**Conceptualization** Cognitive grammar (MT); Cognitive linguistics (MT)
**Condition of satisfaction** Intentionality (H)
**Conflict talk** Applied linguistics (MT)
**Connectionism** (MT); Artificial intelligence (MT); Cognitive psychology (MT); Cognitive science (MT); Language acquisition (H); Psycholinguistics (MT)
**Connectivity** Cohesion and coherence (H)
**Connotation** → Cerebral representation of language
**Consciousness and language** (H); Attention and language (H); Folk pragmatics (T); Perception and language (H); Metapragmatics (MT); Participation (H)
**Considerateness** → Tact
**Consistency-checking device** Manipulation (H)
**Construction grammar** (MT); Case grammar (MT); Emergent grammar (T); Frame semantics (T); Word order (H)
**Constructional analysis** (T); Construction grammar (MT); Constructional analysis (T); Collocation and colligation (H)
**Constructionism** Applied linguistics (MT); Argumentation theory (MT); Cognitive

anthropology (MT); Critical Linguistics and Critical Discourse Analysis (MT); Developmental psychology (MT); Intercultural communication (H); Narrative (H); Social institutions (H)
**Constructivism** → Constructionism
**Contact** (H); Bilingualism and multilingualism (H); Contact linguistics (MT); Creole linguistics (MT); Creoles and creolization (H); Language change (H); Language contact (H); Language maintenance and shift (H21); Superdiversity (H21)
**Contact linguistics** (MT); Bilingualism and multilingualism (H); Contact (H); Creole linguistics (MT); Creoles and creolization (H); Dialectology (MT); Intercultural communication (H); Interjections (H); Language policy, language planning and standardization (H); Sociolinguistics (MT); Speech community (H); Typology (MT); Variational pragmatics (T)
**Context and contextualization** (H); Accommodation theory (MT); Aisatsu (H); Anthropological linguistics (MT); Artificial intelligence (MT); Bateson (H); Cerebral representation of language; Cognitive science (MT); Cohesion and coherence (H); Common ground (H); Communication (H); Communicative style (H); Computational pragmatics (T); Contextualism (T); Conversation analysis (MT); Conversation types (H); Conversational implicature (H); Conversational logic (MT); Dialogical analysis (MM); Discourse markers (H); Ellipsis (H); Emphasis (H); Énonciation (H); Ethnography of speaking (MT); Ethnomethodology (MT); Evolutionary pragmatics (T); Experimental pragmatics (M); Firthian linguistics (MT); Frame analysis (M); Generative semantics (MT); Goffman (H); Gumperz (H); Impoliteness (H); Indexicals and demonstratives (H); Integrational linguistics (T); Intensional logic (MT); Interactional sociolinguistics (MT); Intercultural communication (H); Intertextuality (H); Language psychology (T21); Laughter (H); Literary pragmatics (MT); Metalinguistic awareness (H); Model-theoretic semantics (MT); Motivation and language (H); Narrative (H); Notation in formal semantics (MN); Politeness (H); Polysemy (H); Presupposition (H); Prosody (H); Rhetoric (MT); Stance (H21); Style and styling (H21); Symbolic interactionism (MT); Tactile sign languages (H21); Text comprehension (H); Truthfulness (H)
**Context change** Context and contextualization (H)
**Context modelling** Formal pragmatics (MT)
**Context-of-situation** Context and contextualization (H); Firthian linguistics (MT); Malinowski (H); Register (H); Systemic functional grammar (MT)
**Context-sensitive vs. context-free grammar** Computational linguistics (MT); Functional sentence perspective (H)
**Context-sensitiveness** Context and contextualization (H)
**Contextualism** (T); Context and contextualization (H)
**Contextualization cue** Gumperz (H); Style and styling (H21)
**Continuity** Historical politeness (T)
**Continuity hypothesis** Language acquisition (H)
**Contrast** Functional discourse grammar (T)
**Contrastive analysis** (MM); Developmental psychology (MT); Error analysis (MM); Historical politeness (T); Intercultural communication (H); Interlanguage pragmatics (T); Language change (H); Pragmatic markers (H)
**Contrastive pragmatics** (T); Contrastive pragmatics (T); Ethnography of speaking (MT); Intercultural communication (H); Interlanguage pragmatics (T); Mianzi / lian (H21); Translation studies (T); Typology (MT); Variational pragmatics (T)
**Control** Public discourse (H); Social institutions (H)
**Control phenomena** (H)
**Conventional implicature** Grice (H); Implicitness (H); Truth-conditional pragmatics (T21)
**Conventionality** Adaptability (H); Conventions of language (H); Metaphor (H); Primate communication (H); Speech act theory (MT)
**Conventions of language** (H); Austin (H); Conversational implicature (H); Conversational logic (MT); Grice (H); Speech act
**Convergence** Accommodation theory (MT); Contact (H)
**Conversation** Collaboration in dialogues (H); Conversation analysis (MT); Humor (H); Indeterminacy and negotiation (H); Mass media (H); Narrative (H)
**Conversation analysis** (MT); Age and language use (H); Communication (H); Communicative success vs. failure (H); Computational pragmatics (T); Context and contextualization (H); Conversation types (H); Discourse markers (H); Emphasis (H); Ethnomethodology (MT); Discourse

analysis (MT); Ethnography of speaking (MT); Forensic linguistics (T); Goffman (H); Gumperz (H); Hermeneutics (M); Humor (H); Interactional linguistics (T); Interactional sociolinguistics (MT); Intertextuality (H); Language psychology (T21); Laughter (H); Linear Unit Grammar (T21); Listener response (H); Mass media (H); Notation ′ Systems in Spoken Language Corpora (N); Overlap (H); Prosody (H); Repair (H); Sacks (H); Sequence (H); Social psychology (MT); (The) pragmatic perspective (M); Therapeutic conversation (H); Transcription systems for spoken discourse (MN)
**Conversation types** (H)
**Conversational implicature** (H); Analytical philosophy (MT); Clinical pragmatics (T); Context and contextualization (H); Conversational logic (MT); Ellipsis (H); Experimental pragmatics (M); Grice (H); Implicature and language change (H); Implicitness (H); Interlanguage pragmatics (T); Language and the law (H); Politeness (H); Relevance theory (MT); Speech act theory (MT); Truth-conditional pragmatics (T21); Truthfulness (H)
**Conversational logic** (MT); Context and contextualization (H); Conversational implicature (H); Generative semantics (MT); Grice (H); Philosophy of language (MT); Relevance theory (MT); Speech act theory (MT)
**Conversational move** → Move
**Cooperative principle** Computational pragmatics (T); Conversational implicature (H); Conversational logic (MT); Creativity in language use (H); Grice (H); Humor (H); Implicature and language change (H); Implicitness (H); Irony (H); Silence (H); Politeness (H); Truthfulness (H)
**Copenhagen circle** Structuralism (MT)
**Coreference** Anaphora (H)
**Corpus analysis** (MM); Collocation and colligation (H); Corpus pragmatics (M); Discourse analysis (MT); Language acquisition (H); Leech (H); Pragmatic markers (H); Psycholinguistics (MT); Statistics (MM); Structuralism (MT); Text and discourse linguistics (T); Translation studies (T); Variational pragmatics (T)
**Corpus pragmatics** (M); Corpus analysis (MM)
**Correlational sociolinguistics** (T); Dialectology (MT); Sociolinguistics (MT); Statistics (MM)
**Coseriu** Structuralism (MT)
**Courtroom conversation** Forensic linguistics (T); Interpreter-mediated interaction (H); Language and the law (H)
**Creativity in language use** (H); Authenticity (H); Bühler (H); Cognitive science (MT); Humboldt (H); Language acquisition (H); Think-aloud protocols (M)
**Creature construction** Grice (H)
**Creole linguistics** (MT); Contact (H); Contact linguistics (MT); Creoles and creolization (H); Historical linguistics (MT); Sociolinguistics (MT)
**Creoles and creolization** (H); Contact (H); Contact linguistics (MT); Creole linguistics (MT); Historical linguistics (MT); Intercultural communication (H); Language contact (H); Sociolinguistics (MT)
**Critical Linguistics and Critical Discourse Analysis** (MT); Discourse analysis (MT); Emphasis (H); General semantics (MT); Ideology (H); Intercultural communication (H); Intertextuality (H); Language ideologies (H); Manipulation (H); Marxist linguistics (MT); Mass media (H); Nexus analysis (T); Polyphony (H); Text and discourse linguistics (T); Text linguistics (MT); Truthfulness (H)
**Critical theory** (MT); Intercultural communication (H); Universal and transcendental pragmatics (MT)
**Cross-cultural communication** Intercultural communication (H)
**Cross-cultural pragmatics** Discourse analysis (MT); Listener response (H); Overlap (H)
**Cross-cultural psychology** Cognitive anthropology (MT); Developmental psychology (MT)
**Cross-sectional method** Developmental psychology (MT)
**Crying** Emotion display (H)
**Culioli, A.** Énonciation (H)
**Cultural anthropology** Anthropological linguistics (MT); Cognitive anthropology (MT)
**Cultural model** Cognitive science (MT)
**Cultural scripts** (H); Communicative style (H); Componential analysis (MT); Culture (H)
**Cultural studies** Ethnography of speaking (MT); Literary pragmatics (MT); Translation studies (T)
**Culture** (H); Anthropological linguistics (MT); Behaviorism (MT); Boas (H); Context and contextualization (H); Contrastive analysis (MM); Cultural scripts (H); Default interpretations (H); Ethnography (MM); Evolutionary pragmatics (T); Fieldwork (MM); Gumperz (H); Humboldt (H); Ideology (H); Intercultural communication (H); Interjections (H); Mentalism (MT); Mianzi / lian

(H21); Morphopragmatics (T); Objectivism vs. subjectivism (MT); Ọmọlúàbí (H); Politeness (H); Repair (H); Sapir (H); Semiotics (MT); Sociolinguistics (MT); Style and styling (H21); Whorf (H)
**Curse** Impoliteness (H)
**Cynicism** Irony (H)

**Data collection/coding/analysis** Conversation analysis (MT); Developmental psychology (MT); Grounded theory (M); Historical pragmatics (T); Linguistic landscape studies (T); Statistics (MM); Tactile sign languages (H21); Terms of address (H); Typology (MT)
**Davidson, D.** Analytical philosophy (MT)
**Deception** Truthfulness (H)
**Deconstruction** (MM); Literary pragmatics (MT)
**Deduction** Grounded theory (M)
**Default interpretations** (H)
**Default semantics** Default interpretations (H)
**Deference** Ọmọlúàbí (H)
**Definite articles** Definiteness (H)
**Definite description** Game-theoretical semantics (MT); Reference and descriptions (H)
**Definiteness** (H)
**Degree** Communicative dynamism (H)
**Deixis** (H); Bühler (H); Context and contextualization (H); Énonciation (H); Honorifics (H); Mental spaces (H); Non-verbal communication (H); Peirce (H); Politeness (H)
**Deletion** Ellipsis (H)
**Dementia** Clinical pragmatics (T)
**Demonstrative** Indexicals and demonstratives (H)
**Denotation** → Cerebral representation of language; Polysemy (H)
**Deontic logic** (MT); Epistemic logic (MT); Logical semantics (MT); Modality (H); Modal logic (MT)
**Dependency** Dependency and valency grammar (MT); Frame semantics (T); Polysemy (H); Predicates and predication (H); Role and reference grammar (MT)
**Dependency and valency grammar** (MT); Case and semantic roles (H); Case grammar (MT); Role and reference grammar (MT)
**Derrida, J.** Deconstruction (MM)
**Detention hearing** → Police interrogation
**Deutero-learning** Bateson (H)
**Developmental dyslexia** (H); Clinical pragmatics (T); Developmental psychology (MT); Language acquisition (H); Literacy (H); Pragmatic acquisition (H); Psycholinguistics (MT)
**Developmental psychology** (MT); Bilingualism and multilingualism (H); Cognitive psychology (MT); Psycholinguistics (MT); Vygotsky (H)
**Dewey, J.** Morris (H); Pragmatism (MT)
**Diachrony** Language change (H)
**Diacritic** Phonetic notation systems (N)
**Dialect** (H); Anderson (H21); Dialectology (MT); Dialectology and geolinguistic dynamics (T); Folk pragmatics (T); Integrational linguistics (T)
**Dialect formation** Dialectology and geolinguistic dynamics (T)
**Dialect geography** Dialectology (MT)
**Dialect leveling/loss** Dialectology and geolinguistic dynamics (T)
**Dialectology** (MT); Contact linguistics (MT); Correlational sociolinguistics (T); Dialect (H); Dialectology and geolinguistic dynamics (T); Historical linguistics (MT); Reconstruction (MM); Sociolinguistics (MT)
**Dialectology and geolinguistic dynamics** (T)
**Dialog modeling** Artificial intelligence (MT); Computational pragmatics (T)
**Dialog system** Artificial intelligence (MT); Computational pragmatics (T)
**Dialogical analysis** (MM); Collaboration in dialogues (H); Context and contextualization (H); Foucault (H); Humboldt (H); Interactional linguistics (T); Peirce (H)
**Dialogism** Appraisal (H); Intertextuality (H); Stance (H21)
**Dialogue** Bakhtin (H); Collaboration in dialogues (H); Interpreter-mediated interaction (H); Polyphony (H)
**Diaphor** Metaphor (H)
**Diglossia** Language contact (H)
**Dik, S.** Functional grammar (MT)
**Diminutive** Morphopragmatics (T)
**Direct vs. indirect speech** Reported speech (H)
**Discourse** Argumentation in discourse and grammar (H); Bakhtin (H); Cognitive sociology (MT); Critical Linguistics and Critical Discourse Analysis (MT); Discourse analysis (MT); Discourse markers (H); Ethnography (MM); Foucault (H); Grounding (H); Intertextuality (H); Language psychology (T21); Mental spaces (H); Narrative (H); Neuropragmatics (T); Nexus analysis (T); Polyphony (H); Public discourse (H); Social institutions (H); Systemic functional grammar (MT); Text and discourse linguistics (T); Text structure (H)
**Discourse act** Functional discourse grammar (T)
**Discourse analysis** (MT); Channel (H); Cognitive sociology (MT); Common ground (H);

Conversation analysis (MT); Corpus analysis (MM); Creole linguistics (MT); Critical Linguistics and Critical Discourse Analysis (MT); Geneva school (MT); Grounding (H); Historical pragmatics (T); Ideology (H); Mass media (H); Multimodality (H); Prague school (MT); Rhetoric (MT); Social psychology (MT); Structuralism (MT); Stylistics (MT); Text and discourse linguistics (T); Text linguistics (MT); Truthfulness (H)
**Discourse attuning** Accommodation theory (MT)
**Discourse completion test** Intercultural communication (H)
**Discourse focus** Anaphora (H)
**Discourse genre** Genre (H)
**Discourse linking** Discourse representation theory (MT)
**Discourse markers** (H); Historical pragmatics (T); Interjections (H); Polyphony (H); Pragmatic markers (H); Pragmatic particles (H)
**Discourse mode** Register (H)
**Discourse representation theory** (MT); Default interpretations (H); Game-theoretical semantics (MT); Logical semantics (MT); Montague and categorial grammar (MT); Situation semantics (MT); Tense and aspect (H)
**Discourse sociolinguistics** Critical Linguistics and Critical Discourse Analysis (MT)
**Discourse topic** Consciousness and language (H)
**Discursive ethics** Universal and transcendental pragmatics (MT)
**Discursive formation** Foucault (H)
**Discursive order** Foucault (H)
**Discursive psychology** Authority (H); Language psychology (T21); Motivation (H)
**Dismissal** Impoliteness (H)
**Displacement** Adaptability (H)
**Distinctive feature** Jakobson (H21)
**Divergence** Accommodation theory (MT)
**Diversity** Anderson (H21); Language maintenance and shift (H21); Superdiversity (H21)
**Doctor-patient interaction** → Medical interaction
**Document design** Applied linguistics (MT)
**Donnellan, K.** Reference and descriptions (H)
**Double bind** Bateson (H)
**Drift** Language change (H)
**Ducrot, O.** Argumentation theory (MT); Énonciation (H); Polyphony (H)
**Dummett, M.** Analytical philosophy (MT)
**Dyadic interaction** Conversation types (H); Statistics (MM)
**Dynamic semantic functions** Communicative dynamism (H)
**Dynamic semantics** Presupposition (H)
**Dysphasia** → Cerebral representation of language

**E-mail communication** Computer-mediated communication (H)
**Ebonics** 'Other' representation (H)
**Education** Applied linguistics (MT); Ideology (H); Language learning in immersion and CLIL classrooms (H); Language rights (H); Linguistic landscape studies (T); Literacy (H)
**Egocentric speech** Vygotsky (H)
**Elicitation** (MM); Fieldwork (MM); Interview (MM)
**Ellipsis** (H)
**Embedding** Frame analysis (M)
**Embodiment** (H)
**Emergence** Adaptability (H)
**Emergent grammar** (T)
**Emotion display** (H); Laughter (H); Silence (H)
**Emotions** (H21); Appraisal (H); Emotion display (H); Impoliteness (H)
**Emphasis** (H)
**Endangered languages** Language ecology (H)
**Engagement** Appraisal (H); Nexus analysis (T)
**Engels, Friedrich** Ideology (H)
**English (as a global language)** Linguistic landscape studies (T)
***Énonciation*** (H); Benveniste (H)
**Entailment** Implicitness (H)
**Entrenchment** Conceptual integration (H)
**Enunciation** Benveniste (H); Polyphony (H)
**Environment** Tactile sign languages (H21)
**Epiphor** Metaphor (H)
**Epistemic dynamics** Epistemic logic (MT)
**Epistemic logic** (MT); Deontic logic (MT); Logical semantics (MT); Modality (H); Modal logic (MT); Possible worlds semantics (MT)
**Epistemology** (MT); Austin (H); Foucault (H); Perception and language (H); Objectivism vs. subjectivism (MT); Ontology (MT)
**Epistemology of testimony** (T)
**Erklären vs. Verstehen** Grounded theory (M)
**Error analysis** (MM); Contrastive analysis (MM)
**Ethnicity** Culture (H); Humor (H); Intercultural communication (H); Language dominance and minorization (H); Language policy, language planning and standardization (H)
**Ethnographic semantics** Anthropological linguistics (MT); Taxonomy (MM)
**Ethnography** (MM); Anderson (H21); Anthropological linguistics (MT); Bourdieu (H); Developmental psychology (MT); Ethnography of speaking (MT); Fieldwork (MM); Linguistic landscape studies (T)

**Ethnography of communication** Ethnography of speaking (MT)
**Ethnography of speaking** (MT); Anthropological linguistics (MT); Context and contextualization (H); Conversation analysis (MT); Gumperz (H); Interactional sociolinguistics (MT); Intercultural communication (H); Nexus analysis (T); Phatic communion (H); Style and styling (H21)
**Ethnomethodology** (MT); Cognitive sociology (MT); Context and contextualization (H); Conversation analysis (MT); Interactional sociolinguistics (MT); Language psychology (T21); Phenomenology (MT); Sacks (H); Social psychology (MT); Symbolic interactionism (MT); (The) pragmatic perspective (M)
**Ethnoscience** Anthropological linguistics (MT)
**Ethogenics** Social psychology (MT)
**Euphemism** Morphopragmatics (T)
**Evaluation** Appraisal (H); Emphasis (H); Stance (H21)
**Event-related potential** Cognitive science (MT); Language acquisition (H)
**Evidentiality** Appraisal (H); Authority (H); Modality (H); Stance (H21)
**Evolution (theory)** Adaptability (H); Evolutionary pragmatics (T)
**Evolutionary pragmatics** (T)
**Executive function** Clinical pragmatics (T)
**Exemplar model** Psycholinguistics (MT)
**Expectation** Frame analysis (M); Mediated performatives (H)
**Experimental pragmatics** (M); Experimentation (MM)
**Experimentation** (MM); Cognitive psychology (MT); Cognitive science (MT); Ethnomethodology (MT); Experimental pragmatics (M); Psycholinguistics (MT); Sound symbolism (H); Statistics (MM); Think-aloud protocols (M); Variational pragmatics (T)
**Expertise** Cognitive sociology (MT); Forensic linguistics (T)
**Explaining vs. understanding** → Erklären vs. Verstehen
**Explanation** Linguistic explanation (MM)
**Explicature** Implicitness (H); Truth-conditional pragmatics (T21)
**Expression** → Functions of language
**Extension** → Intension vs. extension

**Face** Impoliteness (H); Goffman (H); Mianzi / lian (H21); Politeness (H); Silence (H)
**Face-to-face interaction** Accommodation theory (MT); Cognitive sociology (MT); Computer-mediated communication (H); Conversation analysis (MT); Intercultural communication (H); Prosody (H)
**False friends** The multilingual lexicon (H)
**Familiarity** Information structure (H)
**Feedback** Adaptability (H); Tactile sign languages (H21)
**Feeling(s)** Appraisal (H)
**Felicity condition** Speech act theory (MT)
**Ferguson, C.** Register (H)
**Field** Register (H)
**Fieldwork** (MM); Anthropological linguistics (MT); Boas (H); Elicitation (MM); Ethnography (MM); Ethnography of speaking (MT); Interview (MM); Malinowski (H)
**Figure vs. ground** Grounding (H)
**Figures of speech** (H); Cultural scripts (H); Emphasis (H)
**File change semantics** Computational linguistics (MT); Discourse representation theory (MT)
**Fillmore, C. J.** Case grammar (MT); Frame semantics (T)
**Firth, J. R.** (H); Firthian linguistics (MT); Register (H); Systemic functional grammar (MT)
**Firthian linguistics** (MT); Context and contextualization (H); Firth (H); Phatic communion (H); Systemic functional grammar (MT)
**Flexibility** Primate communication (H)
**Focalisation** Tense and aspect (H)
**Focalizer** Functional sentence perspective (H)
**Focus** → Topic vs. focus
**Focus structure** Role and reference grammar (MT)
**Folk classification** Anthropological linguistics (MT); Cognitive anthropology (MT); Language ideologies (H); Metalinguistic awareness (H); Taxonomy (MM)
**Folk linguistics** Socio-onomastics (T)
**Folk pragmatics** (T)
**Folk psychology** Philosophy of mind (MT)
**Footing** Frame analysis (M); Goffman (H); Participation (H)
**Foregrounding** Grounding (H)
**Foreigner talk** Intercultural communication (H); Register (H)
**Forensic linguistics** (T); Applied linguistics (MT)
**Form vs. function** Corpus pragmatics (M); Sapir (H)
**Form-function mapping** → Form vs. function
**Formal dialectics** Argumentation theory (MT)
**Formal linguistics** Linguistic explanation (MM)
**Formal pragmatics** (MT); Analytical philosophy

(MT); Logical semantics (MT); Montague and categorial grammar (MT)
**Formality** Conversation types (H); Register (H)
**Formulaic language** → Routine formula
**Formulation** Rhetoric (MT)
**Foucault, M.** (H); Critical theory (MT); Ideology (H); Jargon (H)
**Frame (analysis)** (M); Artificial intelligence (MT); Bateson (H); Cognitive science (MT); Emphasis (H); Frame semantics (T); Goffman (H); Humor (H); Mental spaces (H); Metalinguistic awareness (H); Non-verbal communication (H); (The) pragmatic perspective (M)
**Frame semantics** (T); Collocation and colligation (H); Context and contextualization (H); Dependency and valency grammar (MT); Lexical field analysis (MT); Lexical semantics (T)
**Frankfurt school** → Adorno; Habermas
**Frege, G.** Analytical philosophy (MT); Intensional logic (MT); Reference and descriptions (H); Semantics vs. pragmatics (T); Speech act theory (MT)
**Fremdverstehen** Grounded theory (M)
**Frequency** Markedness (H); Statistics (MM)
**Functional discourse grammar** (T)
**Functional explanation** Linguistic explanation (MM)
**Functional grammar** (MT); Case and semantic roles (H); Case grammar (MT); Mathesius (H); Predicates and predication (H); Prague school (MT); Systemic functional grammar (MT); Word order (H)
**Functional sentence perspective** (H); Communicative dynamism (H); Mathesius (H); Prague school (MT); Word order (H)
**Functionalism vs. formalism** (MT); Autonomous vs. non-autonomous syntax (MT); Cognitive science (MT); Communicative dynamism (H); Emergent grammar (T); Linguistic explanation (MM); Mathesius (H); (The) pragmatic perspective (M); Translation studies (T)
**Functions of language** Bühler (H); Emotion display (H); Evolutionary pragmatics (T); Functional discourse grammar (T); Functionalism vs. formalism (MT); Historical politeness (T); Impoliteness (H); Jakobson (H21); Participation (H); Prague school (MT); Relational ritual (H); Silence (H); Systemic functional grammar (MT)
**Fund** Predicates and predication (H)
**Fuzziness** → Vagueness
**Fuzzy set theory** Categorization (H); Lexical semantics (T)

**Game-theoretical semantics** (MT); Discourse representation theory (MT); Logical semantics (MT); Model-theoretic semantics (MT)
**Gapping** Ellipsis (H)
**Garfinkel, H.** Ethnomethodology (MT)
**Gender** (H); Authority (H); Computer-mediated communication (H); Critical Linguistics and Critical Discourse Analysis (MT); Interjections (H); Laughter (H); Listener response (H); Overlap (H); Silence (H)
**General rhetoric** Rhetoric (MT)
**General semantics** (MT); Critical Linguistics and Critical Discourse Analysis (MT)
**Generalized catastrophe** Catastrophe theory (MT)
**Generalized phrase structure grammar** Computational linguistics (MT); Construction grammar (MT); Interpretive semantics (MT)
**Generative semantics** (MT); Componential analysis (MT); Conceptual semantics (T); Conversational logic (MT); Interpretive semantics (MT); (The) pragmatic perspective (M)
**Generative(-transformational) linguistics** Attention and language (H); Chomskyan linguistics (MT); Cognitive linguistics (MT); Computational linguistics (MT); Creativity in language use (H); Historical linguistics (MT); Interpretive semantics (MT); Language acquisition (H); Language change (H); Lexical semantics (T)
**Genetic linguistics** Historical linguistics (MT); Language change (H); Reconstruction (MM)
**Geneva school** (MT); Discourse analysis (MT); Structuralism (MT)
**Genre** (H); Bakhtin (H); Channel (H); Conversational logic (MT); Conversation types (H); Narrative (H); Tense and aspect (H); Text and discourse linguistics (T); Text type (H)
**Geographical origin** Laughter (H)
**Geolinguistics** Contact linguistics (MT); Dialectology and geolinguistic dynamics (T); Linguistic landscape studies (T)
**Gestalt psychology** Behaviorism (MT); Cognitive psychology (MT); Metaphor (H)
**Gesture** Communication (H); Non-verbal communication (H); Primate communication (H); Prosody (H)
**Given vs. new** Argumentation in discourse and grammar (H); Computational pragmatics (T); Definiteness (H); Functional sentence perspective (H); Information structure (H);

Word order (H)
**Globalization** Language dominance and minorization (H); Dialectology and geolinguistic dynamics (T)
**Glossematics** Semiotics (MT); Structuralism (MT)
**Glottochronology** Historical linguistics (MT)
**Goffman, E.** (H); Frame analysis (M); Conversation analysis (MT); Participation (H); Politeness (H); Public discourse (H); Reported speech (H); Symbolic interactionism (MT)
**Government and binding theory** Chomskyan linguistics (MT); Construction grammar (MT); Interpretive semantics (MT)
**Gradience** Categorization (H)
**Grammar** Argumentation in discourse and grammar (H); Leech (H)
**Grammatical constraints** Code-switching (H)
**Grammatical metaphor** Metaphor (H)
**Grammatical relations** Agency and language (H); Polysemy (H); Role and reference grammar (MT)
**Grammatical status** Grammaticalization and pragmatics (T)
**Grammaticalization** Constructional analysis (T); Emergent grammar (T); Implicature and language change (H); Language change (H); Metaphor (H); Modality (H); Negation (H); Pragmatic markers (H); Predicates and predication (H)
**Grammaticalization and pragmatics** (T)
**Grammatization** Emergent grammar (T)
**Gramsci, A.** Marxist linguistics (MT)
**Greeting** Ọmọlúàbí (H)
**Grice, H. P.** (H); Analytical philosophy (MT); Clinical pragmatics (T); Conversational implicature (H); Conversational logic (MT); Default interpretations (H); Humor (H); Semantics vs. pragmatics (T); Silence (H); Speech act theory (MT); Truth-conditional pragmatics (T21); Truthfulness (H)
**Grounded theory** (M)
**Grounding** (H); Anaphora (H); Computational pragmatics (T); Discourse analysis (MT); Text and discourse linguistics (T)
**Guillaume, G.** Énonciation (H)
**Gumperz, J. J.** (H); Anthropological linguistics (MT); Communicative success vs. failure (H); Culture (H); Ethnography of speaking (MT); Interactional sociolinguistics (MT); Intercultural communication (H); Prosody (H); Register (H)
**Habermas, J.** Critical theory (MT); Ideology (H); Public discourse (H); Universal and transcendental pragmatics (MT)
**Habitus** Anderson (H21); Bourdieu (H); Communication (H); Lifestyle (H)
**Half-truth** Truthfulness (H)
**Halliday, M. A. K.** Critical Linguistics and Critical Discourse Analysis (MT); Firthian linguistics (MT); Genre (H); Jargon (H); Phatic communion (H); Register (H); Social semiotics (T); Systemic functional grammar (MT)
**Harold Garfinkel and pragmatics** (H); Conversation analysis (MT); Ethnomethodology (MT); Metapragmatics (MT); Sacks (H)
**Head-driven phrase structure grammar** Computational linguistics (MT); Construction grammar (MT); Formal pragmatics (MT); Interpretive semantics (MT)
**Hearer** Appraisal (H); Mass media (H)
**Hegemony** Ideology (H); Intertextuality (H); Language ecology (H); Metalinguistic awareness (H)
**Hemisphere dominance** Neurolinguistics (MT)
**Heritage language** Language maintenance and shift (H21)
**Hermeneutics** (M); Analytical philosophy (MT); Anthropological linguistics (MT); Cognitive linguistics (MT); Cohesion and coherence (H); Conversation analysis (MT); Language psychology (T21); Literary pragmatics (MT); Structuralism (MT); Truthfulness (H); Universal and transcendental pragmatics (MT)
**Heterogeneity** Language dominance and minorization (H)
**Heteroglossia** Appraisal (H); Bakhtin (H); Ideology (H); Intertextuality (H)
**Heterosemy** Polysemy (H)
**Historical linguistics** (MT); Borrowing (H); Creole linguistics (MT); Creoles and creolization (H); Dialectology (MT); Historical pragmatics (T); Language change (H); Reconstruction (MM); de Saussure (H); Typology (MT)
**Historical politeness** (T)
**Historical pragmatics** (T); Discourse analysis (MT); Historical linguistics (MT); Interjections (H); Mass media (H)
**Historical sociolinguistics** (T); Correlational sociolinguistics (T); Dialectology and geolinguistic dynamics (T); Historical linguistics (MT); Historical pragmatics (T); Interactional sociolinguistics (MT); Language change (H); Sociolinguistics (MT)
**History** Critical Linguistics and Critical Discourse Analysis (MT); Dialectology (MT)
**Homogeneity** Anderson (H21); Metalinguistic

awareness (H)
**Homogenisation** 'Other' representation (H)
**Homonymy** Indeterminacy and negotiation (H); Polysemy (H)
**Honorifics** (H); Politeness (H); Terms of address (H)
**Humboldt, W. von** (H)
**Humor** (H); Computer-mediated communication (H); Emotion display (H); Irony (H); Laughter (H); 'Other' representation (H); Truthfulness (H)
**Hybridity** Genre (H); Intensional logic (MT); Intertextuality (H); 'Other' representation (H); Presupposition (H)
**Hymes, D.** Anthropological linguistics (MT); Culture (H); Ethnography of speaking (MT)
**Hyponymy** Polysemy (H)

**I-principle** Anaphora (H); Semantics vs. pragmatics (T)
**Iconicity** (H); Jakobson (H21); Language change (H); Sound symbolism (H)
**Identifiability** Definiteness (H)
**Identity** Age and language use (H); Anderson (H21); Dialectology and geolinguistic dynamics (T); Gumperz (H); Ideology (H); Language maintenance and shift (H21); Laughter (H); Life stories (H); Motivation and language (H); Social class and language (H); Superdiversity (H21); Variational pragmatics (T)
**Ideology** (H); Critical Linguistics and Critical Discourse Analysis (MT); Culture (H); Honorifics (H); Manipulation (H); Marxist linguistics (MT); Mass media (H); Public discourse (H); Social psychology (MT); Social semiotics (T)
**Idiolect** Forensic linguistics (T); Integrational linguistics (T)
**Idéologues** Humboldt (H)
**Illiteracy** Literacy (H)
**Illocution** Functional discourse grammar (T); Functional grammar (MT); Indeterminacy and negotiation (H); Intentionality (H); Modality (H); Non-verbal communication (H); Speech act theory (MT)
**Illocutionary force** Speech act theory (MT)
**Illocutionary force-indicating device** Corpus pragmatics (M); Speech act theory (MT)
**Imagined community** Anderson (H21)
**Immersion** Language learning in immersion and CLIL classrooms (H)
**Implicature and language change** (H); Conventional implicature; Conversational implicature (H)
**Implicitness** (H); Cerebral representation of language; Discourse markers (H); Emphasis (H); Truth-conditional pragmatics (T21)
**Impliciture** Implicitness (H)
**Impoliteness** (H); Historical politeness (T); Politeness (H)
**Indeterminacy and negotiation** (H); Ellipsis (H); Integrational linguistics (T); Truthfulness (H)
**Indexicalism** Contextualism (T)
**Indexicality** Ethnomethodology (MT); Jakobson (H21); Language change (H); Language psychology (T21); Metalinguistic awareness (H); Prosody (H); Stance (H21); Truth-conditional semantics (MT)
**Indexicals and demonstratives** (H); Anaphora (H); Context and contextualization (H)
**Indirectness** Conversational logic (MT); Discourse representation theory (MT); Leech (H)
**Individuality** Intentionality (H)
**Induction** Grounded theory (M)
**Inequality** → Power
**(In)felicity** Communicative success vs. failure (H)
**Inferencing** → Cerebral representation of language; Clinical pragmatics (T); Cognitive psychology (MT); Cognitive sociology (MT); Computational pragmatics (T); Conceptual semantics (T); Default interpretations (H); Discourse representation theory (MT); Ellipsis (H); Emphasis (H); Experimental pragmatics (M); Grice (H); Gumperz (H); Figures of speech (H); Implicature and language change (H); Irony (H); Language psychology (T21); Prosody (H); Speech act theory (MT)
**Informal logic** Argumentation theory (MT)
**Information processing** Attention and language (H); Cognitive psychology (MT); Cognitive science (MT); Comprehension vs. production (H); Text comprehension (H)
**Information structure** (H); Argumentation in discourse and grammar (H); Computational pragmatics (T); Discourse analysis (MT); Discourse markers (H); Emphasis (H); Narrative (H); Signed language pragmatics (T); Tense and aspect (H); Text and discourse linguistics (T); Text structure (H); Word order (H)
**Informativeness** Definiteness (H); Humor (H); Information structure (H); Presupposition (H)
**Informing** Mediated performatives (H)
**Innateness** Language acquisition (H)
**Inner speech** Vygotsky (H)
**Institutional role** Laughter (H)
**Institutional setting** Social institutions (H)
**Instructional science** Applied linguistics (MT)

**Instrumentality** Evolutionary pragmatics (T)
**Insult** Impoliteness (H)
**Integration** Language rights (H)
**Integrational linguistics** (T)
**Integrity** Truthfulness (H)
**Intension vs. extension** Intensional logic (MT); Notation in formal semantics (MN)
**Intensional logic** (MT); Logical semantics (MT)
**Intensional semantics** Analytical philosophy (MT)
**Intention** Artificial intelligence (MT); Computational pragmatics (T); Grice (H); Intentionality (H); Irony (H); Mediated performatives (H); Neuropragmatics (T); Philosophy of action (MT); Philosophy of mind (MT); Primate communication (H); Speech act theory (MT); Truthfulness (H)
**Intentionality** (H); Agency and language (H); Communication (H); Impoliteness (H); Philosophy of mind (MT)
**Interaction-organization theory** Metaphor (H)
**Interactional analysis** Multimodality (H)
**Interactional linguistics** (T); Emergent grammar (T); Linear Unit Grammar (T21)
**Interactional sense-making** → Meaning construction
**Interactional sociolinguistics** (MT); Code-switching (H); Communicative style (H); Context and contextualization (H); Conversation analysis (MT); Ethnography of speaking (MT); Ethnomethodology (MT); Gumperz (H); Intercultural communication (H); Metapragmatics (MT); Mianzi / lian (H21); Nexus analysis (T); Sociolinguistics (MT); (The) pragmatic perspective (M)
**Interactive failure** → Communication failure
**Interactive-activation model** Psycholinguistics (MT)
**Interactivity** Computer-mediated communication (H); Deixis (H); Functional discourse grammar (T); Psycholinguistics (MT); Reported speech (H)
**Intercultural communication** (H); Aisatsu (H); Anthropological linguistics (MT); Applied linguistics (MT); Bilingualism and multilingualism (H); Code-switching (H); Communication (H); Communicative success vs. failure (H); Contact linguistics (MT); Context and contextualization (H); Contrastive analysis (MM); Creoles and creolization (H); Critical Linguistics and Critical Discourse Analysis (MT); Critical theory (MT); Culture (H); Ethnography of speaking (MT); Gumperz (H); Interactional sociolinguistics (MT); Interlanguage pragmatics (T); Language and the law (H); Language policy, language planning and standardization (H); Non-verbal communication (H); Text and discourse linguistics (T); Truthfulness (H)
**Interference** Contact linguistics (MT); Language contact (H); Psycholinguistics (MT)
**Interjections** (H)
**Interlanguage pragmatics** (T); Contrastive analysis (MM); Conversational implicature (H); Intercultural communication (H); Politeness (H)
**Internalization** Foucault (H)
**Internet** Computer-mediated communication (H)
**Interpersonal relation** Intentionality (H); Mianzi / lian (H21)
**Interpreter-mediated interaction** (H)
**Interpretive processes** → Inferencing
**Interpretive semantics** (MT); Chomskyan linguistics (MT); Conceptual semantics (T); Generative semantics (MT)
**Interpretive sociolinguistics** Interactional sociolinguistics (MT)
**Interruption** Overlap (H)
**Intersubjectivity** Appraisal (H); Bourdieu (H); Bühler (H); Collaboration in dialogues (H); Communication (H); Language psychology (T21); Peirce (H)
**Intertextuality** (H); Bakhtin (H); Computer-mediated communication (H); Polyphony (H)
**Interview** (MM); Elicitation (MM); Fieldwork (MM)
**Intimacy** Laughter (H)
**Intonation** Communicative dynamism (H); Information structure (H); Markedness (H); Prosody (H)
**Intonation unit** Consciousness and language (H)
**Intuition and introspection** (MM); Cognitive science (MT)
**Involvement** → Affect
**Irony** (H); Experimental pragmatics (M); Frame analysis (M); Humor (H); Polyphony (H)
**Isomorphism** Iconicity (H)

**Jakobson, R.** (H21); Emotions (H21); Participation (H); Phatic communion (H); Prague school (MT); Structuralism (MT)
**James, W.** Morris (H); Pragmatism (MT)
**Jargon** (H)
**Joke** Humor (H); Irony (H)
**Journalism** Mass media (H); Mediated performatives (H)
**Judgement** Appraisal (H)
**Jury instruction** Forensic linguistics (T)

**Kilivila** Malinowski (H)
**Kinesics** Non-verbal communication (H)
**Knowledge** Artificial intelligence (MT); Austin (H); Authority (H); Epistemology of testimony (T); Foucault (H)
**Knowledge representation** Artificial intelligence (MT); Cognitive psychology (MT); Cognitive science (MT); Connectionism (MT)
**Koineization** Dialectology and geolinguistic dynamics (T)
**Kripke, S.** Reference and descriptions (H)
**Kristeva, J.** Intertextuality (H)

L2 → Second language acquisition
**Labov, W.** Correlational sociolinguistics (T); Creole linguistics (MT); Sociolinguistics (MT)
**Language acquisition** (H); Developmental psychology (MT); Discourse analysis (MT); Discourse markers (H); Interjections (H); Irony (H); Jakobson (H21); Literacy (H); Metalinguistic awareness (H); Morphopragmatics (T); Pragmatic particles (H); Psycholinguistics (MT); Repair (H); Text and discourse linguistics (T); Text structure (H); Vygotsky (H)
**Language acquisition device** Language acquisition (H)
**Language and the law** (H)
**Language and thought** Boas (H); Consciousness and language (H); Developmental psychology (MT); Embodiment (H); Humboldt (H); Perception and language (H); Sapir (H); Vygotsky (H); Whorf (H)
**Language attitudes** → Attitude
**Language change** (H); Borrowing (H); Contact linguistics (MT); Correlational sociolinguistics (T); Creativity in language use (H); Creoles and creolization (H); Dialectology (MT); Dialectology and geolinguistic dynamics (T); Discourse analysis (MT); Genre (H); Historical linguistics (MT); Historical pragmatics (T); Historical politeness (T); Implicature and language change (H); Language maintenance and shift (H21); Morphopragmatics (T); Polysemy (H); Pragmatic markers (H); de Saussure (H); Structuralism (MT); Superdiversity (H21); Text and discourse linguistics (T); Text structure (H)
**Language choice** Intercultural communication (H); Language policy, language planning and standardization (H)
**Language comprehension** Comprehension vs. production (H)
**Language conflict** Language contact (H); Language dominance and minorization (H)
**Language contact** (H); Borrowing (H); Contact (H); Language change (H); Literacy (H)
**Language death** Language contact (H); Language ecology (H); Language rights (H)
**Language disorders** → Cerebral representation of language; Clinical pragmatics (T); Neurolinguistics (MT)
**Language dominance and minorization** (H); Language ecology (H)
**Language ecology** (H)
**Language for special purposes (LSP)** Applied linguistics (MT); Genre (H)
**Language game** Game-theoretical semantics (MT); Wittgenstein (H)
**Language generation and interpretation** → Natural language generation and interpretation
**Language ideologies** (H); Bilingualism and multilingualism (H); Bourdieu (H); Ideology (H); Language dominance and minorization (H); Literacy (H); Metalinguistic awareness (H); Speech community (H)
**Language impairment** → Cerebral representation of language; Clinical pragmatics (T); Perception and language (H); Neurolinguistics (MT)
**Language learning in immersion and CLIL classrooms** (H)
**Language maintenance and shift** (H21); Contact (H); Interjections (H); Language change (H); Language ecology (H); Language policy, language planning and standardization (H)
**Language pathology** → Cerebral representation of language; Clinical pragmatics (T); Language acquisition (H); Perception and language (H)
**Language planning** Language maintenance and shift (H21); Language policy, language planning and standardization (H)
**Language policy, language planning and standardization** (H); Applied linguistics (MT); Authority (H); Bilingualism and multilingualism (H); Contact linguistics (MT); Intercultural communication (H); Language ideologies (H); Language maintenance and shift (H21); Linguistic landscape studies (T); Literacy (H); Sociolinguistics (MT)
**Language processing** → Natural language processing
**Language psychology** (T21)
**Language rights** (H)
**Language shift** Contact (H); Interjections (H); Language change (H); Language ecology (H); Language maintenance and shift (H21)
**Language teaching** Applied linguistics (MT);

Error analysis (MM); Ideology (H); Interlanguage pragmatics (T); Language learning in immersion and CLIL classrooms (H); Motivation and language (H); Pragmatic particles (H); Register (H)
**Language technology** Artificial intelligence (MT)
**Language universals** Conversational logic (MT); Dialectology (MT); Humboldt (H); Jakobson (H21); Language acquisition (H); Sound symbolism (H); Speech act theory (MT); Typology (MT); Word order (H); Variational pragmatics (T)
**Language variation** Dialect (H); Dialectology (MT); Variational pragmatics (T)
**Langue vs. parole** de Saussure (H); Structuralism (MT)
**Lateralization** Neurolinguistics (MT)
**Laughable** Laughter (H)
**Laughter** (H); Emotion display (H)
**Learnability** Language acquisition (H)
**Least-effort hypothesis** Semantics vs. pragmatics (T)
**Lect** Dialect (H)
**Leech, G.** (H)
**Left vs. right hemisphere** → Cerebral representation of language; Clinical pragmatics (T); Neurolinguistics (MT)
**Legal language** Applied linguistics (MT); Authority (H); Forensic linguistics (T); Language and the law (H); Sequence (H); Silence (H)
**Legal settings** Forensic linguistics (T)
**Legitimation** Foucault (H)
**Lesion syndrome** Neurolinguistics (MT)
**Lexical bundle/cluster/string** Collocation and colligation (H)
**Lexical decomposition** Componential analysis (MT)
**Lexical field analysis** (MT); Componential analysis (MT); Lexical semantics (T); Structuralism (MT)
**Lexical functional grammar** (MT); Computational linguistics (MT)
**Lexical primitive** → Semantic primitive
**Lexical semantics** (T); Componential analysis (MT); Frame semantics (T); Lexical field analysis (MT); Markedness (H); Metonymy (H); Polysemy (H); Vygotsky (H)
**Lexicalist hypothesis** Interpretive semantics (MT)
**Lexicase** Case grammar (MT)
**Lexico-grammar** Metaphor (H)
**Lexicography** Discourse markers (H); Frame semantics (T); Pragmatic particles (H)
**Lexicometry** Critical Linguistics and Critical Discourse Analysis (MT)
**Lexicon** Collocation and colligation (H); Comprehension vs. production (H); Default interpretations (H); Discourse representation theory (MT); Interactional linguistics (T); Language acquisition (H); The multilingual lexicon (H); Predicates and predication (H); Word (H)
**Lexicostatistics** Historical linguistics (MT)
**Life stories** (H); Narrative (H)
**Lifestyle** (H)
**Linear modification** Communicative dynamism (H)
**Linear Unit Grammar** (T21)
**Linearization** Word order (H)
**Linguicide** Language ecology (H); Language rights (H)
**Linguistic action verb** → Metapragmatic term
**Linguistic atlas** Dialectology (MT)
**Linguistic determinism** Perception and language (H); Manipulation (H)
**Linguistic diversity** Language ecology (H)
**Linguistic dominance** Language ecology (H); Language rights (H)
**Linguistic engineering** Artificial intelligence (MT)
**Linguistic explanation** (MM); Functionalism vs. formalism (MT)
**Linguistic genocide** → Linguicide
**Linguistic hierarchy** Language dominance and minorization (H)
**Linguistic human rights** Language dominance and minorization (H); Language ecology (H); Language rights (H)
**Linguistic imperialism** Language ecology (H)
**Linguistic landscape studies** (T)
**Linguistic relativity (principle)** Anthropological linguistics (MT); Boas (H); Cognitive anthropology (MT); Culture (H); Perception and language (H); Lexical semantics (T); Manipulation (H); 'Other' representation (H); Sapir (H); Speech act theory (MT); Taxonomy (MM); Whorf (H)
**Linguistic repertoire** Gumperz (H)
**Linguistic turn** Analytical philosophy (MT)
**Linking** Conceptual semantics (T)
**Listener response** (H)
**Literacy** (H); Anderson (H21); Applied linguistics (MT); Channel (H); Computer-mediated communication (H); Language acquisition (H); Language ideologies (H); Language policy, language planning and standardization (H); Metalinguistic awareness (H); Multilingualism
**Literary criticism** Figures of speech (H)
**Literary pragmatics** (MT); Bakhtin (H); Context and contextualization (H); Creativity in language use (H); Deconstruction (MM);

Figures of speech (H); Hermeneutics (M); Narrative (H); Rhetoric (MT); Structuralism (MT); Stylistics (MT)
**Localization problem** Neurolinguistics (MT)
**Location** Contact linguistics (MT)
**Logic** Generative semantics (MT); Grice (H); Modality (H); Semiotics (MT); Truth-conditional pragmatics (T21); Wittgenstein (H)
**Logic-based formalism** Artificial intelligence (MT)
**Logical analysis** (MM)
**Logical atomism** Analytical philosophy (MT)
**Logical empiricism/Logical positivism** Analytical philosophy (MT); Grice (H); Morris (H)
**Logical notation** Notation in formal semantics (MN)
**Logical semantics** (MT); Deontic logic (MT); Discourse representation theory (MT); Epistemic logic (MT); Formal pragmatics (MT); Game-theoretical semantics (MT); Intensional logic (MT); Modal logic (MT); Model-theoretic semantics (MT); Montague and categorial grammar (MT); Ontology (MT); Possible worlds semantics (MT); Situation semantics (MT); Truth-conditional semantics (MT)
**Logical typing of communication** Bateson (H); Communication (H)
**Longitudinal method** Developmental psychology (MT)
**Loudness** Prosody (H)
**Lying** Truthfulness (H)

**M-principle** Anaphora (H); Semantics vs. pragmatics (T)
**MTA** Tense and aspect (H)
**Machine translation** Translation studies (T)
**Macro-sociolinguistics** Sociolinguistics (MT)
**Malinowski, B. K.** (H); Anthropological linguistics (MT); Culture (H); Firthian linguistics (MT); Participation (H); Phatic communion (H)
**Manipulation** (H); Truthfulness (H)
**Mapping** Cognitive science (MT)
**Markedness** (H); Emphasis (H); Language change (H); Negation (H)
**Marrism** Marxist linguistics (MT)
**Marx, Karl** Bourdieu (H); Ideology (H)
**Marxist linguistics** (MT); Critical Linguistics and Critical Discourse Analysis (MT)
**Mass media** (H); Argumentation in discourse and grammar (H); Channel (H); Communication (H); Conversation analysis (MT); Critical Linguistics and Critical Discourse Analysis (MT); Discourse analysis (MT); Ideology (H); Manipulation (H); Public discourse (H); Silence (H)
**Materialism** Cognitive science (MT)
**Mathematical linguistics** Communication (H)
**Mathesius, V.** (H); Prague school (MT)
**Maxims of conversation** → Cooperative principle
**Mead, G. H.** Morris (H); Symbolic interactionism (MT)
**Mead, M.** Culture (H)
**Meaning** Analytical philosophy (MT); Austin (H); Cohesion and coherence (H); Deixis (H); Emotions (H21); Firth (H); Grice (H); Integrational linguistics (T); Linear Unit Grammar (T21); Model-theoretic semantics (MT); Phatic communion (H); Semiotics (MT); Situation semantics (MT); Sound symbolism (H); Truth-conditional pragmatics (T21); Wittgenstein (H)
**Meaning construction** Cognitive science (MT); Cognitive sociology (MT); Critical Linguistics and Critical Discourse Analysis (MT); Grounded theory (M)
**Meaning definition** Predicates and predication (H)
**Meaning postulate** Lexical semantics (T)
**Meaning potential** Social class and language (H)
**Mediated performatives** (H)
**Medical interaction** Interpreter-mediated interaction (H); Therapeutic conversation (H)
**Medical language** Applied linguistics (MT); Authority (H)
**Medium** Channel (H); Mass media (H); Mediated performatives (H); Multimodality (H)
**Medvedev, P. N.** Bakhtin (H)
**Membership categorization** Age and language use (H); Sacks (H)
**Memory** Attention and language (H); Consciousness and language (H); Perception and language (H)
**Mental spaces** (H); Conceptual integration (H)
**Mental states** Experimental pragmatics (M); Language psychology (T21)
**Mentalism** (MT); Chomskyan linguistics (MT); Cognitive science (MT); Objectivism vs. subjectivism (MT); Philosophy of mind (MT)
**Mesolect** Creole linguistics (MT)
**Metacommunication** Bateson (H)
**Metalanguage** Corpus pragmatics (M); Impoliteness (H); Reported speech (H)
**Metalinguistic awareness** (H); Adaptability (H); Collaboration in dialogues (H); Computer-mediated communication (H); Consciousness and language (H); Evolutionary pragmatics (T); Folk pragmatics (T); Language acquisition (H); Language ideologies (H); Literacy (H); Metapragmatics (MT)
**Metalinguistic negation** Negation (H)

**Metalinguistics** Bakhtin (H)
**Metaphor** (H); Cerebral representation of language; Cognitive linguistics (MT); Embodiment (H); Emphasis (H); Experimental pragmatics (M); Figures of speech (H); Iconicity (H); Implicature and language change (H); Language change (H); Metonymy (H); Polysemy (H); Silence (H); Truthfulness (H)
**Metaphysics** Grice (H)
**Metapragmatic term** Metapragmatics (MT)
**Metapragmatics** (MT); Agency and language (H); Aisatsu (H); Anthropological linguistics (MT); Cerebral representation of language; Folk pragmatics (T); Interactional sociolinguistics (MT); Language ideologies (H); Metalinguistic awareness (H)
**Metonymy** (H); Figures of speech (H); Implicature and language change (H); Lexical semantics (T); Metaphor (H); Polysemy (H); Speech act
***Mianzi / lian*** **(H21)**
**Micro-sociolinguistics** Sociolinguistics (MT)
**Micro-sociology** Social psychology (MT)
**Mind-body problem** Philosophy of mind (MT)
**Minority** Language ecology (H); Language dominance and minorization (H); Language rights (H); Linguistic landscape studies (T); 'Other' representation (H)
**Misunderstanding** Communicative success vs. failure (H); Truthfulness (H)
**Mitigation** Laughter (H)
**Mixed languages** Language contact (H)
**Modal logic** (MT); Deontic logic (MT); Epistemic logic (MT); Logical semantics (MT)
**Modal particle** Pragmatic particles (H)
**Modality** (H); Appraisal (H); Authority (H); Énonciation (H); Implicature and language change (H); Signed language pragmatics (T); Modal logic (MT)
**Mode** Firth (H); Social semiotics (T); Multimodality (H)
**Model-theoretic semantics** (MT); Game-theoretical semantics (MT); Logical semantics (MT); Montague and categorial grammar (MT); Notation in formal semantics (MN); Possible worlds semantics (MT); Situation semantics (MT)
**Modularity** → Cerebral representation of language; Clinical pragmatics (T); Cognitive psychology (MT); Cognitive science (MT); Conceptual semantics (T); Irony (H); Language acquisition (H); Psycholinguistics (MT)
**Monolingualism** Language dominance and minorization (H)
**Monologizing** Interpreter-mediated interaction (H)
**Monologue** Think-aloud protocols (M)
**Monosemy** Polysemy (H)
**Montague and categorial grammar** (MT); Discourse representation theory (MT); Formal pragmatics (MT); Intensional logic (MT); Logical semantics (MT); Model-theoretic semantics (MT)
**Moore, G. E.** Analytical philosophy (MT)
**Morphology** Deixis (H); Discourse markers (H); Jakobson (H21); Language change (H); Morphopragmatics (T); Word (H)
**Morphopragmatics** (T)
**Morris, C.** (H)
**Motherese** Register (H)
**Motivation** (H)
**Motivation and language** (H)
**Move** Predicates and predication (H); Therapeutic conversation (H)
**Multi-party talk** Collaboration in dialogues (H); Conversation types (H)
**Multiculturalism** Culture (H)
**Multifunctionality** Pragmatic markers (H)
**Multilingual lexicon (The)** (H)
**Multilingualism** Bilingualism and multilingualism (H); Creativity in language use (H); Language contact (H); Language ecology (H); Linguistic landscape studies (T); Literacy (H); The multilingual lexicon (H)
**Multimodality** (H); Computational pragmatics (T); Computer-mediated communication (H); Embodiment (H); Emphasis (H); Genre (H); Historical politeness (T); Metaphor (H); Social semiotics (T); Translation studies (T)
**Mutual knowledge** Common ground (H)

**Name** Linguistic landscape studies (T); Reference and descriptions (H); Socio-onomastics (T)
**Narrative** (H); Appraisal (H); Collaboration in dialogues (H); Discourse analysis (MT); Grounded theory (M); Emotion display (H); Grounding (H); Metalinguistic awareness (H); Reported speech (H); Sequence (H); Text type (H)
**Narratology** Discourse analysis (MT); Semiotics (MT); Text and discourse linguistics (T)
**Nationalism** Anderson (H21); Language dominance and minorization (H)
**Native-nonnative interaction** Discourse markers (H); Intercultural communication (H)
**Nativism** Authenticity (H); Language acquisition (H)
**Natural history of discourse** Metalinguistic awareness (H)
**Natural language generation and interpretation**

→ Natural language processing
**Natural language processing** Artificial intelligence (MT); Borrowing (H); Cognitive psychology (MT); Computational linguistics (MT); Connectionism (MT); The multilingual lexicon (H); Psycholinguistics (MT)
**Natural logic** Argumentation theory (MT)
**Natural semantic metalanguage** Componential analysis (MT)
**Naturalness** Authenticity (H); Language change (H)
**Nature vs. nurture** Cognitive science (MT)
**Negation** (H); Indeterminacy and negotiation (H); Modality (H); Polyphony (H); Truthfulness (H)
**Negotiation** Adaptability (H); Applied linguistics (MT); Indeterminacy and negotiation (H); Prosody (H); Truthfulness (H)
**Neo-Gricean pragmatics** Anaphora (H); Grice (H); Implicature and language change (H); Semantics vs. pragmatics (T)
**Neo-Kaplanean semantics** Semantics vs. pragmatics (T)
**Neogrammarians** Historical linguistics (MT); Lexical field analysis (MT); Prague school (MT); Reconstruction (MM); de Saussure (H)
**Neoliberalism** Ideology (H)
**Network (social)** Computer-mediated communication (H); Language change (H)
**Neuroimaging** → Brain imaging
**Neurolinguistic programming** General semantics (MT)
**Neurolinguistics** (MT); Adaptability (H); Bilingualism and multilingualism (H); Cerebral representation of language; Clinical pragmatics (T); Emotions (H21); Language acquisition (H); Perception and language (H)
**Neurophysiology** Connectionism (MT); Irony (H); Neurolinguistics (MT); Neuropragmatics (T)
**Neuropragmatics** (T); Clinical pragmatics (T)
**Neuropsychology** Cognitive science (MT); Perception and language (H)
**New Left** Bourdieu (H)
**New rhetoric** Argumentation theory (MT); Genre (H); Rhetoric (MT)
**News interview** Mass media (H)
**Newspaper** Mass media (H)
**Nexus analysis** (T); Bourdieu (H)
**Nominalization** Predicates and predication (H)
**Non-literal meaning** Neuropragmatics (T)
**Non-modular grammar** Construction grammar (MT)
**Non-seriousness** Laughter (H)
**Non-verbal communication** (H); Channel (H); Cultural scripts (H); Frame analysis (M)
**Normality** Ethnomethodology (MT)
**Norms** Creativity in language use (H); Ethnomethodology (MT)
**Notation Systems in Spoken Language Corpora** (N); Transcription systems for spoken discourse (MN)
**Notation in formal semantics** (MN)
**Noun phrase** Situation semantics (MT)
**Novelty** Creativity in language use (H)

**Object language** Metalinguistic awareness (H)
**Objectivism vs. subjectivism** (MT); Behaviorism (MT); Epistemology (MT); Foucault (H); Mentalism (MT)
**Observation** Cognitive science (MT); Culture (H); Fieldwork (MM)
**Ọmọlúàbí** (H)
**Onomastics** Socio-onomastics (T)
**Ontology** (MT); Epistemology (MT); Logical semantics (MT)
**Opacity** Mental spaces (H)
**Operationism** Behaviorism (MT)
**Optimality theory** Default interpretations (H)
**Orality** Channel (H)
**Orders of discourse** Critical Linguistics and Critical Discourse Analysis (MT); Ideology (H)
**Ordinary language philosophy** Analytical philosophy (MT); Conversational logic (MT); Grice (H); Indeterminacy and negotiation (H); Metalinguistic awareness (H); Metapragmatics (MT); Pragmatism (MT); Speech act theory (MT); (The) pragmatic perspective (M); Wittgenstein (H)
**Organizational setting** Social institutions (H)
**Organon model** Bühler (H)
**Origins of language** Cognitive anthropology (MT); Evolutionary pragmatics (T); Humboldt (H)
**Orthography** Developmental dyslexia (H)
**'Other' representation** (H); Age and language use (H)
**Other(ing)** Authority (H); Mianzi / lian (H21); 'Other' representation (H)
**Other-repair** Repair (H)
**Othering** 'Other' representation (H)
**Overhearer** → Audience
**Overlap** (H)

**Paralanguage** → Cerebral representation of language; Non-verbal communication (H)
**Paraphrase semantics** Componential analysis (MT)
**Parole** → Langue vs. parole

**Parsing** Computational linguistics (MT)
**Participant observation** → Observation
**Participation** (H); Frame analysis (M); Goffman (H)
**Participation framework** Participation (H)
**Pêcheux, M.** Marxist linguistics (MT)
**Peirce, C. S.** (H); Iconicity (H); Morris (H); Pragmatism (MT); Semiotics (MT); Sign (H)
**Pejorative** Morphopragmatics (T); 'Other' representation (H)
**Perception and language** (H); Austin (H); Embodiment (H); Iconicity (H); Language acquisition (H)
**Perceptron** Connectionism (MT); Psycholinguistics (MT)
**Performance** Computer-mediated communication (H)
**Performativity** Austin (H); Benveniste (H); Mediated performatives (H); Metalinguistic awareness (H); Speech act theory (MT)
**Perlocution** Intentionality (H); Speech act theory (MT)
**Personality** Sapir (H)
**Persuasion** Manipulation (H)
**Phatic communion** (H); Anthropological linguistics (MT); Ethnography of speaking (MT); Evolutionary pragmatics (T); Firthian linguistics (MT); Malinowski (H); Participation (H)
**Phenomenology** (MT); Austin (H); Embodiment (H); Ethnomethodology (MT); Semiotics (MT)
**Philosophy of action** (MT); Action theory (MT); Austin (H)
**Philosophy of language** (MT); Analytical philosophy (MT); Austin (H); Conversational logic (MT); Emotions (H21); Humboldt (H); Speech act theory (MT); Wittgenstein (H); (The) pragmatic perspective (M)
**Philosophy of mind** (MT); Cognitive science (MT); Grice (H); Mentalism (MT)
**Phonetic notation systems** (N)
**Phonetics** Boas (H); Discourse markers (H); de Saussure (H)
**Phonology** Developmental dyslexia (H); Jakobson (H21); Structuralism (MT)
**Phrase-structure grammar** Chomskyan linguistics (MT); Computational linguistics (MT)
**Physical symbol system** Artificial intelligence (MT); Cognitive psychology (MT); Cognitive science (MT)
**Picture-theory of meaning** Wittgenstein (H)
**Pidgins and pidginization** Contact (H); Contact linguistics (MT); Creoles and creolization (H); Creole linguistics (MT); Intercultural communication (H)
**Pitch** Prosody (H)
**Plagiarism** → Authorship
**Planning** Computational pragmatics (T)
**Poetic language** Figures of speech (H); Grounding (H)
**Poetics** Bakhtin (H)
**Point of view** Grounding (H)
**Polarity** Negation (H)
**Police interrogation** Applied linguistics (MT); Forensic linguistics (T); Interpreter-mediated interaction (H)
**Politeness** (H); Aisatsu (H); Conversational implicature (H); Conversational logic (MT); Goffman (H); Historical politeness (T); Historical pragmatics (T); Honorifics (H); Implicitness (H); Interlanguage pragmatics (T); Leech (H); Mianzi / lian (H21); Morphopragmatics (T); Impoliteness (H); Silence (H); Terms of address (H); Truthfulness (H)
**Political correctness** 'Other' representation (H)
**Political language** Authority (H)
**Political linguistics** Critical Linguistics and Critical Discourse Analysis (MT)
**Polyphony** (H); Appraisal (H); Bakhtin (H); Collaboration in dialogues (H); Dialogical analysis (MM)
**Polysemy** (H); Implicature and language change (H); Indeterminacy and negotiation (H)
**Polysystemic analysis** Firth (H)
**Positioning** Stance (H21)
**Possible worlds semantics** (MT); Epistemic logic (MT); Logical semantics (MT); Model-theoretic semantics (MT); Truth-conditional semantics (MT)
**Poststructuralism** Critical Linguistics and Critical Discourse Analysis (MT); Deconstruction (MM)
**Posture** Non-verbal communication (H)
**Power** Authority (H); Cognitive sociology (MT); Critical Linguistics and Critical Discourse Analysis (MT); Foucault (H); Gumperz (H); Honorifics (H); Ideology (H); Manipulation (H); Metalinguistic awareness (H); Politeness (H); Silence (H); Social institutions (H)
**Practice (theory)** Agency and language (H); Nexus analysis (T); Social class and language (H)
**Pragma-dialectics** Argumentation theory (MT)
**Pragmalinguistics** Leech (H)
**Pragmastylistics** Stylistics (MT)
**Pragmatic acquisition** (H); Cognitive psychology (MT); Developmental dyslexia (H); Devel-

opmental psychology (MT); Experimentation (MM); Experimental pragmatics (M); Language acquisition (H); Psycholinguistics (MT)
**Pragmatic enrichment** Truth-conditional pragmatics (T21)
**Pragmatic explanation** Linguistic explanation (MM)
**Pragmatic function** Functional grammar (MT)
**Pragmatic impairment** Clinical pragmatics (T)
**Pragmatic intrusion** Semantics vs. pragmatics (T)
**Pragmatic markers** (H); Discourse markers (H); Pragmatic particles (H)
**Pragmatic norm** Interlanguage pragmatics (T)
**Pragmatic particles** (H); Discourse markers (H); Interjections (H)
**Pragmatic perspective (The)** (M)
**Pragmatic scale** → Scalarity
**Pragmatic transfer** Interlanguage pragmatics (T)
**Pragmaticalization** Pragmatic markers (H)
**Pragmaticism** Evolutionary pragmatics (T); Objectivism vs. subjectivism (MT); Pragmatism (MT); Morris (H)
**Pragmatics** (The) pragmatic perspective (M)
**Pragmatism** (MT); Morris (H); Peirce (H); Semiotics (MT)
**Prague school** (MT); Communicative dynamism (H); Discourse analysis (MT); Functional grammar (MT); Functional sentence perspective (H); Markedness (H); Mathesius (H); Structuralism (MT); Text linguistics (MT); Word order (H)
**Precisification principle** Indeterminacy and negotiation (H)
**Predicate logic** Artificial intelligence (MT); Notation in formal semantics (MN)
**Predicates and predication** (H)
**Preference organization** Repair (H); Sequence (H)
**Prejudice** 'Other' representation (H)
**Prestige** Language dominance and minorization (H)
**Presumptive meaning** Default interpretations (H)
**Presupposition** (H); Argumentation in discourse and grammar (H); Context and contextualization (H); Discourse representation theory (MT); Formal pragmatics (MT); Implicitness (H); Mental spaces (H); Truthfulness (H)
**Primate communication** (H)
**Priming** Psycholinguistics (MT)
**Print** Channel (H)
**Private language** Wittgenstein (H)
**Probabilistic technique** Statistics (MM)
**Problematization** Foucault (H)
**Problematology** Argumentation theory (MT); Rhetoric (MT)
**Procedural semantics** Cognitive psychology (MT)
**Processing** Comprehension vs. production (H); Inferencing; Information processing; Production; Text comprehension (H)
**Production** Conceptual semantics (T); Psycholinguistics (MT)
**Productivity** Creativity in language use (H)
**Projection problem** Presupposition (H)
**Pronoun** Anaphora (H); Creole linguistics (MT); Humboldt (H); Negation (H)
**Proper name** → Name
**Property theory** Intensional logic (MT)
**Propositional attitude** Discourse representation theory (MT); Intensional logic (MT)
**Propositional semantics** Evolutionary pragmatics (T)
**Prosody** (H); Cerebral representation of language; Emphasis (H); Firth (H); Gumperz (H); Information structure (H); Interactional linguistics (T); Language acquisition (H)
**Proto-grammar** Iconicity (H)
**Prototype (theory)** Categorization (H); Cognitive linguistics (MT); Dependency and valency grammar (MT); Language acquisition (H); Lexical semantics (T); Polysemy (H); Taxonomy (MM)
**Proxemics** Non-verbal communication (H)
**Psychiatry** Bateson (H); Therapeutic conversation (H)
**Psycholinguistics** (MT); Bilingualism and multilingualism (H); Borrowing (H); Bühler (H); Cognitive psychology (MT); Comprehension vs. production (H); Connectionism (MT); Developmental psychology (MT); Experimental pragmatics (M); Experimentation (MM); Language psychology (T21); The multilingual lexicon (H); Non-verbal communication (H); Perception and language (H); (The) pragmatic perspective (M); Text comprehension (H); Translation studies (T); Vygotsky (H)
**Psychological anthropology** Cognitive anthropology (MT)
**Psychosemantics** Philosophy of mind (MT)
**Psychotherapy** → Psychiatry
**Public discourse** (H); Goffman (H); Mediated performatives (H); Social institutions (H)
**Putnam, H.** Analytical philosophy (MT)

**Q-principle** Anaphora (H); Semantics vs. pragmatics (T)
**Qualitative methods** Grounded theory (M)
**Quantifier** Model-theoretic semantics (MT); Notation in formal semantics (MN)

**Quantitative method** Statistics (MM)
**Question answering** Computational pragmatics (T); Tactile sign languages (H21)
**Question word** Repair (H)
**Questionnaire** Interview (MM)
**Quine, W.v.O.** Reported speech (H)
**Quotation** Analytical philosophy (MT)

**Racism** Ideology (H); 'Other' representation (H)
**Radical argumentativism** Argumentation theory (MT)
**Radical pragmatics** Grice (H)
**Radio** Mass media (H)
**Rationality** Default interpretations (H); Emotions (H21); Ethnomethodology (MT); Foucault (H); Grice (H); Ideology (H)
**Reading analysis** Critical Linguistics and Critical Discourse Analysis (MT); Text comprehension (H)
**Recall** Collaboration in dialogues (H)
**Reception theory** Literary pragmatics (MT)
**Recipient design** Collaboration in dialogues (H); Communicative style (H)
**Reconstruction** (MM); Dialectology (MT); Historical linguistics (MT); Language change (H)
**Recoverability** Ellipsis (H)
**Reference** Anaphora (H); Definiteness (H); Experimental pragmatics (M); Functional discourse grammar (T); Functional grammar (MT); Information structure (H); Mental spaces (H); Metalinguistic awareness (H); Model-theoretic semantics (MT); Polysemy (H); Predicates and predication (H); Reference and descriptions (H); Tagmemics (MT)
**Reference and descriptions** (H)
**Referential choice** Definiteness (H)
**Referring** → Reference; Reference and descriptions (H)
**Reflection** Communicative success vs. failure (H); Humboldt (H)
**Reflexive** Anaphora (H)
**Reflexivity** Adaptability (H); Ethnomethodology (MT); Foucault (H); Metalinguistic awareness (H); 'Other' representation (H); Style and styling (H21)
**Reflexology** Behaviorism (MT)
**Register** (H); Applied linguistics (MT); Channel (H); Context and contextualization (H); Correlational sociolinguistics (T); Error analysis (MM); Firthian linguistics (MT); Frame analysis (M); Gumperz (H); Honorifics (H); Intercultural communication (H); Rhetoric (MT); Sociolinguistics (MT); Stylistics (MT); Systemic functional grammar (MT)
**Regularity** Relational ritual (H)
**Reinforcement** Emphasis (H)
**Relational grammar** Lexical functional grammar (MT)
**Relational ritual** (H)
**Relevance** Computational pragmatics (T); Conversation analysis (MT); Conversational logic (MT); Irony (H); Relevance theory (MT)
**Relevance theory** (MT); Anaphora (H); Clinical pragmatics (T); Communication (H); Conversational implicature (H); Conversational logic (MT); Emotions (H21); Experimental pragmatics (M); Humor (H); Manipulation (H); Semantics vs. pragmatics (T); Tense and aspect (H); Truth-conditional pragmatics (T21); Truth-conditional semantics (MT); Truthfulness (H)
**Religion** Authority (H)
**Repair** (H); Communicative success vs. failure (H); Conversation analysis (MT); Prosody (H); Sequence (H)
**Repertoire** → Linguistic repertoire
**Repetition** Emergent grammar (T)
**Reported speech** (H); Énonciation (H); Intertextuality (H)
**Representation** Adaptability (H); Conceptual semantics (T); Evolutionary pragmatics (T); Foucault (H); Indeterminacy and negotiation (H); Iconicity (H); Intentionality (H); Metalinguistic awareness (H); 'Other' representation (H); Psycholinguistics (MT); Social psychology (MT); Truthfulness (H); Wittgenstein (H)
**Resistance** Therapeutic conversation (H)
**Resource** Multimodality (H)
**Respect** → Deference
**Response** Ọmọlúàbí (H)
**Response cry** Emotion display (H); Goffman (H)
**Responsibility** Austin (H)
**Rheme** → Theme vs. rheme
**Rhetoric** (MT); Argumentation theory (MT); Discourse analysis (MT); Figures of speech (H); Functional discourse grammar (T); Genre (H); Literary pragmatics (MT); Manipulation (H); Metalinguistic awareness (H); Narrative (H); Social psychology (MT); Stylistics (MT)
**Rhetorical relations** Discourse representation theory (MT)
**Rhetorical structure theory** Artificial intelligence (MT); Computational pragmatics (T); Discourse analysis (MT)
**Ritual** Goffman (H); Relational ritual (H)
**Role and reference grammar** (MT); Case and semantic roles (H); Case grammar (MT);

Dependency and valency grammar (MT)
**Role vs. value** Mental spaces (H)
**Rossi-Landi, F.** Morris (H)
**Routine (formula)** Aisatsu (H); Impoliteness (H); Ọmọlúàbí (H); Relational ritual (H)
**Routinization** Emergent grammar (T)
**Rule** Ethnomethodology (MT); Psycholinguistics (MT); Speech act theory (MT); Wittgenstein (H)
**Rule-based formalism** Artificial intelligence (MT)
**Russell, B.** Analytical philosophy (MT); Definiteness (H); Reference and descriptions (H)
**Russian formalism** Deconstruction (MM); Discourse analysis (MT); Literary pragmatics (MT); Prague school (MT); Semiotics (MT); Stylistics (MT)

**Sacks, H.** (H); Conversation analysis (MT)
**Salience** Anaphora (H); Emphasis (H); Experimental pragmatics (M); Grounding (H); Irony (H); Word order (H)
**Sampling** → Data collection
**Sapir, E.** (H); Anthropological linguistics (MT); Boas (H); Culture (H); Whorf (H)
**Sapir-Whorf hypothesis** → Linguistic relativity principle
**Sarcasm** Irony (H)
**Saturation** Truth-conditional pragmatics (T21)
**Saussure, F. de** (H); Geneva school (MT); Participation (H); Sign (H); Structuralism (MT)
**Scalarity** Conceptual integration (H); Experimental pragmatics (M); Implicitness (H); Negation (H)
**Scale and category grammar** Systemic functional grammar (MT)
**Scenario** Frame semantics (T); Lexical semantics (T)
**Scene** Frame semantics (T); Lexical semantics (T)
**Scene-and-frame semantics** Frame semantics (T)
**Schema** Cognitive science (MT); Frame analysis (M)
**Schizophrenia** Clinical pragmatics (T)
**Schooling** Aisatsu (H); Language acquisition (H)
**Scientific language** Analytical philosophy (MT); Applied linguistics (MT); Text comprehension (H)
**Script** Cognitive science (MT); Frame analysis (M); Frame semantics (T); Humor (H)
**Searle, J. R.** Analytical philosophy (MT); Contextualism (T); Intentionality (H); Reference and descriptions (H); Speech act theory (MT)
**Second language acquisition** Applied linguistics (MT); Contact linguistics (MT); Intercultural communication (H); Interlanguage pragmatics (T); Language learning in immersion and CLIL classrooms (H); Motivation (H); The multilingual lexicon (H); Silence (H); Text comprehension (H)
**Selection restrictions** Predicates and predication (H)
**Self** Authenticity (H); Authority (H); Goffman (H); Laughter (H); Life stories (H); Mianzi / lian (H21)
**Self-repair** Repair (H)
**Semantic differential** Social psychology (MT)
**Semantic field analysis** Lexical field analysis (MT)
**Semantic minimalism** Contextualism (T)
**Semantic network** Artificial intelligence (MT)
**Semantic primitive** Componential analysis (MT); Cultural scripts (H)
**Semantic structure** Role and reference grammar (MT)
**Semantics vs. pragmatics** (T); Anaphora (H); Cerebral representation of language; Discourse representation theory (MT); Emotions (H21); Generative semantics (MT); Grice (H); Implicitness (H); Indeterminacy and negotiation (H); Leech (H); Metalinguistic awareness (H); Metaphor (H); Montague and categorial grammar (MT); Reference and descriptions (H); Semiotics (MT); Structuralism (MT); Truth-conditional pragmatics (T21)
**Semiology** Integrational linguistics (T); de Saussure (H); Semiotics (MT)
**Semiophysics** Catastrophe theory (MT)
**Semiotic resource** Social semiotics (T)
**Semiotics** (MT); Bakhtin (H); Benveniste (H); Iconicity (H); Morris (H); Peirce (H); Pragmatism (MT); Sign (H); Social semiotics (T); Speech community (H); (The) pragmatic perspective (M)
**Sense** Analytical philosophy (MT); Polysemy (H)
**Sensorimotor dysfunction** Clinical pragmatics (T)
**Sentence fragment** Ellipsis (H)
**Sentence grammar** → Cerebral representation of language
**Sentence linearity** Communicative dynamism (H)
**Sentence processing** The multilingual lexicon (H)
**Sentence type** Markedness (H)
**Sequence** (H); Conversation analysis (MT); Grounding (H); Language and the law (H); Notation Systems in Spoken Language Corpora (N); Prosody (H); Relational ritual (H); Repair (H); Stance (H21); Therapeutic conversation (H)
**Sequencing** Sequence (H)
**Sequentiality** Iconicity (H)
**Sexual orientation** Silence (H)

**Shared knowledge** Common ground (H)
**Shibboleth** Anderson (H21)
**Sign** (H); Evolutionary pragmatics (T); Iconicity (H); Integrational linguistics (T); Morris (H); Semiotics (MT); Signed language pragmatics (T); de Saussure (H); Social semiotics (T); Speech community (H)
**Sign language(s)** Language ecology (H); Non-verbal communication (H); Tactile sign languages (H21)
**Signed language pragmatics** (T)
**Silence** (H)
**Silencing** 'Other' representation (H); Silence (H)
**Simile** Metaphor (H)
**Sincerity** Authenticity (H); Truthfulness (H)
**Singular term** Indexicals and demonstratives (H)
**Situated action theory** Cognitive science (MT)
**Situation semantics** (MT); Communication (H); Discourse representation theory (MT); Logical semantics (MT); Model-theoretic semantics (MT)
**Slang** Jargon (H)
**Sluicing** Ellipsis (H)
**Social anthropology** Anthropological linguistics (MT); Cognitive anthropology (MT)
**Social class and language** (H)
**Social cognition** Bühler (H); Language psychology (T21); Social psychology (MT); Style and styling (H21)
**Social difference/inequality** → Power
**Social distancing** 'Other' representation (H)
**Social institutions** (H); Applied linguistics (MT); Authority (H); Cognitive sociology (MT); Communication (H); Conversation types (H); Forensic linguistics (T); Frame analysis (M); Intercultural communication (H); Narrative (H); Politeness (H); Public discourse (H); Therapeutic conversation (H)
**Social organization** Aisatsu (H); Authority (H); Cognitive sociology (MT)
**Social psychology** (MT); Accommodation theory (MT); Bilingualism and multilingualism (H); Conversation analysis (MT); Ethnomethodology (MT); Language psychology (T21); Motivation (H); Nexus analysis (T); Overlap (H); Symbolic interactionism (MT); Terms of address (H)
**Social relationship** → Social organization
**Social science** Grounded theory (M)
**Social semiotics** (T); Appraisal (H); Critical Linguistics and Critical Discourse Analysis (MT); Critical theory (MT); Linguistic landscape studies (T); Literary pragmatics (MT); Multimodality (H); Semiotics (MT); Sign (H)
**Socialization** Aisatsu (H); Developmental psychology (MT); Vygotsky (H)
**Socio-onomastics** (T)
**Sociolect** Dialect (H)
**Sociolinguistics** (MT); Anthropological linguistics (MT); Applied linguistics (MT); Bilingualism and multilingualism (H); Code-switching (H); Cognitive sociology (MT); Contact linguistics (MT); Correlational sociolinguistics (T); Creole linguistics (MT); Creoles and creolization (H); Dialectology (MT); Gumperz (H); Interactional sociolinguistics (MT); Language contact (H); Language dominance and minorization (H); Language maintenance and shift (H21); Language policy, language planning and standardization (H); Lifestyle (H); Linguistic landscape studies (T); Metalinguistic awareness (H); Pragmatic markers (H); Social class and language (H); Speech community (H); Superdiversity (H21); (The) pragmatic perspective (M)
**Sociology** Bourdieu (H); Goffman (H); Gumperz (H)
**Sociology of language** Dialectology (MT); Sociolinguistics (MT)
**Sociopragmatics** Leech (H)
**Sociosemiotics** Social semiotics (T)
**Sonority** Language change (H)
**Sound symbolism** (H); Iconicity (H)
**Speaker vs. listener** Comprehension vs. production (H); Dialogical analysis (MM); Manipulation (H); Participation (H); Terms of address (H); Truthfulness (H)
**Speaker's meaning** Speech act theory (MT)
**Speaking vs. writing** Applied linguistics (MT); Channel (H); Communicative style (H); Computer-mediated communication (H); Discourse analysis (MT); Integrational linguistics (T); Language acquisition (H); Notation Systems in Spoken Language Corpora (N); Register (H); de Saussure (H); Text and discourse linguistics (T)
**Speech accommodation** Accommodation theory (MT); Social psychology (MT)
**Speech act** Adaptability (H); Argumentation theory (MT); Austin (H); Cerebral representation of language; Conventions of language (H); Formal pragmatics (MT); Grice (H); Historical pragmatics (T); Intercultural communication (H); Interlanguage pragmatics (T); Mediated performatives (H); Metonymy (H); Modality (H); Morphopragmatics (T); Neuropragmatics (T); Non-verbal communication (H); Politeness (H); Pragmatic

particles (H); Speech act theory (MT); Truth-conditional pragmatics (T21)
**Speech act classification** Speech act theory (MT)
**Speech act theory** (MT); Analytical philosophy (MT); Artificial intelligence (MT); Austin (H); Benveniste (H); Clinical pragmatics (T); Conversational implicature (H); Conversational logic (MT); Indeterminacy and negotiation (H); Intentionality (H); Language and the law (H); Philosophy of language (MT); (The) pragmatic perspective (M); Truthfulness (H)
**Speech circuit** Participation (H)
**Speech community** (H); Anderson (H21); Computer-mediated communication (H); Gumperz (H); Superdiversity (H21)
**Speech event** Pragmatic particles (H)
**Speech genre** Bakhtin (H); Metalinguistic awareness (H)
**Spelling** Language acquisition (H); Psycholinguistics (MT)
**Spoken discourse** → Speaking vs. writing
**Spoken language corpora** Notation Systems in Spoken Language Corpora (N)
**Sprachbund ('linguistic area')** Contact linguistics (MT); Language change (H); Language contact (H); Sociolinguistics (MT)
**Stance** (H21); Appraisal (H); Emotion display (H)
**Standard language** Dialectology and geolinguistic dynamics (T)
**Standardization** Anderson (H21); Authority (H); Integrational linguistics (T); Language dominance and minorization (H); Language policy, language planning and standardization (H); Literacy (H)
**State of Affairs** Predicates and predication (H)
**State-space search** Artificial intelligence (MT)
**Statistics** (MM); Computational linguistics (MT); Corpus analysis (MM); Correlational sociolinguistics (T); Experimentation (MM)
**Stereotype** 'Other' representation (H)
**Story(-telling)** Narrative (H)
**Strategy** Impoliteness (H)
**Strawson, P. F.** Analytical philosophy (MT); Definiteness (H); Reference and descriptions (H)
**Stress** Information structure (H); Prosody (H)
**Stripping** Ellipsis (H)
**Structuralism** (MT); Autonomous vs. non-autonomous syntax (MT); Benveniste (H); Bourdieu (H); Componential analysis (MT); Corpus analysis (MM); Discourse analysis (MT); Geneva school (MT); Hermeneutics (M); Language change (H); Lexical field analysis (MT); Lexical semantics (T); Prague school (MT); de Saussure (H); Semiotics (MT); Sign (H)
**Style** Communicative style (H); Creole linguistics (MT); Ellipsis (H); Figures of speech (H); Register (H)
**Style and styling** (H21)
**Stylistic stratification** Social class and language (H)
**Stylistics** (MT); Communicative style (H); Discourse analysis (MT); Emphasis (H); Figures of speech (H); Literary pragmatics (MT); Mathesius (H); Rhetoric (MT); Text linguistics (MT)
**Subject** Communicative dynamism (H)
**Subjectivity** Benveniste (H); Énonciation (H); Foucault (H); Implicature and language change (H); Signed language pragmatics (T)
**Substitution** Anaphora (H)
**Superdiversity** (H21)
**Syllable structure** Prosody (H)
**Symbol** Jakobson (H21)
**Symbolic behavior** Evolutionary pragmatics (T)
**Symbolic capital** Bourdieu (H); Social institutions (H)
**Symbolic interactionism** (MT); Bourdieu (H); Cognitive sociology (MT); Context and contextualization (H); Ethnomethodology (MT); Goffman (H); Social psychology (MT)
**Symbolic vs. subsymbolic architecture** Cognitive science (MT)
**Symbolism** Morris (H)
**Symbolization** Bühler (H); Cognitive grammar (MT)
**Symmetry** Language change (H)
**Synchrony** Iconicity (H); Non-verbal communication (H); Structuralism (MT)
**Synergetics** Catastrophe theory (MT)
**Synesthesia** Metaphor (H)
**Syntax** Anaphora (H); Comprehension vs. production (H); Discourse markers (H); Ellipsis (H); Interactional linguistics (T); Language acquisition (H); Language change (H); Grice (H); Polysemy (H)
**Systemic functional grammar** (MT); Appraisal (H); Emphasis (H); Firth (H); Firthian linguistics (MT); Functional grammar (MT); Genre (H); Metaphor (H); Multimodality (H)

**Tact** Leech (H); Politeness (H); Ọmọlúàbí (H)
**Tactile sign languages** (H21)
**Tagging** Corpus analysis (MM)
**Tagmemics** (MT)
**Taxonomy** (MM)
**Telephone conversation** Emotion display (H)

**Television** Argumentation in discourse and grammar (H); Channel (H); Mass media (H)
**Temporal reference** Narrative (H)
**Tenor** Register (H)
**Tense** Modality (H); Tense and aspect (H)
**Tense and aspect** (H)
**Tense logic** Modal logic (MT)
**Terms of address** (H); Honorifics (H)
**Territoriality** Language rights (H)
**Testimony** Epistemology of testimony (T); Interpreter-mediated interaction (H)
**Testing** Text comprehension (H)
**Text** Boas (H); Culture (H); Systemic functional grammar (MT)
**Text analysis** Computational linguistics (MT); Text type (H)
**Text and discourse linguistics** (T); Common ground (H); Text linguistics (MT)
**Text comprehension** (H)
**Text linguistics** (MT); Critical Linguistics and Critical Discourse Analysis (MT); Discourse analysis (MT); Prague school (MT); Stylistics (MT); Text and discourse linguistics (T); Translation studies (T)
**Text structure** (H); Narrative (H)
**Text type** (H); Discourse analysis (MT); Genre (H); Pragmatic particles (H); Text and discourse linguistics (T); Think-aloud protocols (M)
**Theme vs. rheme** Communicative dynamism (H); Functional grammar (MT); Word order (H)
**Theory and theorizing** Firth (H); Grounded theory (M)
**Theory of mind** Adaptability (H); Clinical pragmatics (T); Communication (H)
**Therapeutic conversation** (H)
**Think-aloud protocols** (M)
**Thirdness** Morris (H)
**Threat** Impoliteness (H)
**Timing problem** Neurolinguistics (MT); Neuropragmatics (T)
**Topic management** Laughter (H)
**Topic vs. focus** Anaphora (H); Argumentation in discourse and grammar (H); Functional discourse grammar (T); Functional grammar (MT); Functional sentence perspective (H)
**Topic-comment structure** Computational pragmatics (T); Information structure (H); Signed language pragmatics (T); Word order (H)
**Topicality** Signed language pragmatics (T)
**Toponym** Socio-onomastics (T)
**Trajectory** Sequence (H)
**Transcription** Grounded theory (M); Laughter (H); Phonetic notation systems (N)
**Transcription systems for spoken discourse** (MN); Conversation analysis (MT); Notation Systems in Spoken Language Corpora (N)
**Transformational grammar** → Generative(-transformational) linguistics
**Transitivity** Grounding (H)
**Translation** Interpreter-mediated interaction (H); Pragmatic particles (H); Think-aloud protocols (M); Translation studies (T)
**Translation studies** (T); Pragmatic markers (H)
**Traumatic brain injury** Clinical pragmatics (T)
**Triangulation** Grounded theory (M)
**Troubles talk** Emotion display (H); Laughter (H)
**Trust** Adaptability (H)
**Truth** Austin (H); Grice (H); Ideology (H); Model-theoretic semantics (MT); Speech act theory (MT); Truthfulness (H)
**Truth-conditional pragmatics** (T21); Default interpretations (H)
**Truth-conditional semantics** (MT); Analytical philosophy (MT); Logical semantics (MT); Possible worlds semantics (MT); Relevance theory (MT)
**Truthfulness** (H); Manipulation (H); Ọmọlúàbí (H)
**Turing machine** Computational linguistics (MT)
**Turn(-taking)** Conversation analysis (MT); Frame analysis (M); Intertextuality (H); Language and the law (H); Prosody (H); Silence (H); Tactile sign languages (H21)
**Typology** (MT); Boas (H); Contact linguistics (MT); Deixis (H); Historical linguistics (MT); Language acquisition (H); Language change (H); Language contact (H); Negation (H); Sound symbolism (H); Word order (H)

**UN language system** Language ecology (H)
**Underspecification** → Vagueness
**Understanding** Comprehension vs. production (H)
**Unidirectionality** Language change (H)
**Universal and transcendental pragmatics** (MT); Critical theory (MT); Hermeneutics (M); Truthfulness (H)
**Universal grammar** Language acquisition (H); Language change (H)
**Universals of language** → Language universals
**User modeling** Artificial intelligence (MT); Computational pragmatics (T)
**Utterance** Predicates and predication (H); Speech act theory (MT)

**Vagueness** Indeterminacy and negotiation (H); Polysemy (H); Tense and aspect (H); Truthfulness (H)
**Valency** → Dependency

**Variability** → Variation
**Variable rule** Correlational sociolinguistics (T)
**Variable-rule analysis** Statistics (MM)
**Variation** Adaptability (H); Bilingualism and multilingualism (H); Communicative style (H); Context and contextualization (H); Correlational sociolinguistics (T); Creoles and creolization (H); Creole linguistics (MT); Dialectology (MT); Honorifics (H); Language acquisition (H); Language change (H); Language policy, language planning and standardization (H); Language dominance and minorization (H); Polysemy (H); Register (H); Sociolinguistics (MT); Variational pragmatics (T)
**Variational pragmatics** (T); Contact linguistics (MT); Language change (H)
**Variationist sociolinguistics** Correlational sociolinguistics (T)
**Verb** Communicative dynamism (H)
**Verba dicendi** Reported speech (H)
**Vernacular** Anderson (H21); Authenticity (H); Dialect (H)
**Verstehen** → Erklären vs. Verstehen
**Vitality** Motivation (H)
**Vocabulary** Borrowing (H); Language acquisition (H)
**Voice** Polyphony (H)
**Vološinov, V. N.** Bakhtin (H); Marxist linguistics (MT); Deconstruction (MM); Intertextuality (H); Reported speech (H)
**Vygotsky, L.** (H)

**Whorf, B. L.** (H); Anthropological linguistics (MT); Boas (H); Culture (H); Iconicity (H); Sapir (H)
**Whorfianism** → Linguistic relativity principle
**Wittgenstein, L.** (H); Analytical philosophy (MT); Austin (H); Contextualism (T); Speech act theory (MT); (The) pragmatic perspective (M)
**Word** (H)
**Word order** (H); Negation (H); Typology (MT)
**Word recognition** The multilingual lexicon (H); Psycholinguistics (MT)
**Workplace interaction** Aisatsu (H); Applied linguistics (MT)
**Written discourse** → Speaking vs. writing

**X-bar syntax** Chomskyan linguistics (MT); Computational linguistics (MT); Role and reference grammar (MT)